FOR ALL GOD'S WORTH

For All God's Worth

*True Worship and the
Calling of the Church*

N. T. Wright

WILLIAM B. EERDMANS PUBLISHING COMPANY
GRAND RAPIDS, MICHIGAN

© 1997 Nicholas Thomas Wright
First published 1997 in Great Britain by
Triangle
Society for Promoting Christian Knowledge
Holy Trinity Church
Marylebone Road
London NW1 4DU

This edition published 1997 in the United States of America by
Wm. B. Eerdmans Publishing Co.
255 Jefferson Ave. S.E., Grand Rapids, Michigan 49503

Printed in the United States of America

01 00 99 98 97   5 4 3 2 1

Library of Congress Cataloging-in-Publication Data

Wright, N. T. (Nicholas Thomas)
For all God's worth : true worship and the calling
of the church / N. T. Wright
p.   cm.
ISBN 0-8028-4319-0 (pbk. : alk. paper)
1. Worship.   2. Public worship.
3. God — Worship and love.
I. Title.
BV10.2.W75   1997
248.3 — dc21   97-4926
CIP

Biblical quotations are either the author's own translation or paraphrase,
or are taken from the New Revised Standard Version of the Bible, © 1989,
and are reprinted by permission of the National Council of the Churches
of Christ in the USA.

Quotations from *Heritage and Renewal: The Report of the Archbishops'
Commission on Cathedrals* (London: Church House Publishing, 1994) are
used by permission.

for the musicians of Lichfield Cathedral

Contents

INTRODUCTION

How can you cope with the end of a world and the
beginning of another one? How can you put an earthquake
into a test-tube, or the sea into a bottle? How can you live
with the terrifying thought that the hurricane has become
human, that fire has become flesh, that life itself came to
life and walked in our midst? Christianity either means that,
or it means nothing. It is either the most devastating dis-
closure of the deepest reality in the world, or it's a sham, a
nonsense, a bit of deceitful play-acting. Most of us, unable
to cope with saying either of those things, condemn ourselves to live in the shallow world in between. We may not
be content there, but we don't know how to escape.

This little book is an attempt to say that the way through
is by sheer unadulterated worship of the living and true
God, and by following this God wherever he leads, whether
or not it is the way our traditions would suggest. Worship
is not an optional extra for the Christian, a self-indulgent
religious activity. It is the basic Christian stance, and
indeed (so Christians claim) the truly human stance.
'Worship' derives from 'worth-ship': it means giving God
all he's worth. Hence the title of this book.

For many, Christianity is just a beautiful dream. It's a
world in which everyday reality goes a bit blurred. It's
nostalgic, cosy, and comforting. But real Christianity isn't
like that at all. Take Christmas, for instance: a season of

nostalgia, of carols and candles and firelight and happy
children. But that misses the point completely. Christmas is
not a reminder that the world is really quite a nice old
place. It reminds us that the world is a shockingly bad old
place, where wickedness flourishes unchecked, where children are murdered, where civilized countries make a lot of
money by selling weapons to uncivilized ones so they can
blow each other apart. Christmas is God lighting a candle;
and you don't light a candle in a room that's already full of
sunlight. You light a candle in a room that's so murky that
the candle, when lit, reveals just how bad things really are.
The light shines in the darkness, says St John, and the darkness has not overcome it.

Christmas, then, is not a dream, a moment of escapism.
Christmas is the reality, which shows up the rest of
'reality'. And for Christmas, here, read Christianity. Either
Jesus is the Lord of the world, and all reality makes sense
in his light, or he is dangerously irrelevant to the problems
and possibilities of today's world. There is no middle
ground. Either Jesus was, and is, the Word of God, or he,
and the stories Christians tell about him, are lies.

This is the conviction that has shaped this book. If the
word 'god' refers to anything, and if that anything is anything like the God revealed in Jesus of Nazareth, then we
are bound to take this God with the utmost seriousness.
(There are, of course, all sorts of historical and theological
problems involved in making claims like this about Jesus
and God; I am doing my best to address them elsewhere.)
We can't just acknowledge a God like this at a distance,
and carry on as before. If the stories are true, this God
didn't stay at a distance himself. He took us seriously
enough to come into our world as one of us.

But if we take this God seriously, we find we have to
take ourselves seriously as well. Not, of course, in the
sense that we become gloomy or morbid; rather, in the

sense that we must look at ourselves in the mirror and ask some fairly sharp questions about who we are and what we think we're up to. If God is God, these questions are worth asking. If Jesus is the Word of God, the answers might just take your breath away – and offer you God's breath instead. When that happens, the first result is worship, worshipping God for all he's worth; and the next result will be mission. That movement, that rhythm, is what this book is all about.

Most of this book has grown out of that rhythm as it is expressed in the life and work of Lichfield Cathedral, which, like all cathedrals, is designed to house a community of worship and mission. The second chapter is based on the sermon which I preached at my installation as Dean; several other chapters began in the cathedral as well. The early chapters focus quite narrowly on God and on what worshipping God actually means. The later ones address a range of issues in the mission and unity of the church which arise from that worship. A cathedral, after all, is not a place of retreat from the world, but a place of prayer and of prophecy, a beacon to shine God's light into the world. It is designed as a rich and powerful symbol of the gospel of God's grace.

One of the supreme ways in which a cathedral can be this in reality is by using God's gift of music both in worship and in witness. Hence the dedication: to a group of people whose particular vocation is to enable the rest of us, in the cathedral and further afield, to lift our hearts and minds to the living God in worship and adoration, and to respond to him in love and service. Church musicians sometimes come in for a bad press – from the clergy, for being obstinate and intractable (which of course clergy *never* are themselves!); from the public, either for being out of touch or for being impossibly trendy. I am delighted to report that none of these things apply to our present musicians, from the Organist and Master of the Choristers, Andrew Lumsden, down to the youngest chorister. On the contrary, they exemplify the Lichfield Cathedral motto, *Inservi Deo et Laetari*: Serve God and be cheerful!

Taking daily and weekly worship seriously needs serious resources. All the proceeds from this book will go towards the maintenance and enhancement of the musical life of the cathedral, as we seek to serve the local community, the whole diocese of Lichfield, and the wider church and world. It is my hope that the book will thus, in a small way, help to enable the thing which it commends.

Tom Wright
Lichfield Cathedral

Part One: The God Who is Worthy of Praise

CHAPTER ONE

Worship

What is the most beautiful thing you have experienced this week?

Maybe something you heard. Maybe some beautiful music – perhaps in church, or in a cathedral.

Maybe something you saw in the world of nature: the sun breaking through the mist and making the autumn leaves luminous; the curl of a squirrel's tail as he sat nibbling a nut.

It might be something you smelt: the scent of a rose, perhaps, or the smell of a good meal cooking when you were very hungry.

It might be something you tasted: an exquisite wine, a special cheese, that same meal well seasoned and well cooked.

Maybe something you experienced in work: things suddenly coming together, an unexpected new opportunity.

It might be something you experienced in human relationships: a quiet, gentle glance from someone you love dearly; the soft squeeze of a child's hand.

Hold the moment in your mind. And ask yourself: what does this beauty do to you?

It enriches you; yes. It warms you inside; yes. It makes you more alive; yes. It makes you stronger; yes. It makes you, perhaps, a little humble: you didn't cause this beauty, you didn't make it, it just happened, and happened to you. Yes.

And what does this beauty call out from you?

Gratitude – of course; delight – yes, naturally; a sense of awe – well, perhaps; a sense of longing for something beyond, something just out of reach – quite possibly, though if your experience of beauty was the smell of a good meal I hope it didn't stay out of reach for too long.

What about – *worship*?

Does beauty call out worship from you?

We don't very often use the word 'worship' to describe our attitude to things or people other than God himself. Almost the only place we come across it is in the marriage service in the Book of Common Prayer, where, to my mind utterly appropriately, the man declares to the woman, 'with my body I thee worship'. And, of course, there are good biblical injunctions not to worship, in the fullest sense, anything or anyone except God himself. But the word 'worship' means, literally, 'worth-ship': to accord worth, true value, to something, to recognize and respect it for the true worth it has. And that sets us on a trail that leads us from the squirrel in the garden, the steak in the oven, the singing in the choir, and the squeeze of the hand, all the way to the one who created all of them in the first place.

I want to speak about worship; and that means that I want to talk about God, and about the beauty of God. If we are to worship God truly, it is not enough to think of God's greatness and majesty, his power and sovereignty, his holiness and absolute otherness. That's all enormously important, as part of the story. But we wouldn't ordinarily use the word *beauty* to refer to any of that. I want to suggest to you in this chapter that our ordinary experiences of beauty are given to us to provide a clue, a starting-point, a signpost, from which we move on to recognize, to glimpse, to be overwhelmed by, to adore, and so to worship, not just the majesty, but the beauty of God himself. And, just as we don't very often use the word 'worship' in connection with beauty in the natural world, so we don't very often use the word 'beauty' in connection with God. That is our loss, and I suggest we set about making it good.

Why do I want to talk about worship? Two reasons stand out. First, there are some central passages in scripture which speak of our citizenship in heaven, and which speak of it not least as a constant and delighted experience of worship. The great multitude in Revelation which no man can number aren't playing cricket. They aren't going shopping. They are *worshipping*. Sounds boring? If so, it shows how impoverished our idea of worship has become. At the centre of that worship stands a passage like Isaiah 33: your eyes will see the king in his beauty; the LORD is our judge, the LORD is our ruler, the LORD is our king; he will save us. Worship is the central characteristic of the heavenly life; and that worship is focused on the God we know in and as Jesus.

The second reason I want to talk about worship is that it forms the central task of the church, not least of a cathedral. The Archbishops of Canterbury and York recently commissioned a report on English cathedrals, which was published in 1994 under the title *Heritage and Renewal* (London: Church House Publishing). The report covers many different aspects of the life of Cathedrals. Whatever one thinks of the details in various places, there is, right at the centre, something they got gloriously right. The report states unequivocally and emphatically that the purpose of a cathedral – and this would, of course, apply to any church anywhere – is worship and mission. These two, it emphasizes, belong inextricably together, with management (which it calls 'governance') as the vital means of enabling and sustaining that worship and mission. 'There is unanimity', they say, 'about the priority of worship in the function of cathedrals . . . These great buildings are descriptions of the majesty of God; places of living faith' (p. 8). The Commission stresses that, at the centre of all mission opportunities and management requirements, the primary emphasis is on worship as 'the maintenance of a daily witness to the sovereignty of God in the world' (p. 15). This is linked directly to the cathedral's role in society, and always has a missionary reference: 'in giving glory to God, the primary purpose of worship, those present may be enabled to catch a glimpse of that glory' (p. 17). Daily cathedral worship has been 'the central pillar of the Church's prayer and praise down the centuries, and the spiritual heartbeat not only of the cathedral but of the diocese, the community and the nation' (p. 18). Indeed, it is the worship of God that prevents these buildings becoming mere theme parks or museums: 'Without the warming fire of worship', say the Commission in summing up at the end of the report, 'these elegant buildings would be ancient monuments rather than living temples capable of inspiring the souls of men and women with glimpses of the divine' (p. 173).

It is right, therefore, that from time to time the church should take stock of that which is most central, most important, most vital in our common life together. Though we sing with the tongues of men and of angels, if we are not truly worshipping the living God, we are noisy gongs and clanging cymbals. Though we organize the liturgy most beautifully, if it does not enable us to worship the living God, we are mere ballet-dancers. Though we repave the floor and reface the stonework, though we balance our budgets and attract all the tourists, if we are not worshipping God, we are nothing.

Worship is humble and glad; worship forgets itself in remembering God; worship celebrates the truth as God's truth, not its own. True worship doesn't put on a show or make a fuss; true worship isn't forced, isn't half-hearted, doesn't keep looking at its watch, doesn't worry what the person in the next pew may be doing. True worship is open to God, adoring God, waiting for God, trusting God even in the dark.

Worship will never end; whether there be buildings, they will crumble; whether there be committees, they will fall asleep; whether there be budgets, they will add up to nothing. For we build for the present age, we discuss for the present age, and we pay for the present age; but when the age to come is here, the present age will be done away. For now we see the beauty of God through a glass, darkly, but then face to face; now we appreciate only part, but then we shall affirm and appreciate God, even as the living God has affirmed and appreciated us. So now our tasks are worship, mission and management, these three; but the greatest of these is worship.

And do you see why it's so easy to create that pastiche of 1 Corinthians 13, substituting 'worship' for 'love'? Worship is nothing more nor less than love on its knees before the beloved; just as mission is love on its feet to serve the beloved – and just as the Eucharist, as the climax of worship, is love embracing the beloved and so being strengthened for service.

But this is only true if it's the true God you're worshipping. I was talking to somebody not long ago who said, 'You know, I used to believe in God; but then, as I grew up, I found it harder and harder to think of this old man up there in the sky, so far removed from all the pain and suffering down here in the world.' And I said to him, 'I don't

believe in that god either! The God I believe in is the God I
see in the middle of the pain and the suffering down here in
the world. Without Jesus, the crucified Jesus, sharing and
bearing the pain and sin and suffering of the world, I don't
actually know who on earth, or in heaven, God might be at
all.' You see, if you envisage a god up there in the sky,
detached from the reality of the world, any worship you
offer will simply be a distant acknowledgement of majesty,
like the ploughboy doffing his cap as the great nobleman
rides by ignoring him. And if you go the other route, as my
friend was inclined to, and say that therefore the word
'god' can only refer to the impulse of goodness inside ourselves, then you'll find it pretty hard to sustain any real
sense of worship at all. All you're left with is the ploughboy imagining himself to be a nobleman. But if Jesus is to
be the lens through which you glimpse the beauty of God,
you will discover what it means to worship, because you
will discover what it means to be loved.

Put it this way: if your idea of God, if your idea of the
salvation offered in Christ, is vague or remote, your idea of
worship will be fuzzy and ill-formed. The closer you get to
the truth, the clearer becomes the beauty, and the more you
will find worship welling up within you. That's why theology and worship belong together. The one isn't just a head-
trip; the other isn't just emotion.

I recently read a remarkable testimony to this fact, from
a man called Jason Richards, who at the time was in Park-
hurst prison serving a life sentence for murder. This is
some of what he said:

> I hadn't been long in my sentence and I was very con-
> fused . . . I was carrying an awful lot of guilt. I was
> looking for answers. I read a lot. I read Buddhism. I
> read Islam. I started reading the Bible. And the more I
> read the Scriptures the more I became aware of God.

I didn't believe in God. I was actually an atheist – or at least I thought I was. But I came to believe that God existed. And the more I became aware of God the more I became aware that I was a sinner – and I got more and more desperate.

Then one night . . . I opened the Bible at the very first psalm. I started reading . . . and when I got to Psalms 50 and 51 I realized that God would forgive me. I didn't know [why Psalm 51 had been written] then. But the thing I knew was, 'Save me from bloodguilt, O God, the God who saves me, and my tongue will sing of your righteousness.'

I knew that God could forgive me . . . I didn't know anything about Jesus or the Bible or the Church. I just knew. I read all the rest of the psalms on my knees – and almost from that point for me they became psalms of praise. *It was like I was beginning to worship – and I didn't know what worship was.*

From one point of view that last sentence is no doubt true. He didn't know the dictionary definition of worship. He probably didn't even use the word itself. But I think he did know what worship was, because I think he had met the living God, the loving God, the beautiful God, the God of whom the psalmist wrote when he said:

One thing have I desired of the LORD, that I will require:
That I may dwell in the house of the LORD all the days of my life,
To behold the fair beauty of the LORD, and to visit his Temple.

The beauty of God is the beauty of love; love in creation, love in re-creation of a world spoiled by sin. It is the same love; which is why all the beauty of the world, the beauty that calls forth our admiration, our gratitude, our worth-ship at the earthly level, is meant as a set of hints, of conspiratorial whispers, of clues and suggestions and flickers of light, all nudging us into believing that behind the beautiful world is not random chance but the loving God. He who made the eye, does he not see? He who made the ear, does he not hear? He who created all beauty, is he not himself beautiful? Woe betide those who offer to the creature the worship due to the creator alone; but woe betide those who fail to read the hints, who fail to hear the subtext, who have the experience but miss the meaning, who are deaf to what may be heard, half-heard, in the stillness between two waves of the sea.

St Augustine, in a famous passage, rightly denies that our loves for the material world are the same thing as love for God. Yet, he says, our loves for the material world give us both a sign of, and the vocabulary for, our love for God. And we don't have to apologize for speaking of this love in this way. The world is God's creation, and its beauty is the steady, quizzical pointer to the beauty of God. This is what he wrote:

What do I love when I love my God? Not physical beauty, or the splendour of time; not the radiance of earthly light, so pleasant to our eyes; not the sweet melodies of harmony and song; not the fragrant smell of flowers, perfumes, and spices; not manna or honey; not limbs such as the flesh delights to embrace. These are not the things that I love when I love my God.

And yet, when I love him, I do indeed love a certain kind of light, a voice, a fragrance, a food, an embrace; but this love takes place in my inner person, where my soul is bathed in light that is not bound by space; when it listens to sound that time never takes away; when it breathes in a fragrance which no breeze carries away; when it tastes food which no eating can diminish; when it clings to an embrace which is not broken when desire is fulfilled. This is what I love when I love my God. *(Confessions* 10.6)

People often quote Oscar Wilde's dictum, that a cynic knows the price of everything and the value of nothing. We live in an age of cynics, where 'worth' means 'price' and 'price' means money and money means power. But the gospel of Jesus Christ puts worth back into the world, worth beyond price, worth beyond worldly power; for the gospel of Jesus Christ summons us to worship, to worthship, to lay our lives before the one true and living God, to worship him for all he's worth. Give to this great and loving God the honour, the worship, the love, due to him; celebrate the goodness, the worth, the true value, of the created order, as his gift, his handiwork; and allow that celebration to lift your eyes once more to God himself, to his glory and beauty.

This is, of course, precisely what we do in the Eucharist. Symbols of the natural world become vehicles of the heavenly world, of which we are called to be citizens. And it is utterly fitting that we should surround and celebrate this moment of intense beauty with carved stone and coloured glass, with soaring music and solemn ritual. Worship is what we were made for. Worship is what buildings like churches and cathedrals were made for. If we get this right, we will go to our tasks of mission and management in the right spirit and for the right reason. Worship the LORD in the beauty of holiness; let the whole earth stand in awe of him.

CHAPTER TWO

It Is All God's Work

It is all too easy to suppose that, when we turn from worship to work, we turn from thinking about God to thinking about ourselves. Not so, says St Paul in a magnificent passage in 2 Corinthians 5.11–21: 'It is all God's work' (v. 18). It isn't just us playing ceremonial games; it isn't us forcing our agendas on to people; it isn't a few religious nuts coming unscrewed and rattling around the place. What we are about is the work of God.

Now of course that's an absurd claim. Surely God does God's work; who are we to claim to have even a small hand in it? Well, which god might we talking about? A god who is so lofty and remote that he would never get his hands dirty? That's not the God that great cathedrals were designed to celebrate. A god who is identified with the processes of nature? That's not the God whom the early missionaries went all over the world to proclaim. No: the God we worship here is the God of costly love: 'The love of Christ', Paul wrote, 'overwhelms us, when we consider that one died for all; and his purpose in dying was that those who live should live no more for themselves, but for him who for their sake died and was raised.' In other words, there is a different God to those imagined by so many in the dark ages both of the seventh century, when the first Christian communities were founded in Middle England, and of the late twentieth century. The true God is

God

the one who became human and died and rose again in order to offer a new way of being human, a way of worship and love. Christ died, says Paul, so that we might embody the saving faithfulness of God: 'It is all God's work.'

Now if that isn't true, a building like a cathedral is simply an expensive monument to an impossible dream; and all we do in it is simply an elaborate way of turning over in bed, the better to continue the dream rather than wake up and face reality. But if it is true – if it really is the case that the true God is the one whose love overwhelms us in Jesus Christ – then the appropriate response is celebration, because this God is the reconciler, the healer. Celebration and healing: that is what a cathedral is all about.

'It is all God's work'; celebration no less than anything else. We in the modern West have forgotten *how* to celebrate, probably because we've forgotten *why*. Large meals, lots of drink, and behaving childishly is a parody of true celebration; but it's what you might expect when we forget that our maker is also our lover. That was the condition of Israel in exile, the people addressed in Isaiah 35. Israel was called to be the people of God, but in exile it had all gone stale. People in our society know in their bones that they are made to reflect God's image; but they feel exiled, futile, and stale; so they go in for tired and shoddy celebration, seen only too clearly in the forced frivolity of television programmes over Christmas and New Year. Contrast that mood with the one Isaiah held out to the exiles:

> The wilderness and the dry land shall be glad,
>   the desert shall rejoice and blossom;
> like the crocus it shall blossom abundantly,
>   and rejoice with joy and singing . . .
> They shall see the glory of the LORD,
>   the majesty of our God.

> . . . the ransomed of the LORD shall return,
>   and come to Zion with singing;
> everlasting joy shall be upon their heads;
>   they shall obtain joy and gladness,
>   and sorrow and sighing shall flee away.

When we realize once again that our God is the one who loves us into new life, then we will really know how to celebrate. True celebration, in turn, sustains true humanness. As we glimpse the living God, we are transformed into his likeness.

So it isn't surprising that those who are grasped by this gospel have built cathedrals. People who have forgotten who God is produce concrete jungles and cardboard cities. People who remember or rediscover who God is build cathedrals to his glory, and homes where the poor are cared for; we have both in the city of Lichfield, and they belong together, in celebration and healing. People in our contemporary society are cramped and stifled, fed on a diet of ugliness and noise. They are hungry for beauty, for light, for music. In celebrating and maintaining a wonderful cathedral, we are not a sub-branch of the 'heritage industry'. We are telling real people about the real God: we are saying that there is a different way to be human, a way in which worship and mystery and silence and light and space all play their proper part.

Thus, in a generation whose daily diet is the trivia of muzak and the relentless cacophony of industrial noise, we have the opportunity to celebrate the love of God with some of the greatest music ever written. In doing so, we are not a sub-branch of the musicians' union, but are creating the conditions for real people to be caught up in a rhythm of worship which is beyond their own power, and which can often refresh the parts other styles cannot reach. 'It is all God's work': beauty springs out of naught at the touch o

God. That is why we celebrate; and every gift that God has given us, of art, architecture, music, flower-arranging, theological study, and everything else, is taken up within the total sacrifice of praise. That's what a cathedral is there for. It is all God's work.

But celebration is only the beginning; and in some ways it isn't the most important part of the story. The first time I was shown around Lichfield Cathedral the thing that struck me most forcibly was the way in which the building itself had suffered over the years. The scars are still there; the seams still show, and the stitching is still visible, where devastation in one generation met with reconstruction in the next. Lichfield suffered more than any other cathedral during the Civil War; it was used variously as a military stronghold and as a stable, and it lost its central tower in the process. And there are older tales, too, of massacres and violence. Treasures have been plundered, not least the relics of Chad himself, the first Bishop. Looking wider than just the building, the diocese of Lichfield has suffered various identity crises, being redefined as much because of political intrigue as because of spiritual or pastoral necessity. So, too, the history of both the chapter and the choir reveals all too clearly the folly, as well as the faith, of our forebears. It is even reported that there have been some Deans who were less than the perfect model of Christian piety and wisdom; though one suspects, of course, that here at least malicious legend has been at work.

So what? Is all this something over which we should draw a discreet veil? Should we quietly forget the past, and just enjoy our building and music? No; that would turn the place into a compromise between a museum and a concert hall. Rather, we should embrace the fact that the very stones of such a building speak of a God who takes human wrath and turns it to his praise; who takes even Christian folly and turns it into wisdom; who takes wickedness done in his own name and brings out of it restoration, reconciliation, and new life. If the gospel of Jesus Christ is not about God doing precisely that, it is no good to us. This building embodies the word we need to hear, the word that Isaiah announced to the exiles:

> Then shall the eyes of the blind be opened
>   and the ears of the deaf unstopped;
> then shall the lame leap like a hart,
>   and the tongue of the dumb sing for joy;
> for waters shall break forth in the wilderness,
>   and streams in the desert.

Yes, it is a scandal that Lichfield Cathedral should have functioned as a convenient spot from which to shoot people. Yes, it is somewhat ambiguous that it was restored under Charles II. Yes, it is to our shame that the history of our church is littered with disputes and squabbles. But let's get hold of one thing: St Chad did not come to Lichfield to tell people that if they were already good enough God would be happy to have them on his side. The eighth-century Lichfield Gospels, which we treasure in the cathedral, were not lovingly illuminated because they said that if the people of God were without blemish then God would bring in his kingdom. No. The reason why Chad came to Lichfield, and the reason why an ancient scribe lavished such craftsmanship on those priceless pages, is quite simply that the message *in* those Gospels is even more priceless: the message, that is, that the true God takes our brokenness and in Christ makes us new; that he picks up the pieces of our life, yes, even of our muddled attempts to follow him, and sticks them together again in a new way; that he heals those who are broken in heart, and gives the medicine to heal their sickness; that he promises new life, resurrection life, beyond all our sickness and death. To celebrate precisely here is to celebrate not the wonderful achievements of the church but the healing power of God to build his church with battered and broken building-blocks, including people like you and me. Celebration and healing; it is all God's work.

And what if the seams are still visible? What if the stitching still shows? What if we carry about with us the pain of being half put back together and half still in pieces? What if we have identity crises, if we live with ambiguities and face problems we can't solve overnight? Is that not what being a Christian is all about? As Paul continues, we are taken for imposters, and yet are genuine; dying, and behold we live; in pain, yet always full of joy; poor, yet making many rich; having nothing, yet possessing everything. Paul is not describing an occasional unfortunate lapse from the norm. This is normal Christian existence.

It is because people forget this that much nonsense is spoken and written today. From time to time in the UK certain journalists enjoy mocking the Church of England for having lost its nerve. We are hopelessly divided, they say, heading for ruin, going round in circles like a rudderless ship, with our leaders in disarray and our people in confusion. The evidence they cite consists, often enough, of quotations from each other, and from a suspiciously short list of would-be spokesmen (they're usually men) from the church.

I wonder which world these people live in? Where is it written in scripture that we can expect the church to be free from financial problems, from doctrinal controversy, from difficulties about leadership, from deep personal and corporate anxieties? Where is it written in history that there ever was such a church? Where is it written in theology that God demands such perfection? Go back to Paul's second letter to Corinth and you will find that it concerns exactly these issues. And Paul addresses his readers in Corinth, not with

carping criticism, but with the power of love; not with
sneering put-downs about what a shabby lot they were in
Corinth, but with the gospel of Jesus; not with cynicism,
but with the cross.

And the cross – as the very shape of the cathedral, like
so many churches, reminds us – the cross is the be-all and
end-all of the gospel. It is the cross that generates celebration and offers healing. It is all God's work: the cross
speaks of the God who didn't send someone else to do the
dirty work but came and did it himself; of the God who
lived in our midst and died our death; of the God who now
entrusts us with that same vocation. Because of the cross,
being a Christian, or being a church, does not mean claiming that *we've* got it all together. It means claiming that
God's got it all together; and that we are merely, as Paul
says, those who are overwhelmed by his love. A cathedral
is not the triumphalistic sign of a careless power and
prestige; it is the covenant sign of a suffering love, the
symphony in stone in honour of the Servant King.

And if the seams are still visible – if the stitching still
shows – so what? Those journalists of whom I spoke should
leave their comfortable metropolis for a moment and come
here; come and worship with us, share our life for a few
days; then come round the diocese and see the new green
shoots that are growing through the secular concrete; look
where the blind are seeing, and the lame walking, and the
dumb singing for joy. Let them come and see where the
diocese, whose mother church this is, is standing alongside
those recently unemployed in the mining areas; let them see
that the countryside may be forgotten by the politicians but
is not forgotten by the church; let them see how priests
ordained right here are working with the people of the
street in Walsall and Wolverhampton. Let them come and
see that we, gladly together with all who name the name of
Jesus, are following as best we know how in the way of the

cross. Of course we are in pain on various issues. Of course we sometimes feel as if we're coming unglued. So what? Let them come and see that at the heart of England there is a building whose very stones speak of God's healing love; that at the heart of that building there is a book whose every page is a work of art celebrating that love; and that around that book there is a community of people committed to the one of whom that book speaks, who know themselves called to live not for their own sakes but for his sake who died and rose again. This is our God, the Servant King; he calls us now to follow him.

And if we are to make such an invitation, our immediate task is to consolidate what this community is already good at. No one comes into this cathedral, or into any church, without some pain or fear, without some guilt or grief. But the testimony of many is that when they have come here they have felt welcomed, loved and sustained. That is wonderful, and I thank God for it. People have learned elsewhere today to expect rudeness and even violence as the norm. They are thirsty for gentleness, for kindness, for the sense that they matter. They need to be shown that there is a different way of being human, that the true God embraces them, as they are, with the healing power of the cross and the life-giving breath of the Spirit. That welcome is our work, because it is all God's work, and he invites us to share in it.

We are therefore, in Paul's words, to be ambassadors for Christ. We don't have to be perfect in ourselves. On the cross he dealt with our sin so that he could then work through us, so that we in turn might embody the saving faithfulness of God to all those whom we meet, all those who enter here. And the real mystery of that is that we do it not so much in our triumphs as in our tragedies; not in our strength but in our weakness; not in our success but in our failure. In the real world, it is the wounded who heal.

That is why the chequered history of this cathedral forms such an eloquent statement of the gospel. Celebration and healing: this is to be a place where eyes are opened to truth, where ears long deaf hear their name spoken in love, where those who had forgotten how to sing discover a joy which refuses to remain silent. And when *we* live by that gospel, then tourists may find themselves becoming pilgrims; photographers may stop clicking for a moment and glimpse true beauty; musicians may hear undreamed of harmonies; and historians may come face to face with the one who is Lord of the dead and the living. And so, as celebration leads to healing, healing leads back to celebration. It is all God's work; and those who find themselves called to it must, quite simply, 'serve God and be cheerful'.

CHAPTER THREE

The God I Want?

A few years ago I was browsing in a second-hand bookshop when I came across a book with a title that still makes me think. I confess I didn't buy the book, and haven't read it, so I don't know if I am misjudging it and its author; but the title sums up a particular attitude shared by many people, including many Christians, today. The title was *The God I Want*. I remember thinking then, and I still think now, that that title was silly, and ultimately self-defeating.

The God I Want? Left to myself, the god I want is a god who will give me what I want. He – or more likely it – will be a projection of my desires. At the grosser level, this will lead me to one of the more obvious pagan gods or goddesses, who offer their devotees money, or sex, or power (as Marx, Freud and Nietzsche pointed out). All idols started out life as the god somebody wanted.

At the more sophisticated level, the god I want will be a god who lives up to my intellectual expectations: a god of whom I can approve rationally, judiciously, after due consideration and weighing up of theological probabilities. I want this god because he, or it, will underwrite my intellectual arrogance. He will boost my sense of being a refined modern thinker. The net result is that *I* become god; and this god I've made becomes my puppet. Nobody falls down on their face before the god they wanted. Nobody trembles at the word of a home-made god. Nobody goes

out with fire in their belly to heal the sick, to clothe the
naked, to teach the ignorant, to feed the hungry, because of
the god they wanted. They are more likely to stay at home
with their feet up.

But on one particular day in the year we celebrate the
God whom we didn't want - how could we have ever
dreamed of it? - but who, amazingly, wanted us. In the
church's year, Trinity Sunday is the day when we stand
back from the extraordinary sequence of events that we've
been celebrating for the previous five months - Advent,
Christmas, Epiphany, Lent, Good Friday, Easter, Ascension, Pentecost - and when we rub the sleep from our eyes
and discover what the word 'god' might actually mean.
These events function as a sequence of well-aimed hammer-
blows which knock at the clay jars of the gods we want, the
gods who reinforce our own pride or prejudice, until they
fall away and reveal instead a very different god, a
dangerous god, a subversive god, a god who comes to us
like a blind beggar with wounds in his hands, a god who
comes to us in wind and fire, in bread and wine, in flesh
and blood: a god who says to us, 'You did not choose me; I
chose you.'

You see, the doctrine of the Trinity, properly
understood, is as much a way of saying 'we don't know' as
of saying 'we do know'. To say that the true God is Three
and One is to recognize that if there is a God then of course
we shouldn't expect him to fit neatly into our little
categories. If he did, he wouldn't be God at all, merely a
god, a god we might perhaps have wanted. The Trinity is
not something that the clever theologian comes up with as a
result of hours spent in the theological laboratory, after
which he or she can return to announce that they've got
God worked out now, the analysis is complete, and here is
God neatly laid out on a slab. The only time they laid God
out on a slab he rose again three days afterwards. On the

contrary: the doctrine of the Trinity is, if you like, a signpost pointing ahead into the dark, saying: 'Trust me; follow me; my love will keep you safe.' Or, perhaps better, the doctrine of the Trinity is a signpost pointing into a light which gets brighter and brighter until we are dazzled and blinded, but which says: 'Come, and I will make you children of light.' The doctrine of the Trinity affirms the rightness, the propriety, of speaking intelligently about the true God, while at the same time affirming intelligently that the true God must always transcend our grasp of him, even our most intelligent grasp of him. As St Paul says, what matters isn't so much our knowledge of God as God's knowledge of us; not, as it were, the god we want but the God who wants us. God help us, we don't understand ourselves; how can we expect to understand that Self which stands beside our selves like Niagara beside a trickling tap?

All of this leaves me with two questions. First, do we then need to say anything at all? Isn't it enough just to acknowledge that the whole thing is extremely mysterious and puzzling and leave it at that? Mightn't we just as well say that god is five and one, or fifteen and one, as that God is Three and One? Second, and most important, what difference does it make in what we please to call 'the real world'?

These two questions are in fact intimately linked. We can make 'intelligent' missiles that can make war on one particular building hundreds of miles away, but we don't have an equivalent one that can make peace. Might that be because we have worshipped the gods of war, but have forgotten about worshipping the prince of peace? We can put a few men on the moon, but the few men who were standing between the Tutsis and the Hutus in Rwanda in 1994 had to be withdrawn for lack of funds and political will. Might that be because we have worshipped the gods of technology, the gods who boost our own national security –

the gods we have wanted, in other words – and have forgotten the god who asked Cain, 'Where is Abel your brother?'

You see, what you believe about God makes a difference to the way you respond to this god, and at the same time to the way you are in the world. Let's look at the options. For most people in the Western world today, the word 'god' refers to a distant, remote being. We can't and don't know very much about this being. He may or may not have made the world, though if we say he did we have an uncomfortable feeling that the scientists are going to challenge us (despite people like John Polkinghorne in Cambridge, one of the finest scientists of our generation and also a leading Christian theologian). This god may or may not intervene from time to time in the world, though he usually doesn't. He has, in fact, left us to muddle through as best we can; which usually means looking after our own interests, carving up the world, and perhaps each other, in our own way. The cat's asleep upstairs, and the mice – and perhaps the rats – are organising the world downstairs.

That's why this remote 'god' is the god that the Western world decided it wanted in the eighteenth century: a god to be cooly acknowledged for an hour or so on Sunday mornings, and ignored for the other hundred and sixty-seven hours in the week. No wonder, when they did a survey not long ago, the great majority of people in the United Kingdom said they believed in 'god', but only a small minority regularly go to church. If that's what you believe about 'god' – and it's what a lot of our society still does believe, including (alas) some within the church – then any sense of worship or religious celebration becomes a vague ritual, a meaningless noise, which merely makes us feel a bit better about ourselves. Is it any wonder that the rats are eating the dead after yet another massacre, and the dove is still locked up in the ark? Can such a god really be God?

The problem is that when you banish what you call 'god' up into the remote stratosphere, other gods come clamouring for attention from closer at hand. There are very few out-and-out atheists in the world; those who claim to disbelieve often merely disbelieve in the old high-and-dry god, while happily serving other gods of whom they may be quite unaware, and doing so not just for one hour in the week but with total energy and commitment. I have spoken of the gods of war, of money, of sex. The appalling genocide that still continues in our contemporary world, even within supposedly 'civilized' parts of it, are evidence that millions still give allegiance to gods of blood and soil, of tribe and race. Sometimes they try to invoke parts of Christian tradition to support this; but the fact that they go on killing each other shows clearly enough that it isn't Jesus whom they are worshipping. Christian doctrine isn't a matter of intellectual algebra. It is directly integrated with the way people behave. If the gods you want, and worship, are the gods from below, the local tribal gods, the gods of power and wealth and pleasure, you will destroy yourself and everyone who gets in the way.

But what if we were to take the doctrine of the Trinity seriously? What sort of response, what sort of worship, would that generate? And what sort of agenda, what sort of programme, might arise from such worship?

Before we can address this question, we must face the problem: why on earth should we think in trinitarian terms at all? Isn't this just a bit of muddled dogma, a jumble of dusty ideas which may have meant something to someone many years ago, but about which we must keep a newly open mind today?

The short response to that was given some time ago by G. K. Chesterton. The purpose of an open mind, he said, is like the purpose of an open mouth: that it might be shut again on something solid. Yes, we must be free to ask questions. But when we hear a good answer we must be prepared to recognize it as such, and not be so keen on keeping all questions open that we shy away from an answer because we so like having an open mind. That is the way to intellectual, as well as spiritual, starvation.

But the fuller answer might run something like this. I set it out in three brief stages: it would, of course, take an entire course in systematic theology to work it out in detail.

First, the place of doctrine within Christianity is absolutely vital. Christians are not defined by skin colour, by gender, by geographical location, or even, shockingly, by their good behaviour. Nor are they defined by the particular type of religious feelings they may have. They are defined in terms of *the god they worship*. That's why we say the Creed at the heart of our regular liturgies: we are defined as the people who believe in this god. All other definitions of the church are open to distortion. We need theology, we need doctrine, because if we don't have it something else will come in to take its place. And any other defining marks of the church will move us in the direction of idolatry.

Second, despite what is often imagined, the Trinity grows directly out of Jewish monotheism. It isn't a later corrupt development. The Jewish belief in one god, which was the seed-bed for early Christianity, was never intended as an analysis of the inner being of this one god. Rather, within Judaism in the time of Jesus we find various ideas about the way the one god would act within his world. He would come to live in the Temple. He was present when people studied his law. He breathed with his Spirit on certain persons, to enable them to speak and act with his authority. He spoke his creative Word, and things happened. His divine Wisdom was alive and active throughout the world, but especially in Israel. And it is precisely these ideas – these thoroughly Jewish ways of envisaging the one true and living God – that form the basis of what the earliest Christians said about Jesus and the Spirit. They didn't imagine for a moment that they were abandoning Jewish-style monotheism. They simply used the Jewish categories available to them to describe what it was that they had seen in Jesus, and what it was that they knew of the Spirit. The doctrine of the Trinity is thoroughly present in the very earliest writings of the New Testament, such as Paul's letters: God was in Christ reconciling the world to himself, and entrusting us (by the Spirit) with the message of reconciliation. Trinitarian theology is not a late or strange corruption. It lies at the heart of the very earliest Christianity of which we have evidence.

Third, the particular words we use to express trinitarian theology are of course negotiable. The word 'person', for instance, doesn't mean in modern English what it meant in the Latin from which the phrase 'three persons' is derived. This is the point at which we must be truly open-minded. The doctrine of the Trinity, indeed, is paradoxically the thing which forces us to keep our minds open: having grasped, or been grasped by, the fact that the true god is both three and one we are forced not into closed-mindedness but into true open-mindedness, not because we want to criticize or dispute but because we are hungry for God, hungry to know him better, hungry to love in return the one, and the three, who has loved us into life. The word 'person' in speaking of the Trinity is a way of saying that, from one point of view, there is an irreducible three-ness about the true God, and that the man Jesus of Nazareth is to be identified with one of these three. Likewise, the word 'substance', in speaking of the Trinity, is a way of saying that, from another point of view, there is an irreducible oneness about the true God, shared completely by Jesus and by the Spirit. If we can find better ways of saying the same thing, good luck to us.

I return, then, to my underlying question. What sort of response might belief in this God generate? What sort of spirituality does such worship foster? What sort of agenda might it generate?

To believe in the Trinity is to believe that the true god is the passionate and compassionate God. He is neither the high-and-dry, remote god of so much modern imagination, nor the dark force that drives people into selfish and destructive lifestyles. He is the God who gives himself totally to his world, gives himself in sacrificial love, pours himself out generously, recklessly and prodigally upon his creation. When St John the Divine found himself looking into the open door of heaven, he didn't see the god he might have wanted; he saw all creation worshipping the awesome and majestic creator God; and, when he looked closer, he saw a Lamb that had been killed and was now alive for evermore. The doctrine of the Trinity declares the mystery which is above all else what this broken world needs to hear: that the true God is not detached from the evil of the world, but has come to share it and bear it in his own body. We do not say, 'God so loved the world that he sent somebody else'; we say, 'God so loved the world that he sent his only beloved Son.'

And, as St Paul insists, the God who sent the Son is the God who sends the Spirit of the Son, to put into practice, to implement, what the Son achieved. To believe in the Trinity is to believe that God came in Jesus to the place where the pain was greatest, to take it upon himself. It is also to believe that God comes today, in the Spirit, to the place where the pain is still at its height, to share the groaning of his world in order to bring the world to new life. But the Spirit doesn't do that in isolation. The Spirit does it by dwelling within Christians and enabling them to stand, in prayer and in suffering, at that place of pain. The doctrine of the Trinity is all about prayer, and pain, and prophecy.

It is the doctrine that undergirds the work of a Mother Theresa. It is the doctrine that assures us that our visiting of the sick, our teaching of the young, our creating of beauty, our praying and working for justice and peace in the world, are not simply us doing something for God; they are God acting in and through us.

Moreover, the doctrine of the Trinity assures us that this work is not in vain. Even if, like Jesus himself, we seem to have thrown ourselves away chasing a dream that many dismiss as foolish or impossible, the doctrine of the Trinity insists that out of this death there comes new life, God's own life given to be the life of the world. As we pray for those places in the world which undergo intense and utterly horrible suffering, we stand with those Christians who are at the place of pain right now, continuing through their tears to bear witness to the suffering love of the true God; and we pray for strength to say prophetically to our own government, and to other people's governments, and to the United Nations, that there is a different way of ordering international affairs, and that we must seek and find it with all urgency.

And so it is not as an escape from the world, but as the only truly human stance before the world, that we affirm our faith in the one God who is Father, Son and Spirit. And we do that not just in words, in saying the Creed. We do it, far more powerfully, in the symbol of the Eucharist. The Eucharist is all about God's life given in Jesus Christ to be our life. It is all about God's Spirit, the Spirit of Jesus, given now to be our breath of life. As we eat and drink, we become walking shrines, living temples, in whom the living triune God truly dwells. And if this scary thought should make us take our fellow Christians more seriously as what they really are, it should also make us take more seriously the tasks to which the living God calls us within his world. We cannot worship the suffering God today and ignore him tomorrow. We cannot eat and drink the body and blood of the passionate and compassionate God today, and then refuse to live passionately and compassionately tomorrow. If we say or sing, as we so often do, 'Glory be to the Father, and to the Son, and to the Holy Spirit', we thereby commit ourselves, in love, to the work of making his love known to the world that still stands so sorely in need of it. This is not the god the world wants. This is the God the world needs.

CHAPTER FOUR

God on the Same Scale

When my family and I lived in Montreal, one of our constant sources of amusement was the inability of British visitors to grasp the sheer scale of North America. The province of Quebec alone is the size of Western Europe. To get from Montreal to Vancouver you have a longer journey than to get from London to Montreal in the first place. What we had to do from time to time was to get one of those maps of Canada which have a tiny little map at the side, labelled 'Britain on the same scale'.

Now supposing you had something that worked the other way round. Supposing you had an ordinary map of Britain in an atlas, and then, on the facing page, you had a folded-up insert, which was labelled 'America on the same scale.' You would spread it out on a table, fold after fold after fold, until it filled half the room, completely dwarfing the ordinary map of Britain. No one who had seen that would ever again make the mistake of thinking, as some of our visitors did, that they could pop over to San Francisco in the car for a day visit.

That is the effect that the author of Isaiah 40 intends to create. The people he is addressing have scaled down their god to fit their own stunted imagination. So he starts with their world – the world of geography, of politics, of religion, of astronomy – and he proceeds to sketch, as it were, God on the same scale. There it is, fold upon fold upon fold, laid out before us:

> Who has measured the waters in the hollow of his
> hand, weighed the mountains in scales and the hills in a
> balance?
>   The nations are like a drop in a bucket, like dust on
> the scales;
>   idols are made of wood, plated with gold and silver;
>   earth's inhabitants are like grasshoppers before him;
>   he brings princes to naught, and makes the rulers of
> the world as nothing;
>   he created the stars, bringing them out and counting
> them, calling them by name, checking that they are all
> present.

Get your mind round that, says Isaiah; or rather, open
your mind wider, so that it can take it in. You can't
measure God on the map even of the world's greatest features. Nor is God simply bigger than them, as though God
were a Deist god, simply the most important being in a
sequence of beings. You need a different sort of scale
altogether, a different set of dimensions.

And why does Isaiah write this stunning piece of poetry?
Not as a piece of speculative theology. Not simply in order
to rebuke the small-mindedness of his contemporaries'
theology. He writes in order to lift up the hopes, as well as
the eyes, of a broken and disillusioned people: 'Comfort,
comfort my people, says your God; speak tenderly to
Jerusalem, and cry to her that her warfare is finished, her
penalty paid; she has received from YHWH's hand double
for all her sins.' The greatness of this God does not detach
him from his people; it means, on the contrary, that he is
close enough to comfort them, gentle enough to be their
shepherd, strong enough to give them strength:

He will feed his flock like a shepherd, and gather the
lambs in his arm, and gently lead the mother sheep;
   he gives power to the faint, and strengthens the
powerless.
   Even youths will faint and be weary, and young
people fall exhausted;
   but those who wait for YHWH shall renew their
strength, they shall mount up with wings like eagles;
they shall run and not be weary, they shall walk and not
faint.

The chapter begins with the message of comfort, which
continues by describing the prophetic voice which will ring
out:

In the wilderness prepare the way of YHWH; make
straight in the desert a highway for our God . . .
The glory of YHWH shall be revealed, and all flesh shall
see it together; for the mouth of YHWH has spoken.

The people are in Babylon; but their hearts and spirits
are in the wilderness, in no man's land, in the country
where they think nobody loves them, everybody's forgotten
them, and they have no hope of anything ever being any
different. Listen to it again:

Why do you say, O Jacob, and speak, O Israel, 'My
way is hidden from YHWH, and my right is disregarded
by my god'?

And in this wilderness, their God, the powerful one, the
creator of the ends of the earth, will come to them again,
will come and meet them, come like a shepherd looking
after his lambs, gently leading the mother sheep. He will
reveal his glory, and all flesh shall see it together. This is

the good news that the herald must tell:

> Get up to a high mountain, you herald of good tidings to
> Zion;
>   lift up your voice with strength, you herald of good
> tidings to Jerusalem.
>   Lift it up, do not fear; say to the cities of Judah:
> 'Look! Here is your God!'

The prophet is quite explicit. The people of Israel have got
so used to the map of their own present experience – their
tragedy, their hopelessness, their forgottenness, their exile
– that they have imagined that their god is somehow contained on the same map. They have *tamed* their god; they
have him like a pet, on the end of a lead, and he can't do
them any good. And the prophet unfolds before them this
huge, sprawling map of the untameable God – the creator,
the Lord of the world, the gentle shepherd, the returning
king – and says: Now, here is the one you can lean on.
Here is the one you can trust. He has dealt with your sin,
your failure, your tragedy. From now on he will reveal his
glory, and he will reveal it in saving you and shepherding
you. And Isaiah goes on to explain how God will do this,
in terms of the strange servant-figure, the one who carries
YHWH's saving purposes in his own self into the wilderness, into the exile, to the point of death and out the other
side.

Let me bring this message twenty-five centuries forward,
to our own day. One of those held hostage in Lebanon from
1985 to 1990 was the Irish writer Brian Keenan. In his
awesome book *An Evil Cradling* (London: Vintage, 1993)
he describes how, in solitary confinement, he and John
McCarthy had, to their own surprise, been confronted with
a reality that they had to call God, even though this reality
was far bigger than his upbringing in nominal Christianity

had taught him to expect. Listen to what he says, and think what an indictment this is (God help us) of much would-be Christian talk about God:

> At times God had seemed so real and so intimately close. We [Keenan and McCarthy] talked not of a God in the Christian tradition but some force more primitive, more immediate and more vital, a presence rather than a set of beliefs . . . In its own way our isolation had expanded the heart, not to reach out to a detached God but to find and become part of whatever 'God' might be . . . On occasion there would be discussions on vaguely religious themes, but they were certainly not confined by the dictates of strait-laced doctrines. We had each gone through an experience that gave us the foundations of an insight into what a humanized God might be. (p. 99)

Notice how Keenan equates the Christian tradition with a set of beliefs, and with 'strait-laced' doctrines. One wonders if he had ever heard Isaiah 40 read out in church, or heard a sermon preached on it. The 'god' of his upbringing seems to have been the Deist god: remote, detached, to be described in arid intellectual propositions, not the wild, untameable God of Isaiah, the creator, the Lord of the ends of the earth, who is also the gentle shepherd, the strong one who enables the crushed, the lonely, and the weak to lean on him and find new strength.

One could go further. What Keenan discovered, as he squatted in his solitary cell, coming to terms with his own wilderness, was – irony of ironies – the beginning of the fact of the Trinity, the fact which precedes and underlies all the doctrines. Listen to it again: 'We had each gone through an experience that gave us the foundations of an insight into *what a humanized God might be*.' One might almost think that he had been reading St Mark.

Mark's first fourteen verses appear quite artless: a simple description of John the Baptist and his baptism of Jesus, terse to the point of being almost laconic. He begins with two Old Testament quotations, both about the God who comes to his people at last, after their exile, after the death of their hopes and possibilities. The second of these, which he flags up for us, is by now familiar:

The voice of one crying in the wilderness,
Prepare the way of the Lord,
Make his paths straight.

He applies this, of course, to John the Baptist, coming in the wilderness with his baptism of repentance. And commentators have queued up to say: Silly old Mark, picking a cheap proof-text out of the hat! Just because John was 'in the wilderness', Mark thinks that somehow John is fulfilling Isaiah's prophecy.

But Mark knows exactly what he's doing. Isaiah was talking about the time when, at long last, the exile of God's people would come to an end, when God would comfort them, would feed his flock like a shepherd, would reveal his glory so that all the world might see. Had that happened, between Isaiah's day and the coming of John the Baptist? Virtually all Jews of the time would answer, of course not. They had come back from Babylon, but the great promises hadn't come true yet. They were still ruled over by one pagan nation after another, and YHWH had not returned to live with his people and save them. Isaiah prophesied about how the exile would end: a herald would cry out to Jerusalem and all Judaea that sins were now being forgiven – in other words, that the exile was coming to its end; and that Israel's god himself, YHWH, would come and save her. Mark tells of how John called the people of Jerusalem and all Judaea to his baptism for the forgiveness of sins; and of how he spoke of one coming after, who was stronger than he was, who would complete what he had begun. Anyone reading Mark with Isaiah in mind knows what to expect. We expect YHWH himself, Israel's god, the strong one, the creator of heaven and earth, the gentle shepherd, the coming king.

With breathtaking simplicity, Mark turns our eyes to look at this great sight: and we see – Jesus. In case we fail to get the point, Mark tells us that, at Jesus' own baptism, the voice from heaven addressed him in words echoing, among other passages, the great opening servant-song in Isaiah: you are my child, my beloved one, with you I am well pleased. Like Isaiah's servant (42.1), this strange king is anointed with YHWH's own spirit, to be his person for his task.

This, you might think, is revolutionary enough. But then this king, this YHWH-in-person, this stronger than strong one who submits to Israel's baptism of repentance, is himself driven out by the Spirit into the wilderness, to be tested within an inch of his life by the enemy, the accuser. He goes into the wilderness, because that is where his way has been prepared. He then comes back to Galilee, announcing the good news that Israel's god is at last becoming king. We find ourselves back with Brian Keenan, alone in his private wilderness, discovering a presence more primitive, 'more immediate and more vital', than 'a set of beliefs'. We are back in the prison cell, the place where one is tested to the limit, and, it seems, beyond. We are at the place where one discovers, not some strait-laced doctrine, but 'the foundations of an insight into what a humanized God might be'.

What effect does all this have on our thinking, our praying, and our living in the late twentieth century? There has recently been a small renaissance in trinitarian theology. We were confidently told by some theologians in the 1960s

that the Trinity was out-of-date nonsense; but the doctrine
is now being rediscovered as a source of power and illumi-
nation. But God forgive us if we ever forget that the doctrine is simply a shorthand for the story, and that the central character in the story is more primitive, more
immediate and more vital than any set of beliefs. The doctrine of the Trinity is the carefully chosen frame that
enables us to view the actual picture to best advantage.
Some, like a myopic guide in a museum, have spent so
much time talking about the frame that they have forgotten
to point to the picture. Others, like people subjected to such
nonsense, have concluded that if the frame is so boring the
picture can't be worth looking at. But when, even for a
moment, you just glimpse the picture – Isaiah's picture,
Mark's picture, of the God whose scale dwarfs all our little
maps – then you may find that the old frame does well
enough, provided you use it as a frame should be used, that
is, to let the picture itself be seen to best advantage.

And when you stand in front of this picture, the picture
not of a strait-laced doctrine but of the humanized God, you
realize, with Isaiah, that all geography, politics, religion,
and astronomy is like so much stubble, like a bunch of twit-
tering grasshoppers. God has to sweep away all our ideas,
including all our ideas about God, in order to draw us,
unwilling as we are, face to face with the reality, which is
both greater and gentler than we can imagine. And if that is
true in our praying and thinking – if it is true that we have
to be stripped of our own noisy jumble of thoughts in order
to hear afresh the word of the triune God – it is just as true
in our living. We are summoned, again and again, to be
found by God where he has promised to meet us, that is, in
the wilderness.

It's lonely in the wilderness. Most of us aren't equipped
for it. We like our world populated, and our creature comforts close at hand. Even when we choose solitude, we

people it with books, music, and pictures; if we don't have them to hand, we retain them in our hearts. Most of us haven't even really begun to strip away the busyness and over-population of our mental furniture and to enter the wilderness, where, like Brian Keenan, we are alone, lonely, exposed, naked. But when we do find ourselves there, which may happen to any of us at any time, we find two figures to tell us the way. Isaiah and John the Baptist remind us that when we find ourselves in exile, at a loss, frightened, anxious beyond anxiety, crushed by our circumstances, our surroundings, our sin – then we are summoned to hear a fresh word of comfort. The doctrine of the Trinity is not meant to be part of a forbidding set of dogmas, however true those dogmas are. It is a doctrine of comfort; of healing and forgiveness; of waiting for the Lord, and discovering him to be, as we go out to face an unknown future, the one who gives power to the faint.

And we discover this God precisely as we look at Jesus. If Isaiah has given us a map of 'God on the same scale', Mark offers us a guide to the map; and more than a guide: one in whose face, in whose very self, the living and true God is present to save, to comfort, to strengthen. If you want to mount up with wings as eagles, you know what you have to do.

CHAPTER FIVE

The Glory of the Lord

He was a good man, and he had exhorted the people to lead righteous lives, to practise justice towards their fellows and piety towards God. When the crowds around him began to increase, becoming extremely aroused by his powerful preaching, the king became alarmed. Eloquence with such great effect might lead to rebellion. The king therefore decided to strike first . . .

Those are the words of Josephus, the first-century Jewish historian (*Antiquities* 18.116-18). The king was Herod Antipas, the son of Herod the Great. The people were of course the Jews, in or around AD 28. And the good man, whose powerful preaching alarmed the king with the thought of sedition, was of course John the Baptist, who featured in our previous chapter.

The gospels' portrait of John the Baptist is filled out by this quite independent account. Underneath the story we all know, of Herod's dancing daughter and John's head on a platter, we find the dark undercurrent of political fear. As far as Herod was concerned, John was dangerous.

Well, of course he was. He was a voice, a voice that would not be silent; a voice in the wilderness, a voice of warning, a voice of promise, a voice in which some came to believe they had heard the voice of God. Voices like that are threatening to those with vested interests.

He was a different voice. He came from a priestly family, yet he was not himself living and working as a priest,
but instead conducting a strange initiation ritual down by
the Jordan. That very action, quite apart from anything he
said, strongly implied that people could be true members of
God's people, not by adherence to the Temple and the other
Jewish symbols, but through his own work. Voices like that
are worrying to those whose prestige is bound up with the
current institutions.

He was a prophetic voice, in line with the prophets of
old. Amos and Micah had warned the people about God's
judgement falling on those who ignored basic principles of
justice. Ezekiel and Jeremiah had predicted, and witnessed,
the devastation of Jerusalem, as the people refused to heed
their warnings. God had spoken through the prophets; and
John, by his clothing, his food, and his habit of life seems
to have been conscious of standing in that great and risky
tradition. Risky, because kings tend not to like prophets.
Voices that tell uncomfortable truths usually get silenced.

But what was the truth that John was telling? What was
the message that was so urgent that he had to get it across
even at the risk of his life? It was the news that all would
be well at last; that the long night was nearly over, and that
the day was about to break; that the God who had
apparently abandoned his people was coming back: coming
to rule, coming to judge, coming to save, coming to forgive. It was the Advent message.

It was, in other words, the message of Isaiah 40. This
passage, which we were considering from a different angle
earlier in this book, is one of the most memorable parts of
the Old Testament; in our culture it has been made even
more so by the fact that George Frederick Handel created
no less than five pieces in his *Messiah* out of the first
eleven verses alone. Handel starts where the chapter starts:

Comfort ye, comfort ye, my people
says your God;
Speak comfortably, tenderly, to Jerusalem,
and cry to her
that her warfare is accomplished, her iniquity pardoned;
that she has received from the LORD's hand
double for all her sins.

For the Jew in the first century the message would be
plain. The long night of exile is really over at last. Israel's
trials and tribulations at the hands of the pagans are coming
to an end. God has, somehow, dealt with her sin, the sin
because of which all her misery had come upon her. Now it
is time for comfort, for God to woo her again (when the
prophet says 'speak comfortably', or 'tenderly', he literally
says 'speak to her heart'; this is the language of wooing, of
engagement, of the tenderness and delicacy of gentle human
love). This is the first thing that we must stress, if we are
to understand Isaiah 40, and so to understand John the Baptist. Rough old John, with his camel-hair cloak and his
locusts and wild honey, seems an unlikely messenger to be
carrying God's love-letter to his forsaken and grieving
people, but that's the role he adopts. His is the message of
Advent, of the arrival of the Bridegroom – that is, of God
himself, coming at last to claim his bride and turn her waiting into dancing, her mourning into joy. This is exodus-
language. God will betroth Israel to himself once more, as
he did when he called her out of Egypt. This is why the
very creation itself must now get ready:

A voice cries,
'In the wilderness prepare the way of the LORD;
make straight in the desert a highway for our God.'
Every valley shall be lifted up,
and every mountain and hill be made low;

the uneven ground shall become level
and the rough places plain.

Why all this flattening out of the very surface of the earth? What's the big fuss? The answer – and this is the second thing that must be stressed – is that the Bridegroom is on his way home; God himself is returning to his people; and creation itself must roll out the red carpet to greet him. Then

the glory of the LORD shall be revealed;
and all flesh shall see it together;
for the mouth of the LORD has spoken it.

I suspect that when we read those words, or hear them sung by the choir in the first chorus of the *Messiah*, we don't at once see the picture. To get it right we would have to go back through the Old Testament to the passages which speak of the glory of the LORD being revealed. Sometimes this is in the Temple, as with Isaiah himself, and with Solomon when the Temple was first dedicated. But the most striking time is at the exodus, when Moses begs God to show him his glory, and God declines, revealing himself by hiding himself, letting Moses see only his back. Now we find the prophet declaring that in the wilderness, the exodus-place, God will at last reveal his full glory, his true glorious self; and not just to one or two favoured people, but to the whole world. 'All flesh shall see it together.' This is emphasized again a few verses later, in yet another piece that we can't read without thinking of George Frederick Handel:

Get up to a high mountain,
O herald of good tidings to Zion;
lift up your voice with strength,

lift it up, don't be afraid;
say to the cities of Judah
'Behold your God!'

What can all this mean, since, as the Old Testament
stresses, no one can see God and live? And what can John
the Baptist mean, by casting himself as the voice, the voice
that cries, the herald whose words make the princelings
tremble?

Our first thought is no doubt that the prophet envisaged
God coming in, as we say, a blaze of glory. Perhaps he
imagined that God would appear, shining like the sun, sitting on a throne or a chariot, surrounded by millions of
angels. But we might begin to have some doubts about that.
We have already discovered that the prophet speaks of God
wooing his people gently, coming to them as a bridegroom
to his bride. Appearing in blazing glory on a throne is
hardly the way to speak to the heart of your beloved. And
at the end of the passage, in yet another *Messiah* passage,
we find this description of what God will do when he
comes:

He will feed his flock like a shepherd,
he will gather the lambs in his arm,
he will carry them in his bosom,
and gently lead those that are with young.

Again, that's hardly the 'blaze of glory' that we might
expect. How then is God going to appear?

The answer is the strangest thing you could think of. As
we read on in Isaiah 40—55, we find that the coming of
God focuses increasingly on the work of the Servant of the
Lord. God will come to woo and win his people. But he
will come, like the prince in the story, in the disguise of a
beggar:

Who would have believed such news?
To whom has the Arm of the LORD been revealed?

He had no form or beauty that we should desire him;
[He did not come in a blaze of glory,
sweeping all before him,
with angels singing Hallelujah;]

He was despised and rejected by men,
a man of sorrows, and acquainted with grief.
Surely he has borne our griefs, and carried our sorrows;
he was wounded for our transgressions,
he was bruised for our iniquities;
the chastisement of our peace was upon him
and with his stripes we are healed.
All we like sheep have gone astray
we have turned every one to his own way;
and the LORD has laid on him the iniquity of us all.

We love these passages, and meditate on them each year
as Holy Week comes round. But what we often fail to see is
that, within their literary context, they form the climax of
that great sustained passage of prophecy which purports to
speak of how the living God returns to woo and win his
people. What will it look like when God comes back to
Jerusalem? Isaiah's answer is that it will not be a blaze of
glory. It will not be in the form of a great military display
of power. It will be in the life of one who takes upon himself the form of a servant, and is obedient unto death. This
is how God will comfort his people; this is how the
bridegroom will return to Zion; this is why Advent is good
news, why we know that God is a shepherd who carries the
lambs in his bosom, and gently leads those that are with
young. To a world besotted with the love of power, Isaiah's
God reveals himself in the power of love.

The Advent message, Isaiah's message for his hearers, is that this God is coming to judge the world by the law of love. There is always a danger that when we speak of God's judgment we imagine God as a fierce, bullying, domineering God. I suspect that many people in our society today, if they use the word 'God' at all (other than as an expletive), think of God basically like that. That's why so many of them have rejected him. There are quite enough fierce bullies in the world already without having one up in the sky as well. But the reason that the true God will come to right all wrongs in the world (and that's what 'judgment' really means) is not because he's a fierce bully but precisely because he is the bridegroom who wants to woo and win his bride; because he is the shepherd who longs to carry the lambs close to his heart; because he is the servant who is wounded for our transgressions and bruised for our iniquities. If this is what the true God is like, it's the fierce bullies – the Herods of the world – who are in for a shock. This is the God whose coming judgment will be based upon love. This is the God whose word will stand for ever, while the grass withers and the flower fades.

And what about old John, who cast himself in the role of the Voice that had to announce this Word, to herald the coming of this God? How much of all this did he understand?

Bits and pieces, I think. It is very revealing that, in the first chapter of John's gospel, he refuses to see himself as Elijah, let alone as the Messiah or the great final Prophet. He seems to have thought that Jesus was going to be Elijah; Jesus seems to have returned the compliment. Perhaps part of the strange vocation to be Elijah, to get the people ready for the coming of God, was precisely that one would not know the significance of one's own work. I suspect that a lot of vocation works like that. The only role John will accept, as we saw at the beginning, is that of the Voice: I

am the voice of one crying in the wilderness, Make straight
the way of the LORD. That is almost all he knows.

It is enough. Enough to create around him a community
of the true Israel, on tiptoe with expectation for God to
come and save and judge; a community among whom were
people called Peter and Andrew, a community in whose
midst there was one whose sandal-strap John was not worthy to untie. Enough to make Herod tremble on his throne
at the thought that the old rumours of Israel's God coming
back might after all be true, or at least that enough people
might believe them to make life very difficult for his own
shaky kingdom. Enough to challenge those who lived by
the love of power with the old message, half-forgotten but
never quite obliterated, of the power of love.

Enough, too, to challenge us in our own little kingdoms,
and our own responsibilities. We, too, live on and live by
the promised coming of God. We who live on the farther
side of Christmas, Calvary, Easter and Pentecost stake our
lives on the belief that, in the man Jesus, Isaiah's promise
about the coming of the bridegroom to woo and win his
people came true in literal human history. But if we believe
that, we are also committed to the belief that this same God
comes to us again week by week, in bread and wine, to
woo and win us, to carry the lambs in his bosom, gently to
lead the mother sheep. And we are committed to the belief
that he will come again, finally, to judge and save his
weary old world once and for all.

And our calling, therefore, as those who celebrate his
strange and beautiful coming, is once again to be a voice.
The church is here to be the Voice to the world; the Voice
that does not claim great things for itself, but simply urges
the world to get ready for the God who comes in the power
and judgment of love. We are to live, and we are to speak,
in such a way as to do for our generation, more or less,
what John did for his: to demonstrate and to announce that

there is a different way of being human, the way of love,
the way of God, and so to bring to the world the news
(good news for the weary, bad news for the bullies) that the
creator of the world is also the comforter of the world:

Comfort ye, comfort ye, my people,
says your God;
speak comfortably to Jerusalem –
to London and Lichfield
to Birmingham and Bristol
to New York and Tokyo
to Rwanda and Bosnia
to Ireland
and, yes, to Jerusalem now as then;
and cry to her
that her warfare is accomplished
her iniquity is pardoned.
Prepare in the wilderness the way of the Lord;
make straight in the desert,
in the slum, in the high-rise,
in the swamp, in the battlefield,
in the palace, in the penthouse,
in the broken hearts of the world
a highway for our God.

CHAPTER SIX

The Face of Love

The scene is set in a prison cell. The prisoner, a man in early middle age, is writing a letter to a close friend. It's a tricky letter to write, because the friend has been very badly treated by a third party, and the prisoner, who has come to know the third party, is appealing for a reconciliation.

He makes two basic moves. First, he stresses the friendship which means that prisoner and free man are bonded together with ties of love: you and I belong together, he says, as one. In the same breath, he stresses that he and the third party have also become very close, like father and son. The friend, reading thus far, discovers that if he values the prisoner's friendship, he is going to have to take the wrongdoer along with him. Then, second, he faces the question of the wrongdoing itself. All right, he says, there has been trouble; but whatever it was, I want you to put it down to my account, not his. Blame me for it; I'll repay you any damages he owes you. And by the end of the letter the friend really has no choice. He is faced with sheer love; and he would have to have a stony heart indeed not to respond as the prisoner indicates.

In case you haven't recognized him, the prisoner is of course St Paul; the friend is Philemon; the wrongdoer is the runaway slave Onesimus. The prison is probably in Ephesus, on the Turkish coast, about a hundred miles from

Philemon's home in Colosse, up the Lycus valley. And I want to suggest to you that if the little letter from Paul to Philemon, one of the shortest books in the New Testament, was the only scrap of evidence that we had about early Christianity, we would still have to conclude that something very remarkable had happened in the first century which had radically changed the way people looked at themselves, at one another, and at the world.

There are other letters in antiquity which speak about runaway slaves and similar problems. Normally they adopt a patronizing and condescending tone: the slave or equivalent is of course irrelevant, scarcely human, but, my dear fellow, you might want to show what a good chap you are and give the rascal a second chance. (That would be at the most generous end of the scale.) Paul's letter breathes a totally different air. He and Philemon are brothers in Christ. He and Onesimus are brothers in Christ. Paul stands between the two of them, with both arms outstretched, to embrace and unite both master and slave. He becomes, in himself, the bond of love that will unite them. He becomes the place where, and the means by which, the pain and anger and guilt of their relationship is snuffed out and dealt with.

Paul would have seen, better than we do, the significance of the posture: a human being with arms outstretched, bearing the shame and the pain, and effecting healing and reconciliation. This is a new idea, and much more than an idea, a new fact, a new way of being, a new force let loose in the world. And where it comes from is quite clear. It comes from Calvary, where Pontius Pilate's most famous prisoner stretched out his arms to embrace Jew and Greek, slave and free, male and female; and, beyond that, to embrace and reconcile God and humanity, the creator and his runaway slave, the creator and his runaway world. Paul gives us our earliest written evidence of the first and, in a sense, the main thing I want to say in this chapter: that the cross of Jesus *changed the world.*

And I want to say this particularly in order to guard against the belittling of the cross which can so easily creep in to our thinking, and even to our praying and our devotion. The cross of Jesus is such a huge reality, standing in the middle of the world and of history, that we are often at a loss to know how to respond to it, what we're supposed to think or do when we're confronted with it. When we try to say that the cross means this, or that, or the other thing, we usually end up doing something analogous to playing a Beethoven symphony on a mouth-organ. We bring it down to the level of our own thinking and feeling, instead of allowing it to lift our thinking and feeling – yes, and our praying and living and loving – up to its own level.

I don't pretend for a moment that what I say here will escape the same problem. But I want to try to point beyond words, including my own words, so that our eyes rest on the fact itself. And the fact is, as I say, that the cross of Jesus *changed the world.* It didn't just create a new possibility for human devotion. It didn't just reveal an aspect of the character of God. It wasn't just the most wonderful example of a terrible death bravely suffered. It changed the world.

How, more particularly? The cross and resurrection of Jesus didn't just happen at some miscellaneous moment in the past. They came as the culmination of a long history, in which the creator God had been preparing his great plan for the saving of his world. The time is fulfilled, said Jesus, and now at last God is becoming King. When the time had fully come, said Paul, God sent forth his Son to redeem the world. Jesus' life, and supremely his death, simply don't make sense if we see them as the action of one man standing in the middle of nowhere. They only make sense when seen as the climax of the creator's plan to save the world.

In particular, they only make sense if we understand the plight of the world in its most radical form. Those who have looked most deeply into the face of this world's evil have regularly concluded that evil is something more than simply the sum total of individual acts of wrongdoing. Evil exerts a destructive power which goes beyond even those who implement it. Pontius Pilate was a little man swept along by the tradition and ethos of a ruthless empire. Annas and Caiaphas were little men who happened to be at the leading edge of a two-thousand-year-old national way of life. Herod was a little man who held on to power in the way that little men do, by blustering and bullying. Even the emperor Tiberius, brooding back in Rome, was only ultimately a little man. Something bigger than all of them was at work; and that something was decisively challenged by the one person of all time who was not a little man; the man who had grasped a secret which the world's rulers never knew, that to be great you must be the slave of all, that the power of love is stronger than the love of power.

And the result was inevitable. They did to him what they often did to runaway slaves: they crucified him. He took upon himself, literally and historically, the force and weight of the evil systems of the world, that reveal their evil nature by crushing human beings, human freedom, human love. It is not merely a theological or spiritual truth that Jesus bore the sin of the world: on the first Good Friday, it was politically and historically true. That is why it changed the world.

The truth of the cross is therefore bigger than, and logically prior to, all our devotion, all our sense of pity and awe and wonder at the suffering of the Son of God. If it were not, our keeping of Good Friday would become roughly the same sort of thing as the horror and sympathy we feel when confronted with Rwanda, or Sarajevo, or Dunblane. Good Friday transcends that level, important though it is in itself. It is about the moment when the principalities and powers over-reached themselves. As Paul says in another letter, the powers that run the world didn't understand what they were doing when they crucified the Lord of Glory. Pride, greed, fear, arrogance and ultimately violence stay in circulation because when they operate they create more of themselves: one person's pride begets another person's jealousy, one act of violence begets another. In this case, the pride and fear and violence of all the world – the greatest empire the world had ever seen, the highest religion the world had ever known – did their worst to Jesus. And he prayed, 'Father, forgive them; they don't know what they're doing.' And, in dying without bitterness, without pride, without retaliation, he changed the world. He acted out the victory of love over evil.

Ah but, you say, the world isn't changed. Pride and violence still exist. We are still subject to them – even we who believe in Jesus. At this point it would be easy to say: yes, well, but Jesus has opened up the possibility for men and women to live in a different way, and our task as individuals is to do so as best we can. No doubt that is true, so far as it goes.

But the cross, as expounded in the New Testament, speaks of a victory that goes deeper than that. Just as evil is more than the sum total of individual acts of wrongdoing, so Jesus' victory over evil is more than the sum total of subsequent individual acts of selfless love. Christian faith, faith in the crucified Jesus, is more than my individual belief that he died for me, vital though that is. It is the faith that on the cross Jesus in principle won the victory over sin, violence, pride, arrogance and even death itself, *and that that victory can now be implemented*. This faith refuses to accept that violence, greed and pride are unassailable and unchallengeable. This faith will go to work to challenge and subvert those destructive forces, in ourselves, in our local communities, in our corporate and political life, in the belief, albeit often in the teeth of the evidence, that they have been defeated and that the power of God's love is stronger than they are. To say that the cross changed the world is a statement of faith; but it is not blind faith, whistling in the dark. It is faith that looks up at the creator God and knows him to be the God of love. And it is faith that looks out at the world with the longing to bring that love to bear in healing, reconciliation, and hope.

You see, if the cross of Jesus changed the world, there is a sense in which, also, the cross of Jesus *changed God*. Now don't misunderstand me. I'm not saying (though some have said it) that prior to the cross God was an angry, vindictive tyrant, and that after the cross he became a loving father once again. Those two great theologians of the cross, Paul and John, both insist that the cross was an action from God's own side, an act of the greatest and deepest love. The cross, from that point of view, reveals what was always true: that God so loved the world, that God was in Christ reconciling the world to himself. Yes, but in the process, if we may so speak, God *became* on the cross what God always was. I may have it in me, in ability and desire, to climb Mount Everest; but until I actually go into training and do it it remains latent. You may have it in you to be a brilliant concert pianist; but until you get down to practice and performance, all that brilliance remains latent. God always was the God of love – generous, spontaneous, free and cheerful self-giving love; but until God, if we dare put it like this, gets down to practice and performance, that love at its deepest level remains latent. On the cross God at last performs the score composed before the foundation of the world. On the cross God at last scales the highest of the peaks. It isn't just that the cross *reveals* God's love in the most striking way. It reveals it because it *enacts* it. It becomes part of, indeed the most central part of, the personal history of God. God becomes the prisoner in the condemned cell, writing in his own blood the letter of reconciliation.

And so, as at creation God worked for six days, completing on the Friday the loving and generous work of creation, and resting on the seventh day, the Saturday, so on Good Friday God finally completes the loving and generous work he had set himself to accomplish. The last chord dies away, and the pianist leaves the keyboard, exhausted. The sun goes down on the mountain, and the mountaineer is taken home, totally spent. The letter is sent, and does its work, even as the prisoner is led away to the gallows. God rested in the tomb on the seventh day, the great Holy Saturday, the time of stillness, when passion and compassion had done their work, had completed their task. He had at last become what he always was: the world's true lover.

And now, to all eternity, the cross remains at the heart of God, stands as the truest symbol of God, offers the most exact and precise exposition of God. Part of the point of the doctrine of the Trinity is that what happened to Jesus of Nazareth on the first Good Friday happened to God; and, having happened to God, it has, so to speak, made God decisively and in practice, once and for all, what he always was in principle. That is why, on Good Friday, those who come to church do so, not to venerate a piece of wood (that, after all, would be the grossest pagan folly), but to use the cross as the truest possible icon of the living and loving God. As with any icon, the point is to look through it at the reality, of which, like all true symbols, the cross speaks more deeply than words.

And, as we look, and worship, it is not only the world that is changed; it is not only God who is changed; *we ourselves are changed*. We are changed, after all, by a smile from a stranger; how can we not be changed when we look at the face of Love himself? We find ourselves caught and

held in the outstretched arms of the divine prisoner; we are
captivated by the music of his stretched sinews; we are
swept up to the mountain-tops, from which we see the
whole world in a new way. And we ourselves, made
prisoners in our turn by that love, discover that we have a
new identity. As we are set free by that love from our own
pride and fear, our own greed and arrogance, so we are
free in our turn to be agents of reconciliation and hope, of
healing and love. We are to be the prisoners who will write
the letter; we are to reach out to God and the world and
hold them together in our own very selves, our own
actions, our own words, our own lives. This is what praying for the world is all about. This is what Christian political action is all about. This is what visiting the sick and
dying is all about. This is what marriage counselling is all
about. It is what being a Christian in the thousands of walks
of life to which we are called is all about.

And none of this is dreamed up, or drummed up, by our
own effort or will-power. It follows from, and flows from,
the fact that the cross of Jesus changed the world once and
for all, and that since Calvary the creator of the world has
been known by the symbol of the cross.

And as we engage in this cross-shaped ministry of reconciliation, we must not be surprised if from time to time it
feels as though we ourselves are being pulled apart. We
talk of 'taking up the cross' or 'having a cross to bear' as
though God somewhat arbitrarily gave each of us some pain
or trouble just to make things difficult for us, to stop us
having too easy a life of it. Not so. Just as evil is more than
the sum total of human wrongdoing, and just as God's victory over evil is more than the sum total of subsequent
human loving, so our ministry of reconciliation is more
than simply the words we speak and the physical acts we
perform. We ourselves, as whole persons, are caught up in
the process in ways beyond our understanding, so that our

suffering, whatever it may be, becomes part of Christ's own passion, of God's own passion, and as such brings healing and reconciliation at levels and depths beyond our imagining. Our task is to be faithful to the calling of the cross: to live in God's new world as the agents of his love, and to pray that the cross we carry today will become part of the healing and reconciliation of the world. We will not understand in the present time how it is that our pain, our illness, our heartbreak, our deep frustration, is somehow taken up into the pain of God and the healing of the world; but if we offer it back to God that is precisely what will happen.

What we do on Good Friday, therefore, is more than the fuelling of private devotion, though it should be that as well. It is more than the learning of some theological truths, though it is vital to do that also. It is looking into the face of Love, that we may reflect that Love into the world. It is allowing ourselves to be changed into the image of the God who was himself changed on Calvary, so that the world which was decisively changed on the first Good Friday may finally be changed until it reflects the love, the justice and the peace which met and embraced on the cross. It is learning the meaning of life from the condemned prisoner. It is discovering reconciliation in the outstretched arms of God.

CHAPTER SEVEN

No Bones About It

On Palm Sunday 1996 the *Sunday Times* ran a feature about
the tomb of Jesus. At least, it was supposed to be about
Jesus' tomb; but actually nobody made the claim explicit.
There were, predictably, some misleading headlines. Some
suggested that the discovery threatened the basis of
Christianity. One spoke of 'The tomb that dare not speak its
name' – which was silly, because that was precisely what
the tomb did, which was why there was a story at all. Other
newspapers got in on the act. The radio stations chattered
away about it all week.

What happened was this. Two BBC producers went
looking for fresh material for the Easter Sunday edition of
the programme *The Heart of the Matter*. They wanted to
stimulate discussion on the nature of the resurrection. Supposing, they wanted to ask, someone actually found the
bones of Jesus lying around in Palestine: what would that
do to Christian faith? So they looked for ossuaries – bone-
boxes. They found one that said 'Jesus, son of Joseph'
(actually, they found more than one, but they only followed
one up). It had been found in a family tomb; and in the
same family tomb were other boxes, labelled Joseph, Mary,
another Mary, a Matthew, and someone called Judah,
described as 'the son of Jesus'. Actually, the boxes were
empty: vandals had apparently got there first, possibly in
antiquity. There were, so to speak, no bones about it. But

journalists are good at putting two and two together and making seventeen. Could this be Jesus' tomb? Would it cast doubt on the very foundations of Christianity?

The first thing to say is that, even if nobody had ever said Jesus of Nazareth had been raised to life, the probability is still enormously high that this would not have been the tomb of the Jesus, Mary and Joseph we know from the gospels. 'Mary' is by far the most common female name in the period; 'Joseph' and 'Jesus' are two of the most common male names, with Judah – or Judas – not far behind. So discovering a tomb with these names in one family is rather like someone coming across an English tombstone with a Tom, Dick and Harry all in the same family. Or, more sharply, it's like an archaeologist two thousand years hence finding an English tomb with parents called Philip and Elizabeth and children called Charles and Anne, and claiming that this must be the British royal family. The Israeli archaeologists, none of them interested in defending Christianity, were the first to pooh-pooh the idea of this being the tomb of Jesus of Nazareth.

The second thing to say is that, if it had been the tomb of Jesus and his family, there are serious oddities. Why is it in Jerusalem, when the family lived in Nazareth, where (presumably) Joseph had died some time before Jesus' public ministry? Why is there no mention of James, Jesus' most famous brother, or of Joses and Simon (as listed in Mark 6.3, along with some unnamed sisters)? And why on earth is there a *son* of Jesus? There is no evidence whatever that Jesus had children, whether in or out of wedlock; and we need to remind ourselves that his family – that is, his brothers and nephews – were well known in the early church. Sixty years after Jesus' death, his great-nephews were accused by the Roman emperor Domitian of being part of a would-be royal family. If Jesus had had a son, people would have known. It would have mattered.

But the most serious problem is yet to come – and this points forward to the real message of Easter, which I want to focus on here. Bone-boxes, ossuaries, were used in the *second* stage of a two-stage burial process. Many first-century Jews were buried this way. First they were laid on a slab, wrapped in cloth with spices. The tomb was a cave, not a hole in the ground. It would have a movable stone door; the family and friends would in due course lay other bodies on other shelves in the same cave. Then, a year or more later, when all the flesh had decomposed, relatives or friends would return to collect the bones and place them in an ossuary, a box roughly two feet by one foot by one foot, which would then be stored away either in recesses within the same cave or somewhere else. In other words, the burial of Jesus as recorded in the gospels was only the first stage of an intended *two*-stage burial.

So: did anyone ever think of going back to the tomb to collect Jesus' bones and put them in an ossuary? No, they didn't! The whole early church knew that Jesus' body wasn't in the tomb. They believed that God had raised Jesus to life again, transforming his body in the process. This wasn't a resuscitation, a journey back into the present life; it was a resurrection, a going on through death and out the other side into a new mode of physicality, the beginning of God's new creation. If the disciples had believed that what they called the 'resurrection' was just (what we would call) a 'spiritual' event, leaving the body in the tomb, someone sooner or later would have had to go back to collect Jesus' bones and store them properly. They couldn't and wouldn't have left a skeleton just lying there on the ledge, with only the first stage of burial complete. The tomb was designed, like most such tombs of the period, as a family tomb. As further family members died, the relatives would in due course have come again with their bodies, to lay them elsewhere in the tomb. The ledge where

Jesus had been laid would be needed again. But of course, if anyone had at any stage gone back to tidy up Jesus' bones and put them in an ossuary, that would indeed have destroyed Christianity before it had even properly begun. Even those contemporary scholars who deny that Jesus was raised bodily from the dead are clear that all the early Christians thought he had been, and that they made it the basis of their whole life.

So the question of the ossuaries, when we explore it thoroughly, provides paradoxically a sort of negative evidence in favour of Jesus' resurrection. Not only is the tomb the journalists are highlighting not Jesus' tomb. By drawing attention to the two-stage burial process, they have reminded us of how impossible it is to imagine Christianity getting off the ground at all if the second stage of the burial process had ever been carried out. Make no bones about it. In their eagerness to find news, the journalists have accidentally highlighted the good news.

You see, belief in Jesus' resurrection was never simply belief in a life after death. Someone on a radio show in Holy Week, after the original article, declared that it didn't matter if Jesus' bones were still lying around Palestine somewhere, because, he said, 'I expect to go to heaven when I die, and I won't be taking my bones with me; so I don't see why Jesus shouldn't have done the same.' I suspect that that idea, or something like it, is quite widespread, and it's worth pointing out the mistake. Belief in Jesus' resurrection is *not* the belief that Jesus has simply 'gone to heaven' after his death, as though Jesus were like a great saint or martyr whom God has received into his presence with honour. Jews believed that about all sorts of people; it wouldn't have been new; it wouldn't have been *news*. Easter faith always was the belief that Jesus went through death into a new sort of bodily existence, in which his original body was transformed into a body with new characteristics and properties. When St Paul, the first Christian to write about the resurrection, draws conclusions from Jesus' resurrection to ours, he says that those who are still alive at the end of time will have their bodies *changed*. He talks about seeds and plants, about acorns and oaks. Our bodies won't be abandoned; they will be transformed. That is what Paul, in common with all other early Christians, thought had happened to Jesus.

So what was the resurrection all about, as far as the early Christians were concerned? And what on earth – and I mean *on earth* – does it mean for the world and the church at the end of the twentieth century?

The early Christians very quickly came to understand what had happened to Jesus in terms of the old Jewish, biblical belief that the living God was one day going to solve the problem of Israel's exile and oppression, and by doing so was going to solve the problem of evil and injustice in the whole world. That is what it means to say that the resurrection took place 'according to the scriptures': it was the fulfilment of prophetic promises and long-cherished hopes. Putting it crudely, the resurrection demonstrated that the cross was a victory, not a defeat. As St Paul says, if Christ is not raised, your faith is futile, and you are still in your sins. But if Christ has been raised, then this shows that on the cross he defeated death, and hence sin, and hence all evil and injustice, once and for all. Easter isn't just about one person going through death and out the other side, as a sort of crazy maverick event unrelated to anything else, a sort of one-off display of supernatural power. It is the unveiling of God's answer to the problems of the world.

You see, just as that early Christian belief in the resurrection of Jesus was a belief about something that actually happened within this real world, not simply a belief about a transcendent dimension, a spiritual or other-worldly reality

which leaves this world behind, so the continuing message
of the resurrection is precisely *not* that 'there is a life after
death'. There is, and all God's people will inherit it; but
the point is that it won't be what most modern Westerners
think of as 'life after death'. It will involve God's people
being given new bodies, like Jesus' body, to share in the
new heavens *and new earth* that God will make. The message of the resurrection is that this present world matters;
that the problems and pains of this present world matter;
that the living God has made a decisive bridgehead into this
present world with his healing and all-conquering love; and
that, in the name of this strong love, all the evils, all the
injustices and all the pains of the present world must now
be addressed with the news that healing, justice and love
have won the day. That's why we pray 'Thy Kingdom
come, *on earth as it is in heaven*'. Make no bones about it:
Easter Day was the first great answer to that prayer.

You see, if Easter faith is simply about believing that
God has a nice comfortable after-life for some or all of us,
then Christianity becomes a mere pie-in-the-sky religion
instead of a kingdom-on-earth-as-it-is-in-heaven religion.
Or, if Easter faith is simply about believing that Jesus is
risen in some 'spiritual' sense, leaving his body in the
tomb, then Christianity turns into a let-the-world-stew-in-
its-own-juice religion, instead of a kingdom-on-earth-as-it-
is-in-heaven religion. If Easter faith is only about me, and
perhaps you, finding a new dimension to our own personal
spiritual lives in the here and now, then Christianity
becomes simply a warmth-in-the-heart religion, instead of a
kingdom-on-earth-as-it-is-in-heaven religion. It becomes
focused on me and my survival, my sense of God, my
spirituality, rather than outwards on God, and on God's
world that still needs the kingdom-message so badly. But if
Jesus Christ is truly risen from the dead, Christianity
becomes what the New Testament insists that it is: good

news for the whole world, news which warms our hearts
precisely because it isn't just about warming hearts. The
living God has in principle dealt with evil once and for all,
and is now at work, by his own Spirit, to do for us and the
whole world what he did for Jesus on that first Easter day.

That is why we who celebrate Easter do so with material
things: water (not least when people are baptized at an
Easter vigil, as in the ancient Christian custom); bread and
wine at the Eucharist. Easter is about the living God claiming the world of space, time and matter as his own. That is
why Christians celebrate it with candles and flowers and
incense and processions and banners and, above all, music:
the world of creation has been reclaimed by the living and
healing God. That is why we who celebrate Easter after a
Lenten fast do so not with a guilty sense of going back to
things that are tainted with sin, but with the joyful sense of
celebrating the goodness of God's good creation in all its
rich variety. That is why the celebration of Easter calls us,
one and all, to delight in God's way of holiness: not a
negative, gloomy holiness, but a positive giving of ourselves to God in the knowledge that his way is the way of
true delight, of true fulfilment. And that is why the celebration of Easter, in a world, a country, and a region where
injustice, violence, degradation and all manner of wickedness are still endemic, makes the most powerful symbolic
statement that we are not prepared to tolerate such things –
that God is not prepared to tolerate such things – and that
we will work, and plan, and pray, and vote, with all the
energy of God to implement the victory of Jesus over them
all. True Easter faith, true Easter celebration, and true
Easter holiness, must issue in true Easter agendas. Let's
make no bones about it.

You see, the old jibe of Karl Marx and others that
Christianity lulls people into being content with their lot,
and content to look on other people's misery and injustice,

because it speaks only about a spiritualized heaven in the future and a spiritual experience here and now – that jibe is a fair critique of that watered-down Christianity which tries to say that Jesus' body, like John Brown's, stayed a-mouldering in the grave while his soul went marching on. But it misses entirely the point of the true Christian belief in the resurrection. Here's an interesting thing: notice how, in the gospels, all the first witnesses of the resurrection *run.* Half the references in the gospels to people running occur in the resurrection stories: the women run *from* the tomb, Peter and John run *to* the tomb, the disciples in Emmaus hurry back to Jerusalem. Where is that energy in the church today, a god-given energy that can't wait to get the good news out and to implement it in the world? If it is lacking, could it have something to do with the fact that far too many Christians have been lulled into thinking that God isn't really concerned with this world, so that the resurrection of Jesus isn't about something happening within this world, so that the only thing that matters is my private other-worldly salvation?

You see, the bodily resurrection of Jesus isn't a take-it-or-leave-it thing, as though some Christians are welcome to believe it and others are welcome not to believe it. Take it away, and the whole picture is totally different. Take it away, and Karl Marx was probably right to accuse Christianity of ignoring the problems of the material world. Take it away, and Sigmund Freud was probably right to say that Christianity is a wish-fulfilment religion. Take it away, and Friedrich Nietzsche was probably right to say that Christianity was a religion for wimps. Put it back, and you have a faith that can take on the postmodern world that looks to Marx, Freud and Nietzsche as its prophets, and you can beat them at their own game with the Easter news that the foolishness of God is wiser than men, and the weakness of God is stronger than men.

Those who celebrate the mighty resurrection of the Lord
Jesus Christ, therefore, have an awesome and non-
negotiable responsibility. When we say 'Alleluia! Christ is
Risen', we are saying that Jesus is Lord of the world, and
that the present would-be lords of the world are not. When
we sing, in the old hymn, that 'Judah's Lion burst his
chains, and crushed the serpent's head', are we ready to put
that victory into practice? Are we ready to stand alongside
our fellow Christians, even in civilized Britain, whose
churches are regularly desecrated and vandalized? Are we
ready to speak up for, and to take action on behalf of, those
even in our own local community, let alone further afield,
who are quietly being crushed by uncaring and unjust
systems? Are we ready to speak up for the truth of the
gospel over the dinner-table, and in the coffee-bar, and in
the council-chamber? Let's make no bones about it: if
Easter isn't good news, then there is no good news. But if
it is – if it is true that Jesus Christ is risen indeed – then
Easter day, and the Easter message, is the true sun which,
when it rises, puts all other suns to shame:

The sunne arising in the East,
Though he give light, and th' East perfume,
If they should offer to contest
With Thy arising, they presume.

Can there be any day but this,
Though many sunnes to shine endeavour?
We count three hundred, but we misse:
There is but one, and that one ever.

(George Herbert, 'Easter: The Song')

Part Two: Reflecting God's Image in the World

CHAPTER EIGHT

Remember

When *The Lord of the Rings* was first published, at least one reviewer accused its author, J. R. R. Tolkien, of writing 'escapist' literature. 'All right,' replied Tolkien, 'who is it who doesn't want people to escape? I'll tell you: *Gaolers*.' It's a good answer: but will it do for us? Here we are, with parts of the world ripping themselves apart in sectarian or ethnic violence; here we are, with the nameless horrors of civil wars being flashed on to our television screens from other parts of the global village; here we are, with wars and rumours of wars all round the globe, cheerfully kept going by those in our own civilized countries who supply them with weapons. We, for our part, when we want, officially as it were, to remember wars and rumours of wars, put on paper poppies and sing magnificent Magnificats. What do we say to the charge of 'escapism'? How do we answer the voices singing in our ears, as Eliot said of the Wise Men, insisting that this is all folly?

Let's go back to the book of Exodus. Moses had run away and escaped. He had cherished the dream of freedom for the captive Israelites. He had begun the process by killing an Egyptian. It hadn't worked; he was in deep trouble, and he left town fast. His instant solution had just made matters worse. But while he was in the wilderness, living as a shepherd, the plight of the Israelites became so appalling that they cried to their God in their misery; and, we are told, God heard their cry, and God *remembered* the covenant he had made with Abraham, Isaac and Jacob. Our remembering often turns into nostalgia or recrimination; God's remembering turns into action. The next thing we know, Moses is standing before a bush, a desert shrub. The bush is on fire, but the fire is not burning the bush.

Moses had heard about God before. He had even tried to act on behalf of God before. Now he finds himself in the presence of God, and suddenly everything looks rather different. Moses, like Adam in front of another tree, is afraid and hides. But the God who is revealed as fire is not to be escaped. He has words to speak to Moses, words which tell of his great compassion for his suffering people, words full of hope and promise and covenant love. And Moses is called to stand in awe before the beauty and power and majesty of God – in order that he may then stand without fear before the pomp and might of Pharaoh, king of Egypt, and in the name of the one true God demand the release of the true people of God.

Later on in the story we are told that Moses was very *meek*. Don't misunderstand that; the word 'meek' doesn't mean 'weak'. It's the word you'd use of a wild horse that's been tamed. Young man Moses, charging off to do God's will, killing the Egyptian: there's the wild horse, worse than useless. Mature Moses, standing before Pharaoh: he doesn't even have to raise his voice. There's the wild horse, tamed. The secret of the difference is what happened at the burning bush, where Moses stood and trembled in the very presence of the living God.

Moses, then, had escaped into the wilderness, away from the problem. But he hadn't escaped from God. And when we widen the angle again, and see the whole story of which the burning bush is a part, we see what was going on. Moses met God at the bush *because* God had heard the cry of his people and had remembered his promises; and he met God at the bush *in order that* God could call him to be his agent in putting those promises into effect. His earlier failure was not just overlooked. It was actually part of the training. Moses already knew that there was a wrong way of going about setting people free. He was now to discover the right way, by listening to the voice that came from inside the fire.

I want now to suggest that Western society has got to the same stage that Moses had got to when he found he had to leave Egypt in a hurry; that what our society desperately needs is a fresh vision of the living God; and that what we do when we come to worship, so far from being escapism, is actually designed to fuel and fire that vision. Vision without action would indeed be escapism; action without vision is blundering folly. We have a fair amount of both in the church and the world at the moment, perhaps more of the latter (action without vision) than the former. When God remembers his promises, though, he will act through people whose actions are grounded in vision, the burning vision of his saving covenant love.

First, then, where we've got to as a society. We haven't lost all moral sense, as some would say. Ours is in fact a very moralistic age: consider the sheer moral fury of those who protest about (for instance) fox-hunting. It's just that we've changed the moral targets. People who would be horrified to have an older sexual morality imposed on them 'for their own good' are eager to impose a new ecological morality on others 'for their own good'. This is a recipe for moral confusion, and there's plenty of that about right now.

Take some examples. We are all passionately in favour of justice, but somehow it slips through our fingers. We all long for peace in the world, but nobody quite knows how to achieve it. When we did decide to do something, as in the Gulf War, we ended up protecting and liberating some of the most oppressive regimes in the world, while leaving the Kurds to freeze in the mountains, and the Shiites to be gassed in the marshes. Since the collapse of the Berlin Wall, which had at least provided us with the illusion that we knew how the world was to be run, with a fatally easy goodies-and-baddies analysis, the West has looked suspiciously like Moses, doing the right thing for the wrong reason, the wrong thing for the right reason, and, as often as not, the wrong thing for the wrong reason. And, all over the Western world, people are asking where on earth we go from here.

Meanwhile, the cry of the poor gets louder. And if the living God heard the cry of his people in Egypt three and a half thousand years ago, he surely hears the cry that rises now from the bereaved in Belfast, the dispossessed in Palestine, the starving in the Sudan, and those in Bosnia and elsewhere who face another winter of freezing homes and hospitals, of battered and shattered lives. And if God hears this cry, and remembers his promise that the wolf shall lie down with the lamb, that swords will be beaten into ploughshares, that the whole earth will be filled with his glory, his justice and his peace, then how is he going to act? What is he going to do? When God remembers his promises, his memory moves him to action: as the Red Queen said, it's a poor memory that only works backwards. But God's way of action, now as then, is through a people, maybe even through an individual, who have glimpsed a fresh vision of his fire, and have heard for themselves his words of promise. They will almost certainly be unlikely people. Like Moses, they won't be expecting it. They may well not want it. But if they will only stand in fear before the living and burning God, they will be enabled to stand without fear before the Pharaohs of today.

So where do we learn to stand in fear before this God? In our worship. Many movements in the modern church try to make the worship of God more accessible; often all they succeed in doing is to trivialize it. Of course there must be understanding, of a sort, if worship is not to degenerate into mumbo-jumbo. But when you are confronted by fire, the proper response is not rational analysis, or 'will-the-people-in-the-pew-understand-it?', or a lowest-common-denominator levelling of words or music, but falling on your face. And, without mincing any words, people are more likely to be confronted by the majesty and awesomeness of God when the music and drama used in worship was written and is performed with that in mind.

This, to be sure, places an awesome responsibility on the musicians and liturgical organizers. Church music is meant to be a polished silver chalice, in which the strong wine of God's love is given to the rest of us. It is meant to be a burnished brazier which allows the congregation to warm themselves at God's fire. Woe betide, of course, the chalice or brazier that forgets what it is there for; but woe betide those who scoff at the polish or the burnishing because they cannot see what lies within. There is, after all, no escape from the temptation to professionalism: those whose churches eschew traditional choirs, and are filled instead with sound-systems and electronic gadgets, still need their professionals, who concentrate on their microphones and switches, as traditional choirs and organists concentrate on their minims and crotchets, so that the others may worship unhindered. No: what matters is that in worship we should enter the presence of the living God. And the music, if it is appropriate, can be a vital element in that awesome event.

But we meet with the high and holy one, the God of

fire, in order that we may ourselves be transformed and be his agents for the healing of his world. The God we worship is the God who hears the cry of his people, who remembers his promises, and who therefore desires to act not only for us but also through us. To enjoy worship for its own sake, or simply out of a cultural appreciation of the 'performance' (whether of Byrd or heavy rock), would be like Moses coming upon a burning bush and deciding to cook his lunch on it. No: we too need to cultivate a memory that works forwards as well as backwards. We remember, with due solemnity, events in the past which have shaped our national, social and personal life. But, as we do so in the presence of the living God, we must listen also for the voice which says: 'I have heard the cry of my people; and so I am sending *you* to *Pharaoh*.' We are not escapists, when we come to worship the true God and to pray for his bruised and bleeding world. On the contrary. We come so that, in whatever ways God calls us, small or great, we can be his agents in rescuing the world that still lies in gaol and cries for freedom. We, after all, stand before a yet more glorious tree: the tree of Calvary, which speaks, more truly than any words, of the fire of love which still burns at the heart of the living God.

CHAPTER NINE

Doing What He Was Told

He was only doing what he was told, after all.

One of the oldest tricks in the bureaucratic book is to tax people when they move from place to place. In Vancouver international airport you buy your ticket, you check your bags, you go through Customs, and then, when you think you're clear, you pass another little booth where they take a further ten dollars' airport tax off you. (This was true in 1995; I hope they soon scrap the system, if they haven't already.) Of course by then you're committed to travelling, and what's ten dollars compared with the price of the ticket? So you grumble inwardly and you pay up outwardly.

It can't be much fun to be the person collecting that ten dollars from thousands of people every day. You're on the receiving end of the veiled anger – and sometimes not so veiled – of those who feel it's a bit of a con. It's a bit like being a traffic warden. Or a prison warder. But there it is. It's their job. They're only doing what they're told.

Now if they'd had aeroplanes in the first century, you can be quite sure they'd have had an airport tax. One of the reasons Herod the Great could afford to rebuild the Temple in Jerusalem (here's something I bet you didn't know) was because he built a new harbour and forced all sea traffic to go through it, paying him a tax for the privilege. But when Herod the Great died, around the time Jesus was born, he divided his large kingdom between his sons. What does dividing a kingdom mean, when it comes to airport taxes or their ground-level equivalent? It means a lot more of them. Imagine if you had to pay a toll every time you crossed a county boundary while travelling around Britain. You'd think twice before driving fifty miles.

And where did you pay these taxes in Jesus' day? Not on the border itself; it would be dangerous to have a little booth stuck out by itself miles away from anywhere. No; the tax collection centre was in the first town you would come to once you'd crossed the border. After the death of Herod the Great, the northern part of his kingdom was divided between Philip and Antipas, east and west; and if you travelled west, from Philip's territory to Antipas', you would cross the border by crossing the Jordan just above the Sea of Galilee. And the first town you would come to on the western side was Capernaum. And in Capernaum there would be waiting for you a man called Levi ben Alphaeus, with a fixed smile and an outstretched hand. And you would think much the same thoughts as people think today in Vancouver international airport; only you would think them somewhat more bitterly, because you would know that Levi, Alphie's boy, made his living on the mark-up he chose to set between what he was supposed to charge and what he actually charged. And he would know that you would know. And you would know that he would know that you would know. And so on.

He was only doing his job.

But think what it does to you on the inside, if you're putting on that fixed smile six days a week, fifty weeks a year, allowing for Passover and the odd other holiday. It's not a great way to be a human being. It does things to you. It shows on your face. It shows in your voice, the superficial politeness with the threat of anger lurking underneath. It probably shows at home, with your wife and children.

And the trouble is that Levi, Alphie's boy, may well not have wanted very much to be a toll collector. The system needed someone, and found him. And so the social isolation, the cold shoulder from polite society, was probably reflected in the way he felt about himself. Because he had to get on with the job, he probably didn't very often confront the way he felt about himself. That does things to you, too. It's remarkable how many people are frightened of looking inside themselves, because of what they suspect they'll find. And if I'd been Levi, Alphie's son, I'd have been frightened of doing that, too.

Now we have to do all that ancient history, and all that amateur psychology, simply in order to get on the map of the story of Levi (Mark 2.13-17). Mark's first readers would have known all of that in their bones with the very first sentence. They would have seen instinctively, intuitively, what we have to come at by this more roundabout route. They would have felt the shock, the sense of a whole little world being turned upside down, when Jesus of Nazareth, who was going around announcing that God was at last becoming King, looked right inside Levi, Alphie's son, and said 'Follow me!'

In Matthew's gospel this story is part of a string of stories, most of which are healing miracles. There's a good reason for that: this story, too, is a healing miracle. When Jesus goes off to dinner in Levi's house, and the self-appointed guardians of tradition grumble (because if you're announcing the kingdom of God you don't associate with people like that), Jesus replies with a medical metaphor. Those who are well don't need the doctor; it's those who are ill who need the doctor. It's a healing miracle, all right. Levi, Alphie's son, was never the same again. Somebody had treated him as a human being. Somebody had *wanted* him. Did he even dare recognize that somebody had *loved* him? True healing begins in the heart, and I reckon that's where Jesus' words and action touched and found Levi, Alphie's boy.

In Mark's gospel, this story is part of his build-up of showing that the work of Jesus is bringing into being God's whole new order, his new world. It's the new wine that is going to burst the old bottles. Now that the sun has risen, you can blow out the candles. Now that Jesus is here, everything is to be stood on its head. That's what Mark is saying. But the new way, the Jesus revolution, isn't just novelty for novelty's sake. It was the new thing for which Israel had been longing. And she'd been longing for it for at least eight centuries, ever since the prophet Hosea penned these haunting words (14.1–4):

> Israel, come back to the Lord your God;
> your iniquity was the cause of your downfall.
> Provide yourself with words
> and come back to the Lord.
> Say to him, 'Take all iniquity away
> so that we may have happiness again
> and offer you our words of praise . . .'
> I will heal their disloyalty,
> I will love them with all my heart,
> for my anger has turned from them.

This is a prophecy of God restoring Israel; and of Israel recognizing that her sins have caused her ruin, and turning back to the God who still loves her freely and faithfully. Now ask yourself: what would that prophecy look like if it were to clothe itself in flesh and blood? Might it not look like a young man going around Galilee making all things new by loving the unlovable, by healing the unhealable, by welcoming the outcasts? It's not the healthy who need a doctor, but the sick; I didn't come to call the righteous, but sinners. That's the great joke of the gospel. The minute you think you're good enough for God, God says, 'I'm not interested in people who are good enough for me.' And the minute you think you're too bad for God, God says, 'It's you I've come for.'

There are two things which come bubbling out of this happy and subversive little story which I think we should grasp. The first is obvious and well known and central. (I sometimes worry about insulting people's intelligence by telling them things they already know very well; but, just as I don't get tired of hearing Schubert's Mass in G and Mozart's *Ave Verum* on a regular basis, and indeed would grumble if I didn't, so I hope we don't get tired of hearing what is, to me, the theological equivalent, and indeed the theological basis, of those two astonishing pieces.) When we come to worship, and to the Eucharist in particular, we come into the presence of Almighty God, and to feast at his table, not because we are good people, but because we are forgiven sinners. We come, as we come to a doctor, not because we are well but because we are sick. We come, not because we've got it all together, but because God's got it all together and has invited us to join him. We come, not because our hands are full of our own self-importance or self-righteousness, but because they are empty and waiting to receive his love, his body and blood, his own very self.

This is as basic to Christianity as the ball is to football. And, just as you have a rotten game of football if people ignore the ball and simply tackle the opposition, or even the crowd, so you have a pretty poor time in church if you forget for a moment that we are here because we don't deserve to be. And when that truth gets hold of you, and sinks down inside you like a hot drink on a cold day, then the effect on the whole life of the Christian community is quite marvellous. We are all here by grace alone: so we can relax. You don't have anything to *prove* in the presence of God; you shouldn't have anything to prove, either, in the

presence of your fellow Christians. You don't have to
pretend in the presence of God; no more should you need
to pretend in the presence of your fellow Christians. The
ground is level at the foot of the cross; the only people who
are excluded from the party are those who exclude themselves, by supposing they don't need the cross, don't need
God's forgiveness, don't need the free love of Jesus, in the
first place.

So the first thing that comes at me out of the story of
Levi, son of Alphaeus, is the simple basic truth that God in
Christ loves and accepts us as we are, and invites us into
fellowship with him, and with each other, on the basis of
that love rather than anything in ourselves:

> Love bade me welcome: yet my soul drew back,
>   Guiltie of dust and sinne.
> But quick-ey'd Love, observing me grow slack
>   From my first entrance in,
> Drew nearer to me, sweetly questioning
>   If I lack'd any thing.
>
> A guest, I answer'd, worthy to be here':
>   Love said, 'You shall be he.'
> 'I, the unkind, ungrateful? Ah, my dear,
>   I cannot look on Thee.
> Love took my hand, and smiling did reply,
>   'Who made the eyes but I?'
>
> 'Truth, Lord; but I have marr'd them; let my shame
>   Go where it doth deserve.'
> 'And know you not,' says Love, 'Who bore the blame?'
>   'My dear, then I will serve.'
> 'You must sit down,' says Love, 'and taste my meat.'
>   So I did sit and eat.
>
> (George Herbert, 'Love')

The other point that comes out of this story to me forms a direct challenge to the contemporary church. Think back to Hosea's prophecy for a moment. 'I will heal their disloyalty, I will love them with all my heart, for my anger has turned from them.' What would that prophecy look like if it were to become flesh and blood *today*? Answer that question, and we have written ourselves an agenda for mission. 'It isn't the healthy that need a doctor, but the sick.' What sort of things might the church be doing if we needed to explain them with an aphorism like that? If we aren't doing anything that needs that sort of explanation, then we need to ask ourselves whether we are in fact presenting the gospel of Jesus Christ to today's world. We must be ready to challenge society in Jesus' name. Jesus himself, after all, challenged his own society by overturning its expectations, and celebrating the kingdom of God with, as it seemed, all the wrong people.

What matters, as we consider our mission and how to go about it, is that we should be considering where the real need is in our society, and how we can meet that need. This is partly, of course, to do with money. When, as a church community, not least in a cathedral, we raise money, part of what we pledge goes of course to important charitable causes elsewhere. Part of what we spend on the cathedral itself goes precisely to make it place a place of welcome, of love, of gospel for all who come. One of the reasons I dislike the idea of cathedrals balancing their books by charging tourists for admission is that I believe we should present to our visitors the welcome of Jesus, not the outstretched hand of Levi, Alphie's son. But if we are to manage that, and so enable such buildings to exercise their unique mission (English cathedrals see more of the unchurched population than all other 'religious' buildings in the country put together), those who regularly use them (whether their regular congregation, their local community, or their diocese) need to be supporting their gospel mission from their own resources and initiatives as far as they can.

But, though money is important, it's not all-important. Everybody gave Levi money; Jesus gave him something else. He gave him back his humanity. We need to look around us and discover where people are being dehumanized – by their jobs or their lack of jobs, by their homes or their lack of homes, by their families or their lack of families. We need to find ways of communicating to them what Jesus communicated to Levi ben Alphaeus: that they are human beings, that they are valuable, that they don't need to prove anything, that they don't need to pretend. We need to communicate to them that God loves them.

A well-designed church or cathedral is put together in order to say that, but we need to be sure that it does. Most churches could do more than they do through exhibitions and displays; but the human welcome that people receive is far and away the most important thing. Church music is designed to express the richness and wonder of God's love, and church musicians need to be supported in giving us this priceless gift day by day and week by week. But these are only a beginning. There are many other ways of telling people that God loves them. There are projects for the homeless, for those below the poverty line. There are people in prison who need visiting. There are hospitals and hospices that depend very considerably on volunteer help. And so on. This usually means doing things more than saying things. Remember what St Francis said to his friars as he sent them out: 'Preach the gospel of Jesus by every means possible; and, if it's really necessary, you could even use words.'

And it all comes down to the little command which Jesus gave to Levi, Alphie's son, that strange day in Capernaum. The one thing people didn't want Levi to do was to follow them. They wanted to leave him behind, to forget about him, to put him out of their minds, to concentrate on the nice people, the lovable people, not those who made them angry, or ashamed, or afraid. And Jesus said, 'Follow me.' Follow me, Levi ben Alphaeus; follow me to the party, where the love of God flows like new wine and everyone can drink as much of it as they want; follow me to the table where we all look into one another's eyes without pretending and without needing to prove anything. But, Levi, this party isn't just for you. Once the doctor has cured you, you must in your turn become a doctor. Follow me to where people are feeling like you used to feel. Follow me to the people with hard faces and with sad faces, with hard hearts and with bitter hearts. Follow me to the rich people who are afraid of the poor, and to the poor people who are jealous of the rich. Follow me to the people who weep every day, and to the people who have forgotten how to weep. Follow me, and do as I do, love as I love.

Jesus didn't ask much of Levi ben Alphaeus. He asked everything, because he had just given everything. And Levi, perhaps to his own and certainly to the onlookers' astonishment, got up and followed him.

He was only doing what he was told.

CHAPTER TEN

Bethany

Come with me to Bethany. It's not far to go, if you're in Jerusalem; but it's quite a steep walk. If you came this way, taking the route you would be likely to take, from the place you would be likely to come from, you would go down: down into the Kidron valley, across the brook, and past the garden of Gethsemane; then up, steeply up, further up than you'd gone down before, until you would stand at last, out of breath, on the summit of the Mount of Olives, looking back at Jerusalem the golden. It's only a mile or so, but it's quite a climb. That was the route taken at night by the broken king, David, when Absalom rebelled. It was the route travelled by Jesus and his disciples, night after night during Holy Week, until, for reasons Jesus knew but they did not, they remained on the last night down in Gethsemane, and waited. And, night after night, from the crest of the Mount of Olives they would go on just a short way more, inside another mile, and would arrive at Bethany.

And there they went on that last day, the day Luke describes at the end of his gospel. 'Then he took them out as far as Bethany, and lifting up his hands he blessed them. Now as he blessed them, he withdrew from them and was carried up to heaven.' And let's not be fooled, while we're on the subject, by the naive literalism of certain paintings of the ascension, and for that matter certain hymns, which speak of Jesus going 'to his home above the skies', as though Jesus were some kind of primitive space-traveller. Heaven, as I have said elsewhere, is not a place thousands of miles up, or for that matter down, in our space, nor would it help us if it were. It is God's dimension of ordinary reality, the dimension which is normally hidden but which we penetrate mysteriously, or rather which penetrates us mysteriously, in prayer, in the scriptures, in the breaking of the bread. So when you stand on the outskirts of Bethany, and think of Jesus' withdrawal from the disciples, you are not here to verify, instruct yourself, inform curiosity or carry report. You are here to kneel where prayer has been valid.

And prayer is indeed valid here, on the Mount of Ascension, because Jesus' ascension is the great symbol of prayer. It isn't just that the ascended Lord is constantly interceding for his people before the Father's throne, true though that is. It is, more, that his ascension sums up what prayer actually is. A human being goes through the thin veil into the very presence of God, there to be welcomed, to worship, to love, to intercede. As so often in Christian theology, the best definition is not an abstract formula but a human being, indeed *the* human being, Jesus. That is why we pray *to* the Father *through* Jesus the Son. He is, quite literally, the Way. That is what the ascension is all about. And the journey to this point is always short, but steep.

So let's allow Bethany to stand for the rest of the gospel story, and ask again who it is that is the Way, who it is that is now enthroned as Lord of the world. What else happened at Bethany? Well, that's where Jesus got the donkey, for a start. No doubt there is much we could learn from that, but I want to choose three other Bethany incidents, three little vignettes which put some flesh and blood on the otherwise somewhat abstract doctrine of the ascension. When we think of the ascended Lord as the Bethany Jesus, what picture do we get?

Bethany was, first, the home of Mary and Martha. Think back to Luke chapter 10, the well-known Mary-and-Martha story. Jesus is visiting the sisters, and precipitates a domestic crisis. What's the problem? We normally regard Mary and Martha simply as typical of the passive and the active personalities, or, in Christian terms, of the life of devotion on the one hand and the life of service on the other. That may well be one level of the story, but it isn't the whole truth. The problem is not simply that Mary is so starry-eyed, listening to Jesus, that she forgets to help with the washing-up. The problem is that in that culture men and women belong in different parts of the building, and Mary has shamelessly gone across the short but steep gulf that separates male and female space.

What's more, she has assumed the posture of a disciple, a learner. She is sitting at Jesus' feet; which is the equivalent, in that culture, to somebody sitting at a desk in a classroom in modern Western life. You sit at the feet of a rabbi, like Saul of Tarsus sitting at the feet of Gamaliel, in order that one day you may be a rabbi yourself.

So Martha's excuse about the washing-up looks like a coded way of saying: 'stop this shameless behaviour and leave our social world intact.' She is telling Jesus to reproach Mary, but actually she is reproaching Jesus too. And Jesus, there in Bethany, declares that Mary has chosen the better part. Jesus quietly and calmly dismantles a major social taboo and leaves the onlookers open-mouthed in amazement. This is the Bethany Jesus; should we be surprised to find that the Lord of the world has the right to turn the world upside down?

And not only the world, but life and death themselves. Come back to Bethany some time later, and find the same two sisters in the very depth of shock and grief. 'Lord, if you had been here, my brother would not have died.' They both say it, with the reproach of grief: Lord, we needed you and you weren't here! (Have you ever said that?) And the Bethany Jesus, the one we know as the ascended Lord, finds his own grief welling up in sympathy with these dear sisters, and we have that awesome little verse in John 11.35: 'Jesus wept.' And, still greatly distressed, he comes to the tomb of Lazarus, and tells them to take away the stone.

Martha objects – she's always telling Jesus off, bless her, and he is so gentle with her – Lord, there'll be a smell! He's been dead four days! But they remove the stone anyway. Jesus prays a prayer, not of intercession but of thanksgiving, presumably *because there isn't a smell*; he has already prayed, and knows he has been heard. And then he shouts, 'Lazarus; come out!' And Lazarus makes the short but steep journey from death to life. We die with the dying: see, they depart, and we go with them. We are born with the dead: see, they return, and bring us with them. This is the Bethany Jesus; this is the ascended Lord: the one who has identified totally with the pain of the world, the one who has total authority over life and death, and the one who now prays to the Father for his grief-stricken people. The ascended Lord is the one who disturbs the comfortable and comforts the disturbed.

And then another scene we all know very well. Jesus is again in Bethany, sitting at table, and a woman comes with a costly jar of ointment, and anoints Jesus with it. Matthew and Mark tell the story, but don't tell us who it was; John reveals that this, too, was Mary of Bethany. Well, she would, wouldn't she? (This probably isn't the same story as the one in Luke, where a woman who is a sinner comes and anoints Jesus and is assured of forgiveness. But the point is not far off.) Mary has discovered that Jesus is worth everything she's got: she has attained that condition of complete simplicity, costing not less than everything. She has made the short but steep journey from being around Jesus to

being totally devoted to him. She is worshipping him for all
he's worth.

And, as always, when people are worshipping Jesus with
everything they've got, some other people find this distaste-
ful and disturbing. This time the coded message comes in
terms of money, always a powerful argument for maintaining the *status quo* and the stiff upper lip. It needs to be
heard as blustering, embarrassed self-importance: 'This
ointment – this ointment – this ointment could have been
sold for hundreds of pounds and – and – and given to the
poor!' Mary's uninhibited worship has shown up the
onlookers' cold formality, has knocked at the door of deep
emotion that they had carefully locked up. People resent the
Bethany Jesus; they resent, too, the way other people react
to him.

We find this blustering self-importance today when
people criticize the church for spending money on new silver vessels or on fabulous music. We find it when people
lose their inhibitions and want to raise their arms in the air
and sing in tongues, or when they want to swing incense
around so that the building, like the house in Bethany, is
filled with the lovely smell. I suspect we all reach a point
where somebody else's enthusiasm strikes us as over the
top. But, let's face it, the whole point of enthusiasm is that
it's over the top; and if you're not enthusiastic about Jesus,
or are tempted to mock at somebody who is, look around
within this story and see what company you're keeping.

This, then, is the Bethany Jesus, part three: the Jesus
who, on his way to the cross, is worthy of such total and
costly devotion that those who don't understand will regard
it as crazy. When the ascended Lord comforts the disturbed
and disturbs the comforted, the result is reckless adoration.
That's what Ascensiontide is all about.

Where have we got to so far, following this Bethany
Jesus, this ascended Lord? He is the Lord who turns the

world upside down. He is the one who sympathizes totally
with us in our sadness, our failure, our grief. He is the one
whose prayer to the Father brings life out of death. And he
is the one who deserves our most costly devotion. Let
Bethany stand for all the other incidents in the gospels, and
this is the story of Jesus in miniature. These are, of course,
some of the traditional themes of Ascensiontide: Jesus the
ruler of the world, Jesus the great high priest, Jesus ever
living to make intercession for us, Jesus the object of our
love and worship. But there is one more, which Luke
would not have us forget. And to find it I want to take you
once more on that short but steep journey.

Some years ago, at Ascensiontide, I was in Jerusalem,
teaching at the Hebrew University. I used to walk out of
the old city, across the head of the Kidron valley, and up to
the campus on Mount Scopus, just to the north of the
Mount of Olives. And one afternoon, as I was half-way
through my lecture, we heard three muffled but quite loud
explosions.

Now in Israel you often hear odd noises. Sometimes it's
military planes breaking the sound barrier; it's such a small
country, so they have to train over built-up areas. Sometimes it's fireworks, when someone's having a party.
Sometimes it's gunfire. These explosions weren't quite like
any of those. We looked at one another, shrugged our
shoulders, and I went on with the lecture (which, ironically
enough, was on Romans 9—11, Paul's classic statement
about God's struggle with Israel). It was only that night, on
the television news, that I discovered what had happened.
The Israeli army had caught three teenage Arab boys who,
as part of their regular protest against the occupation of
their territories, had been throwing stones at the soldiers.
The army did what they usually did. They went to the boys'
homes. They ordered everybody out. They packed the three
houses with explosives. And they blew them up. Three sad,

squat piles of rubble, containing the thousand little things that make a house a home. And the village where this took place, on that bright, sunny afternoon, was of course Bethany. (And do you know, when I told my Israeli friends what I thought of this barbaric behaviour, they told me with a wry smile that it was a trick they had learned from the British in the 1940s.)

And I wanted to say – Lord, if only you had been there! Lord, if you're the Lord of the world, why are people still blowing up each other's houses? Lord, isn't it time for this barbaric behaviour to be broken through just like you broke through the old taboos? And Bethany, of course, stands once more for the whole story: for Bosnia, for Rwanda, for Ireland, for Somalia, for Central America, the litany that becomes so familiar that the pain is dulled and we shrug our shoulders and walk away. And I go back to Luke's story of the ascension, and I find the answer staring me in the face.

One of the last things that Jesus said to his followers before they went on that short and steep journey to Bethany was this: that, in his name, 'repentance and forgiveness of sins should be preached to all the nations, beginning from Jerusalem' (Luke 24.47).

Now, listen: we have trivialized that message. We have reduced it in scale; we have brought it down to our level to make it bearable. We have thought that it meant simply that I should repent of my sins, and you of yours, and that God would forgive us. And of course it does mean that, and without that there is no personal gospel; but it means much, much more. What is the announcement that the church must make to the world? It isn't simply that every individual is a sinner and needs to repent, true though that is. It is that the way the world lives is out of joint with the way that God intends; and that God in Christ is holding out a different way to live, a way which is characterized, at every level, by forgiveness. When people glimpse the forgiveness of God in Christ, they are set free from the need to clutch at their own security and to blow up those who threaten them, even when they're boys throwing stones. Forgiveness is the most powerful thing in the world, because it is the gift of the ascended Lord not only to his church but also to his bombed-out world.

Think how it works. The world, like Martha, says: 'We must do things this way; this is the only way we know how to live.' No, says the Bethany Jesus, there is a different way to live, which will turn your world upside down. The world, like Martha and Mary, stands weeping at the tomb, saying there's no point opening this all up because it'll only stink. No, says the Bethany Jesus; I have prayed to the Father, and there is life hidden in that tomb. The world, like Judas, stands mocking at those who worship Jesus with everything they've got; what use will that be in addressing the problems of society? Every use possible, says the Bethany Jesus: it has been written that the Messiah should suffer and rise again, and that, as Lord of the world, he should send out his heralds to announce to the world that there is a different way of living, a different way of being human, a way characterized by forgiveness through and through.

This is what it means for the ascended Lord to entrust his church with the task of evangelism. Evangelism is not simply a matter of bringing individuals to personal faith, though of course that remains central to the whole enterprise. It is a matter of confronting the world with the good, but deeply disturbing, news of a different way of living, which is the Bethany way, the way of love. With the drawing of this Love and the voice of this Calling, we shall not cease from exploration, and the end of all our exploring will be to arrive where we started and know the place for the first time.

The Bethany Jesus comforts the disturbed and disturbs the comfortable. He wants us to be his agents in doing so. For this, we need to know that he is the ascended Lord of the world; and we need to be indwelt by his Spirit. The life of heaven, through the prayer of the ascended Lord, is to become the life of earth.

Come with me, then, to Bethany. It's a short journey, but a steep one. From here, on a clear day, you can see for ever.

CHAPTER ELEVEN

When I am Weak

Nearly twenty years ago I found myself at a large conference, and I bumped into a man I vaguely knew. He had just been appointed as principal of a small seminary in the United States. He was looking for some new junior faculty members, and asked me if I was interested. I suppose I must have given him some encouragement, because his next question was: 'Do you have a copy of your *curriculum vitae*?'

I was astonished. He seemed to think that the average person, or at least the average academic, would naturally be walking around with a *curriculum vitae* handy on the off-chance that someone might want to see it. This struck me then, and strikes me still, as faintly absurd. It makes sense only in a society where too many people take themselves too seriously. I sometimes think that every time one has to make up a *curriculum vitae*, for a job or whatever, one ought at the same time to make up, at least for one's own benefit, an inverted list: the exams I didn't pass, the jobs I didn't get, the short story no one would publish.

For America, read Corinth; for the inverted *curriculum vitae*, read 2 Corinthians 11 and 12. To get the flavour, imagine me presenting to my over-solemn acquaintance that upside-down list of all my failures and disappointments. You see, the Corinthian church had started to take themselves too seriously. Now that they'd been Christians for a

little while they wanted to go up-market. They'd had some
new teachers in town, who had given them the idea that
they could aspire to higher standards of wisdom, to higher
levels of spiritual attainment, to more dramatic experiences,
to greater triumphs for the gospel. This was very exciting;
it was also very beguiling. Instead of being regarded as the
lowest of the low, as a little group of crazy fanatics that
had dropped off the bottom of the social ladder, maybe this
new teaching, this new wisdom, might actually advance
their social standing just a bit. Maybe, with these new
teachers, their church would be famous, looked up to . . .

And where did that leave Paul? Well, Paul had been
their own evangelist and founder, they couldn't deny that.
But, in the light of all that they'd heard from these new
teachers, they were tempted to look at Paul in the way that
young people, spending a week in the big city, may be
tempted to think of the folks back home: a bit boring, a bit
shabby – just a bit dull. And the new teachers seem to have
suggested that actually Paul was more interested in his
other churches anyway; after all, it was a long time since
he'd been to see them . . .

Paul was clearly hurt by this nonsense, but he was far
more worried at the sheer pride – social pride and spiritual
pride – that he detected in Corinth. And what the
Corinthians didn't know was that he had just come through
something like a total nervous breakdown, and in any case
had only just got out of prison in Ephesus, so he wasn't in
great shape to sail straight over and sort them out face to
face. So he travelled round the north end of the Aegean,
and as he travelled he thought and prayed and worried. And
then at a certain point I think I see a slow smile coming
across his face, as he starts to plan the letter he will write to
them.

He has some specific things to say anyway. He is collecting money on behalf of the poverty-stricken Christians

in Judaea, and he wants to make sure the Corinthians have got enough laid by to put up a decent sum. But the bulk of the letter is an explanation of what being an apostle really means. All right, he says. You want my *curriculum vitae*. You want my up-to-date testimony. You want my full credentials as an apostle. You want to know all the wonderful things I have done for God, all the battles I have fought and the victories I have won in the service of the kingdom, all the things that will enable you to hold your heads high in front of your pagan neighbours. Very well, get a load of this. I am the most superior apostle imaginable – because I'm a habitual jailbird; I've lost count of my beatings; I've been through humiliating punishments, I've been stoned, three times I've been shipwrecked, I've been constantly in danger, and I'm always anxious about all the churches. Paul's *curriculum vitae* is upside-down. He's boasting of all the wrong things. They want his successes, not his failures. They want his triumphs, not his disasters. They want him to play the hero, and he plays the fool.

But they are the real fools. They have exchanged the gospel of the crucified Messiah for the gospel of success; and the only way Paul can get through to them is through this shameless tease, exposing their pride for what it is. And this brings us to 2 Corinthians 12. They want his up-to-date spiritual testimony, do they? They want to know what splendid visions and revelations he has been experiencing, do they? They want an account of his great supernatural power, do they? Fine, here we go. I know a man in Christ – he won't even say it's himself to begin with – who *fourteen years ago* [come on, Paul, we want something more up-to-date than that!] was caught up into the third heaven, and – well, actually, I don't know much about what was going on, he says, and I'm not allowed to tell you what I heard. Yes, it was wonderful, but that's about it. (It reminds me of when Einstein was asked when he normally had his original ideas. He replied that actually he hadn't had that many.)

And then Paul comes to the crunch. 'To keep me from being too elated, I was given a thorn in the flesh.' He won't even say what it was, but it was clearly an unpleasant affliction. 'Three times', he says, 'I prayed to the Lord about this, that it would leave me' [yes, yes, think the Corinthians, now we're getting there – a great healing miracle coming up] – 'but he said to me, "My grace is sufficient for you; power is perfected in weakness." So where does this leave me? I will boast gladly of my weaknesses, so that Christ's power may dwell in me. I am content with weaknesses, insults, hardships, persecutions, and calamities for Christ's sake; for when I am weak, then I am strong.'

I like to imagine the scene in the Christian assembly in Corinth as this letter is read out. There they are, fifty or sixty of them perhaps, crammed into the house of one of the few wealthy Christians in the town. They have just watched their new ideas dismantled from behind with breath-taking skill by the one they regarded as a bit old hat, a bit dull. But the whole point of what he's been saying is that skill and strength and pride and power aren't where it's at. Do we follow a crucified Messiah, or do we follow some happy hero-figure?

And do you see what Paul has achieved, in fact, through this letter, through this astonishing irony and teasing? We often think of Jesus Christ as the great healer, but this passage sounds as though it should be entitled 'When Christ Refused to Heal.' But what Paul has done is in fact to effect a healing miracle at a much deeper level. Who cares whether the thorn remains in the flesh or not, if the body of Christ is deeply sick with spiritual pride? Who cares about private visions and revelations if the community of the people of God cares more for status and prestige than for the shameful gospel of the cross?

What was their disease? The Corinthians had not, perhaps, gone very far down the road along which their new teachers had enticed them. A mile or two further on, they would have prided themselves on being *Corinthian* Christians, rather than those backward heretical Philippians or Ephesians. A little way beyond that, they would have become syncretistic, picking up every new spiritual experience they could find, whether it had anything to do with Jesus and the cross or not. And before very long they would have set up on their own; or rather, they would have broken up into different groups, because once you contract the Corinthian disease you become vulnerable to personality cults (disguised, of course, as doctrinal or ethical debates); or perhaps to battles between different cultural styles in worship (disguised, of course, as the distinction between the truly spiritual and the merely aesthetic).

And what is the remedy? It's no good Paul giving them a lecture, bullying them or harrying them into line. Silly old Paul, they'll say; we're bored with you. Nor will it simply do for him to back off, to sit and sulk, or perhaps pray, in Ephesus or wherever. The love of Christ, as he says in 2 Corinthians 5, leaves him no choice. He must come to the place where they are; he is on his way, physically, but in this letter he is coming to meet them emotionally and spiritually and deeply personally. He is coming, out of his own pain, both emotional and physical, to apply his own love, his own upside-down wisdom, his own humour and irony, his own knowledge of Christ, to the place where the disease has got hold of them. He stands in the middle, holding fast to Christ with one hand, and holding fast to them with the other, even though it stretches him into the agonizing but familiar position that suggests the healing is starting to work. This, as we saw in chapter 6 of the present book, is what he means when he talks about the ministry of reconciliation.

How would you like to be Paul? Not a lot, I should think. Shipwreck, beating, worry, danger, prison: forget it.

But it's not so good not being Paul either, when you think about it. How do you cope when the world is out of joint? When *your* world is out of joint? When people you love are at odds with one another or with you? When you can see people, perhaps people you care for very deeply, going off in the wrong direction while claiming that it's you that's heading the wrong way? The temptation is either to yell at people, or to back off and sulk in a corner. That's the way of not being Paul; it's not very effective, and it's not much fun.

But what does it mean to be Paul in such situations? It means thinking right into the problem and the pain of the situation you face, even if that means allowing some of your own raw nerves, some of your own vulnerability, to be exposed. It means being weak in order to be strong. We live in a world full of people struggling to be, or at least to appear, strong, in order not to be weak; and we follow a gospel which says that when I am weak, then I am strong. And this gospel is the only thing that brings true healing.

The calling to imitate Paul is obviously the calling to imitate Christ. From the whole way we have come at it, this is obviously the call to be Christ's agents in working healing miracles: not necessarily in healing physical ailments, though that can and does happen today (never predictably, always humblingly), but also in healing personal, emotional, psychological, social, cultural wounds and scars. Please note, if Paul is anything to go by (and he is), you don't have to be healthy to be a healer. It is the wounded surgeon who plies the steel most successfully; 'beneath the bleeding hands we feel the sharp compassion of the healer's art.'

What is our calling, then? We are called, simply, to hold on to Christ and his cross with one hand, with all our might; and to hold on to those we are given to love with the other hand, with all our might, with courage, humour, self-abandonment, creativity, flair, tears, silence, sympathy, gentleness, flexibility, Christlikeness. When we find their tears becoming our own, we may know that healing has begun to happen; when they find Christ in being held on to by us, whether we realize it or not, we are proving the truth of what Paul said: God made him to be sin for us, who knew no sin, so that in him we might embody the saving faithfulness of God.

This calling comes in at least three varieties, or levels. We are all called to the first; and such insight as we gain from that will help those who aren't called to the second and third to pray intelligently, at least, for those who are.

The first level of calling, in many ways the most important, comes to all human beings, men, women and children in Christ. Wherever you are, whoever you are with, you are called – we are all called – to hold on to Christ firmly with one hand and to hold on to those around with the other, in prayer, discussion, generosity, gratitude, teaching or learning, caring or being cared for. You will never meet anybody, and you will never meet any group of people, that does not need healing in some respect or other; and God will see to it, whether you realize it or not, that their pain and yours are often remarkably similar, so that all you may have to do, to share the work of Christ the healer, is to hold on and pray in silent sympathy. There will be other times when the work of healing will require all your resources of courage, to confront and challenge folly and wickedness, but to do it as one who knows their power and allure. There will be times when healing will come through humour, through cooking, through play. Paul had to call on all his rhetorical skill, not in order to teach but in order to heal. Whatever skills God has given you, be prepared to use them as instruments of the gospel.

But the second level of calling, which may, and I pray will, come to some of you, is the calling to be all this for the church. It is the call, in other words, to full-time Christian ministry at whatever level, including that of ordination. Ordination isn't the be-all and end-all of Christian ministry; but the church desperately needs ordained clergy, needs them now as much as ever, and I would be surprised if out of the readers of a book like this God were not calling someone, perhaps several, to give their life in imitation of Paul in imitation of Christ: to hold on to Christ with one hand and hold on to the church with the other, to share and feel the agony of the church's follies and failings, and to know the power of Christ to restore and heal the church and set her feet back on the right path. That is a vocation not to be lightly dismissed.

The church, after all, needs leaders who can break new ground for others to follow. The church needs teachers who can expound the scriptures and find fresh ways of presenting the story of God's love. But, above all, the church needs healers who can be channels of God's peace and love, who can be for her today what Paul was for Corinth, a wise and faithful friend who wounds in order to heal, who tells the truth not to hurt but to mend, who rejoices with the joyful and weeps with the mourners, who teases and plays, who agonizes and prays, who shares the priestly and healing work of Christ. The church doesn't need people who know it all, or can do it all, or want to control it all. When I am weak, then I am strong.

The third level of calling ought to be in our prayers especially at times of crisis, such as we face in many parts of the Western world at the moment. There is a desperate need for people to do for the world, for society as a whole and in its various parts, what Paul did for Corinth.

Our hearts go out to those who suffer through terrorist action, through war and civil conflict, and through the countless waking nightmares that we see and hear in the news media day by day. And what is needed, in so many areas of national life as well, such as prisons, health services, schools and colleges, inner cities, racial minorities, the unemployed, and of course politics itself – what is needed all over our society is the one thing the Thatcherite and Reaganite revolution forgot to cater for: healers.

Why healers? We don't need people to yell at these situations or to bully them. We don't need people to back off and pretend it's somebody else's problem. We need Christian people to work as healers: as healing judges and prison staff, as healing teachers and administrators, as healing shopkeepers and bankers, as healing musicians and artists, as healing writers and scientists, as healing diplomats and politicians. We need people who will hold on to Christ firmly with one hand and reach out the other, with wit and skill and cheerfulness, with compassion and sorrow and tenderness, to the places where our world is in pain. We need people who will use all their god-given skills, as Paul used his, to analyse where things have gone wrong, to come to the place of pain, and to hold over the wound the only medicine which will really heal, which is the love of Christ made incarnate once more, the strange love of God turned into your flesh and mine, your smile and mine, your tears and mine, your patient analysis and mine, your frustration and mine, your joy and mine.

This isn't a matter of having all the answers or taking control of the world. Indeed, it's just the opposite. When I am weak, then I am strong. We must pray for the Middle East; for the countries of the former Soviet bloc; for Northern Ireland; and for so many other situations we could name around the world. We must pray that God will raise up a new generation of strong weaklings; of wise fools; of wounded healers; so that the healing love of Christ may flow out into the world, to confront violence and injustice with the rebuke of the cross, and to comfort the injured and wronged with the consolation of the cross.

Somebody said on the television recently, concerning Northern Ireland, that it would take a miracle to sort things out now. Yes, indeed, and that, once again, is what Jesus specializes in; but miracles come in all shapes and sizes. 'My grace is sufficient for you, for power is made perfect in weakness.' Please God there may not be lacking men, women and children of holy courage in Northern Ireland, in Bosnia, in the Middle East, and elsewhere, who will be that miracle in their lives, their love, their hope and their faith. And please God may we, in whatever vocation he calls us, be that same miracle there. For when we are weak, then we are strong.

CHAPTER TWELVE

Getting Back on the Road

The newspapers always like a good religious story. Actually, what they like is a good religious *controversy*; a scandal, an argument, another variation on the old 'trads v. rads' theme. But there's one theme that they don't touch these days. Even during the Week of Prayer for Christian Unity, they never seem to talk about the quest for church unity, the ecumenical movement.

Well, they wouldn't, would they? The ecumenical movement is no longer news. The heady days of the sixties and seventies, when for a while it looked as though major steps towards visible union were going to come about, have passed. Ecumenical projects have come and gone. Many ordinary Christians in the Western world have become accustomed to praying for the unity of all Christian people in the way that many pray for the eventual coming of the kingdom – something greatly to be desired, no doubt, but it doesn't seem to affect particularly what we actually do from week to week.

I believe it is time to get things back on track. If we worship the one true and living God, how can we not grieve over disunity in the church? If we worship the God of love revealed in Jesus, how can we not long for the loving unity of all those who respond to that love? If we worship the God revealed in the life-giving Spirit, why shouldn't we invoke that Spirit to bring us together?

To this end, I'm going to look at one of the great Pauline passages that speaks of the unity of the church, namely, a quite remarkable text in Galatians chapter 2. Here is Paul, talking about himself, but even more about someone else:

> I have been crucified with Christ; and it is no longer I who live, but Christ who lives in me. And the life I now live in the flesh I live by faith in the Son of God, who loved me and gave himself for me. (Galatians 2.19–20)

You might suppose that this is simply a rather lavish way of describing Paul's conversion and its permanent consequences. What had happened to him could only be described as dying and coming back to life – or rather, going on through death and out into a new sort of life. In recognizing that the crucified Jesus was the Messiah, Paul came to see that he, as a zealous Jew, had to regard himself as completely identified with, and loyal to, this Messiah. And that meant that he, Saul of Tarsus, had in one sense to lose his identity completely, in order to find a new identity as 'a man in Christ'.

But what has that, in turn, got to do with Paul's vision for the unity of the church? Well, from Paul's point of view, everything. Paul isn't just indulging in a bit of autobiography for its own sake. This description of his dying and rising with Christ is the climax of a long paragraph, in which Paul tells of the confrontation he had had with Peter in Antioch. And that confrontation was all about the unity of the church.

Let's back up a bit and consider what was at stake. Galatians 2 is all about the question: who are Christians allowed to eat with? This was a major issue for the early church. Paul's response remains enormously important.

Paul's altercation with Peter arose like this. Peter had been visiting the church in Antioch (Paul's home church), where Jewish and Gentile Christians used to eat together perfectly happily; and Peter had joined in without scruple. Until, that is, certain persons came from James, in Jerusalem; whereupon Peter separated himself and ate only with other Jews, presumably Jewish Christians. Who was right? Peter or Paul?

Paul addressed the question in terms of the doctrine we have come to call 'justification by faith', ending with the remarkable passage I quoted a moment ago. Justification, of course, has been for four hundred years one of the main sticking points in discussions between Protestants and Catholics. Paul's point, however, is this: if you understand justification by faith, you will be left in no doubt about who you may sit down and eat with. The whole discussion is about *community definition*. The thrust of it all for us today, I believe, is that the original Pauline doctrine of justification *is not only something that all Christians might be able to agree on, but, ironically, that it is in itself the original and the strongest ecumenical doctrine*. It isn't just that if we really try hard in our doctrinal discussions we might come up with a formula which enables us to bury the hatchet from centuries of acrimonious debate about justification; justification is itself the doctrine that tells us *that* we *should* bury the hatchet and, moreover, tells us *how* we might do it.

You see, Saul of Tarsus and his pre-Christian Jewish friends didn't just sit around discussing religious doctrines. They were eager for Israel's God to act, to bring in his kingdom; and this would consist, they believed, of the victory of God over the pagan, Gentile nations. All their praying and their politicking were bent to this end. And, as zealous Jews to this day believe, the only way this would happen was if Israel stopped flirting with paganism and maintained herself as the holy people of God, true to the law, separate from the rest of the world. Saul of Tarsus had been longing for a national and ethnic liberation in which Israel would become, publicly and visibly, the true people of the one true God.

So, in the church in Antioch, within a very few years of Pentecost, Peter found himself caught in the cross-fire between two clearly thought out positions.

The Jerusalem Christians were quite clear. They were Jewish Christians; and because of their zeal for God, and their hostility to Gentiles, they were unwilling to share fellowship with Gentile Christians unless they became circumcised. The hope of ethnic Israel was still paramount. From their point of view, failure to get circumcised represented a lack of seriousness about the Gentiles' commitment to the God of Abraham, Isaac and Jacob.

Paul's position was equally clear, and far more radical. The renewed people of God in Christ were a single people, he insisted; they were called, in principle, from every nation under heaven, and did not require any racial or cultural qualification. Their belief in the gospel of Jesus was the only badge of membership. That's what 'justification by faith' was all about.

And poor old Peter is embarrassed. He is caught between the two. And, when he draws back, and decides not to eat with the Gentile Christians any longer, the other Jewish Christians in Antioch withdraw as well, including even Barnabas, Paul's close associate and travelling companion.

Paul, telling the Galatians what he said to Peter, puts his finger on the critical issue (2.14). Peter is a Jew; fine. But Peter, who had believed all along that Jesus was the Messiah, had come to realize that this meant crucifixion and resurrection. Peter had himself pioneered the mission to the Gentiles, accepting freely and without racial constraint those who believed in Jesus. Now, Paul says, by your own action you are saying to your Gentile fellow Christians that they are second-class citizens; if they want to become full members of God's people, they must get circumcised and become adopted into the Jewish people. That, from Paul's point of view, was a contradiction in terms.

So, in addressing Peter, Paul articulates the all-time basis for the unity of all Christian people. Membership in God's family is not by race, but by grace. It is not by moralism, but by the forgiving love of God. It is not tied to a particular culture or class or gender; the ground is level at the foot of the cross. As he sums it up a chapter later, there is neither Jew nor Greek, slave nor free, male nor female; all are one in Christ Jesus.

The only badge of membership, therefore, is that which is the same for us all: the saving act of God in Christ Jesus, and the helpless acceptance of that by the believer, simply in the act of believing itself. That's justification by faith. And that, not just a private spiritual experience, however dramatic, is what Paul is talking about in the passage with which I began (vv. 19–20):

> Through the law I died to the law, so that I might live to God. I have been crucified with Christ; it is no longer I who live, but Christ who lives in me. And the life I now live in the flesh I live by faith in the Son of God, who loved me and gave himself for me.

Paul, not for the last time, is using himself as the example of what happens to the typical Jew when fully faced by the revelation of the living God in the face of the crucified and risen Jesus Christ. He is, quite simply, turned inside out.

Let's go through, step by step, the thrust of what he's saying, not just about himself but about the whole purposes of God. The Messiah represents Israel; the Messiah has died and been raised: so those who recognize him as Messiah discover that God's plan was always cross-shaped; they are co-crucified with the Messiah, and given a new life, the Messianic life, which redefines their identity. They are no longer labelled by their ethnic, territorial or cultural setting, but simply as 'the Messiah's people', people 'in Christ'. Jewish Christians have come out of the defining context of the Jewish law; that is no longer where their identity lies. Gentile Christians have come out of the defining context of their social and cultural worlds. That is no longer where their true identity lies.

Jew and Gentile alike have thus come alive in a new way to the living God. The life they have is not, however, that which their parents bequeathed them, circumscribed by family, land, and tribal taboos. The life all Christians have is defined by faith in, or perhaps by the faithfulness of, the Son of God; and the Son of God is known as 'the one who loved me and gave himself for me'. As so often in Paul, at the heart of the doctrine there is no cold mind, but a warm heart; no abstract system, but the act of love and the response of love.

For Paul, therefore, to step back even for a second into a world where one is defined in terms of race, geography, cultic taboos and the rest is to transgress against love, against the light and truth of the gospel, and against grace. 'I do not nullify the grace of God!' he says (v. 21). 'If membership in God's people came through the law, then Christ died for nothing.' The death of Jesus was the great messianic act of love and liberation, in which the God of Israel had acted once and for all to save his people and, through them, the whole world. To go against this is to go against the loving, gracious act of God.

You see, the whole point of the gospel for Paul, as he makes clear in several passages, is that through the achievement and announcement of King Jesus the principalities and powers, the local and tribal deities that have carved up the world between them, have had their power shaken to the roots. A new kingdom has been set up in which the old tribalisms, and the ideologies and idolatries that sustain them, have been declared redundant. And woe betide anyone who names the name of Christ but persists in worshipping, at least by implication, at the shrine of any of those old loyalties, no matter how venerable they may seem.

All of which brings us, none too soon, to the thrust for today of all this wonderful Pauline theology. I return to the central point: justification by faith is not simply something which, if we work at it, we ought to be able to agree on; it is, in fact, the doctrine which declares that *all who believe in the Messiah Jesus belong at the same table, no matter what their ethnic, geographical, gender or class background*. There is neither Jew nor Greek, slave nor free, male nor female, for you are all one in Christ Jesus. Paul's doctrine of justification is *the* ecumenical doctrine.

Galatians 2 gives us, therefore, not just a truth to glimpse but an agenda to act upon. The way forward is unlikely to be merely a matter of doctrinal definition. It will mean going wider, into the world that, properly understood, doctrine reveals: the world of symbol and praxis. Let me say a word about each of these.

At the heart of Galatians 2 is not an abstract individualized salvation, but a common meal. Paul does not want the Galatians to wait until they have agreed on all doctrinal arguments before they can sit down and eat together. Not to eat together is already to get the answer wrong. The whole point of his argument is that all those who belong to Christ belong at the same table with one another.

The relevance of this today should be obvious. The differences between us, as twentieth-century Christians, all too often reflect cultural, philosophical and tribal divides, rather than anything that should keep us apart from full and glad eucharistic fellowship. I believe the church should recognize, as a matter of biblical and Christian obedience, that it is time to put the horse back before the cart, and that we are far, far more likely to reach doctrinal agreement between our different churches if we do so within the context of that common meal which belongs equally to us all because it is the meal of the Lord whom we all worship. Intercommunion, in other words, is not something we should regard as the prize to be gained at the end of the ecumenical road; it is the very paving of the road itself. If we wonder why we haven't been travelling very fast down the road of late, maybe it's because, without the proper paving, we've got stuck in the mud.

But isn't this to elevate something we *do*, as opposed to something we *believe*, to the supreme position? The understandable Reformation emphasis on 'faith' as opposed to 'works' has often, paradoxically, emasculated the clear thrust of Pauline theology: that we should express our unity by working together with one mind for the spread of the gospel, that is, for the announcement of the Lordship of Jesus Christ to all the world, not least to the principalities and powers that keep people locked up within their local and tribal divisions. We have seen once again in the 1990s what happens when tribalisms, including those that proclaim a would-be Christian allegiance, go unchecked. The gospel itself stands against all attempts to define ourselves as Catholic or Protestant, Orthodox or Methodist, Anglican or Baptist, still less by national, cultural or geographical subdivisions of those labels. Our definition must be that we are in Christ; the praxis that goes with that is love for one another and the loving announcement of Jesus Christ to the whole world.

Thus, wherever we find tribalisms distorting the truth of the gospel (whether it be in Bosnia or Birmingham, in the

West Bank or in Wolverhampton, in Staffordshire or South Africa), we must name them for what they are, and must announce that in Christ all are one. Evangelism, properly conceived, ought to be the most ecumenical of endeavours. If we are looking out at the world for which Christ died, rather than at ourselves and all our problems and muddles, we are more likely to find those problems and muddles put into their proper perspectives. To turn away from our own jealously hoarded private identities, and to discover that we are all redefined in and by Christ, and by him alone: that is the vision. I am crucified with Christ; nevertheless I live; yet not I, but Christ lives in me; the life I now live I live by faith in the Son of God, who loved me and gave himself for me.

Stand back now from Paul, and think about the New Testament as a whole. It is all about the wonderful things that God has done in Jesus Christ, revealing his power, presence and glory. What do you think would reveal to the world today the power, the presence, and the glory of God? Well, how about the coming together of all those who name the name of Christ, in love, and unity, and mission? That might take a miracle, I hear someone say. Well – isn't that, once more, what Jesus seems to have specialized in?

CHAPTER THIRTEEN

The Older Brother

It was cold that December in New York; so cold that the young boy, another victim of the Great Depression, put newspaper inside his clothes before going out, and cardboard in his thin shoes to protect his feet. He walked dozens of long freezing city blocks to queue outside Macie's, the large downtown department store. (This, by the way, is a true story.) He wanted to meet Father Christmas. He wasn't sure whether he believed in him; but he knew there was something exciting and mysterious going on, and he wanted to be part of it. Finally it was his turn. The white-bearded figure looked him up and down. 'This ain't for you, Jew boy,' he said. 'Go to your rabbi.' In a fury, the boy spat at him; Father Christmas flung him off, the other children kicked him, the store attendants hustled him out into the bitter streets, and he ran home crying, thinking that this was what it meant to be a Jewish child, in a Christian world, at Christmastime.

Come forward half a century, to England just a year or two ago. Fired with a determination not to make the same mistake as that misnamed Father Christmas, an organization committed to welcoming Jews into the love of Jesus Christ bought advertising space on the London Underground. The message was simple: 'Jews for Jesus? Why not? After all, Jesus is for Jews.' Almost at once some leaders of the London Jewish community lodged a forceful complaint with the transport authorities. They used words like 'harass-ment' and 'targeting'. The advertisements came down.

Which side are you on? Do you agree with the New York Father Christmas: that whatever Christmas is about it isn't for Jews? Or do you agree with the organization behind the posters: that the love of Jesus is for all without distinction, Jew as well as Gentile? Is there a third pos-sibility? What are we going to do with this nice little nest of theological nettles?

The one thing you can't do is ignore it. I saw a rather different poster not long ago in the London Underground, advertising a film about the awfulness of modern marriage. The caption read something like this: 'Marriage is like the Middle East. There's no solution; you just keep your head down and hope the problems will sort themselves out.' The present state of the Middle East has become a byword for political insolubility. One of the crucial dimensions of the situation is of course religion. One vital element in the reli-gious dimension is that it was deemed essential in 1948 to give the Jews part of their ancient homeland as a permanent dwelling-place, because there wasn't anywhere else for them to go, after the Holocaust. And to this day many argue, with plenty of apparent evidence, that a major cause of the Holocaust was Christian anti-semitism.

So how are we going to line up the issues and try to think Christianly about them? I am going to take three steps which seem to me demanded by the combination of biblical Christian faith on the one hand and the contemporary situa-tion on the other. If we are committed to worshipping the God revealed in Jesus, the God of Advent and Christmas, of Good Friday and Easter, these are questions we cannot ignore.

The first thing to say is that without the Jews and Judaism Christianity wouldn't exist in the first place. It isn't simply the case, as Christians sometimes seem to

imagine, that Jesus had to belong to some race and it just
happened to be the Jewish one. No; *Jesus only makes sense
as a Jew.*

Think about it. Take the standard Advent Carol Service,
now becoming increasingly popular in many church circles.
Every single one of the regular Advent carols celebrates the
fact that Jesus is the fulfilment of the hope, not of the
world *per se* – the world wasn't hoping for anything much,
except less war and lower taxes – but of Israel. 'O Come,
O Come, Emmanuel, and ransom captive Israel': every line
of that great hymn shouts that Jesus is the fulfilment of all
that Israel had longed for. If Advent means anything it
means the coming of the Messiah to Israel. 'Hark the glad
sound! The Saviour comes, the Saviour promised long';
'Israel's strength and consolation, hope of all the earth thou
art'; and he is the hope of all the earth simply and only
because he is Israel's strength and consolation. It is *Zion*
that hears the watchmen's voices; it is *Jerusalem* that is
awoken by Bach's great *Wachet Auf*. When we read Isaiah
40 each Advent – Comfort, comfort my people, says your
God – we are claiming that, in the coming of Jesus, God
has finally fulfilled his word of promise to Israel.

And it isn't only Advent. The same is true at Christmas.
'O Come ye, O come ye to Bethlehem'; because that is
where the Jewish royal family comes from. 'To you in
David's town this day is born from David's line a Saviour,
who is the Messiah . . .' – but many who sing those words
unthinkingly would be shocked if someone displayed the
Star of David outside their church. 'Hail the Sun of
Righteousness' – in other words, the one whom the prophet
Malachi foretold as the great hope of the Jewish people.
Christmas, like Advent, only means anything if we are
celebrating the birth of the Jewish Messiah. If we're not
making that claim, then we might as well sing 'Deck the
hall' and 'We wish you a merry Christmas' and call it

quits. It would be a nice old pagan festival for the winter solstice.

Ah but, you say, Jesus Christ is the saviour of the *world*, not just of the Jews. Yes, indeed. But that belief is itself a profoundly *Jewish* belief. Epiphany, which follows hard on the heels of Christmas, only makes sense because the kings of the earth are coming to do homage to the *Jewish* boy-king. 'Earth has many a noble city; Bethlehem, thou dost all excel: out of thee the Lord from heaven came to rule his Israel.' The kings come to the King of kings; and he is King of kings because, and only because, that's what *Israel's* kings were always supposed to be. Read the Psalms and you'll see it again and again. King of kings and Lord of lords – what does that remind you of? Handel's *Messiah*, of course. But did you ever notice that about 90% of the libretto for Handel's *Messiah*, including the bulk of the story of Jesus himself, comes not from the New Testament but from the prophecies in the Old Testament? When you worship Jesus you are worshipping a Jew. When you pray to Jesus you are praying to a Jew. When you celebrate the Eucharist you are celebrating a Jewish liberation-party in memory of the Jewish Messiah. Take away the Jewish hope and Christianity is left looking like the grin on the Cheshire Cat when the cat itself has gone. And the grin becomes increasingly sinister.

We could in principle follow the story right through, from Christmas and Epiphany to Good Friday and Easter, to Ascension and Pentecost. The same thing is true throughout. The whole Christian scheme only makes sense insofar as it is claiming to be the fulfilment of all that Israel longed for. Sometimes theologians have tried to minimize that; but whenever they do, the proper response has been that they are cutting off the branch they're sitting on. The funny thing is that many Christians don't even notice when that happens, or even when they reconstruct it as something quite different: a pagan, non-Jewish parody of Christianity which requires, and alas usually receives, a paganized Jesus. And you can usually tell when that process has been going on. One of the signs is the rise, within the would-be or self-styled Christian community, of anti-semitism.

The Jewish roots of Christianity, finally, are woven into the liturgy which many churches, including Anglicans, sing and say week after week. 'He, remembering his mercy, hath holpen his servant Israel; as he promised to our forefathers, Abraham and his seed for ever.' Take that away, and you've robbed the Magnificat of its great climax. Then of course, there is the Nunc Dimittis: 'Mine eyes have seen thy salvation, which thou hast prepared before the face of all people; to be a light to lighten the Gentiles' – yes, indeed, but only because this child is first and foremost 'the glory of thy people Israel'. Take away the claim that Christianity is the fulfilment of the hope of Israel, and you lose Christian liturgy as well as Christian theology.

This, then, is my first point: the central Christian claims all involve, non-negotiably, the claim that Jesus is the one promised to Israel. Jesus is the saviour of the world *because* Israel was called to be God's means of saving the world, and because (Christians claim) Jesus has fulfilled that great hope.

Mentioning the tendency to anti-semitism brings me to my second point. Throughout Christian history, the potential for anti-semitism has been present, but it isn't in fact a genuinely Christian phenomenon. Christians have connived at it, have contributed to it, have even spurred it on its way; but in doing so they have been acting as pagans, not as Christians. This needs spelling out just a little.

Within the first century there were several different groups that, claiming to be the genuine Israel, condemned all other Jews as renegades. That's what the Essenes did. That's what the Pharisees did. That's what the various revolutionary groups did. 'We are the true heirs of the promises to Abraham, and all other claimants are bogus.' Now tell me: were the Pharisees anti-semitic, for making such a claim over against all other Jews? Of course not. Were the Essenes anti-semitic, for making such a claim? Of course not. They were claiming to be the true Jews; they were opposed, not to Judaism, but to groups that, in their eyes, had forfeited the title 'Jew' because of their beliefs or behaviour. When Christianity emerged, making a very similar claim, it was of course controversial, but in no way was it anti-semitic or anti-Jewish.

The Essenes and the Pharisees hoped that more Jews who were at present outside their movement would join them. They no doubt prayed that this would happen. Was that an anti-semitic thing to hope? Of course not. The Christians hoped that non-Christian Jews would join them in their celebration of being the true Israel, and they, too, prayed that this would happen. Was that anti-semitic? Of course not. One of the best-known contemporary Jewish apologists in the UK, a scholar named Hyam Maccoby, claimed on a TV programme not long ago that Paul's belief in Jesus' resurrection was the foundation of anti-semitism. He meant, of course, that the early Christians, claiming to be the fulfilment of Israel, opened the way to look down on the Jews as inferior. But you couldn't say that about the first generation of Christians. They knew that Christianity was a Jewish movement. When it went out into the world it was perceived as a variety of Judaism. It was far, far more like Judaism than it was like anything in the pagan world. It wasn't anti-semitic. It was, basically, anti-pagan.

But at the same time, of course, Christianity needed to define itself in relation to Judaism; and that has, down the years, produced a crop of disasters. From the Greek church father John Chrysostom in the early period to the sixteenth-century reformer Martin Luther, and on to the renowned

New Testament scholar Gerhard Kittel in Nazi Germany, there have been great thinkers and teachers within the Christian tradition who have denounced the Jews in ways which make our blood run cold today. And our blood runs cold, of course, not least because of the Holocaust.

But how did the Holocaust happen? There are plenty of voices today that blame it on Christianity. But the anti-semitism that sent six million Jews to their deaths in civilized Europe a mere fifty years ago had its real roots, not in the New Testament, but in the pagan teachings of various European philosophers and the pagan culture of Richard Wagner. The church's part in all of this is tragic: because the New Testament contains a striking and central passage, Romans 9—11, which warns in no uncertain terms against the possibility that the church might go down the road of pagan anti-semitism. And the tragedy is that Romans 9—11 was marginalized by the Reformers' concentration on chapters 1—8; that the corporate thrust of the gospel message, and its implications for Israel, were marginalized by the Reformers' concentration on individual salvation; so that, when the church should have stood up and objected to what was going on, she had lost the key to a vital part of her armoury. The church, instead, was seduced into paganism. Failing to practise Christianity herself, she failed to shine the light of Christ upon his own people. Think of the nominally Christian 'heroes' of *The Merchant of Venice*, standing by as Shylock acts the real tragic hero:

> O father Abram, what these Christians are,
> Whose own hard dealings teaches them suspect
> The thoughts of others! (Act II scene 1)

> What's his reason? I am a Jew. Hath not a Jew eyes?
> Hath not a Jew hands, organs, dimensions, senses, affec-
> tions, passions, fed with the same food, hurt with the

same weapons, subject to the same diseases, healed by
the same means, warmed and cooled by the same winter
and summer, as a Christian is? If you prick us, do we
not bleed? If you tickle us, do we not laugh? If you
poison us, do we not die? And if you wrong us, shall we
not revenge? If we are like you in the rest, we will
resemble you in that. (Act III scene 1)

There is the real tragedy. Vengeance, the very thing which
the Christian gospel renounces with all its power, became
enshrined in supposedly Christian society, until even the
Jews learned it from these wolves in sheep's clothing, these
pagans mouthing Christian words. The charge of anti-
semitism is a charge properly levelled against paganism,
whether in ancient Rome, the early church, mediaeval or
nineteenth-century Europe, twentieth-century Stalinist Russia or Nazi Germany – or, alas, twentieth-century Britain,
France, America, Japan and other major leaders of what
passes for contemporary civilization. And many of these
paganisms have claimed to be Christian. It's a first-rate
smoke-screen.

Thus, as the Christian culture in the Western world
declines today towards more explicit neo-paganism, both in
its materialism and in its New Age ideologies, so anti-
semitism rears its ugly head once more. We should, perhaps, have seen it coming. The scurrilous anti-Jewish literature that we associate with Hitler's propaganda is on sale in
increasing quantity all over Europe, Russia and its former
satellites, in the Arab countries of course, and even in
Japan. There are sinister groups in America who not only
deny that the Holocaust happened but propagate the very
teachings that made it happen.

Let me be quite categorical: I'm not nearly so interested
in post-Holocaust theology as I am in *pre*-Holocaust theology. *It could happen again.* That's not scaremongering; it's

sober realism. We recently watched so-called 'ethnic cleansing' in a country not too far from where the Holocaust happened, and the West had no idea what to do about it. And if violent anti-Jewish activity breaks out again, then we as Christians must make the right response this time. We must stand up and say that it is blasphemous. Anti-Jewish behaviour is a pagan vice to which Christians should be opposed as much as they should be to extortion, or fornication, or witchcraft. To the extent that Christians have connived at anti-Judaism, they have accommodated their faith to paganism.

My second point, then, is this: Christianity is not itself anti-semitic or anti-Judaic, but it has often been lured into guilty association with it, and must learn its lesson.

What, then, thirdly and finally, is the proper Christian response to this sorry state of affairs? One approach would be through Paul's letter to the Romans, which I've already mentioned. Why has Israel not believed in the Messiah, and what is God doing about it?

In those great chapters, Romans 9—11, Paul, the one-time hard-line Pharisee, wrestles with this issue in the presence of God, and comes up with an astonishing and theologically brilliant answer. God wanted to save the whole world, by drawing its evil on to himself in the person of his Son and so exhausting its power. For this to happen, he chose a people and prepared them to be the family into which the Son would be born. This people, as part of the plan, were themselves sinful like the pagans, so that when the Messiah came he would be born into, and would die under, the full weight of the world's sin. But if this people focused their attention on their own special status, and not on their vocation, they would reject the Messiah whose Jewish vision was to rescue the whole world; and that is what had happened and was still happening. As Paul says, they didn't understand God's strange purpose, and they were trying to establish a private purpose and status of their own. But the Messiah brings God's strange purpose to its completion, so that all humans, not just Jews, can become God's chosen people.

What then about the Jews themselves? Are they to miss out at last? Was Christianity meant to have one generation of Jews only, and then no more? Were ex-pagans, now become Christians, going to be able to look down at Jews and say, 'The kingdom of God now belongs to us, and you have no part in it?' How could that possibly be correct? Paul's answer is categorical. All humans are sinful, Jews as well as Greeks, and all need humbling at the gate of God's kingdom: Gentiles, by being invited to join an essentially Jewish family; Jews, by being invited in to a family which was theirs in a sense, but into which a large number of Gentiles have been adopted with equal rights. 'God has subjected all (Jew and Gentile alike) to disobedience, so that he may have mercy on all.' And, says Paul, this means that in every generation God longs for Jews to come to faith in Jesus Christ – perhaps more and more. To say anything different (to suggest, for instance, that Jews are not now welcome in the kingdom of God) would be the real anti-Judaism, the real pagan arrogance.

Thus far Paul. But we must put some flesh and blood on this somewhat abstract though very profound theology; and, to do so, we go back in conclusion to one of Jesus' best-known parables (Luke 15.11–32). It's often known as 'the Prodigal Son'; one of many better titles might be 'the Two Lost Sons'.

In Jesus' original story, the Prodigal Son represented the outcasts whom Jesus was welcoming into the kingdom, and the older brother represented the Pharisees and scribes who grumbled at this scandalous behaviour. But in Luke's retelling of the parable, there is perhaps another level of meaning. This time, the Prodigal is the pagan world, welcomed into the kingdom through the church's Gentile mission; and the older brother is the Jewish people, who are at the moment refusing to join in the party. What the story then says is that the Gentile Christians are like the younger brother, welcomed home by the father in an astonishing act of grace, with new clothes, new shoes and a huge banquet. Those who were partying with the pagans a year ago, and pigging it on the farm a week ago, are now welcomed as long-lost children.

But what about the elder brother? What attitude should the younger brother have towards him? In the parable, the father tries to persuade him to come in and join the party. We aren't told whether the appeal was successful. In Jesus' day it mostly wasn't. In Luke's day it mostly wasn't.

So how might the story go on, if we were to bring it down through history and up to date? We need to increase the size of the family a little to see the range of options clearly.

Once upon a time there was a man with five children. The oldest stayed at home and worked hard, while the other four – two boys, two girls – went off with as much loot as they could, lived it up, went bust, and came home with their tails between their legs. The father welcomed them all back with amazing generosity, and gave them a party, while the elder brother sulked outside.

The morning after, the four younger ones got together over a pot of black coffee to talk it through.

'What are we going to do about Judah?' said the first, whose name was Constantine. 'He was so snooty last night – stalked off with his nose in the air as though we were something the cat had brought in. He made me so mad. Why don't we all get together and beat him up, and teach him a lesson?'

'Hey, steady on,' said the second, who was called Portia. 'He is our brother, after all. I've got a better idea.

Let's have a wild party again tonight, and we'll pick him up and drag him in by force and *make* him enjoy himself.'

'Oh, I don't know,' said the third, whose name was Enlightenment. 'I think he's so different from us, it would be better to leave him alone entirely. He can go his way and we can go ours. It would be very arrogant of us to attempt to say anything to him or even about him. If we just ignore him . . .'

'*Ignore* him?' said the fourth, whose name was Pauline. 'Look: I couldn't sleep last night. I was so sad when Judah went out (and I can quite understand why he did); it was as though part of me went with him. I don't think we'll feel like a proper family again until he comes back. But he'll have to come back in his own way and his own time. We certainly can't put pressure on him. We mustn't project our own guilt on to him. But what we can do, perhaps, is to try to live here in such a way that he'll *want* to come back. We can hold the sort of party *he* would enjoy. We can let him know how sorry we are, and make it clear he's really welcome, that we really do want him back. And I'll tell you something else. Perhaps we should ask Father to have another go at persuading him. That's probably the best way of all.'

If you have ears, then hear. If you have knees, then pray.

CHAPTER FOURTEEN

Living Truth

Come with me now to Galilee; and up, away from the lake and into the hills.

We don't know which hill in particular heard the first preaching of the Sermon on the Mount. That hasn't stopped zealous pilgrims from settling on a site, building a church there, surrounding it with a beautiful and tranquil garden, and calling it 'The Mount of Beatitudes'. It's an attractive spot, just up the hill from Capernaum, where the monks and the archaeologists are busily turning the little village into as much of a tourist trap as they can. Everything about the site, its setting, its garden, its church, and the carefully carved Beatitudes which greet you inside (blessed are the poor in spirit, the mourners, and so on), is designed to tell you what the Sermon on the Mount in general, and the Beatitudes in particular, are all about. The whole place resonates with what is, I suppose, the normal Christian reading of those remarkable phrases. And I think they've got it more or less exactly wrong.

The symbolism of the place, the church, the garden, the decoration, all combines to say to you, before you've even stopped to think of the particular texts: here is a way of life which is tranquil and peaceful; here is a gentle, unfussy spirituality, that doesn't disturb anyone or anything; a way of life which consists in being nice to everyone, concentrating on being heavenly minded and quietly detached from

the world. Here is a way of life which insulates you from
the pressures of everyday life, and prepares you for heaven
after you die. It communicates, that is to say, a certain style
of piety which has been popular in the church from time to
time, and was, I think, pretty clearly in the minds of the
people who chose the site – which, I suspect, had more to
do with its proximity to the regular tourist trail along the
north side of the lake than to any suggestion of history –
and who carefully built and adorned the pretty little church.

Now come back down the hill for a moment, and into
one of the villages by the lake. Come back a few years –
say, around two thousand. What are the people concerned
about? What is eating at them? What makes them tick?
What sort of a teacher, and what sort of a message, would
get them to down tools and set off hiking up a hill after
him?

Not, I suggest, a tranquil message about a detached
spirituality, a general niceness, and pie in the sky when you
die. No. They were anxious and pressurized about many
things. Life was tough – politically, economically, and
socially tough. Israel was in deep trouble, living under the
rule of the pagan Romans, with all kinds of social and
financial problems swirling around as a result. I see nothing
to suggest that lots of people in that situation would have
welcomed, or followed enthusiastically, the sort of Jesus
that the present so-called Mount of Beatitudes is designed to
symbolize.

But suppose we went to a rather different mountain for
symbolism? Suppose we went a few miles further west, still
within view of the lake, but further round? There we would
find, not a gentle slope in a pastoral landscape, but steep
crags and rough caves. And those hills, to a first-century
Galilean, would symbolize revolution. This was where the
holy brigands had lived a generation earlier. They had
gathered, a band of desperate men, longing for the kingdom

of God, too urgent in their eagerness for it to be content
with eking out a living in the valleys and hoping for better
times. They prayed and fasted, they lived lives of intense
holiness based on the Jewish law interpreted at its fiercest,
and they planned and they plotted how to overthrow, in
God's name, the wicked rulers who were compromising the
hope of Israel by doing deals with the pagans. Sounds
familiar? Tragically, yes.

Not surprisingly, the authorities weren't too keen on
groups like this. It was from the descendants or associates
of that group that there emerged the movement which the
Jewish writer Josephus calls the Fourth Philosophy, the
violent holy revolutionaries, whose slogan was that there
should be 'no King but God'. They were the people who
longed passionately for God to renew his covenant at last,
to liberate Israel so that they could inherit the promised
land at last, and be masters in their own house, to establish
his justice for Israel and, through her, for the whole world.

Not surprisingly, again, they made great demands on
their followers. This was an all-or-nothing venture; you
couldn't be half-hearted about it. They were noble and
brave in spirit, daring everything, risking everything,
hoping everything, enduring everything. The high,
inaccessible mountain was not only a safe place for such
people, away from the authorities except when someone
like Herod determined to smoke them out. It was also an
excellent symbol of their fierce piety, their exclusive holiness, their determination to claim the kingdom of heaven as
their own. God's kingdom would come, and his will would
be done, on earth as it was in heaven.

This mountain gives us a very different sort of clue to
how Jesus' message would have been perceived, and to
why people chose to leave their homes for the day and
climb up the hills with him. He had been talking cryptically, in the valley and by the lake, about the kingdom of

God. They had been fascinated, but often a little puzzled; some of his stories left them scratching their heads. They knew he was trying to tell them something, and the kingdom of which he spoke was certainly what they all most deeply wanted; so when he told them to follow him up into the hills, away from prying eyes and ears and the possibility of unwelcome interruption, where they could hear a fuller and more explicit version of his kingdom-agenda, they naturally were eager to do so. Their eagerness had little to do with a desire for a deeper piety or a more secure grasp on other-worldly realities, and a great deal to do with the longing for God's kingdom to come on earth as it was in heaven.

The format of the Sermon on the Mount answers pretty exactly to these expectations. This revolutionary kingdom-teacher, when he gets them off away from the lakeshore, is much more explicit about the kingdom. No cryptic parables here; instead, the terms of the covenant which God was at last remaking with his people. Let's take a bird's-eye view of the 'Sermon' and see how it works out.

Think of the covenant in Deuteronomy: a list of solemn blessings on those who kept the commands of God. Blessings on you when you do this, and that, and the other; blessed are you when you keep this law, and that one, and the other one. This is an agenda for Israel, a covenant-agenda, summoning her after all these years to be the people that her God intended her to be: you are the light of the world, the salt of the earth, so let's get on and be that, let's stop being half-hearted about it. This was a summons to an intensification of the law; the Pharisees hadn't gone far enough, but now we were going to get it right, and be the true Israel that the law and the prophets had envisaged. Thus far, the material in (what we call) Matthew 5.

Within this, in Matthew 6, there is a reordering of piety. Don't play-act at piety like the hypocrites; get it right, and pray this simple, direct and urgent prayer that God's kingdom would come and his will be done on earth as in heaven. Trust God, put his kingdom before all else, and he will do it! And then, in Matthew 7: watch out for imposters; accept no man-made imitations of the true kingdom which is now being inaugurated. We are the true revolutionaries; all other groups are deluded.

Finally, the great warning, that would have made Herod and Pilate shiver in their shoes (or at the very least send out a detachment of commandos) if they'd heard it. This is the only way to build the house on the rock; a house built on anything else will fall with a great crash. The 'house on the rock' is Temple-language. Jesus is announcing, cryptically but quite emphatically, his intention and expectation that his movement will turn out to be the true one, and the rule of Rome, of the puppet King Herod, and of the jumped-up pseudo-aristocrats who run the Temple itself, will prove to be transient and ruinous.

When you read the Sermon in this setting, it makes a whole lot of sense. It was the sort of thing Jesus' hearers were expecting. It wasn't so much 'teaching', in the sense of imparting information about religion or ethics or anything else for that matter. It was an agenda, and a revolutionary one at that. The whole shape and format of the Sermon says: we are the people through whom the one true God is going to establish his kingdom. Let's get on and do it. When Jesus first gave the teaching we now call the Sermon on the Mount, he was staging something like what we would call a political rally. He was like someone drumming up support for a new movement, a new great cause.

But wait a minute. That's what the format says; and that's what they were hoping to hear. The Sermon is indeed revolutionary. But when we look at the content of the Sermon, we discover that it is actually doubly revolutionary. Jesus is not simply offering another variation on the well-worn theme: keep the law more strictly, and prepare for military revolt. He is not whipping up hatred for the pagans and the compromisers, urging his followers to beat their ploughshares into swords and their pruning-hooks into spears. His revolution is upside down. The two symbolic mountains we have examined so far are both too small. Maybe there is a higher one standing behind both of them.

Jesus is calling and challenging his contemporaries to be the people of God in a truly radical new way. He solemnly announces God's blessings – but he blesses all the wrong people. Blessed are the poor in spirit; that's who the kingdom will belong to. Blessed are the mourners; they will be comforted. Blessed are the meek; they're the ones who will inherit the land. Blessed are those who long for God's justice to rule; their hunger will be satisfied. Blessed are the merciful; they will receive God's mercy. Blessed are the pure who are pure not just in outward rule, but in the heart; the vision of God (denied even to Moses) will be theirs. Blessed are the peacemakers; they will be called God's children, the true Israel. Blessed are those who are persecuted for the sake of God's justice; the kingdom belongs to them. This is the revolutionary agenda all right, but now with a decisive twist at its heart.

When the real revolution comes, Jesus seems to be saying, the ordinary revolutionaries won't get a look in. This is a dangerous message, an exciting, deeply subversive challenge. It's not only the authorities, the Herods and Pilates, who would be disturbed if they heard what Jesus was teaching. The strict revolutionary groups, and the Pharisees who leaned in the same direction, would be appalled. How can we mount a serious resistance movement, how can we make Israel holy enough for the kingdom, with someone going around letting the side down like this? The Sermon on the Mount, and the Beatitudes at its head, is doubly revolutionary, doubly subversive.

We need both halves to get the full effect. If you just have the first revolution without the second, you reduce Jesus to the status of another would-be freedom-fighter. Many historians have tried to do that; but of course you can achieve that portrait only if you systematically screen out the deeper revolution at the heart of it all. Equally, if you have the second revolution without the first you reduce Jesus to a quietist, a teacher of private piety and eternal verities, someone that Herod and Pilate would pass in the street without noticing, let alone without being threatened. Many have tried to make Jesus that sort of figure; not least those who planned the symbolism of the so-called 'Mount of Beatitudes' for the pilgrims and tourists. But you can do that only if you systematically screen out the first revolution; if, in other words, you subtly alter the words of the Lord's Prayer, which lies at the heart of the Sermon, so that it reads, 'Thy kingdom come, thy will be done, in heaven as it is in heaven.' But the Sermon as it stands, and the prayer as it stands, do not leave us that option.

Jesus, then, stands in the prophetic tradition, summoning Israel to repentance and restoration, to a new way of being Israel, a way which goes beyond the regular round of worship and is committed to living in such a way as to reflect the love and justice of God into his world. The echoes from the Sermon go back deep into Israel's roots:

> Hear, you mountains, the controversy of the Lord, his controversy with his people . . .
> He has told you, O mortal, what is good. What does the Lord require of you, but to do justice, to love mercy, and to walk humbly with your God? (Micah 6.2, 8)

The prophet Micah denounced the rulers of his day, holding out a vision of God and of his people which deeply subverted their whole way of life. Jesus did the same.

The Sermon is a covenant-agenda, a revolutionary manifesto, summoning Israel prophetically to a radically new way of being God's people, a way that would overturn the normal power structures but also challenge at its heart the normal sort of revolution. This, and not the simple revolutionary dream, is how Israel is to be the salt of the earth, the light of the world. Blessed are the poor, the mourners, the meek; blessed are the hungry, the merciful, the pure; blessed are the peacemakers, the persecuted, the insulted. Yours is the kingdom, the comfort, the land; yours is the plenty, the mercy, the vision of God; yours is the sonship, the kingdom, the reward. This is a different dream for the people of God, because it represents a different vision of God, a vision as different as the Father in the parable of the Prodigal Son was from what most fathers would be like. No wonder they hung on his words, and repeated them to one another as they went back down the mountain, forged into a strange new sort of revolutionary group, ready to live in Jesus' new kingdom-way.

And the question that comes to us, as we read all this in our own day, is: what would it look like if the church were to announce this same message to the world today? The world usually wants the church to announce one or the other revolution, but not both. Both the mountains we looked at retain popularity. Some in the world want the church to be a typically revolutionary body, supporting every trendy or radical or politically correct cause that comes along; and, in various countries today, there are plenty of people in the church only too eager to oblige. Some in the world want the church to be a typically quietist body, advocating detachment from the world and its concerns, seeking a kingdom simply and solely in a *post mortem* heaven rather than praying for the kingdom to come on earth as in heaven. Again, there are plenty of people in the church only too eager to oblige.

But the Sermon, and the Beatitudes, do not leave us with either of these shrunken options. We must have the full thing: the truly, the doubly revolutionary message. What might it look like today?

We have to learn how to translate Jesus' message to his contemporaries so that it becomes our message to our contemporaries. The Sermon isn't just Jesus' challenge to the church. It ought to be the church's challenge to the world. But our world is not expecting covenant renewal, with a list of blessings, an intensification of the Jewish law, a newly deepened piety. Our world is not wanting to rebuild a temple, a house on the rock. We cannot simply throw at our contemporaries the same language and imagery that Jesus used in his day and hope it will somehow stick. We have to take the difficult, but exhilarating step of *working out where our contemporaries are and translating the message into their language and setting*.

At one level, this is a matter of experiment and improvisation, risky though that will always be. At another level, it is a matter of total fidelity to Jesus' doubly revolutionary message. If we are announcing the Kingdom in such a way that it simply echoes what certain groups in the world are saying, we have climbed one wrong mountain; if we announce it in such a way that it challenges nobody and nothing in our world, we have climbed another wrong mountain. We need the higher mountain that stands behind both. This is the vision that Paul embraced when he said,

> Jews demand [revolutionary] signs, and Greeks seek wisdom; but we proclaim Christ crucified . . . God chose what is foolish in the world in order to shame the wise, God chose what is weak in the world to shame the strong, God chose what is low and despised in the world the non-existent things, to reduce to nothing the things that are. (1 Corinthians 1.22f., 27f.)

This is doubly revolutionary. It doesn't fit anyone else's categories, though it exercises a strange and compelling fascination for people of all sorts. You might almost think Paul had been reading the Sermon on the Mount.

So how can we do for our day what Paul was doing for his, translating the message and challenge of Jesus into categories and language appropriate for a different culture and place? Each church must, of course, labour at this in its own setting; but here are what I regard as the ground rules.

If we are addressing Gentiles, as we mostly will be, we are not called to remind people that they are Israel, the light of the world and the salt of the earth. We cannot assume that our hearers are already struggling to keep the Jewish law, and need to know how to keep it from the heart. We cannot assume that they already practise a piety which needs to be deepened and integrated. We cannot, that is, assume any of the things that Jesus could assume in his hearers.

But we can and must assume that our hearers are human beings, made in the image of God, designed to tremble at his word, to respond gladly to his love, and to reflect his wise care and justice into his world. We can and must assume that humans know in their bones that they are made, as Genesis insists, for relationship, stewardship and worship. People don't have to be told that they are made for these things; they know it deep within themselves, and they are puzzled, and often grieved, that it doesn't work out like it should. Our task is to speak the language they speak, in symbol and story as well as in articulate theory; to offer them the revolution they know they need; and to urge and invite them to follow us as we move forward with the hope that God's kingdom will come on earth as in heaven. At the same time, in so doing, we must tell them and show them that the revolution, the justice and peace, the restoration of creation, will come about only if we are worshipping the true God of heaven and earth, the one made known in Jesus Christ.

There are two signs that we will be more or less on the right track. The message must be so related to the actual needs and problems of the day that the rulers of the world will think we are being subversive. But it must be so grounded in the worship and love of the God revealed in Jesus Christ that the normal revolutionaries will regard us as having sold the pass. Jews demand signs; Greeks seek wisdom; we preach Christ crucified. The foolishness of God is wiser than human wisdom; the weakness of God stronger than human strength.

Once we make this translation – which I have only begun to hint at, and which it is up to every church to work out for itself – we will discover that the old Beatitudes resonate again, not with a private piety, but with a deep and rich welcome for those in our world whose hearts are breaking, whose lives are breaking, who need God's kingdom and who need it now. As we read them, we should ask what they might mean in terms of our own agendas. Such questioning might run as follows.

Blessed are the poor in spirit; yours is the kingdom of heaven! What could the church *do*, not just say, that would make the poor in spirit believe that? Blessed are the mourners; they shall be comforted! How will the mourners believe that, if we are not God's agents in bringing that comfort? Blessed are the meek; they shall inherit the earth. How will the meek ever believe such nonsense if the church does not stand up for their rights against the rich and the powerful, in the name of the crucified Messiah who had nowhere to lay his head? Blessed are those who hunger and thirst for God's justice; how will that message get through, unless we are prepared to stand alongside those who are denied justice and go on making a fuss until they get it? Blessed are the merciful; how are people to believe that, in a world where mercy is weakness, unless we visit the prisoner and welcome the prodigal? Blessed are the pure in heart; how will people believe that, in a world where impurity is big business, unless we ourselves are worshipping the living God until our own hearts are set on fire and scorched through with his purity? Blessed are the peacemakers; how will we ever learn that, in a world where war in one country means business for another, unless the church stands in the middle and says that there is a different way of being human, a different way of ordering our common life? Blessed are those who are persecuted and insulted for the kingdom's sake, for Jesus' sake; how will that message ever get across if the church is so anxious not to court bad publicity that it refuses ever to say or do anything that might get it into trouble either with the authorities, for being so subversive, or with the revolutionaries, for insisting that the true revolution begins at the foot of the cross?

I wish I could say that I knew of a church, somewhere in the world, that had really grasped this strange agenda and was struggling to live by it. I am sure there are some, and I regret that I don't often come across them. It is so desperately easy to choose one mountain or the other, the pietist one or the simplistic revolutionary one, and to miss the larger vision which Jesus was holding out. But I am full of hope, because even if we don't know where precisely the Sermon was first preached, we do in fact know the location of the mountain which, symbolically, draws the other two together. The Lord who preached the Sermon in Galilee went to the hill called Calvary, outside Jerusalem, there to disarm the principalities and powers once and for all; and in rising again he established for all time the house on the rock, which shall stand as a beacon of hope until the day when our prayers are answered, when God's intention in creation is finally fulfilled, when God's kingdom does come, and his will is done, on earth as it is in heaven.

Until that day, we worship, and pray, and work, and proclaim, and celebrate. And, in particular, we break the bread and we share the wine, to hold together the death and the coming kingdom of the one who said, 'Blessed are they who hunger and thirst, for they shall be satisfied.' And we respond, in turn, with our own beatitude: 'Blessed is he who comes in the name of the Lord! Hosanna in the highest!'

Reviewers love Alan Bradley's New York Times
bestselling
Flavia de Luce series!

The GRAVE'S *a* FINE
and PRIVATE PLACE

New York Times bestseller
Publishers Weekly bestseller
Indie bestseller

"Outstanding . . . As usual, Bradley makes his improbable
series conceit work and relieves the plot's inherent darkness with clever humor."
—*Publishers Weekly* (starred review)

"There's only one Flavia. . . . Series fans will anticipate the
details of this investigation, along with one last taste of
Flavia's unorthodox family life."
—*Library Journal* (starred review)

"Bradley's unquenchable heroine brings 'the most complicated case I had ever come across' to a highly satisfying
conclusion, with the promise of still brighter days ahead."
—*Kirkus Reviews*

"As those of us with Flavia-mania know from previous
books, the plucky adolescent is terrifically entertaining—
the world's foremost braniac/chemist/sleuth/busybody/
smarty-pants. Nobody can touch her in that category."
—*The Seattle Times*

"Provides all her fans with their Flavia fix . . . The Flavia de Luce books fall into that somewhat rare category for me. I delight in the witticisms and language and the flavor and color of the well-developed characters, wanting to read slowly, savoring every word, but then there is the mystery to be solved, so I find myself rushing to the end. Only one solution I can come up with: Read them again . . . and again."

—*The Fredericksburg Free-Lance Star*

"[Bradley] lets Flavia be her hilarious, inimical best, and perfectly captures village life in 1950s Britain. Historical fiction and mystery readers alike are sure to rejoice at getting to spend another afternoon in Flavia's agreeable world."

—Shelf Awareness

"Bradley's style of writing is quick-witted, fact-laden and extremely fun to read. . . . A wonderful series for most ages."

—Killer Nashville

THRICE *the* BRINDED CAT
HATH MEW'D

New York Times bestseller
USA Today bestseller
LibraryReads pick

As CHIMNEY SWEEPERS COME *to* DUST

"Eleven-year-old Flavia de Luce, perhaps **contemporary crime fiction's most original character**—to say she is Pippi Longstocking with a Ph.D. in chemistry (speciality: poisons) barely begins to describe her—is finally coming home."

—*Maclean's*

"Plot twists come faster than Canadian snowfall. . . . Bradley's sense of observation is as keen as gung-ho scientist Flavia's. . . . The results so far are **seven sparkling Flavia de Luce mysteries**."

—LibraryReads

"Even after all these years, Flavia de Luce is still **the world's greatest adolescent British chemist/busybody/ sleuth**."

—*The Seattle Times*

The DEAD in THEIR VAULTED ARCHES

SPEAKING FROM AMONG *the* BONES

"The precocious and irrepressible Flavia **continues to delight.** Portraying an eleven-year-old as a plausible sleuth and expert in poisons is no mean feat, but Bradley makes it look easy."

—Publishers Weekly (starred review)

"Bradley's Flavia cozies, set in the English countryside, have been **a hit** from the start, and this fifth in the series continues to charm and entertain."

—Booklist

"An excellent reminder that crime fiction can **sparkle with wit, crackle with spirit and verge on the surreal** . . . Flavia, once more, entertains and delights as she exposes the inner workings of her investigative mind to the reader."

—National Post (Canada)

I AM HALF-SICK *of* SHADOWS

"**Every Flavia de Luce novel is a reason to celebrate,** but Christmas with Flavia is a holiday wish come true for her fans."

—USA Today (four stars)

"This is a classic country house mystery in the tradition of Agatha Christie, and Poirot himself would approve of Flavia's skills in snooping and deduction. Flavia is everything a reader wants in a detective—she's smart, logical, intrepid and curious. . . . This is a **refreshingly engaging read.**"

—*RT Book Reviews*

"This is a **delightful read through and through.** We find in Flavia an incorrigible and wholly lovable detective; from her chemical experiments in her sanctum sanctorum to her outrage at the idiocy of the adult world, she is unequaled. Charming as a stand-alone novel and a guaranteed smash with series followers."

—*Library Journal* (starred review)

A RED HERRING *Without* MUSTARD

"**Bradley's third book about tween sleuth Flavia de Luce will make readers forget Nancy Drew.**"

—*People*

"Think preteen Nancy Drew, only savvier and a lot richer, and you have Flavia de Luce. . . . Don't be fooled by Flavia's age or the 1950s setting: *A Red Herring* isn't a dainty tea-and-crumpets sort of mystery. It's shot through with real grit."

—*Entertainment Weekly*

"**Delightful** . . . The book's forthright and eerily mature narrator is a treasure."

—*The Seattle Times*

"Bradley's characters, wonderful dialogue and plot twists are a most winning combination."

—*USA Today*

The WEED *That* STRINGS *the* HANGMAN'S BAG

"Flavia is incisive, cutting and hilarious . . . **one of the most remarkable creations in recent literature.**"

—*USA Today*

"Bradley takes everything you expect and subverts it, delivering **a smart, irreverent, unsappy mystery.**"

—*Entertainment Weekly*

"The real delight here is her droll voice and the eccentric cast. . . . **Utterly beguiling.**"

—*People* (four stars)

"**Endlessly entertaining** . . . The author deftly evokes the period, but Flavia's sparkling narration is the mystery's chief delight. Comic and irreverent, this entry is sure to build further momentum for the series."

—*Publishers Weekly* (starred review)

The **SWEETNESS** *at the* **BOTTOM** *of the* **PIE**

**THE MOST AWARD-WINNING BOOK
OF ANY YEAR!**

WINNER:
Macavity Award for Best First Mystery Novel
Barry Award for Best First Novel
Agatha Award for Best First Novel
Dilys Award
Arthur Ellis Award for Best Novel
Spotted Owl Award for Best Novel
CWA Debut Dagger Award

BY ALAN BRADLEY

Flavia de Luce Novels

The Sweetness at the Bottom of the Pie

The Weed That Strings the Hangman's Bag

A Red Herring Without Mustard

I Am Half-Sick of Shadows

Speaking from Among the Bones

The Dead in Their Vaulted Arches

As Chimney Sweepers Come to Dust

Thrice the Brinded Cat Hath Mew'd

The Grave's a Fine and Private Place

Flavia de Luce Stories

The Curious Case of the Copper Corpse

The GRAVE'S *a* FINE
and PRIVATE PLACE

BANTAM | NEW YORK

The GRAVE'S *a* FINE and PRIVATE PLACE

A Flavia de Luce Novel

ALAN BRADLEY

• • •

2018 Bantam Books Trade Paperback Edition

Copyright © 2018 by Alan Bradley
Excerpt from *The Golden Tresses of the Dead* by Alan Bradley
copyright © 2018 by Alan Bradley

Published in the United States by Bantam Books, an imprint of Random House, a division of Penguin Random House LLC, New York.

BANTAM BOOKS and the HOUSE colophon are registered trademarks of Penguin Random House LLC.

Originally published in hardcover in the United States by Delacorte Press, an imprint of Random House, a division of Penguin Random House LLC, in 2018.

This book contains an excerpt from the forthcoming book *The Golden Tresses of the Dead* by Alan Bradley. This excerpt has been set for this edition only and may not reflect the final content of the forthcoming edition.

LIBRARY OF CONGRESS CATALOGING-IN-PUBLICATION DATA
Names: Bradley, C. Alan, 1938– author.
Title: The grave's a fine and private place : a Flavia de Luce novel /
Alan Bradley.
Other titles: Flavia de Luce novel
Description: First edition. | New York : Delacorte Press, 2018.
Identifiers: LCCN 2017031500 | ISBN 9780345540003 (trade paperback) |
ISBN 9780345540010 (ebook)
Subjects: LCSH: De Luce, Flavia (Fictitious character)—Fiction. |
Child detectives—England—Fiction. | Serial murder Investigation—
Fiction. | False testimony—Fiction. | BISAC: FICTION / Mystery &
Detective / Historical. | GSAFD: Mystery fiction.
Classification: LCC PR9199.4.B7324 G73 2018 | DDC 813/.6—dc23
LC record available at https://lccn.loc.gov/2017031500

Printed in the United States of America on acid-free paper

randomhousebooks.com

2 4 6 8 9 7 5 3 1

Text design by Diane Hobbing

To Shirley, my inspiration

The grave's a fine and private place,
But none, I think, do there embrace.

—Andrew Marvell, *To His Coy Mistress* (1681)

The GRAVE'S *a* FINE
and PRIVATE PLACE

·ONE·

I AM ON MY deathbed.

Again.

Although I have done everything in my power to survive, it has not been enough. A human being can only bear so much.

I turn my face to the wall in bitter remembrance.

Father had died suddenly at Christmas, leaving a colossal vacuum which we quickly realized would never—could never—be filled. In some strange way, he had been the secret glue which held us all together, and with his passing my sisters and I, never friends at the best of times, had now—and quite inexplicably—become the most deadly of mortal enemies. Each of us, wanting desperately to be in charge—to gain some control over her shattered life—found herself at odds with the others at every turn.

Words and crockery were thrown with equal carelessness. It didn't seem to matter much who was hit.

With our family on the verge of breaking up, Aunt Felicity had come down from London to sort us out.

Or so she claimed.

In case we had forgotten it, we were quickly reminded of the fact that our dear auntie was—as *The Book of Common Prayer* so charitably puts it—a woman who followed the devices and desires of her own heart.

In short, she was at best a stubborn old woman and at worst a bully and a tyrant.

Buckshaw was to be sold at once, Aunt Felicity insisted, even though in law it was mine to do with as I pleased. Feely was to be married off to her fiancé, Dieter Schrantz, with all haste—or at least as quickly as possible—as soon as a respectable period of mourning had been observed.

Daffy would be sent up to Oxford to read English.

"Who knows but that, given time, you might even become a gifted teacher," Aunt Felicity had said, upon which Daffy had thrown her teacup and saucer into the fireplace and stormed out of the room.

Tantrums were useless, Aunt Felicity had told us icily. Tantrums solve no problems, but only create new ones.

As for me, I was to be taken up to London, along with my cousin Undine, to live with Aunt Felicity until she could decide what to do with us. In my case, I knew that meant sending me somewhere to continue those studies which had been interrupted when I was chucked out of Miss Bodycote's Female Academy, in Canada.

But what of Dogger and Mrs. Mullet? What would become of *them*?

"They shall be paid off and each given a small pension in proportion to their years of service," Aunt Felicity had decreed. "And I'm sure they will both be very grateful."

Dogger fobbed off with a pension? It was unthinkable. Dogger had given us almost his entire life: first to my father, then to my mother, and later to my sisters and myself.

I pictured him sitting on a quaint wooden bench by a river somewhere, dressed in a rough-spun pensioner's jacket, forced to beg bread from the passing tourists, who took occasional snapshots of him to send home to their cretinous relatives.

Dogger deserved better than that.

And Mrs. Mullet?

Left to cook for total strangers, she would languish and die, and we would be responsible.

Our lives were looking exceedingly grim.

Then, at the beginning of February, to make matters worse, King George had died: King George VI, that lovely man who once sat and chatted so happily with me in our drawing room as if I were his own daughter; and with his passing, the entire nation—indeed all of the Commonwealth countries, perhaps even the whole world—joined in the shock and sadness of our own recent bereavement.

And what of me? What of Flavia de Luce?

I would perish, I decided.

Rather than submit to a lifetime locked in some dismal pigeon-infested London square with an aunt who valued

the Union Jack more than her own blood, I would simply
do away with myself.

And as an authority on poisons, I knew precisely how
to accomplish it.

No cyanide for me, thank you!

I knew the symptoms all too well: the vertigo, the diz-
ziness, the burning in the throat and stomach and, as the
vagus nerve becomes paralyzed, the difficulty in breathing, the cold sweat, the feeble pulse, the muscular paraly-
sis, the crushing heaviness of the heart, the slobbering . . .

I think it was the slobbering, more than anything, that
put me off the cyanide. What self-respecting young
woman would want to be found dead in her bedroom
drowned in her own drool?

There were easier ways of joining the Heavenly Choir.

And so, here I am on my deathbed, all warm and cozy,
my half-closed eyes moving slowly for the last time across
that ghastly red-clotted mustard-yellow wallpaper.

I shall simply fall asleep and they will never find so
much as a trace of what it was that did me in. How clever
of me to have hit upon it!

They'll be sorry, I thought. *They'll all be sorry.*

But no! I mustn't let it end like that. Mustn't let it end
with such a commonplace expression. That was the kind
of platitude milkmaids died with—or match girls.

The death of Flavia de Luce demanded something
greater: some great and noble words to hold in my mind
as I stepped across the threshold of the universe.

But what were they to be?

Religion had been done to death.

Perhaps I could conjure up some great insight into the peculiar electron bonding of diborane (B_2H_6), for instance, or the as yet unsolved atomic valences of Zeise's salt.

Yes, that was it!

Paradise would welcome me. "Well done, de Luce," the vast crystal angels would say, flickering with frozen fire as I set foot upon their doorstep.

I hugged myself, cuddling in my own warmth.

How comfortable death was when properly done.

"Miss Flavia," Dogger said, breaking in upon my pleasant thoughts. He had stopped rowing the skiff for a few moments and was pointing.

I snapped out of my reverie in a split second. If it had been anyone but Dogger, I'd have taken my sweet time about it.

"That's Volesthorpe over there," he said, pointing. "St. Mildred's is just to the left of the tallest elm."

He knew I wouldn't want to miss it: St.-Mildred's-in-the-Marsh, where Canon Whitbread, the notorious "Poisoning Parson," had just two years ago dispatched several of his female parishioners by lacing their Communion wine with cyanide.

It had been done for love, of course. Poison and Passion, I have discovered, are as closely connected as Laurel and Hardy.

"Looks a harmless enough place," I said. "Like something from the pages of *Picturesque England.*"

"Yes," Dogger said. "Such places often do. Horrific crimes can sometimes bleed a location of all feeling."

He fell into silence as he gazed across the water and I knew he was thinking of the Japanese prisoner-of-war camp in which he and Father had been so badly abused.

As I have said, Father's death, six months ago, was the reason we were now adrift on the river: my sisters, Ophelia and Daphne, and, of course, me, Flavia.

Undine, as originally planned, had already gone up to London with Aunt Felicity.

In the bow, her face damp with mosquito repellent, Feely lay languishing on a couple of striped pillows, staring down at her own reflection in the still water just ahead of our punt. She had not spoken since we set out this morning. The fingers of her right hand hammered out a tune on the gunwales—one of Mendelssohn's *Songs Without Words:* I recognized it by the rhythm—but her face was a perfect blank.

On the raised wicker seat, Daffy sat hunched over a book—Robert Burton's *Anatomy of Melancholy*—oblivious to the glorious English landscape sliding slowly by on either side.

Father's sudden and unexpected death had knocked our family into a kind of coma, brought on, I believe, by the fact that we de Luces are constitutionally incapable of expressing our grief.

Only Dogger had broken down, howling like a dog in the night, then silent and impassive in the long and tortured days that followed.

It was pitiful.

The funeral had been a shambles. Denwyn Richard-

son, the vicar and one of Father's oldest and dearest
friends, had been seized at the outset by uncontrollable
sobbing, unable to continue, and the service had to be
halted until a stopgap clergyman could be found. In the
end, poor old Canon Walpole was located in the next
village, dragged from his sickbed, and rushed to St. Tancred's, where he finished what his colleague had begun,
barking from a rattling chest cold at the graveside like a
hundred hounds.

It was a nightmare.

Bent on taking charge, Aunt Felicity had (as I have
said) swooped down from London, the death of her
only—and younger—brother having driven her into a
frenzy, during which she treated us all like particularly
dim-witted galley slaves, slinging orders about like a grill
cook:

"Straighten those magazines, Flavia. Put them in al-
phabetical and then in chronological order, right side up,
in the cupboard. This is a drawing room, not a jackdaw's
nest. Ophelia, fetch a mop and pull down those spider's
webs. The place is like a tomb."

Then, realizing what she had said, she went all fretful
with suppressed shame, and made even more hurtful remarks, which I will not report here for fear of her reading
them someday and taking revenge.

Am I overdramatizing the situation? Not entirely.

"You look like a school of slugs," Aunt Felicity had
told us. "You need something to burn away the slime."

And so it was decided—I'm still not entirely sure by

whom—that we all of us needed a holiday: something with charabancs and gaily striped deck chairs by the sea, or at least exposure to the great outdoors.

It was Dogger, I think, who had come up with the idea of a boat trip: of lazy days on the river, of cold-meat hampers with flasks of lemonade and ginger beer from Fortnum & Mason, of goose-down mattresses at night and hot beef roasts in an ever-changing string of country hotels.

"Think of *Huckleberry Finn*," Daffy had said. "Who knows, Flavia? You might even be fortunate enough to find a dead body in a floating house."

It seemed unlikely, but anything was better than staying at Buckshaw, which now seemed likely to remain in mourning until the last day of the last month of the end of time.

There now seemed to be a sudden damp dustiness about the house that I had never noticed before: a certain staleness of the air, as if the ashes of generations of de Luces had been shaken from the bag of a hoover and allowed to settle wherever they wished. In fact, it was Daffy who had pointed this out to me:

"It's like the moldy little church in the park in *Bleak House*," she had said with a shiver, pulling her cardigan closer about her shoulders, and referring to the book which she claimed to have been reading obsessively again and again since she was in a pram, beginning anew each time she finished. "'There is a general smell and taste as of the ancient Dedlocks in their graves.' Gaak!"

The "Gaak!" was Daffy's, not in Dickens's original.

Feely's marriage to Dieter Schrantz, which had been planned for June, was postponed out of respect to Father. There had been scenes of dinnerware thrown, wallpaper ripped, upholstery gutted, and so forth, but all of it had been in vain.

"For the death of a parent, a heavy mourning period of six months is laid on," Aunt Felicity said, betraying her military attachments, no matter how top secret they were supposed to have been. "And not a day less. And all your shrieking cuts no ice with me."

And that was that.

What should have been a time of bliss now became a nightmare as Feely's nerves, fear, and anger seized reason by the throat and shook it dead. The result was a spectacular series of split-ups and reconciliations with Dieter, followed by suddenly renewed outbreaks of hostility that would have put even Genghis Khan to shame.

Through it all, Dieter had been a brick, but had at last, as all heroes must sooner or later do, retired to lick his wounds.

And so it came to pass that we had packed up with little ado—except on the part of Dogger, who was never ill-prepared—and set out on what was hoped would be a time of healing.

But things didn't turn out that way.

By the time we were finally able to make our first escape from Buckshaw, Father had been dead for nearly six months, during which it had seemed, at least in the beginning, as if Dogger had lost some essential part of his soul. But as the days went on, it became ever more apparent—to me, anyway—that he was gaining something greater.

In the past several weeks especially, Dogger had been acquiring a glow. It's hard to describe, but I'll do my best.

It was not a superficial effect, as if he had just shaved and patted his face with a bay rum lotion, for Dogger would never stoop to such artifice.

No, it was as if he had begun to grow a nimbus: that pale radiance which, in paintings of the medieval saints, is portrayed as a gold halo about the head, as if the saint in question were wearing an inverted brass kettle.

There are, in fact, no halos in the Bible—just as there are no cats or accordions. If it's halos you're after, you'll have to look them up in the *Encyclopaedia Britannica*, where they come between "Hallucination" and "Halogens." Physical halos, such as those observed around the moon or sun, are caused, as everybody knows, by the reflection and refraction of light by ice crystals suspended in the atmosphere. But for the halos of saints, no cause is given—although one can easily imagine. At least, I can.

In Dogger's case, it was a kind of glow, or glory, which was coming upon him only gradually. I had made a point of going into the kitchen first thing every morning to observe him closely, although I was, of course, discreet about it.

There was a rather growing pinkness of the cheeks, and I had worried at first about stramonium poisoning, or plague. But since Dogger knew better than to handle the potted Datura plant (*Datura stramonium*) that grew in my chemical laboratory, and because the Black Death had been extinct in England since a last reported case near Ipswich had taken the life of a Mrs. Bugg in 1918, I decided that Dogger's growing radiance could be only for the good.

And so it was. On this particular morning in June, sitting dead center in the skiff, digging the blades of the sculls firmly into the warm muddy river water, Dogger was as handsome and as healthy as I had ever seen him: like a cinema star, in fact. If this were a film, rather than real life, he would be played perhaps by John Mills, squinting knowingly with a slight smile into the morning sunshine as if he saw already what lay just round the next bend. And perhaps he did.

"Have you ever been here before, Dogger?" I asked. "On this particular stretch of the river, I mean?"

"Many years ago, Miss Flavia," he answered, "but that was in another life."

And I knew enough to leave it at that.

I gazed across the water at the rich and comforting shades of the churchyard.

Most people probably never stop to think about why our burial places are so green. But if they ever did, their faces might turn the very shade of that graveyard grass, for underneath the picturesque moss and lichen, and beneath all those weathered stones, is a slowly simmering chemical stew, bubbling and burbling away in the dark earth as our ancestors and neighbors, with the help of a little chemistry, are returned to their Maker.

"For dust thou art, and unto dust shalt thou return," the Bible tells us.

"Ashes to ashes, dust to dust," says *The Book of Common Prayer*.

But both of these books, having been written mostly in good taste, fail to mention either the stinking jelly or the oozing liquids and the gaseous phases through which each of us must pass on our way to the Great Beyond.

The average churchyard is a first-rate meat tenderizer.

Shocking, perhaps, but true.

In an issue of *The Illustrated London News* from several years ago—which I found abandoned under a sofa in the drawing room at Buckshaw—it was reported that an extract of the humble papaya fruit was now being marketed to soften the squire's steak.

What a colossal waste! I had thought. *A faster and much more powerful and effective product could be easily manufactured simply by bottling—*

By now, we were drifting along just feet from the edge of the churchyard, and St.-Mildred's-in-the-Marsh loomed above us, the shadow of its square tower blocking the morning sun. A sudden chill came into the air, and it wasn't just from the light wind which had suddenly sprung up, signaling a change in the weather.

"It was just there by the old dock, wasn't it, Dogger, that Canon Whitbread chucked the poisoned chalice into the river?"

I knew perfectly well that it was. I had pored for ages over the photographs in *News of the World*, memorizing the details: the path, the dock, the sloping riverbank, the reeds . . . all helpfully labeled, with arrows, for the convenience of the bloodthirsty reader.

He had thrown the vessel into the river in the belief that it would sink to the bottom and remain there in the mud until Judgment Day. He hadn't counted, however, upon the villainy of some earlier churchwarden who had replaced the original silver with a thinly plated alloy replica which, unfortunately, floated and remained bobbing among the reeds for a farmer's boy to find.

"He oughtn't to have dumped it on a moonless night," I said aloud.

"Just so, Miss Flavia," Dogger said, easily able to read my thoughts. "He might have seen that it hadn't sunk."

"It might have, though," I said excitedly. "It could have been brought back up by some punter's pole or a heavy oar."

"Could have," Dogger said. "But not likely. I believe the police rejected that theory on the grounds of fragility. The rather frail replica would almost certainly have been dented by such an instrument, but it was not."

"Odd, then," I said, "that Canon Whitbread had never noticed the lightness of the substitute chalice."

"Unless it was he himself who swapped it," Dogger said.

I slapped the surface of the water in excitement, my heart thrilling at the idea that it was here, at this very spot, that the traces of cyanide and strychnine had been washed away. Perhaps some of the molecules still remained—vastly diluted, of course, but still, if the homeopathic theories of Samuel Hahnemann were to be believed, deadly effective.

"Flavia!" Daffy shouted. "You flaming idiot! You've soaked my book!"

Daffy's magnificent vocabulary always failed her when she was genuinely angry.

She slammed the volume shut and jammed it into the wicker picnic basket.

There was a blessed—but slightly tense—silence along the river now as we drifted beneath the arches of the willows. Now and then the glassy surface would be broken by a fish's bubbles. (*Do fish break wind?* I idly wondered.)

We were not far from one of the great universities. Surely someone there would know: some famous scientist—some ichthyologist, to be precise. Some young up-and-coming ichthyologist with a square jaw and curly blond hair, a pipe and blue eyes. I could drop in to consult with him about some rarefied chemical question . . . one that would make him realize instantly that I was no rank amateur . . . *The Dispersal of Cyanide and Strychnine in Riverine Fish Habitats.* Yes! That was it!

Roger, his name would be. Roger de something-or-other, to suit my own . . . from an ancient Norman family with enough arms, crests, flags, banners, and blazons to shame a secondhand automobile mart.

"Roger," I would say—

No, wait. *Roger* was too commonplace. Something you might call a dog. His name needed to be Llewellyn, pronounced the proper way: Thew-ETH-lyn, the way they do in Wales.

Yes, Llewellyn.

"Llewellyn," I would say, "if ever you have a case of piscine poisoning to solve, I should be happy to help."

Or was that too forward?

I had never actually performed an autopsy on a fish, but it couldn't be all that different from dissecting bloaters at the breakfast table.

I sighed with pleasure and let my hand dangle languidly over the side.

Something touched it. Something grazed against my fingers and I instinctively made a grab.

Was it a fish? Could I possibly have caught a fish by hand?

Had some dim-witted chub or stupid pike mistaken my trailing fingers for a bit of floating food?

Not wanting to lose the opportunity to go down in history as "Fishhook Flavia," I hung on for dear life, hooking my fingertips firmly behind the hard ridge of bone I could now so easily feel. I planted my thumb for a firmer grip. This catch was not going to become "the one that got away."

"Hold on, Dogger," I said, trying to keep my voice level and matter-of-fact. This story was going to be handed down for generations, and I wanted to make sure that my coolheadedness was properly noted. "I believe I've caught something."

Dogger stopped rowing and let the skiff drift. I could feel the dead weight of the thing dragging at my arm. It must be one of those gigantic fish—famous in local lore— that lives for centuries at the bottom of a pool. "Old Moldy," or some such name, the villagers would call it. Would they be outraged to hear that I had caught their beloved monster with my bare hands?

I smiled at the thought.

Whatever it was, it wasn't putting up much of a fight.

Although Daffy and Feely were pretending to be disinterested, both had turned toward me.

Holding on with all my strength, I gave my extended arm a good shake, taking care not to let go of my prey—whatever it might be.

I had seen photographs in the picture magazines of the American author Mr. Hemingway battling a giant marlin on the end of a ridiculously slender pole. Even *he*, I'll bet, had never landed such a fish by hand.

Flavia, I thought, *you're about to become famous*.

As the boat slowed and the water cleared, a shadow—and then a brighter patch—appeared just beneath the surface. *A fish's belly?* It was certainly light enough.

I hauled it in for closer inspection.

Although the object was upside down, it was now easily recognizable.

It was a human head—and attached to it was a human body.

My fingers were inserted firmly in the corpse's open mouth, locked behind its upper teeth.

"We'd best make for the pier, Dogger," I said.

· T W O ·

BRINGING THE SKIFF ALONGSIDE the pier behind the church was not so easy a task as it might have been.

For one thing, Daffy was busily disposing, over the gunwales, of every bite she had eaten since last Thursday fortnight. If you've ever seen those cinema newsreels in which a trawler dumps its nets, you'll know what I'm talking about. To say that her gorge was rising would be a gross understatement. Hurling her guts out was more like it. To be honest, it was awe-inspiring.

If it hadn't been for the seriousness of the situation, it might even have been amusing.

Dogger, to his great credit, said not a word. A single glance over his shoulder told him all he needed to know, and he reacted accordingly. Slowly, but steadily, we edged in silence—except for Daffy's retching, of course—toward the riverbank.

Nearby boaters, of whom there were several, would assume that a young lady had been taken ill. Paste sandwiches that had gone over, perhaps, or a bit of bad tongue. It would not do to stare, and no one did. None of them could see, of course, what I was dragging by its open mouth.

As the skiff bumped against the wooden dock, Dogger handed me the tartan picnic blanket we had intended to sit upon for tea. I knew at once what he wanted me to do, and I did it.

Without attracting attention, I took the blanket with my left hand, unfolded it, and spread it casually over the floating corpse. Having made fast the skiff, Dogger stepped out into the shallow water, took hold of the shrouded figure, lifted it gently in his arms, and waded to the grassy bank beside the pier.

In another moment he had laid the body in the grass at the edge of the churchyard.

I couldn't help noticing the bruise on the back of the neck, as if the man had somehow stumbled, banged his head, and fallen into the water. Dead men don't bruise, I remembered.

"Artificial respiration?" I asked, trying to think logically.

Dogger had once told me of his studies in the Kanō system of Jiu-Jitsu, in which drowning victims had been restored to life by a sharp blow across the soles of the feet.

"I'm afraid not, miss," Dogger said, lifting a corner of the blanket. "It's too late for that. The fish have already been at this poor fellow."

And he was right: The earlobes and the nose had certainly been nibbled.

As for the rest of the face, the dead man had been handsome enough. Those long, lank red locks, now plastered down by the wet, must once have curled fetchingly enough about the lace collar of his ruffled silk shirt.

I am not making this up: It really *was* silk, as were the blue trousers, which were fastened by buttons and silken ribbons at the knee.

I had the strange impression that I was looking at someone from the eighteenth century: some time traveler who had slipped playfully beneath the surface of the water in the days of King George III, perhaps, and decided just now that enough was enough.

My next thought was this: Had anyone gone missing from a masquerade? Or from the cast of a cinema film?

Surely such a thing would have been widely reported, and yet here was this healthy young specimen (aside from being dead, of course) laid out like a trout on the riverbank as if it were the most natural thing in all the world.

He was almost too beautiful: like the *Blue Boy* of Gainsborough's famous painting, but rather more pale.

But wait! It *was* a painting he reminded me of—yet it certainly wasn't a Gainsborough. No, it was a work by a much less well-known artist named Henry Wallis.

The Death of Chatterton, it was called, and it depicted the body of that sad young poet who had poisoned himself in 1770 at the age of seventeen, having been exposed as a literary forger.

I ought to have realized this at once, but I didn't, even

though a large framed reproduction of the original had been hanging for years in a place of honor on my bedroom wall.

It is one of my favorite works of art, I must admit.

In the painting, Chatterton, his flesh an awful fish-belly white, lies stretched upon a shabby couch in his rented garret, the fingers of his left hand seeming to bare the breast in which his heart had quite recently been beating.

His right hand lies stiffly clutched on the floor, near the empty arsenic bottle.

All art ought to be this fascinating.

"Please remain where you are, Miss Ophelia and Miss Daphne," Dogger said, pulling me out of my thoughts. "Keep a sharp eye out, both up and down the river."

What a clever man, I thought. He meant to keep them occupied; keep them from going into hysterics; keep them from trampling the evidence.

It is a remarkable fact that orders given in a firm voice at the scene of a tragedy are invariably obeyed.

"If you'd be good enough to stay here, Miss Flavia," he said, "I shall go for the police."

I gave him a brisk nod and he was off, scrambling up the grassy riverbank toward the church, the wet turn-ups of his trousers sloshing round his ankles, but still dignified in spite of it.

As soon as he was gone, I lifted the corner of the blanket.

The pale blue eyes, which were half open, the pupils

dilated, gazed up at me in surprise—as if I had suddenly snatched a coverlet from the face of a light sleeper. The irises matched the color of his lips and the silk ribbons at his knees.

I sniffed the lips—actually touched them with the tip of my nose—but could detect nothing but the brackish smell of river water.

I leaned low over the corpse and drew up into my nostrils the smell of his eyeballs.

I was already half expecting it: the odor of apples.

Potassium cyanide, I recalled, is quite odorless until mixed with water, in which it freely dissolves to form an alkaline solution, from which prussic acid is abundantly evolved, which, when exposed to air, volatilizes to produce the smell of apples.

The tissue of the eyes, being the thinnest and softest in the body, not only are more absorbent of chemical odors than are other parts of the body, but retain them longer. If you don't believe me, take a whiff of your own tears an hour after you've eaten onions.

Also, the eyes, having been fixed in a half-closed position, would have been better protected from the diluting effect of the water than the nose and lips.

His complexion was—well, let's just say that it was interesting. Although the features were somewhat bloated, there was remarkably little lividity: a sure sign, I remembered, either that the body had not been in the water for long, or that it had been sunken in the cooler depths for several days. The fact that it had now floated up to the

surface, though, was a likely indication of gaseous putrefaction. There were other possibilities, of course, but that
was the most likely sequence of events.

Further physical signs (which I could have checked)
might also be present, but examining these would have
involved stripping the body, which, I decided, would not
be decent. Besides, there wasn't time: Dogger would be
returning with the police at any moment.

In drowning, it is sometimes the internal evidence
which turns out to be most crucial. Obviously, I couldn't
conduct a full-scale postmortem here on the riverbank. I
would have to settle for the next best thing.

Placing both hands in an overlapping position on the
dead man's chest, I threw all my weight into a powerful
straight-armed push.

I was amply rewarded: A surprisingly rich flow of frothy
broth, followed by what I took to be water, streamed out
from between his blueish lips.

Reaching for my handkerchief, I blotted up the mess,
folded it inward in a ball to avoid contamination, and
returned it to my pocket.

Certain people—such as Mrs. Mullet, for instance—
kept going on about the importance of always carrying a
clean handkerchief about one's person, and for once they
were right.

A quick look round told me that I had not been observed.

Returning to my physical examination of the corpse, I
felt the palms of the dead man's hands for looseness of

skin, the "glove effect" which would indicate a longer immersion in the water, but they were remarkably firm.

Almost without thinking, I raised my fingertips to my nose.

It's remarkable, really, how much we ignore our sense of smell: until, that is, we detect one extreme or another, fragrant or foul—either roses or rot. The human olfactory system has trained itself to ignore anything that doesn't matter.

I sniffed my fingers.

Aha! I hadn't really expected anything out of the ordinary, but my nose was picking up an unmistakable smell.

Paraldehyde, by all that's holy! Good old, jolly old $(CH_3CHO)_3$,—a foul-smelling, foul-tasting, but colorless liquid which can be easily produced by treating aldehyde with sulfuric or hydrochloric acid. The stuff was first synthesized in 1829, and had once been combined with extract of vanilla, syrup of raspberries, and chloroform to treat insomnia. It had also been used, mixed with equal parts of cherry-laurel water, to administer subcutaneous injections to the insane.

But because of the lingering reek of the breath it produced in the patient, paraldehyde had generally been abandoned a hundred years ago. Although I had overheard someone remark that there were still those—particularly among the aristocracy—who had gone beyond alcohol and become addicted to the stuff.

I sniffed my fingertips again to reinforce my memory of the facts.

Paraldehyde poisoning, if I recalled correctly, *contracted* the pupils, whereas this poor man's were dilated. It didn't quite add up. There wasn't that sudden "click" of certainty.

It would have to wait until later. There was no time now.

I returned my attention to the lower parts of the body.

On one of the feet, which stuck out slightly beyond the far end of the blanket, was what I can only describe as a red ballet slipper. The other foot was bare. He was not a tall man, I judged: somewhat less than five and a half feet, perhaps, although it was difficult to estimate with him lying on his back and partly covered.

Yes! That was it: The man was a ballet dancer, which would account for his costume.

I was proud of myself. He had come down to the river-bank in the night, perhaps to practice his pirouettes away from prying eyes. *Swan Lake*, probably.

What a sight that must have been beneath the weeping willows and the sleepily flowing river—until he had misjudged—or tripped—and fallen into the dark water.

Or been pushed.

Had he become entangled in reeds or duckweed? I folded back more of the blanket. There was no vegetation clinging to his body.

Perhaps some of it had become caught up in his clothing. I decided to search him.

Have you ever stuck your hands into the pockets of a corpse? Perhaps not. I myself have done it on only a couple of occasions, and I can tell you that it's not always the most pleasant of occupations.

Who knows what may be lurking in the crevices of the clothing? With a drowning victim, you're at risk of eels, water snakes, crabs, and so forth, and I tried to recall quickly which species of these—such as the Chinese Mitten Crab—had been known to make their way upstream from the tidal waters of the Thames. When it comes to crabs you can never be too cautious.

I needn't have worried. Except for a wad of wet lint and a folded bit of soggy blue-lined paper from his trousers, the corpse's pockets were empty. I fished out the paper between my first and second fingers, noting as I did so that I would need to give my hands a jolly good scrubbing later because of the slime.

Smoothing it carefully with my thumb to avoid disintegration, I slowly unfolded the scrap. Something had been written upon it in pencil: a series of numbers.

54, 6, 7, 8, 9

A date perhaps? The year 1954—with 6, 7, 8, and 9 representing the months of June, July, August, and September? If so, it was still some two years in the future, since we were now in June of 1952.

People don't usually make appointments *that* far in advance.

Or could it be the combination to a safety lock? That seemed unlikely, since a series of four small numbers in strict numerical sequence would be extremely difficult to dial accurately—if it could be done at all. As Dogger had taught me, during one of our sessions devoted to the art of lock-picking, combinations generally contain at least two widely spaced numerals.

Or was it a telephone number? I couldn't be sure which exchange was represented by the first two digits, but one could always ring the number and see who picked it up on the other end.

The possibilities seemed endless, which made it all the more exciting, since possibilities are so much more thrilling than certainties—or so I've always thought.

I was about to stuff the wadded paper back into the corpse's pocket when a sudden shadow blocked the sun and fell upon the body. An electric chill shot through my bones.

I twisted round and put my hand up to block the light, but could see only a black silhouette hovering over my shoulder.

"What are you doing to Orlando?" demanded a voice, and I nearly leapt out of my liver. The speaker was seated in an antique wicker bath chair, and had rolled up in such silence that I hadn't heard her coming.

"What are you playing at? Is this a game? Another one of your larks? Get up at once, Orlando—you're soiling your silks."

"I'm sorry," I said, scrambling to my feet. "I'm afraid—"

"And well you might be, you shameless girl. What are you playing at? Answer me at once!"

My first impression of the woman was that she had a beak like a battleship: forward-jutting and powerful enough to slice through the most fearsome Atlantic breakers as if they were runny cheese.

Her snow-white hair was tied up so tightly into a large

bun at the back of her head that it gave her face the appearance of a squeezed pimple in the instant before it bursts.

The toe of a riding boot peeked out from under a lap robe, and an old school tie flopped out of a Norfolk jacket onto her ample chest. The woman seemed all odds and ends.

"What are you staring at?" she asked. "Didn't your parents teach you not to gawk?"

That did it. My parents—both of them now deceased, God rest their dear departed souls—had taught me the most important thing of all, which was to show some spine in the face of bullying.

I know that I ought to have been a fountain of condolences, a rock of sympathy in a sea of sadness, but this woman had stepped across my line of decency. I couldn't bring myself to touch her, let alone hug her.

"Orlando is dead," I informed her. "He drowned. We found the body."

I could tell she was not listening to me.

"Orlando, get up at once," she commanded. "The Hawthorne-Wests will be arriving in an hour, and you know how Parthia hates to be kept waiting."

Orlando's already pallid complexion was tinted an even more awful green by the closeness of the grass, and I couldn't help noticing that a couple of dandelions beside his ears were reflecting little yellow bruises onto his cheeks, like dabs of rancid butter.

"That's enough, Orlando," the woman said, releasing a foot from its stirrup beneath the lap robe and giving his shoulder a prod. "Get up now and come along."

I seized her arm.

"Better not touch him," I said. "He's dead. The police have been called."

The woman looked up at me—then back at the corpse—then back at me again. Her eyes widened and her vast and lightly whiskered upper lip curled back as a horrible wail shattered the quiet air—rising and falling like a demented air-raid siren.

Her ear-splitting screech caused Feely and Daffy to swivel their heads in our direction—but only for a quick glance, returning at once to scouting the river as Dogger had instructed them to do.

"See no evil, hear no evil" was their motto, and some small part of me didn't blame them. Being embroiled with bodies is not so simple as some people seem to think it is.

Looking away is easy, but staring Death in the face takes more than a strong stomach.

Dogger, I saw, was now returning through the church-yard, accompanied by two other persons. One, it was obvious by his uniform, was the village constable; the other, by his dog collar, the vicar, a roly-poly, jolly-looking gentleman.

Thank heavens, I thought. I would no longer have to deal with this howling harpy on my own.

"Stand back, please," the constable said, as I knew he would. I was happy to obey by getting to my feet and shuffling backward to a point where I could watch without being watched. Of such small tools from one's bag of tricks are great investigators made.

I know how stuffy that must sound, but it's true.

Dogger and I stood looking on as the constable—gingerly, I thought—peered under the corner of the blanket. Having satisfied himself that he was dealing with a dead body, he tugged at his jacket, straightened his tie, turned to us, and said, "Yes. Well, then . . ."

He jabbed his thumb vaguely toward the church and, presumably, the high street.

"I'd be obliged if you'd all step across to the Oak and Pheasant. The landlord lays on a good spread of pickled hocks and cheese, if you feel up to it, that is. I shall be along in due course."

If we felt up to it? I suppose he meant to sound solicitous. Or was it supposed to be humorous? Whose leg did this village idiot think he was pulling?

I had half a mind to tell him that there was nothing I loved more than gorging on cold ham while examining a particularly juicy corpse.

I caught Dogger's eye before I replied.

"That's very thoughtful of you, Constable," I said. "I think I could stand a whiff of smelling salts about now."

Because it was expected of a girl my age, I flashed him a quick but slightly sickly grin, leaving him to work out what I meant.

"Have we seen everything that we need to?" I asked Dogger from the corner of my mouth, as we walked to fetch Feely and Daffy from the punt.

"We have, indeed, Miss Flavia," he said. "More than enough."

·THREE·

"How perfectly icky!" Daffy whined when we were seated round a table in the saloon bar of the Oak and Pheasant.

I hadn't the faintest idea whether she was referring to the pub, the corpse, or the wailing woman in the bath chair we had left to the tender mercies of the constable on the riverbank.

Nor did I particularly care.

Feely shifted uneasily in her chair, giving quick, darting glances round the room. I knew at once that she was unable to hide her discomfort at being seated with a servant.

I don't know what she was worried about. The only other patrons in the pub were a group of rather shabby men of assorted sizes, all wearing colored kerchiefs round

their necks, all busily poking one another in the chest
and laughing loudly at the others' jokes.

Not that Dogger would have minded. We were on holiday, and so was he. Rank and station were forgotten—or
were supposed to be. Things were different since the war.
Feely had been brought up in a different world, and it
showed.

I pitied my sister. Her life had not been an easy one—
especially recently. She was mourning Father and moping
over her postponed marriage. To someone used to getting
her own way, it must have seemed like the Apocalypse.

"What'll it be?" the landlord asked, his pencil poised.
"Ploughman's lunch all round?" In his apron and shirt-
sleeves he was the very picture of an innkeeper in a cartoon from *Punch*.

"A pint of Guinness, please," Feely said, and I nearly
fell out of my chair. It was the first time she had spoken
since breakfast.

"Are you over eighteen?" the landlord asked. "Sorry,
miss, but I'm obliged to inquire."

"I can vouch for her," Dogger said.

"I'll have the same," Daffy blurted, and the man was
too taken aback to repeat his question. She was evidently
even more shaken than I had thought.

"Ginger beer for me," I said. "And if it's not too much
trouble, I'd like it warmed on the back of the cooker for
three minutes."

It's always a good idea to demand some quirky service,
to let them know that you're not just anybody.

I knew that with an investigation getting under way over against the churchyard wall, we were bound to be in this village for quite some time, and it was essential to establish priorities at the outset. You can't command respect after the starting whistle's been blown—especially among strangers.

The landlord gave me a squinty eye, but he wrote down my order.

"And you, sir?" he asked, turning to Dogger.

"Milk," Dogger replied. "A small glass of milk. It's pasteurized, I presume?"

"Pasteur-*ized* and past your ears, sir!" The landlord laughed, slapping his knee. I could have slapped his face. "You've never seen milk so pasteurized as our own. Why, just yesterday I was saying to Mr. Clemm, our vicar, 'You'll get no trade from *our* kitchen!'—meaning, of course, in the funeral department. He wasn't amused—like Queen whatsername."

I stopped listening. I knew all too well the dangers of unpasteurized milk.

The chemist Louis Pasteur was, after all, one of my great heroes. I had eagerly memorized the symptoms of tuberculosis—also known as consumption, or phthisis—and how the bacillus responsible caused the victim's lungs to turn into a kind of weeping cheese: the features becoming livid and darkening as the blood retains excessive carbon, the hectic fevers, the racking cough, the racing pulse, the wasting muscles, the night sweats, and the agitated delirium—the mind, however, remaining cruelly clear and focused almost until the very end.

There had been a time when, after first reading up on these horrors, I had refused to drink so much as a drop of milk without first taking it to my chemical laboratory and pasteurizing it personally, then examining it closely under the microscope for rogue bacilli.

Nowadays, of course, since the discovery of penicillin in 1928 by Alexander Fleming, no one dies of consumption except in the cinema, where its onset is invariably signaled by tragic glances, sprayed-on perspiration, soot rubbed below the eyes, dramatic coughing, and spitting of fake blood always—conveniently—into spotlessly white handkerchiefs.

My fascinating train of thought was interrupted by the arrival of our drinks.

"Cheers!" Daffy said quietly, raising her glass to each of us in turn. She was showing off—not giving a thought to the seriousness of the situation. Even if taste and decency are chucked out the window, there is one rule that remains: keeping a long face in the presence of death.

I shot her a wet-blanket look.

"Sorry," she said, surprisingly humbled.

In the silence that followed, I let my mind drift across the room, out the door, across the road, and through the churchyard to the riverbank.

Who was the dead man, and how had he come to drown? Had it been an accident, or—

"I want to go home," Feely said suddenly. "I'm not feeling well. I've had enough."

Oddly enough, I knew exactly what she meant. It wasn't just the finding of a corpse on the river. As I have said, Father's death had told terribly upon her, and the continued postponements of her wedding date, and the resulting battles, even more.

Poor Feely, I thought. Her life had been a will-o'-the-wisp, with true happiness always just beyond her grasp.

I had an idea, but it would keep until after we had eaten. I touched her arm as a kind of "message received" signal.

Was the look that she returned a grateful one? With Feely, one could never know.

Dogger, as I knew he would, ordered the ploughman's lunch, Feely a small salad, and Daffy a small dish of steamed carrots.

"I'm sorry," she said, "but I simply can't face meat."

I plumped for plain old chutney, cheese, and pickled onions, a favorite dish, which I had secretly named "The Embalmer's Breakfast." It was as like a chemical lab as you could get when away from home.

We ate in silence. The things that Dogger and I might have talked about were not suitable for my sisters' ears, while the topics I might have discussed with them were unfit for his.

As we were finishing our meal, the door of the public bar next door burst open, and a loud, breathless voice announced: "Somebody's drowned! They've fished a dead 'un out of the river!"

A general hubbub arose at once as chairs and boots grated noisily on the floor. Before you could say "Nine-pins!" the place had emptied, and the only sound was that of a few retreating voices.

"Come," I said, tugging at Feely's arm. It was time to put my plan into execution.

"I'm not going back there," she said. "I don't feel well. I want to go home."

"I know," I told her, not loosening my grip. "But think—what's across the road?"

"A drowned body," she answered, shuddering.

"Besides that." She looked up at me dumbly.

"A church!" I said. "And where there's a church, there's an organ. No smoke without fire, and so forth. Come on, let's go. My ears are parched. I need a bit of Bach."

Something dawned on Feely's face. It wasn't exactly happiness, but it would do.

As she got to her feet, I took her forefinger and led her toward the door. It was the first time I had willingly touched my sister's hand since I was nine months old and learning to walk.

Outside, the June weather was glorious, and we both had to shield our eyes against the summer sun.

We crossed the road and approached the church along the gravel path.

St.-Mildred's-in-the-Marsh, it said on the weathered signboard, and I gave a shiver of pleasure. The ghost of Canon Whitbread might, even at this moment, be peeping round one of those old, weather-blasted tombstones, looking over my shoulder.

As I stared up at the square tower, I had the distinct feeling that someone was watching us, but in a moment it had passed. Churches can do that to you.

In the porch, Feely made a beeline up the curving stone steps to the organ loft, and I took a pew at the front on the center aisle.

There is nowhere you can feel the presence of the dead more than in the damp dimness of an empty church. If you listen, you can hear them breathing. I know that makes no sense, because the dead don't breathe—at least in an earthly way. But you can hear them nonetheless.

I turned up the volume on my almost supernatural hearing. This was a trait I had inherited from my dead mother, Harriet, which, although generally a pain in the ear, sometimes came in handy.

But if the dead were whispering today, they were not addressing me. Perhaps the lady victims of Canon Whitbread were gathering round the Communion rail for a jolly good chin-wag. Wasn't it, after all, the very spot where they had been poisoned?

I stared at the altar with new interest. Was there a slight shimmering of the air? If so, it was nothing you could put your finger on. A thermal of warm air, perhaps, set into motion by the outside temperature: a silent gust from one of the underfloor heating ducts.

It was either moving air or ancient holiness, and if I had to make a bet, I'd put my money on a cold draft.

After a few hollow knocks and the rustle of paper somewhere at the back of the church, the organ began to speak. I recognized the melody at once: Johann Sebastian Bach's *The Art of Fugue*.

It began with the note of a single pipe, which sounded

at first like a dry bone singing itself to sleep in a crypt somewhere in the night. But it wasn't long before the other bones joined in—Bach's playful organ notes rising and flitting about high up among the rafters and hammer beams like a squadron of deliriously happy bats. An apt comparison, if I do say so myself, since the word *fugue* means *flight*.

Oh, it was delicious!

I sighed, took a deep breath, and closed my eyes.

Old Johann Sebastian, I decided, must have had a mind like mine, capable of being everywhere at once.

I have always found organ music to be great fertilizer for thoughts. With Bach in my ears and no distractions, my mind accelerated like a greyhound let off the leash.

Who was the dead Orlando, and who was the woman in the bath chair? What was the relationship between them? Why had she reacted so vigorously when I told her he was dead?

More important, what was the meaning of the numbers I had found in the corpse's pocket?

My eyes popped open at the thought, and were drawn immediately to the numbers posted on the hymn boards above the pulpit and the lectern. These were, of course, the hymns which were to be sung at the next service—or *had* already been sung at the last one.

Three only were listed: Hymns 289, 172, and 584.

I swiveled round and plucked a copy of *Hymns Ancient and Modern* (*Ancient and Laundered,* as Daffy calls it) from the rack on the back of my pew.

I thumbed my way to Hymn 289:

Days and moments quickly flying
Blend the living with the dead;
Soon will you and I be lying
Each within his narrow bed.

How I adore hymns! They have a sense of perspective that's all too often missing in everyday life.

Not much correspondence, though, with the numbers in the corpse's pocket. I called to mind the wrinkled bit of paper: 54, 6, 7, 8, 9, it had said.

Well, the 8 and the 9 of the first hymn number were the same but it wasn't enough. Two numbers out of six wins nothing on the lottery, and it didn't here, either.

I turned to Hymn 172:

Praise to the Holiest in the height
And in the depths be praise

This was more like it. I couldn't help but think of the dead Orlando, whom I had dredged from the depths, although I doubt if he was doing much praising about his predicament.

But for this hymn, only the 7 tallied. Worse odds than the previous one.

What if the numbers referred to Hymns 54, 67, and 89? My thumbs became a blur.

Hymn 54 seemed promising:

When shades of night around us close
And weary limbs in sleep repose . . .

But from there, it quickly wandered off into pity, guilt, and misery.

I flipped to Hymn 67.

The third verse had blood and water, and the fourth something about landing on the eternal shore.

I sighed and went on to 89.

Which was about Moses, fasting. Not particularly promising.

But then I remembered: *Hymns Ancient and Modern* wasn't the only flounder in the sea. No, indeed! The church, for as long as I could remember, had been tinkering with the hymnal and the prayer book so much as to make your head spin. Sunday morning services were like a steeplechase as we fanned pages in the next jump to get to the proper place.

And then, of course, there was *The English Hymnal.* That in itself was an entirely *different* kettle of fish.

Were all these fishy thoughts a kind of blasphemy? I decided not: Wasn't the fish, after all, as much a symbol of Christianity as the cross?

I twisted round again in my seat—actually got onto my knees on the pew—so that, facing backward, I could dig more deeply—I was going to say "fish," but I won't—in the book rack behind me.

And yes, as I somehow knew it would be, not far from my searching fingertips was a rather tattered copy of *The English Hymnal.*

This was larger—fatter—than *Hymns A & M,* due of course to the fact that it contained not only the words of the hymns with their titles in Greek and Latin, but also the music, as well as footnotes.

This was an industrial-sized hymnbook, intended for experts.

I turned to Hymn 54:

Ye clouds of darkness, hosts of night,
That breed confusion and affright
Begone!

Et cetera.

Could it have been a warning? That seemed unlikely.

I paged ahead to number 67:

Now is the healing time decreed.

Healing, perhaps, but disappointing.

Now only Hymn 89 was left.

My fingers were already feeling defeated.

But wait—here it was:

Soul of Jesus, make me whole,
Meek and contrite make my soul;
Thou most stainless Soul Divine,
Cleanse this sordid soul of mine.

I gave an involuntary shiver. Could this be a personal message from the universe to Flavia de Luce?

Was it like one of those oracles where you stuck your finger into the pages of the Bible at random and read out the text from wherever it landed?

I had seen Feely do this once—but only once.

"What shall I wear when Dieter takes me to the cinema on Saturday night?" she had asked, but when the Bible had replied: "My flesh is clothed with worms and clods" (Job 7:5), she had let out an unearthly shriek and canceled her date.

The hymn went on to talk about curses and ransoms, but not until the later verses. In my opinion, no one sending an encrypted threat would make use of any but the opening words. Otherwise, it would be too obscure. The intended victim would become bored and give it up before getting to the message.

I could see that the hymnbook idea was a washout, and I returned it to its rack.

Beside the two hymnals was a third book, thick and black, loose and battered from much use.

Not expecting much, I picked it up.

The Holy Bible—King James Version. It was as heavy as a brick.

Acting upon a sudden impulse, I shoved my forefinger in among its pages.

> Her princes within her are roaring lions; her judges are
>   evening wolves; they gnaw not the bones till the
>   morrow.

Zephaniah, chapter 3, verse 3.
So much for oracles, I thought.
But, believe it or not, at that very instant, an idea came flying out of nowhere and landed on my head, like a pigeon on Lord Nelson's statue.

I turned to the front of the Bible, praying desperately for a table of contents.

Yes! Here it was—just as you would expect—at the beginning.

Genesis . . . Exodus . . . Leviticus . . .

A cold hand touched my bare arm. I leapt at least two feet into the air, and my pounding heart cowered behind my kidneys.

"I thought I'd find you here," said a voice at my ear, and I spun round in a state that was close to terror.

It was the woman from the riverbank. Once again, she had rolled up behind me in utter silence.

With my back turned to the altar, and the music from the organ, I had not seen or heard her bath chair coming. She must have entered the church through the transept.

"We got off on the wrong foot out there," she said, jerking a thumb toward the churchyard. "My fault entirely. You were only trying to help poor Orlando. I should have realized that at once."

She must have seen my astonishment. Could this be the same person who, not all that long ago, had been tearing out her hair on the riverbank?

"You must have been longing to slap my face, mustn't you? Oh, go ahead, admit it. I shouldn't have blamed you if you had."

I gave her one of those grim fishhooks-in-the-corners-of-the-mouth smiles, and turned my attention back to the open Bible.

Genesis . . . Exodus . . . Leviticus . . .

"Tell me you forgive me," she said, giving my arm a

tug. "The vicar and the constable advised me to come into the church and compose myself. Which is what I am attempting to do. But you must help me."

I tried to ignore her, but it was not easy.

"Here," she said, shoving a hand in my face. "Shake. I'm Poppy Mandrill. And who, pray tell, are you?"

"Titania Bottom," I replied, as I sometimes do when I'm annoyed.

The woman threw back her head and laughed—a surprisingly rich, warm, throaty laugh that flew up and joined the flitting notes of the organ.

"Come off it," she said. "I've directed enough Shakespeare in my time to know when my leg's being pulled."

She tapped her right knee—or at least, where her right knee ought to have been, but wasn't. I noticed for the first time that she was lacking a leg. Until now, the blanket in her lap had hidden the missing member.

"I—I'm sorry," I said, feeling like a chump.

"Don't be," she replied. "*I'm* not. It's curiously liberating, in a way. Oh, don't give me that look of pitying skepticism. I'm sick and tired of people looking at me like that. They don't know what to make of me. I may be lacking a leg but there's nothing wrong with my brain."

I had to admit to myself, grudgingly, that there was something in this woman I admired. I made a sudden decision and thrust out my hand.

"Flavia de Luce," I said, looking her in the eye as I gave her a firm old handshake to make up for my insolence.

"Tell me about Orlando," I went on, while our palms were still touching. "I feel so sorry for him."

She studied my face closely.

"And besides, I'm curious," I added.

"Fair enough," she said. "I believe you. Orlando was my . . . protégé."

An interesting word, that. I knew that it came from a French word meaning *to protect*. Feely's organ teacher, Mr. Collicutt, always referred to her as his protégé. At least, he always did before he was murdered.

But if Mr. Collicutt ever fancied he was protecting Feely from *anything*, he must have had the brains of a trilobite. My sister was born with the defensive instincts of a tiger shark.

No, there was another sense to the word, meaning a student, or pupil. That must be it.

"You were his teacher?" I asked.

Miss Mandrill sized me up before answering.

"In a sense, yes," she said at last.

I had learned some years ago by observing my friend Inspector Hewitt, of the Hinley Constabulary, that the best way to elicit further information is by keeping one's mouth firmly shut.

I said nothing—and by Jehoshaphat, it worked!

"Orlando was a very talented actor," she explained. "He might have become the greatest of our age—or of any other—had he lived. Another Gielgud—who knows? Perhaps even greater than Gielgud. He had the sensitivity and the steel combined: that precious alloy so lacking in so many of today's footlight trotters.

"All he lacked was opportunity, and now even that seems to have been snatched away from him."

By whom? I wondered grammatically. *By Fate?*

Or was Miss Mandrill suggesting that something much more sinister had taken place?

I thrust my face slightly forward to indicate intense interest.

"Well," she continued, giving her head a shake, "wherever he is now, he will be laughing at his own tragedy. That's how it's done, you know. *That* is the secret of true greatness."

She's right, I thought. I don't know how many times I've laughed aloud at the very thought of my own not inconsiderable talents.

I smiled modestly.

"And where do *you* suppose he is?" I asked, sneaking the question in under the wire, so to speak.

"Orlando?" She spoke his name with a little laugh. "Oh, he'll be perching on the edge of some mauve-tinged cloud, wiggling his toes, sipping a glass of absinthe, and chummying up to one of our more outré dead novelists. Ronald Firbank, or one of that lot."

"Not Shakespeare?" I asked, surprised.

"Shakespeare?" Miss Mandrill repeated, making a prune mouth. "Good lord, no! Orlando detested Shakespeare. 'High-blown muck,' he used to say. 'The lot of it. Like an explosion in a pigsty.'"

I couldn't help sucking in my breath. *Good thing Daffy isn't here,* I thought. She would have pulverized the woman for even repeating such sacrilege.

"I detect your disagreement," said Miss Mandrill. "It's written all over your face. Oh, well. I suppose there are people you can talk sense with, and others whom you can't."

How was I going to deal with this woman? One moment she was confiding in me like an old pal, and the next she was shooting at me with flaming arrows.

I couldn't afford to stalk off in "high dungeon," as Mrs. Mullet once put it, nor could I waste time playing on-again-off-again with such a wandering mind. It was like playing at bowls on a teeter-totter. Of course the woman was upset. Who wouldn't be to find their protégé dragged drowned from the drink and spread-eagled on a patch of grass?

"Had he any relatives?" I asked. "Anyone who ought to be informed?"

"Ha!" she barked.

And left it at that.

Feely by now had reached one of the quieter parts of *The Art of Fugue*, and the organ's notes, rather than flying and fluttering about, now roosted, whispering, up among the ancient timbers. In the near-silence, I heard the sound of approaching footsteps on the wooden floor.

And it wasn't the sidesmen bringing the collection plate to the altar rail.

It was the police.

"Constable Otter, miss," said an onion-scented voice at my ear. "A word outside, if you please."

I gave an eye-shrug to Miss Mandrill, crossed myself ostentatiously (you never knew), got to my feet, and followed the constable up the aisle and out into the sunshine, blinking madly at the glare.

I noted at once that the constable had had the good sense to come for me alone.

"Now then . . ." Constable Otter said, flipping open the pages of his notebook and licking the end of an indelible pencil, and I knew that I was, so to speak, home free.

·FOUR·

I CANNOT PRETEND THAT it was unpleasant to be questioned by the police. I had in the past become quite accustomed to occasional quiet chats with Inspector Hewitt: chats during which, as often as not, I was able to set the inspector straight on some of the finer points of chemistry and even, on one or two occasions, certain other matters as well.

Although I would have preferred to be grilled by the Detective Branch, I was nevertheless quite gracious to the uniformed Constable Otter. I put him at his ease at once.

"Ah! You've tracked me down at last," I said in an admiring voice. "Nothing like a mysterious death to liven up a lazy summer day, eh, Constable?"

I'd show him that I was an old hand at this sort of thing.

He gave me rather an odd squint. *Is it the sun?* I wondered. *Or have I misjudged the man?*

"Mysterious, miss?" the Constable asked.

Careful, Flavia! I thought. This man was quicker on the uptake than I had given him credit for.

"Well, you know what I mean," I improvised. "Drowned but not reported missing."

"And how do you know that?"

I could tell at once that Constable Otter was far from being the dullest blade in the drawer. In fact, I was already foreseeing great things for him in the future.

"By deduction," I said. "One would expect to find searchers on the banks, the river being dragged, and so forth."

Constable Otter scratched the tip of his chin with the point of his pencil. It left a small indigo mark, but I didn't point it out to him.

"Well, miss," he said, "I expect we ought to leave such deductions, as you call them, to the professionals: the chaps with the brains and the microscopes."

The constable was being witty, but I pretended not to notice.

He must have misread the look on my face, because he added: "A microscope, miss, in case you didn't know, is a device for magnifying small or minuscule objects. It makes a flea's eye look as broad as a barn."

Obviously, he did not realize that he was speaking to a person who had at home, in her own personal chemical laboratory, one of the finest binocular microscopes ever crafted by Ernst Leitz of Wetzlar, and that she bloody well knew how to use it! *Idiot!*

"No! *Really?*" I asked, letting the words writhe out of my mouth like a snake from a basket, and letting my jaw fall open the regulation three inches.

"Hmmm," he said, giving me that narrow look of his again. "Are *you* a professional, miss?"

His unexpectedly perceptive question caught me off guard.

"Well . . . yes," I said. "In a way, I suppose, you could say I am."

My reply was greeted with silence. This man had all the makings of a chief inspector. I'd better watch my step.

More important, I'd better get on the right side of him.

"You're very good at what you do, you know," I said.

Better not butter him up too much, though, I thought, *otherwise I might slip and fall on my face.*

He was giving me *that* look again, but I was saved from embarrassment by a cry from the water's edge.

"Constable! Constable Otter!"

It was the vicar and he was waving his arms in rather an unholy manner: more like a railway guard, I thought.

With great deliberation, Constable Otter returned his notebook and pencil to the breast pocket of his uniform. He was not a man to be stampeded.

With one last quizzing look at me, he turned and strode off purposefully along the path, his police boots crunching without mercy on the gravel.

Naturally, I followed. He had not instructed me to stay where I was.

Although our skiff was still at the riverbank, Dogger and Daffy were nowhere in sight. They must be still at the Oak and Pheasant, where Dogger would be doing his best to distract Daffy: to keep her mind—and eyes—away from the corpse. In spite of her steel-hard exterior, my sister was the tenderest of us all. She simply hated to show it.

When the cards were down, Daffy was always the first to fold. Anything truly gruesome, such as an arm or a leg broken in a tumble from a tree, or a toad speared on the tines of a garden fork, would reduce Daffy to a quivering, helpless jelly. The sight—or even the smell—of blood caused her to drop her dinner on the spot: as if her brain and belly were connected by a string.

But books were another matter. As long as it was only described in print, with no pictures, my sister could stomach anything.

Hadn't she read aloud to me with great enthusiasm, when I was still a child, the scene from *Crime and Punishment* in which Raskolnikov hacks two women to death with an ax? And she had positively burbled with delight at the death by pistol of Vladimir, in *Eugene Onegin*, in which his blood gushed, smoking, from the wound.

Books served Daffy as an insulation between the real world and her tender heart.

As for me, I was not like that at all. No, not in the least.

To me, an unexamined corpse was a tale untold: a knotted ball of a tale that was simply crying out to be unraveled until the last strand had been picked free. The fact that it was also a study in progressively putrid chem-

istry simply made it all that much more lively and interesting.

My point is that although there were obviously certain
similarities between Daffy and myself, there were also
insurmountable—in this life, at least—differences.

The vicar was still making wigwag signals with his
arms as I approached, just a few steps behind Constable
Otter.

"I thought you ought to see this," he was saying, holding out a sodden slipper.

It was red: a perfect match for the single one the corpse
was wearing.

"Where did you get this, then?" the constable demanded in rather a gruff voice. It had been my experience that the police do not like evidence to be discovered
by anyone but themselves.

"There," said the vicar, pointing a semi-accusing finger
at a rather ragamuffin lad who stood nearby beside the
wreckage of a sodden kite. I hadn't even noticed him.

"Hob Nightingale," the vicar said.

I turned my attention to this grubby child who was
staring attentively down at his oversized boots. Just a
couple of years younger than me, he might well have
been a porter at Covent Garden market; an orphan waif
from one of Daffy's Dickens novels. From his peaked cap
and baggy rumpled trousers, I knew at once that he almost certainly had an older brother—and no mother.

"What you starin' at, then?" he asked, looking up and
meeting my eye aggressively.

"Sorry," I said, and I meant it. I have a tendency to gawk when I'm fascinated.

He tossed his head and looked away. People who have been offended are entitled to a short sulk, as long as it doesn't drag on too long. I would have to wait a while to see if my apology had been accepted.

"Young Hob, here, was flying his kite," the vicar said. "A little gust brought it down among those reeds."

He pointed to a brackish bit of riverbank where a stretch of reeds and pondweed lined an indent in the river's course.

"Just over there," the vicar said, pointing.

"Floating, was it, the slipper?" Constable Otter asked. "In the water, like?"

The vicar nodded.

"And who fished it out, then?" the constable asked slyly.

"Why, I did," the vicar replied sheepishly, and I noticed for the first time that his trouser legs were rolled up to reveal a stretch of white ecclesiastical legs and a pair of fish-white feet. "Hob pointed it out. I waded in to retrieve it.

"He's just a child," he added. "I didn't want him to tumble in."

"I see," Constable Otter said, weighing the dripping slipper in his hand. "So you fished it out yourself? With your own hands?"

The vicar nodded meekly, and the constable, producing pad and pencil with the flourish of a stage magician, made a note in his book. There would be no catching out this stickler for detail at the inquest.

"Now then," the constable said, turning to the scowling Hob Nightingale. "What were you up to? No fibs, mind, else I'll tell your dad. He'll know what to do with you."

I blanched on the boy's behalf. I knew all too well what it felt like to be on the receiving end of a naked threat.

But I needn't have bothered.

"Go ahead and tell him. I don't care," Hob said, staring Constable Otter in the eye. "I wasn't doing anything wrong. Since when is it a crime to fly a kite?"

The constable was as taken aback as I was. He removed his helmet and scratched the back of his head with his pencil. I wondered idly if he'd placed an indelible mark up there, as well.

"Since when?" Hob persisted, his voice rising slightly: just enough to threaten a full-scale tantrum.

"Now then, little laddie," the constable said. "No need to get your nappies in a knot."

He turned to the vicar, expecting a smile at such rapier wit, but his little joke died on the vine. The vicar stared at him as blankly as if he were one of Einstein's equations on a blackboard.

"Well, then," Otter said. "Run along home now. If I need anything else, I know where to find you."

And suddenly I saw the way. As if the sun had popped out from behind a black cloud and lighted a path through the woods.

"I'll take him home," I said. "I can help carry his broken kite."

I almost stressed the word *broken*, but was able to suppress the urge before it passed my lips. I had spotted a shape beneath the rumpled paper that was certainly not part of the flying apparatus.

"You don't even know where I *live*," Hob protested.

"Never mind, sweetie," I said, hating myself as I said it. "You can show me the way. I'm a wizard with broken kites."

I bent and gathered up the soggy bundle of balsa wood, paper, and string (of which there seemed to be an exceptional mess), taking care to keep the object beneath it out of sight. As a safeguard, I wrapped the long tail of paper bows around my forearm to seal the bundle shut.

"Lead on, then, Hob," I said, in a mock dramatic voice.

Tossing his head up and his shoulders back, as if he were leading an army out of captivity in one of those stirring war films, Hob strode off through the churchyard, and I, with the shattered kite bundled awkwardly in my arms, followed him humbly.

No one would ever suspect me of removing evidence from the scene of a crime.

Hob did not so much as glance back at me. I might have been a mere servant carrying the train of his robe.

We made our way past the church, into the high street, and then into a narrow passageway that ran between a greengrocer's and an undertaker's. On the right was a brick wall and on the left a tall wooden fence.

"In here," Hob said, speaking for the first time since leaving the churchyard.

I stopped in my tracks, staring up at the painted sign on a weathered board above an open gate.

F. T. NIGHTINGALE, it read. FUNERALS ETC.

"Wait—" I said, but Hob shushed me with a finger raised to his lips.

"Keep it down," he whispered. "I don't want Da to hear us."

"Da?" I whispered back.

"My father," he said, pointing up to the sign. "The undertaker."

You could have knocked me over with an ostrich feather. It's not often that Fate deals you a winning hand, but I'd just been given four aces and a joker up my sleeve.

"The undertaker," I murmured. "Fancy that!"

"Nothing to be afraid of," Hob said, miming the words in an exaggerated manner with his lips.

"Are you sure?" I mimed back.

He did not reply, but, beckoning me with a curled fore-finger, led the way into the fenced area.

Inside was a broad cobbled courtyard and I found myself in another century. From the gas lamp above the back door of the premises to the cast-iron hitching posts, it was clearly a place where funerals had been marshaled before their procession to the graveyard.

I could imagine the black horses standing patiently as they were harnessed for the hearse, which would have been a shellacked and solemn thing on slender wooden wheels, with unnerving slabs of glass all the way round, so that those fortunate enough to be still alive could have a jolly good gawk at the coffin as they envisioned its grisly contents.

There would have been cockades attached, of black-dyed ostrich feathers, designed to ruffle in the breeze like the feathers of dead birds—which they were—to generate a primitive shudder in the spectators and remind them of their own mortality; there would have been mutes in tall black hats to pace numbly alongside the hearse and catch the eye of anyone they could, as if to say, "You! You there! Yes, you—You Who Might Be Next."

Oh, for the good old days, I thought, *when Death was an everyday equal and not to be padlocked away like some dimwitted relative whom nobody wanted to see or spend time with.*

Today, at the door where once the horses were persuaded not to prance, stood a rather elderly and down-at-the-heels motor hearse. An Austin, I noted, which had apparently served in a former life as a London taxicab.

Looking round, it was obvious to me that this courtyard was the rear of the undertaking premises and not meant for public viewing. Wooden coffin cases leaned heavily against the fence, and boxes full of empty bottles were stacked in every corner. *Embalming liquids,* I noted appreciatively.

I leaned over for a closer look at one of the weathered labels.

Aha! Just as I suspected: formaldehyde, mercury chloride, arsenious acid, with a pinch of good old sodium chloride (table salt) plus a couple of drops of thymol, oil of cinnamon, and oil of cloves, to mask the stink.

I recalled with a delicious shiver that arsenious acid, in the form of arsenic trioxide, is one of the deadliest of poisons, and is often used to dispatch rats.

"Hurry up!" Hob hissed.

He was standing in an open doorway fanning frantically with his hands. I followed eagerly.

I let out a low whistle. We were in a large workshop, at the far end of which was a raised loft or gallery. Coffins and parts of coffins in various stages of construction were everywhere: resting on wooden trestles, leaning against walls, piled in corners. Planes, hammers, saws, and chisels covered every level surface, and the air was sweet with the smell of sawdust and wood shavings.

To a girl of my interests, the place seemed like Heaven.

It was like being in on the Creation!

Hob was already halfway up the ladder that led to the loft.

"Up here," he said. "Hurry up. Hustle your bustle."

I obeyed, dragging myself unsteadily up, rung by rung, with the crumpled kite pressed against my bosom. I must have looked like an apprentice paperhanger.

Hob reached out a hand to help me up onto the platform.

Without any further ado, he took the crashed kite from my clutches and threw it into a corner, revealing a black and boxy object, which he placed carefully atop a highly polished coffin.

I gave the hard finish a couple of sharp taps with my fingernail. Shellac, dissolved in methylated spirits: a coffin of the highest quality. Certainly not one of the cheaper finishes of linseed oil and lampblack to which a bit of gold size in turpentine has been added.

This box was meant for someone important.

From my own personal experience I knew a thing or two about the various varnishes and their qualities. An emergency repair of a seventeenth-century refectory tabletop at Buckshaw—ruined by my roller-skating on its polished surface—had once needed to be completed and invisible before Father got home from London.

At the thought, a twinge touched my heart.

"I hope this camera's not busted," Hob said, "or Pippin's going to slaughter me when he comes home."

Pippin? Who was this Pippin? I wondered. I raised my eyebrows.

"My brother," he said. "He's a pilot. Photo reconnaissance. He's mapping northern Canada for the Geological Survey. He used to fly a Spitfire. It's *his* camera. I nicked it for an experiment."

I could see the pride in Hob's eyes as the words came bubbling out of his mouth.

Reflected in the polished gloss of the coffin, the camera had rather an unearthly look: a strange scientific instrument from another planet sent, perhaps, to spy with its single, ever-open, all-seeing eye upon our backward world.

And yet at the same time it was a perfectly ordinary Kodak Brownie Six-20. There were plenty of them about. Every tourist in every English village had one strapped around his or her neck, clicking away madly here and there at every quaint cottage, every tithe barn, and every duck on every village green.

But this camera was different. A tiny hole had been drilled in the shutter release lever, to which had been fastened a length of fishing line that passed through a couple of small brass rings attached to the side of the camera.

"Have you got it worked out yet?" Hob demanded, hopping from one foot to the other with excitement.

"It's a cable release," I said. "A kind of remote control."

"Aerial photography!" he exploded, unable to contain himself any longer. "I knocked it together myself. Do you like it?"

"Extraordinary," I said, feeling much older than my actual years.

"Altogether ripping!" I added, more for my own benefit than for Hob's.

Hob fairly basked in the glow of my approval and I knew in that moment that he hadn't many friends.

"I have an idea," I said. "Let's take the film to the chemist's to be developed. I'll put it in my name and you can put your brother's camera back wherever you found it. That way, he'll never know you even pinched it."

"You're brilliant!" Hob said, and I had to agree.

A few moments later, the roll was in my pocket, along with my handkerchief and whatever remained of the fluids from the lungs of the late Orlando.

As I was giving myself a mental pat on the back, a door at the end of the loft swung silently open and a man dressed entirely in black came into the room. He must have moved on oiled castors, I thought. Even my keen hearing had not detected his approach.

He seemed almost as surprised to see us as we were to see him.

"Hob!" he said. "What are you doing here? I thought you were out playing. And who's this you've brought home?"

I saved Hob the trouble of explaining. Stepping forward in the most ladylike manner I could summon up, I offered him my hand and gave him a firm shake.

Remarkably strong, I thought, *for an undertaker.* And yet an undertaker had to be capable—when you got right down to it—of manhandling bodies as if they were so many sacks of potatoes.

His suit was clean but shabby, the cuffs slightly frayed. *From rubbing against so many coffins,* I thought. An honest workingman.

"I'm Flavia de Luce, sir," I said. "Hob had a bit of a prang with his kite and I helped him get it home."

"I'm much obliged to you, Miss de Luce," he said. "Most grateful."

He extracted an old-fashioned pocket watch from his waistcoat, glanced at it, and said: "But now you must excuse me. I'm afraid I have some rather urgent business to attend to, and—"

I knew what he was referring to even before he finished speaking.

Orlando! It had to be Orlando!

What else could be so urgent in a small town on a lazy summer afternoon? How many deaths were likely to come to light within the space of a single hour?

I fancied myself something of an expert on that topic. I knew, for instance, that most deaths in quiet country towns were due to old age, and that most of the elderly, when their time was up, tended to die quietly in the night and be discovered before breakfast.

Deaths in the afternoon, on the other hand, were much more likely to be due to causes such as heart attacks among hardworking farmers, or road accidents involving young drivers with an appetite for alcohol and speed.

There were other factors, of course, but these were the most likely.

"Of course, sir," I said, offering another shake. "It's been most pleasant to meet you."

Pleasant! You genius, Flavia! Even old Peter Mark Roget, the thesaurus boffin, couldn't have come up with a better word himself. Not in a hundred years. Not in an eon!

Mr. Nightingale adjusted his widower's cuffs, and I knew I'd been approved.

But just to make sure, I added: "I know you're extremely busy, sir, but I wanted to compliment you on your French polishing."

I touched the gleaming coffin lid with appreciative fingertips.

"I noticed by the bottles in the courtyard that you use shellac and methylated spirits. I love the luster it gives."

I caressed the highly polished wood.

Mr. Nightingale straightened his tie.

"Sometime, when you have a minute, sir, you must give me your views on the use of bullens as an ornamental device. I realize there's a great deal of controversy—especially in Dissenting parishes—but . . ."

I allowed my words to trail off.

Bullens were the square-headed brass nails beloved of undertakers who wished to make a bit of easy profit at little expense. I had read up on them with great interest in *Coffins and Coffin Making,* a well-thumbed copy of which was kept on a high shelf in the Bishop's Lacey Free Library.

I excused my boldness by forcing a slight but pretty blush, which isn't as easy as it sounds. It's a matter of holding one's breath while forcing air from the lungs toward the head without appearing to do so.

"I am flattered, Miss de Luce," the undertaker said. "Perhaps another time."

I inclined my head graciously and gave him a coy smile. It was jolly good luck I didn't have a fan in my hand!

Had he clicked his heels together, or was it my imagination?

At any rate, he was suddenly, smoothly, and gracefully gone, just as you would expect from someone of his standing.

"What a lovely man your father is, Hob," I remarked. He was grinning from ear to ear.

"Now then," I told him, dropping my duchess pose. "Let's go find out what's on that film."

·FIVE·

FORTUNATELY, THE CHEMIST'S SHOP was in the opposite direction from the church, so we were at little risk of
running into anyone I knew. It simply wouldn't do to be
stopped and ordered about by the police, although even
that would have been better than coming face-to-face
with Feely or Daffy.

Feely! I had completely forgotten about her. I had
walked out of the church with Constable Otter, and left
my sister producing a Niagara of notes on the church
organ. For all I knew, she might still be at it. Old Johann's
Art of Fugue, uninterrupted, could run on for as long as an
hour and a quarter, especially if my sister was upset and
had recently eaten.

"Musick has charms to sooth a savage breast," William Congreve had once written, in his play *The Mourning Bride*.

"'Musick *and* chicken sandwiches,' he ought to have said," Daffy once remarked as Feely had stormed away from the dinner table and taken refuge in one of the most beautiful and heart-wrenching of the piano sonatas by Beethoven.

"Did you say you were going to pay for this?" Hob asked, interrupting my thoughts.

"Yes," I told him. "But let's hurry before I change my mind."

If we cracked on with the film processing, I might be able to get back to the church and slip into a pew before Feely even noticed I was gone.

"What's the hurry?" Hob asked, shooting me a most penetrating look.

"Nothing really," I told him, biting my tongue. "It's just that I'm awfully keen on aerial photos. I haven't laid eyes on a good old aerophoto in simply ages. They used to print tons of them in *The Illustrated London News*, but that was before the war. Nobody gives a tinker's curse about them nowadays. Except you, of course—and me."

I shot him a beaming smile and he beamed back.

The chemist's was next door to a butcher's shop in the high street. WANLESS & SONS DISPENSING CHEMISTS, it said in peeling black and gold above the door and on the little bow window, in which were displayed two glass globes of tired-looking colored water.

A bell tinkled brightly as we stepped into a dim, cramped Aladdin's cave of bottles, flasks, tins, bags, and boxes. There was barely enough space in the place to turn around, and it smelled of sulfur; of lavender and mint; of bath salts and smelling salts; of licorice and aloes and *nux vomica;* of castor oil and oil of cloves (for toothache).

The atmosphere, I realized with a sudden start, was that of a sickroom—but the sickroom of a patient who had quite recently departed this life.

I didn't want to think about it.

Behind an arched wire wicket, the chemist, tall, thin, and white-jacketed like a London tearoom attendant, didn't bat an eye as I handed over the film.

"Prints?" he asked, his pencil poised.

"One of each," I told him.

"Name?"

"Flavia de Luce," I said. There was no point in lying about it.

"Are you from our neighborhood, Miss de Luce?" he asked.

"We're staying at the Oak and Pheasant," I said, "but we're expecting to leave tomorrow. Do you think they'll be ready by then?"

This was pure invention. I had no idea when we were leaving, but I wanted the prints as soon as possible.

The chemist frowned.

"I can't promise anything. We process every day except Sundays, of course. But this is our busiest time of year . . ."

He didn't say "because of the tourists" but I knew that's what he meant.

I formed my mouth into a little pout to indicate that I might take my business elsewhere.

"Sometimes," the chemist added reluctantly, "they're ready the same day, but only rarely. We're rushed off our feet this time of year, you know."

I put on a guilty look, as if it were all my fault.

He stared at me intently for a moment and then, as if having come to some momentous decision, turned away and began to paw with his right foot at the wooden floorboards, as if he were a maddened bull who had just spotted the matador in the ring.

"Howland!" he shouted in a new and alarmingly loud voice, quite unlike the one in which he had been speaking to me. "When can you do a roll of six-twenty?"

Howland, whoever he was, must be remarkably hard of hearing.

From under the floor there came an angry subterranean grumble, as if the gods of the underworld were suffering badly from indigestion.

I could not make out any of the words.

I peered round the edge of the wicket at which I was standing. Sure enough, there was a trapdoor beneath the chemist's feet. The invisible Howland must have his photo darkroom in the cellar.

"In due course," the chemist said, turning back to me.

"Thank you," I replied, baring my teeth and rewarding him with a full-on but well-chosen grin from my inner grab bag of smiles.

"I know you'll do your best," I said, and somehow I knew that he would.

Outside in the high street I said my goodbyes to Hob.

"I must get back," I said, "otherwise my sister will be frantic. She worries about me too much. You know how it is."

A little untruth never hurt a casual acquaintance.

Hob nodded and made off along the high street.

Only after he was gone did I realize how few words he had spoken.

As I walked back toward the church I heard the unmistakable sound of a hurdy-gurdy. Was it a wandering organ grinder with his monkey? I wondered. A "peripatetic pest," as Daffy would call him?

My question was quickly answered as I came to a short passageway on the left side of the street. Through a brick archway was a cobbled lane that led to an open space beyond which were fields. I knew by the ancient stone cross and cattle troughs that this was the town marketplace, now taken over by a small traveling fair.

A canvas banner announced that this was SHADRACH'S CIRCUS & MENAGERIE: THE GRANDEST LITTLE SHOW ON EARTH.

The music was coming from a small merry-go-round, its gaudy horses, pigs, griffins, and a single (but fierce) fire-breathing dragon spinning endlessly in the warm summer sunshine. There were no more than a handful of small riders astride these handsome beasts, and one of those, a red-faced little chap, was holding on for dear life and wailing for his mother.

Nearby, a bored-looking elephant, shackled at the leg, munched half-heartedly on a mound of hay.

Arranged round the four sides of the market square

were the usual stalls: a coconut pitch and a pieman, a ring-toss, and an Aunt Sally. Directly across from these was a shooting gallery, with flying mechanical ducks, grouse, partridges, and a leftover portrait of Neville Chamberlain flying jerkily across a crudely painted landscape. Someone had painted a happy grin on Chamberlain's exhausted-looking face with lipstick.

Beyond, in a row of side stalls, were games of Crown and Anchor, Under and Over, and, in spite of the ban on casino games at village fairs, a surprisingly large illuminated roulette wheel. A hand-lettered sign on a stick said No Children Please.

For the little ones, there was a fishpond with magnetic hooks to pull worthless trinkets from a cellophane "pool."

"Hello there!" someone said behind me, and I spun round to find myself face-to-face with one of the men I had seen in the pub. The largest one. I recognized him by his polka-dot kerchief.

"Haven't we met before?" he asked. "Your face is familiar."

I knew better than to fall for a line like that. Daffy had coached me in dealing with strange men who claim that you have a familiar face. Her instructions ranged from the sharp retort and rapid departure all the way up to a swift kick in the colonies.

"You have to show them you mean business," Daffy had said.

I shook my head and turned away. But the man was not so easily discouraged. He shuffled round in front of me, blocked my way, and held out a roll of colored tickets.

"Take a chance on the Lucky Draw," he coaxed. "Sixpence each, six for a shilling. What could be fairer than that?"

"Go away," I said quite loudly. That was Step A.

"Come on," he persisted. "You look like a sport—a girl who likes to take a chance."

"Go away," I repeated. That was Step B.

"Can't win if you don't enter," he said, going into a faint whine.

Step C was not to be executed unless the man physically laid hands upon you, but if he did—even so much as a finger—he was fair game.

"I'm warning you—" I said.

A hand touched my upper arm. I swung round, spotted my target, and—

"Let's go, Flavia," Hob said, tugging at my sleeve. "You can buy me a candy floss."

I had come within an ace of flattening him. Had the little dickens been following me?

I gave him a raised eyebrow.

"You know as well as I do that sweets are still rationed."

"I *do* know that as well as you do"—Hob grinned—"but I have a ration book."

And so it was that the two of us, our faces covered with cobwebs of pink sugar, strolled back into the high street, licking our chops like butcher shop cats, and wiping our sticky fingers on the leaves of overhanging trees.

Gorging on sweets together creates as strong a bond between two people as being in love. Or so it seems to me, although I've never been in love. Nor am I much accustomed to sugar. The war had seen to that.

And yet, walking along with Hob, both of us inhaling spun sucrose like a pair of jet engines, we became, almost instantly, old pals.

"How does it feel to have an undertaker for a father?" I asked.

It was a question I had been dying to ask him since the moment we met; a question to which, for some strange reason, I desperately required an answer.

"Do you really want to know?"

"Of course I do," I said, picking strands of pink fiber off my chin. "It's the kind of thing that interests me. I wish *my* father had been in the trade."

"Wasn't he?" Hob asked.

"No. At least not directly."

I was thinking of Father's wartime service, when he and Dogger had been shipped out to the Far East in order to dispatch foreigners to an early grave.

"Anyway," I said, pulling myself back into the moment, "you haven't answered my question."

Hob shrugged.

"Well," he said, "they tease me about it at school."

"I'd rip their hearts out," I said, suddenly fiercely defensive of this tiny creature.

"Oh, I don't mind," Hob said. "Da says that life is full of death, and that it's better to make friends with it than fight it."

Oh! The wisdom of the man!

It was as if the heavens had suddenly opened and a disembodied arm had handed down to me the Secret of the Universe, scribbled on a slip of wrinkled paper.

A weight had been lifted from my shoulders: a weight of which I hadn't been aware until it was gone.

I wanted to hug someone. I wanted to burst into glorious song.

"Hmmm," I said. "Yes. I suppose that's one way of looking at it."

I hadn't noticed until now that Hob had stopped strolling and begun cantering. Yes, *cantering!*

It seemed as if a little of my elation had rubbed off on him.

"What do you know about Poppy Mandrill?" I asked suddenly.

In my experience, it is often a bolt from the blue that shakes loose the biggest avalanche.

"Everyone's afraid of her," Hob replied, without batting an eye.

"Everyone?"

"Well, I'm not, of course," Hob said, jutting his chin out. "But I only know her to see her."

I couldn't resist.

"Then how do you know everyone's afraid of her?"

"Because I keep my ears open," Hob said. "At funerals."

I realized at once, of course, that I had, almost accidentally, tapped into a vast reservoir. If there's one place where people speak with unguarded tongues, it's at a funeral. Emotion—and especially grief—loosens tongues even more than alcohol.

I'll bet there have been more truths told over an open coffin than in all the confession boxes in Christendom.

"Do you really?" I asked admiringly.

Hob fairly preened.

"Mrs. Perry said that to Mrs. Belaney at old Mr. Arkwright's funeral. As soon as Poppy Mandrill came into the room, everybody moved away from her—as if she had the Black Plague or something."

"Perhaps it was respect?" I suggested.

"Phah!" Hob said. "They were afraid of her. Mrs. Perry leaned over and whispered to Mrs. Belaney: 'They're all afraid of that—'

"I'm not allowed to say the next word, but you must know the one I mean. I heard it with my own ears."

"You're a very clever lad, Hob," I said, and he nearly burst into flames.

"I knew it!" he said, hugging himself. "I knew it!"

"Well, you are," I assured him. "What else have you heard? About Poppy Mandrill, I mean. We can get to the others later."

"She's with the Puddle Lane Little Theatre." Hob rolled his eyes as if I would understand. "They put on plays in the Town Hall. Pantomimes at Christmas. You know."

I did indeed. We suffered in much the same way at Bishop's Lacey with the same kind of dreary and awkward—but compulsory—comedies.

But why on earth would the dead Orlando be dressed for a Christmas pantomime? It was June, for goodness' sake! Rehearsals wouldn't even begin for months, and as for *dress rehearsals*—well, they were simply out of the question at this time of year.

"Is anyone holding a masquerade?" I asked.

"I don't know that word," Hob said.

"A masquerade? A dress-up party. Costumes. Highwaymen, for instance. Gents in powdered wigs, ladies in silk dresses like tents at the fête, and black beauty spots stuck on their cheeks."

"Ugh," Hob said. "Doesn't sound very beautiful to me. I've never heard of such a thing."

"Why are they afraid of Poppy Mandrill?" I asked, trying to get my line of questioning back onto the track.

"She's bossy," Hob said. "Always giving people orders."

"Isn't that what a theater director is supposed to do?" I asked, only half seriously.

"Not in church!" Hob exclaimed, his eyes widening and his hackles rising visibly.

"Did you actually see that happen?" I asked.

Hob nodded several times to make his point. "Only once," he said. "She shouted out at the vicar, right in the middle of his sermon."

"Good lord!" I blurted. Even *I* wouldn't have dared such sacrilege. "Do you remember what she said?"

"She said 'Cut the cackle, Vicar. I've a train to catch.'"

"Was this on Palm Sunday, by any chance?" I asked. "About three months ago?"

"How did you know that?" Hob asked. "We all had our

The GRAVE'S a FINE and PRIVATE PLACE · 77

palm fronds in our hands. Lizzy Pleasance tried to strangle me with hers. I took mine home and made a straw soldier out of it."

I couldn't help wondering idly what Hob would have thought if I'd told him I usually twisted my own annual palm frond into a hangman's noose.

Actually, naming the date was a brilliant bit of deduction on my part. I knew by bitter experience that the Palm Sunday morning service was the longest in *The Book of Common Prayer*. The Gospel was taken from Matthew, chapter 27.

Which, as I recalled, ran more than a thousand words. I knew this because I had counted them, one by one, following with my index finger, as our own vicar, Denwyn Richardson, had read them aloud on several Palm Sundays, back home in Bishop's Lacey.

"You lot are getting off easily," he had told us at Confirmation class. "Had you been unfortunate enough to have lived in about 1550, in the time of King Edward the Sixth—who died at the age of fifteen . . . younger than you, there, Ted Pullymore . . . yes, you, Ted . . . and who died coughing up green, black, and pink matter, leading some to believe he had been poisoned—you'd have had to sit still three times longer than we do nowadays. In those days, the Gospel reading for Palm Sunday combined Matthew chapters 26 *and* 27, and would have lasted somewhere between twenty minutes and half an hour. Fortunately, the many editors of *The Book of Common Prayer*, in their wisdom, took mercy upon our poor, aching sitters and slashed the reading substantially."

That's what I loved about Denwyn Richardson: He simply oozed history.

"And what about the dead man?" I asked Hob. "Orlando. Did you know him?"

"Orlando?" Hob snorted noisily. "Everybody knew Orlando."

"Everybody except me," I said. "I don't even know his last name."

"Whitbread," Hob said. "Orlando Whitbread. His father used to be the rector of St.-Mildred's-in-the-Marsh."

Whitbread?

You could have knocked me over with a bit of goose down.

"Canon Whitbread?" I asked. "Not *Canon* Whitbread? Not the one who—"

"Choked on a rope?" Hob said. "Yes, that's the one. I helped Daddy embalm him."

· S I X ·

WHAT CAN YOU POSSIBLY say to a child who has helped
his father pump preservatives into the carotid artery of a
hanged murderer?

Precious little, I discovered. There are no words suitable for the occasion; no words to convey my shock, my
awe, my admiration, or my jealousy.

"Are you surprised?" Hob asked. "You seem surprised."

"Not at all," I said, leaping madly aboard the opportunity. "Tell me about it."

"You look surprised," Hob persisted.

"All right, then. I'm surprised. Astonished. Flabbergasted, in fact. Tell me about it."

"Perhaps when I know you better," Hob said.

Where did this little lad get his spunkiness from? What
crazy corner of the universe animated his mind?

"All right," I said. "I don't mind. I'm really not all that interested anyway."

Hob said nothing, but gave me a look that suggested I'd just been caught poaching his father's chickens.

If undertakers, in fact, *had* chickens. I could think of various reasons why they might and might not keep poultry, none of them suitable for discussion with anyone other than the most confidential friends. And even then . . .

But before I could stop him, Hob was loping off toward home.

"Farewell," he called back over his shoulder.

Had I scared him off by being too familiar?

Well, no matter.

But I didn't think of the obvious question until he had already disappeared round a corner.

"Hob! Wait!" I called, but he didn't hear me. Or pretended not to.

I could have run after him, but there was no time. *Never mind*, I decided, *there will be other opportunities*.

Meanwhile, Feely, Daffy, and Dogger would already be worrying about me. Or would they? I could never quite be sure.

In any case, I needn't have bothered. By the time I got back to the church, Feely was still lost in *The Art of Fugue*, which was now nearing its end—or what passed as its end, since J. S. Bach had never finished the thing. At the point where he had abruptly given it up, Bach had noted on the manuscript that, at this point, the composer had died. Which was, Daffy said, a colossal joke that no one had yet spotted: that somewhere up among the stars, Bach was still waiting for someone to laugh.

I gave a quiet chuckle at the thought, and old Johann Sebastian, from somewhere beyond Pluto, raised two fingers and gave me the "V for Victory" sign.

Dogger and Daffy were sitting side by side in a back pew, eyes closed, hands folded on tummies like a pair of well-fed pigeons on a ledge at Westminster Abbey, listening contentedly to the music.

I slid in quietly beside them, and although Dogger opened the corner of one eye, Daffy may as well have been somewhere in the far-off Fiji Islands.

I walked my fingers slowly and quietly across the pew as if they were a hump-backed spider.

With my forefinger, I tapped out a message in code on the back of Dogger's hand: a quick touch for a dot and a long touch for a dash. Jolly good thing I had been forced to learn the Morse system at Miss Bodycote's, in Canada.

Dot-dash-dash-dot, dot-dash-dot, dash-dash-dash, and so forth, until I had spelled out the letters *P-R-O-G-R-E-S-S.*

For just a fraction of a moment I thought he hadn't got it, but then I saw his head incline by about a sixty-fourth of an inch. If you hadn't known Dogger, you'd have sworn he hadn't budged.

Now his hand was lightly touching mine: *E-X-C-E-L-L-E-N-T,* his fingers tapped.

A warm glow came over me, and I hoped I wasn't flushing. I sneaked a glance at Dogger, but his eyes were still closed. How noble he looked! How like a god.

The Art of Fugue ended abruptly as I knew it would: cut off in mid-flight—just like Orlando Whitbread.

And, come to think of it, just like his father, late of St.-Mildred's-in-the-Marsh.

As the music came to a stop, the organ made the usual little dying noises as the air left its lungs. Somewhere behind the tall ornamental pipes, leather bellows collapsed, and all the tiny tin and wooden arteries, deprived of wind, wheezed into a restless silence.

For a moment, the three of us, Daffy, Dogger, and I, sat in that uneasy vacuum that always comes into existence when the music ends, each one of us reluctant to be the first to speak.

In the end, it was me.

"We'd better get back to the Oak and Pheasant," I said. "We'll need to book rooms. I don't expect we'll be going home until further notice."

"Those arrangements are already seen to, Miss Flavia," Dogger said. "I shall go fetch the car."

We had left the Rolls parked a short distance up the river at the boat rental establishment.

"Good old Dogger," I said, patting his hand. "You are the one fixed point in a changing age."

He smiled and vanished.

"Sherlock Holmes," Daffy said, her eyes popping open. "'His Last Bow.' 'There's an east wind coming all the same, such a wind as never blew on England yet. It will be cold and bitter, Watson, and a good many of us may wither before its blast.'"

Even though she was quoting from memory, Daffy's

words shook me to the core. I was seized with a sudden crawling chill. Instead of the word "England," she might have said "such a wind as never blew on *us*," *us* meaning the de Luce family.

With Father's death, the blight had already begun. This happy holiday was no more than the gentle and deceiving slope at the lip of the pit.

There was a clatter behind us on the stone steps, and Feely appeared.

"Come along, slugs," she said, meaning Daffy and me. "I'm famished."

Feely was like that. She could switch her attention from Gregorian chant to the state of her own gut in half of a horsefly's heartbeat.

I had come to realize that I simply didn't understand my older sister, and I never would.

As we came out of the church, I noticed that Orlando's body had been removed from the riverbank. Constable Otter was nowhere in sight. Nor was Miss Mandrill.

A cluster of women in housedresses stood on—or close to—the spot where Orlando had until lately lain leaking into the grass. Even at this distance, and against the wind, I could hear the sound of their magpie chatter.

Back at the inn, we found that our rooms had already been assigned. Feely was to be given the best bedroom: a low-timbered chamber at the front of the building, which faced the church and in which, or so it was said, Queen Elizabeth I had slept on one of her many Progresses round her kingdom.

"Is there a single bedroom in all of England in which

she didn't?" Daffy asked sourly, but the landlord, who was accustomed to such impertinence, shot back:

"Yes. Mine."

Daffy had the good grace to laugh, although I knew her well enough to recognize that it was insincere.

Daffy had been given a cozy little chamber, up one step on the west side of the building, which, in the days of Good Queen Bess, had been a small country house.

"Longer daylight for reading," she said.

Although she had spotted a small library, which was little more than a couple of shelves banged together halfway up the stairs, she had written it off at a glance.

"Anthony Hopeless," she said. "Ouida . . . Sabatini . . . Michael Arlen . . . Rider Haggard . . . and not so much as a single scribble by the Divine Charles."

Meaning Dickens, of course, to whom she had constructed a small shrine in her bedroom at Buckshaw. Before coming away on our holiday, I had suggested she have the whole setup mounted on an oxcart as they did with their portable altars in the Middle Ages.

"We can tow it behind the Rolls," I told her. "Think how handy it would be to have the whole lot of it: portrait of the Divine Charles, candles, snuffers, incense, first editions of *Bleak House* and *The Pickwick Papers* all right there at your fingertips in case you suffer withdrawal symptoms."

Whereupon I had been driven from the breakfast table in a hail of bath buns, which, considering that they had been baked by Mrs. Mullet, was a good deal more life-threatening than it sounds.

As for me, I was to be quartered in a tiny room at the rear of the inn, which had once, the landlord assured me, been a small minstrel's gallery.

"Don't worry if you hear strange voices singing in the night," he told me in a confidential tone. "They're mostly harmless—even though the last lady wot heard 'em went stark mad," he added, dropping into a dialect stage whisper, "an' 'ad to be put in a straitjacket!"

I ignored him.

A glance out of the narrow single window told me that the only voices I was likely to hear would be those of the old gaffers sitting round the trestle tables in the sunken garden with their tankards of ale.

I raised the flyblown Holland blind to let more light into this murky chamber.

The furnishings were sparse, to say the least: a small bed complete with a chamber pot, a cheap wooden table with ewer and pitcher, a safety lamp with candle and glass chimney—presumably for emergencies in the night—a chair that was straight out of a painting by Vincent van Gogh, a sink that had seen goodness-knows-what, a hot plate and tin kettle, and an oval mirror with yellowed glass.

Dogger was already back, bringing with him my small traveling case from the Rolls. Unlike Daffy, who had insisted on dragging along a wooden packing case containing *The Works of Charles Dickens,* complete in twenty-six fat, red, heavy leather-bound volumes, I had brought only the bare necessities: a toothbrush, and Taylor's *Principles and Practice of Medical Jurisprudence.* In order to keep down the weight, I had selected only the second volume of that great work: the one containing the poisons.

I waited until the landlord, with his hand-rubbing ghost stories, was out of earshot, and even then, I closed the door.

"Dogger," I asked, "where do they bury executed murderers?"

"Well, Miss Flavia," he said, "that depends upon the times. In the eighteenth century, they were sometimes left hanging on the gibbet. The birds took care of the rest."

I gave a delicious shiver at the thought.

"Some were buried at a crossroads," Dogger went on, "as were suicides, until the practice was abolished by an Act of Parliament in the 1820s."

"Why a crossroads?" I asked.

"It was believed that the meeting of four ways would reduce the chance of the ghost finding its way back home."

"And nowadays?" In my excitement, I could hardly get the question out.

"Nowadays," Dogger replied, "the bodies of executed murderers are the property of the Crown. They are buried in perforated coffins in unmarked graves within the precincts of the prison in which their sentence was carried out."

"Not handed over to the family? Not turned over to the undertaker?"

"Not unless directed otherwise by the sheriff of the

county," Dogger answered. "Once buried, exhumation requires a formal license from the Home Office, which must be signed personally by the Home Secretary. Although I understand that this is frowned upon, and would be granted in only the most extraordinary circumstances."

My mind was floundering to stay afloat.

Unless Hob was a downright liar, it was simply not possible for him to have been present at the embalming of Canon Whitbread.

In the first place, if the canon had been hanged at one of His Majesty's prisons, the body would not have been embalmed. A perforated coffin could mean only one thing: that the speediest possible decomposition was desired. Embalming would only prolong it.

Which left only a handful of possibilities: that the body of the hanged canon had been turned over to the family after execution but before burial, upon receipt of a direct order from the sheriff; that the body on Mr. Nightingale's slab had not been Canon Whitbread; or that Canon Whitbread had not, in fact, been executed.

I couldn't contain my excitement.

"Where was Canon Whitbread buried?" I asked.

"Ah," said Dogger. "That is the question, is it not? We shall have to find that out."

We! Dogger and me. The two of us, on the case together.

My heart began to glow like a potbellied woodstove in a logger's cabin.

"Where shall . . . we . . . begin?" I managed to say.

"With the parishioners of St. Mildred's," Dogger answered. "It is a fact often overlooked by the law that when it comes to murder, the parishioners know all the answers."

"Did you say *murder*, Dogger?"

"I did indeed."

Now, suddenly, I was glowing like the midsummer sun. Dogger had—independently—come to the same conclusion I had.

"We mustn't discuss specific details," I whispered. "In order not to contaminate each other's evidence."

"Of course," Dogger agreed. "I was about to say the same thing myself, Miss Flavia."

I let out a long, noisy breath—a hiss of almost serpent pleasure.

The murderer of Orlando Whitbread was doomed. From that very moment, he hadn't the chance of a snowman in Hades to escape the team of Dogger and De Luce.

I desperately wanted to rub noses with my new partner but I didn't dare. Eskimo kisses would have to wait until we were more firmly established.

"And now, miss," Dogger said, turning to my single piece of luggage, "shall we unpack the poisons?"

· S E V E N ·

THE "POISONS" TO WHICH Dogger referred were those discussed in the fat blue volume of Taylor's *Medical Jurisprudence*, in its Ninth Edition, which I believe I have already mentioned.

"Sorry for the weight," I said, as Dogger hoisted my suitcase onto the bed. I knew perfectly well that mine was nothing compared with the oxcart of books dear Daffy had dragged along. I trusted that, in Dogger's mind, I would seem thoughtful by comparison.

"'A good book,'" he said, squaring up the heavy volume reverently on the bedside table, "'is the precious lifeblood of a master spirit, embalmed and treasured up on purpose to a life beyond life.'

"Or so, at least, says Mr. Milton in his *Areopagitica*," he added.

I nodded wisely in agreement, even though I wasn't

quite sure who Mr. Milton was, what he meant by the remark, or what his *Areopagitica* might happen to be.

Still, any quotation with the word *embalmed* in it can never be a bore.

"Dogger," I said, "what do you think—"

But Dogger stuck up a warning hand, palm toward me: the universal symbol for "Hush!"—or perhaps "Shut up!"

I shut up.

Incredibly, I had not heard the footsteps on the stairs outside. Fortunately, Dogger had.

"I shall find a tackle shop, Miss Flavia," he said, keeping his hand in the air, "and some suitable rods. If we are to be detained for a day or two in order to assist Constable Otter, I am quite confident there can be no harm in a bit of fishing."

On the last word, he gave me a broad wink, and I had to clap a hand over my mouth to keep from giggling.

"Oh, must we?" I said, falling into the role as Jean Simmons might have done. "I *detest* fishing."

"I daresay," Dogger replied with a poker-straight face, "that you will feel quite differently when you catch something."

I hugged myself with delight. *This* was living! The shadows of the past six months—at least most of them—vanished at the prospect of . . .

Well, I wasn't quite sure what, but reeling in a murderer would certainly keep our minds occupied.

"I suppose you're right," I said, trying to inject unwillingness into my voice, but even as I spoke, Dogger was moving slowly and silently toward the door. When he reached it, he seized the knob and gave it an easy, fluid twist.

"Oh, Mrs. Palmer!" he said. "You startled me. I didn't realize you were here."

You old fox, I thought. *You clever old fox!*

"Oh, Mr. Dogger," the landlord's wife said. "I was just about to say the same. We've gone and startled one *another,* haven't we? I was just coming up to see if anything was required."

Another old fox, I thought. Or, rather, *Another old vixen.*

I was keenly aware that I was watching two Old Masters at work.

"Nothing, thank you," Dogger said, pretending to brush a fleck of dust from the suitcase.

"And you, dearie?" Mrs. Palmer asked, fixing me with the most awful, leering counterfeit grin. "Anything to make you comfy?"

I had once made a solemn pledge to flay alive and use their skin for a horse blanket the next person who dared to call me "dearie."

Her awful word hung in the stale bedroom air. And then:

"Just a bit of quiet, thank you," I heard my mouth saying. "I have the most awful headache."

It was the first time in my life I had ever used this Neanderthal excuse but I knew, even as I said it, why at least two thousand generations of females have employed those very words—or, at least, their equivalent—in whatever language they may have spoken.

As an argument, the phrase was unassailable: a conversational stone wall. Who, for instance, could ever prove you hadn't one?

As a sword shrouded in velvet—a gentle weapon—it was probably unequaled.

Six simple words, of which all but two were of a single syllable, and yet which fairly oozed accusation: "*I have the most awful headache.*"

I knew that it was unfair: a cheat, a deceit, and—well, why not put it plainly?—a lie.

At the same time, I rejoiced in knowing that it had wandered in from some distant room in my brain.

"I shall be all right," I said. "It's just . . . just . . . the . . . shock of . . ."

I let my voice trail off into nothingness.

Flavia! You fibber!

"There, there, dearie," Mrs. Palmer said. "I understand. I've been taken that way myself on many an occasion."

There was that word again.

I had somehow to restrain myself.

In my mind, I pulled from my pocket a needle and a reel of fishing line. I imagined popping the end of the tough black fiber into my mouth to moisten it, then squinting as I pushed it through the eye of the needle, which I shoved in through my lower lip, out through my upper lip, pulled it tight, followed with another loop—and another—and another. When I was finished, my mouth looked like one of those stitched-up shrunken heads that are brought back by explorers from the Amazonian jungle.

I was proud of my handiwork. Against all odds, I had managed to keep my mouth shut.

Mrs. Palmer was giving me what I believe is called a quizzical look.

Shoo! I told her with my mind. *Buzz off! Go away! Vanish! Vamoose! Get lost! Take a powder!*

And, by the jawbone of Jupiter, it worked!

Mrs. Palmer blinked.

"I'd best be getting back, then, if there's nothing I can do," she said, dusting her hands as if to signal she was finished with me.

"Thank you, Mrs. Palmer," Dogger said, and I thought I heard a muffled "humph" as she clumped noisily down the stairs.

"Back to the poisons," I said when she was gone and the door was firmly shut.

"Back to the poisons," Dogger echoed.

I have to admit that I was reluctant to tell him what I'd done, but after only a couple of false starts, I found myself explaining in detail how I had used my handkerchief to swab a sample of liquid from the corpse's lips.

I needn't have worried.

"Excellent," Dogger said. "You were thinking of the diatoms, no doubt?"

"No," I admitted. "I was thinking of potassium cyanide, prussic acid, and paraldehyde."

Dogger nodded.

"Quite right," he said. "The three P's. Very proper. We shall test for those also."

"Tell me about the diatoms," I said.

When the speaker was Dogger, I was more than willing to be instructed.

"The diatoms," Dogger explained—and I could see that he was enjoying this—"are a vast species of microscopic algae belonging to the class *Bacillariophyceae*, which are notable for secreting a hard outer skeleton of siliceous matter—"

"Hold on," I said. "Are you telling me they secrete a shell of sand?"

"Well, virtually—in its hydrated form, of course. Their cell walls are of the same material."

"Like tiny army tanks!"

"Precisely."

"The point being?" I could hardly contain myself.

"The point being that, in cases of drowning, the presence or absence of diatoms in the lungs may well indicate whether or not the victim was breathing when he or she went into the water."

I wrinkled my brow.

"I don't quite follow you," I said.

Dogger reached into an inner pocket and pulled out a small black notebook. After flipping through a great many pages upon which were written a great many notes in his tiny, meticulous hand—O! How I wish I could have read it all!—he came at last to a blank page.

Unscrewing the cap of his fountain pen, he began to draw a series of small triangles, ellipses, and circles, then filled them in with elaborate but regular patterns of cells and chambers: some like snowflakes—or miniature honeycombs—or snooker balls in their triangular racks—or the hugely magnified fly's eyes in one of those endless instructional films we were made to watch in St. Tancred's parish hall.

"Diatoms are abundant in both fresh and salt water," Dogger said. "If we analyze the residue on your handkerchief—"

And suddenly the light went on!

"We can tell if he was breathing. We can tell if he was murdered!"

"Perhaps," Dogger said. "Putting aside the bruise on the neck for a moment, there were no marks of restraint on the visible parts of his body. It is remarkably difficult to hold an unwilling victim under water. Ropes are usually required."

"Or handcuffs," I added.

"Or handcuffs," Dogger agreed. "Although it's the extremities of the limbs that flail about, so that abrasions generally tend to be found on the wrists and ankles."

"That makes sense," I said, and it did. How did Dogger know all these things?

"All that remains," said Dogger, "is a proper chemical analysis."

"We'd better get on with it," I said, "before the evidence evaporates."

"Possibly, with reference to the cyanide, the prussic acid, and the paraldehyde, but as for the diatoms, there is no urgency whatever. The frustules for which we are searching consist virtually of glass, which will last for millions of years. I suggest we have time for tea."

"But I don't want tea," I protested. "I want to roll up my sleeves and get to work."

It took me a moment to see what Dogger was smiling at. In my light summer dress, I had no sleeves worth speaking of to *roll* up.

"And so do I, Miss Flavia," he said, "but first we shall have to assemble certain . . . ah, philosophical instruments."

Because "philosophical instruments" was the phrase used by Dr. Watson to describe certain of Sherlock Holmes's chemical apparatuses, I knew what Dogger meant.

"Of course," I said. "We must assemble our philosophical instruments."

Not yet having the faintest idea what these might be.

"Well, we can boil our own water, anyway," I said, pointing to the electric hot plate and tired-looking tin kettle that sat on a table in front of the window.

"An excellent start," Dogger said, rubbing his hands together. "I shall be back in a jiff."

Back in a jiff? What was the world coming to? That Dogger should use such slang was unthinkable. But before I could remark upon it he was gone.

I went to the window and peered down through the curtain. A few seconds later, Dogger appeared in the inn yard, walked casually to the parked Rolls, removed a couple of items from the boot, and retraced his steps.

"You're very cheerful, Dogger," I twitted him as he came back into the room. "Did you win something on the dogs or the horses?"

"I am not a betting man, Miss Flavia—except upon

the great game of Life and Death. In my own turns at the table, I have been most fortunate to date."

I ought to have known better.

"I'm sorry, Dogger," I said. "I didn't mean to—"

"Nor did I," said Dogger. "It is time, I think, to make our first move."

And with that he placed two objects on the bed. The first was a man's black leather travel case; the other I recognized as the first-aid kit from the boot of the Rolls.

From his pocket he produced the powerful torch normally kept in the car's glove box.

"Now then," he said, "one thing more . . ."

He opened the door and, after looking both ways, stepped into the hall and vanished to the left, which direction, I knew, led only to the WC. Otherwise, it was a blind corridor.

There was a silence, and then came the gush of a flushing toilet.

There are times when it isn't polite to listen, but the proximity of the water closet to my bedroom at the Oak and Pheasant made such niceties difficult to observe.

A moment later Dogger was back.

"Always flush when you are up to no good," he said with a solemn face. "It puts them off the scent."

I couldn't believe my ears. Was Dogger making a joke? He was talking to me almost as if I were an equal.

From behind his back he produced a yellow metal tin.

"There is no good landlord—or landlady, for that matter—from Land's End to John o' Groats who doesn't lay in a good supply of drain cleaner."

He held out the tin for my inspection.

"Drain Bane," I read aloud. "Is that really the name of it?"

"Unhappily, yes," Dogger said. "But fortunately for us, it is nothing more than sodium hydroxide putting on airs."

Sodium hydroxide! I clapped my hands together. Caustic soda to the masses, but good old NaOH to those of us who are lucky enough to be chemists.

As if I were home again in my lab at Buckshaw, a great calm came over me.

"Where do we begin?" I asked, suddenly breathless at the prospect.

"I suggest we prepare the diatoms," Dogger replied.

I dug into my pocket and extracted the handkerchief, taking great care to keep it balled up to protect the evidence.

I handed it over to Dogger, realizing, even as I did so, that this frail bit of linen might well become the noose round the neck of some person or persons as yet unknown.

It was an eerie feeling—but a pleasant one. It would be nice to believe that Justice plays no favorites.

To my surprise, Dogger set the handkerchief aside. Well, not exactly aside, but he pushed it gently into a glass drinking tumbler which he took from the black travel case.

"First things first," he said. "First things, in this case, being distilled water."

He half-filled the kettle with water from the small sink in the corner, and placed it on the hot plate. Setting aside the lid, he replaced it with the glass chimney from the candle holder, capping this with a second tumbler from the travel case.

"Almost a perfect fit," he said, switching on the hot plate. "It will do."

"You've done this before," I observed.

"No," Dogger said. "I'm afraid I am improvising."

"Improvising is half the fun," I said. "If it works."

"It is, indeed," Dogger agreed.

·EIGHT·

IT WASN'T LONG BEFORE the kettle's steam began rising into the lamp chimney and condensing on the colder glass. Dogger let it boil for two and a half minutes before switching off the hot plate, by which time the inside of the chimney was completely filled with steam, its inner surfaces streaming water droplets like a rain-lashed window.

With a swift movement, Dogger seized the makeshift apparatus and, removing it from atop the kettle, flipped it over and placed it gently on the table. The drinking glass was now on the bottom, the inverted chimney on the top. Already the condensation was forming beads, running down the inside of the glass, dripping into the tumbler.

"That's our distilled water," I said, ticking it off on my fingers.

"We shall set aside a bit of it for our cyanide and paral-dehyde experiments," he said, tipping a couple of ounces into a drinking glass from the bedside table.

"Do we have enough?" I asked.

"We shan't require a great deal," Dogger said, decant-ing the remaining water carefully into the glass contain-ing my handkerchief, and tamping it down with the end of his fountain pen until the whole wad was thoroughly wetted. "The evidence is microscopic."

"What's next?"

"We shall leave it to percolate for a while," Dogger said.

Time becomes glacial when you're impatient, and after just a few minutes I found myself sitting on my hands to keep from fidgeting.

"Shall we get on with our cyanide and paraldehyde testing?" Dogger suggested with a gentle smile, as he took down a white stoneware soap dish from a shelf above the sink.

I hugged myself with joy.

Because potassium cyanide (KCN) would have been converted by Orlando's stomach acids to prussic acid (HCN), these tests were simple. We could, of course, have produced the required picric acid with a handful of aspirin tablets in sulfuric acid, but we quickly decided upon an easier method: A couple of grams of sodium bi-carbonate and a few drops of picric acid antiseptic, both from the first-aid kit Dogger had brought from the Rolls, would do the trick nicely.

I watched as Dogger carefully washed and dried the

soap dish, tipped into it an ounce or so of the solution in which my handkerchief was soaking, then added a few drops of the antiseptic to the sample.

As I was half expecting it would, the fluid, due to the formation of potassium iso-purpurate, quickly took on a faint reddish brick color.

"Interesting," I said, trying to contain my excitement. "Cyanide. The presence of which would, in itself, suggest accidental poisoning, suicide, or murder."

Dogger nodded.

"And now for the paraldehyde. I've also taken the liberty of siphoning a small quantity of battery acid— sulfuric, of course—from the Rolls," he said, producing a small glass bottle which I recognized at once as having formerly contained smelling salts in the car's glove box.

"You are amazing, Dogger!" I clapped my hands together.

"Thank you, Miss Flavia," he said. "'*Amazing*' is a word for wizards. I prefer to think of myself as merely practical."

Because Dogger's gentle rebukes were always as warm as honey, I treasured them. I vowed never to use the word again.

"Would you care to do the honors?" he asked, and I knew that I was forgiven my momentary indiscretion.

After heating the bottle gently in the steam from the kettle, I removed—with great care—the stopper of the salts bottle and decanted a few drops of the sulfuric acid into the soap dish, which contained the small sample of what I now thought of as my handkerchief water.

Just as the picric acid signaled the presence of cyanide by turning red in the first sample, so did the sulfuric acid tell us we were in the presence of paraldehyde by going yellow with a greenish tinge.

Dogger and I looked at each other: snug as two bugs in a rug.

"Cyanide," I said again. "*And* paraldehyde."

"It certainly seems so," Dogger agreed. "And now for our friends the diatoms. If you will be so good as to prepare a solution of the sodium hydroxide—a couple of cubic centimeters ought to be sufficient."

Taking the now-empty drinking tumbler from our makeshift distilling apparatus, I placed it in the bottom of the sink and poured into it some of the remaining hot water from the kettle.

One needed to be extremely careful at this game. Dogger nodded approvingly as I raised the window sash.

Sodium hydroxide crystals, upon contact with water, generate sudden tremendous heat—the so-called exothermic reaction—resulting in a furious foaming, which explains why they are so highly regarded in the unclogging of stubborn drains.

Because of the caustic nature of the stuff, it is necessary to protect the skin and clothing from unexpected splashes. I loved it that Dogger didn't tell me to be careful.

"May I borrow your driving gloves?" I asked.

Did Dogger raise an eyebrow?

Perhaps by the width of a hair, but he hid it well.

"Of course you may, Miss Flavia," he replied, and fished them from his jacket pocket.

As I slipped them onto my hands, I marveled at the soft luxury of the gloves, which Dogger had once told me were stitched from the skins of young hornless goats from the Cape of Good Hope.

Poor babies! I thought as I wiggled my fingers into position. *I'd better be careful not to damage them.*

Uncapping the tin of Drain Bane, I tipped a few crystals of the stuff into the glass of water from the kettle. They sank to the bottom. A few more crystals and they began to fizz. A few more and—

I stopped abruptly. Like a dose of stomach salts, the stuff was suddenly foaming fiercely up the sides of the glass, but fortunately it stopped just before reaching the lip.

"Perfect," Dogger said. Until that moment I hadn't realized he was watching me.

"As for the required glassware, I have taken the liberty of bringing up the bud vase from Miss Harriet's Rolls-Royce."

How I longed to hug him! Not just for thinking of how to provide a makeshift test-tube, but for still thinking of the Rolls as belonging to my late mother.

In the days when she was still alive, this small glass trumpet from Liberty's had been one of two in the car, which my father had kept perpetually supplied with roses from the garden at Buckshaw.

The thought of it tugged at something inside me, but I didn't want to give in to emotion in front of Dogger.

"Brilliant!" was all I could manage. "What shall we use for a stopper?"

But Dogger had already thought of that. "Candle wax,"

he said, reaching for the hand lamp whose glass shade we had already put to such good use.

He plucked the candle from its socket, held its butt end over the hot plate, and turned on the switch. Rotating it as it warmed, he soon had a teardrop of wax the size of a penny ready to drop.

"If you'll be so kind as to hold this for a moment," he said, and taking the glass containing the submerged handkerchief, he gave it a final stir and a good poke with his pen.

Having done so, he poured some of the liquid contents into the bud vase and handed it to me.

With thumbs and first two fingers, I worked the wax to form a perfect plug, then pressed it into the top of the vase.

"Watertight!" I said, and Dogger nodded.

"Now for a centrifuge," he said quietly, almost as if to himself.

Centrifuge?

At home, in my laboratory at Buckshaw, I had the lovely professional centrifuge that had been brought from Germany by my late uncle Tarquin. With an electrical motor powerful enough to swing an ox until Doomsday at 2000 revolutions per minute, or until the electrical power was cut off, whichever came first.

But here in a miserable bedroom at the Oak and Pheasant? What were we to do?

A small light dawned in my brain. I was already grinning from ear to ear.

"The blind cord!" I blurted. Then gaining control of

myself, I said in softer tones—and with considerably less volume: "I think the cord from the blind will serve admirably."

The look on Dogger's face was worth a sultan's ransom, as if his horse had won the Derby. If this wasn't pride, it was something very much like it.

"Quite right," he said. "I'm sure the good Mrs. Palmer won't mind, as long as we leave everything as we found it."

He stepped to the window, lowered the blind, brought out his penknife, selected the smallest blade, and before you could say "I name this racehorse Jack Robinson," had detached the flaxen cord.

With a firm reef knot—left over right, right over left; granny knots begone—he fastened the cord firmly to the tapered neck of the bud vase.

"Now for the acrobatics." He took up a position at the foot of the bed. "Please sit in the corner and mind your head."

As I retreated to the chair in the corner, Dogger seized the cord in its center and, like an American cowboy about to lasso a calf, began swinging it—and the bud vase with its precious cargo—in a circle round his head.

As the speed accelerated, Dogger let out more and more cord until the glass was coming within a foot of each of the walls.

I watched for a while until—as always happens when you're watching someone swing a rope—I began to grow bored.

"How long will it take?" I asked.

"Fifteen minutes, I reckon," he said.

"I reckon"? Was this meant to be a joke? And a cowboy joke, at that? Was I supposed to laugh?

I smiled to cover all the possibilities and returned to my watching.

I understood perfectly what was taking place, of course. Inside the bud vase, the diatoms (if there were any), because of their relatively heavy siliceous composition, were overcoming both buoyant and frictional forces of the liquid solution as centrifugal force rammed them relentlessly and tightly into the very bottom of the bud vase.

"Shall I spell you for a while?" I asked Dogger, and he nodded with a look of what I guessed was gratitude.

I ducked in under the rope and synchronized my motions with his. Like a country stationmaster handing off the right-of-way token to the engine driver of the Flying Scotsman at speed, the transfer was perfection.

Dogger stepped neatly out of the way and perched on the edge of the chair.

"This is harder than it looks," I said after a couple of minutes. My arm was already beginning to ache.

"Sustained muscular action often is," Dogger said. "Without prior training, that is. Such fatigue is due largely to a surplus of chloride, potassium, lactic acid, and magnesium, caused by muscular contraction, and a simultaneous insufficiency of creatine phosphate, glycogen, and adenosine triphosphate."

Why had no one ever put it so plainly? It suddenly made such perfect sense.

Muscle power needed to be chemically provided and, at the same time, muscular waste products efficiently removed, to allow Harry Plunkett to lift his father's Clydesdale horse, Colossus, clear off the ground for charity every August at the Hinley Goose and Gooseberry Show.

My arms were feeling suddenly less heavy.

Round and round the bud vase flew on the end of its cord, producing an audible humming noise.

I was an angel and the glass container my oversized halo. But wait! I was now being transformed into a helicopter on the verge of lifting off!

If I could, I would fly out the window, across the road to the church, and hover there, an eye in the sky, getting a firsthand view of the landscape in which Orlando Whitbread had met his bitter end. There would be no need to wait for Hob's aerial snapshots from the chemist's.

"That ought to be sufficient," Dogger said, snapping me abruptly out of my daydream.

I slowed the high-speed missile, letting it descend gently, little by little, until it came almost to rest, rotating slowly and idly, at the end of the cord.

"Now then," Dogger said. "The sodium hydroxide ought to have digested any organic matter which was present in your sample—"

By my "sample," he was referring to the slimy liquid I had wiped from Orlando's mouth.

"—leaving only the siliceous cell walls and outer skeletons of the diatoms—presuming, of course, that diatoms *were* present."

As he spoke, he poured off into the sink the excess

liquid—which was quite clear—leaving only the slightest trace of a foggy residue in the bottom of the bud vase.

"And if they weren't present?" I asked, knowing the answer perfectly well, but wanting to hear it again from Dogger's lips.

"If they weren't present, then we can certainly make the case that our deceased friend was already dead when he entered the water. All that remains for us now is to improvise a microscope."

Improvise a microscope? I think my heart stopped. Was all this to be for nothing?

"Which is quite easily done," Dogger said, ignoring my open mouth.

Taking the torch, he switched it on and stood it on the table so that its beam was striking the ceiling.

Then, slipping two fingers into his waistcoat pocket, he removed a tiny object and held it up for my inspection.

"A paper clip?" I asked.

"Indeed. The humble paper clip, in certain circumstances, can be of more practical use than a magic wand."

And without another word, he opened out one end of the metal clip and, with fingers as deft as any surgeon's, twisted it into a tiny loop. From the first-aid kit he removed a small jar of petroleum jelly, into which he dipped the wire circle.

"Now," he said, taking a deep breath, "shall we rake out the contents of our vase—whatever they may be— onto the bottom of . . . this?"

"This" was a small graduated measuring glass, which

he was removing from the first-aid kit. He turned it upside down and placed it on the table beside the torch.

With a wooden tongue depressor—also from the first-aid kit—I scraped out the residue from the vase and spread it thinly on the bottom of the glass.

Dogger picked up the glass and slipped it, inverted, over the glowing lens of the torch. Drawing the loop of his paper clip along the inside of the glass lamp chimney, which still contained a small puddle of distilled water, he pulled it out and held it up for my inspection. Suspended in the loop of the clip was a single drop of water, which sparkled like a diamond in the light from the window.

"Wonderful," I said, and I meant it.

It was the petroleum jelly, of course, which held the water drop in place. How clever of Dogger to have thought of it!

"Our objective lens," Dogger said, moving it into position just above our smudge of residue on the bottom of the glass.

"What do you see?" he asked.

I bent at the waist until I was directly above the drop of water, which was illuminated from below by the torch. Several tiny grains, fringed with many colors, shimmered before my eyes.

"Are those diatoms?" I asked. "They're quite tiny."

Dogger reached into the pocket of his resourceful waistcoat and pulled out his reading glasses. "Use these as a magnifying eyepiece."

I slipped them onto my nose and ears.

Gently, so as not to dislodge the drop of water, I took

the paper clip from Dogger's fingers, moving it up and down until the image in the water drop was clear.

Success! The reading glasses more than doubled the magnification of our homemade microscope.

I drew in a breath.

"What do you see?" Dogger asked.

"Stars," I told him. "Triangles . . . circles . . . rods . . . strings . . . tiny seashells. It's like a kaleidoscope."

Dogger leaned in for a look.

"Diatoms," he said in a quiet voice. "Definitely diatoms."

"Meaning?" I asked.

"Death by drowning."

Drat! I had been counting on cyanide to be the killer.

"Oh, well," I said, trying to hide my disappointment. "At least it was an interesting chemical experiment."

"Indeed it was, Miss Flavia. How is your headache now?"

I had completely forgotten my fib.

"It's gone away," I said.

Dogger nodded wisely.

"Yes," he said. "Chemistry has that effect, has it not?"

·NINE·

THERE WENT ALL MY theories: shot down in flames.

So much for death by prussic acid. So much for the paraldehyde.

Death by drowning, Dogger had said.

Orlando, the idiot, had probably caught his foot on a plank while practicing his dance on the dock behind the church. He might easily have suffered a dizzy spell, fallen, and banged his head, or had a heart attack, or, suddenly tired of life, had sipped a bit of cyanide and hurled himself into the water and, by sheer determination, had kept his head beneath the surface until it was too late to be rescued.

That was easy enough to do. Virginia Woolf, Daffy had told me, loaded the pockets of her overcoat with stones and waded into the River Ouse.

I had a sudden sinking feeling. Had I checked Orlando's pockets?

I had, and had found nothing but wet lint and that mysterious bit of paper.

Perhaps I had overlooked something.

"Dogger," I asked, "did you by any chance check the pockets?"

There was no need to explain whose pockets I was talking about. That was the great thing about Dogger: He could follow my train of thought as easily as if he owned the railway.

"I could feel them, Miss Flavia, as I carried him ashore. No stones. And now, if you'll excuse me—"

He needn't have asked, as both of us knew perfectly well. His sense of duty was calling him to check up on my sisters. He had spent enough time with me.

Not that they needed him, of course. My two sisters were as tough as a pair of old blacksmith's boots, but still, they enjoyed going through the motions of helplessness.

I knew that in a matter of minutes, Daffy would be sending Dogger off on a search of the local library for the second volume of John Forster's *The Life of Charles Dickens*, the only book missing from the deluxe morocco-bound set in our library at Buckshaw.

Or should I say *my library*?

Because Buckshaw was now legally mine, lock, stock, and barrel, so, supposedly, were all the books in that vast mountain range of printed matter, *including* the missing Forster—wherever it might be.

Perhaps upon our return I would gift wrap the two sur-
viving volumes and present them to Daffy with my com-
pliments. I might even go so far as to inscribe them on
their flyleaves.

But no—that might be a bit presumptuous: as if my
name deserved to be displayed beside Dickens's. Besides,
an incomplete set of anything was hardly a decent gift,
was it? That would be like presenting an avid golfer with
a set of antique clubs that were missing the niblick, or the
mashie, or whatever those iron bludgeons were called.

I would bide my time.

As for Feely, she would be sending Dogger trotting off
to the chemists with instructions to replenish her stock of
Dekur Bonne Nuit Turtle Oil Cream, Rubinstein's Valaze
Blackhead and Open Pore Paste, oatmeal cream, and a
couple of Crinofricto Depilatory Stones.

The fact that she continued to medicate her hide indicated—to me, at least—that despite their most recent
crockery-tossing split-up, she still had plans of making it
up with Dieter.

As I made my way down the narrow creaking stairs, I
heard piano music. Someone was singing:

"I'm the girl that makes the thing that drills the hole
that holds the ring that drives the rod that turns the knob
that works the thing-ummy-bob . . ."

I looked in through the glass door of the saloon bar and
saw that it was Feely. She was seated at a rather battered
piano, surrounded by three men in kerchiefs: the same

three men we had seen when we first arrived at the pub. I had seen the one with the polka-dot handkerchief again at the fair.

> *"I'm the girl that makes the thing that holds the oil*
> *that oils the ring that takes the shank that moves the crank*
> *that works the thing-ummy-bob."*

I couldn't believe my eyes. Feely was evidently having the time of her life and never had she had a more appreciative audience.

The three men hung on her every word, nodding along, tapping their feet and fingers and occasionally joining in to roar with her, as they raised their glasses of ale, the words at the end of each line:

> *". . . that works the thing ummy bob!"*

I recognized the song, of course. It was one of Gracie Fields's wartime classics: the one about the girl in the munitions factory making the parts for some top-secret but important machine whose function is a mystery.

Feely's voice was high and clear, rising like a skylark above the coarse, rumbling voices of the three men who hemmed her in. Could this possibly be the same person who had, less than two hours ago, sat at the organ and summoned up the mathematical ghost of Johann S. Bach?

In spite of living with her all my life, there were still sides of my sister I had never seen before. She had as many facets as an icosahedron, that twenty-faceted form

into which Plato believed—wrongly, as it turned out—
the water in our human bodies decayed when we were
dead.

There were faces of Feely which, like the far side of the
moon, were always turned away. Perhaps this came of
looking at herself in mirrors so much. Perhaps parts of her
had, like Alice, slipped through to the other side of the
looking-glass.

The song came to a sudden end:

"... *that works the thing-ummy-bob!*"

Feely looked around the room as if she had just awak-
ened from a long trance and found herself on another
planet. She got up from the piano, clasped her arms, and
hugged herself in the way that she always does when she's
ashamed.

"You're a corker, gal!" said one of the men. "Gi' us another!"

"'Kiss Me Goodnight, Sergeant Major,'" demanded
the tallest one, leering and wiggling his ginger mustache
at her as he spoke. "Do you know that one?"

Feely looked from one of the men to another with startled eyes.

"No, she doesn't," I interrupted, flinging open the glass
door and stepping into the saloon bar.

Six eyes—eight counting Feely's—swung round and
fixed me in their glare.

"Come along, Ophelia," I said, putting on a pretentious

voice. "You're wanted at Miss Wilberforce's bedside. She's taken rather a nasty turn and you're needed at once."

Who Miss Wilberforce was, or from what horrid malady she was suffering, I hadn't the faintest idea. It was intended to extract Feely from the predicament she was in, and to brook no argument.

But it didn't work.

Feely gave me one of her ten-ton looks.

"What do you mean by barging in here!" she shouted, her face already going the color of brick.

As if to defend her, one of the men put his arm around her shoulders and pulled her toward him.

"Well?" he demanded, in a parade-square voice.

I marched over to Feely, seized the man's hand between my thumb and forefinger as if it were a stinking fish, and lifted it from my sister's shoulders.

I could smell the alcohol on his breath.

It was a showdown of sorts:

"What's going on here?" a voice demanded: a voice that I would know anywhere. Anywhere! Even on the darkest desert night.

I dropped the offending hand and spun round.

Dieter, Feely's forsaken fiancé, was standing in the doorway, his face frozen at the scene before him.

"Dieter!" I shouted and flew into his arms. I wanted to squeeze him until nothing was left but a husk.

The room fell suddenly silent.

The three men with kerchiefs all let their hands fall to their sides, as if to be within handy reach of their holsters.

They stared at Dieter, as if afraid to be the first to unlock eyes.

Dieter stared back at them.

And then, on the other side of the room, a whine began: low at first, like a distant air-raid siren, then rising in pitch and volume from a whisper to a buzzing scream.

It was, all in all, an amazing vocal performance.

"Dieterrrrrrr!"

Feely's shriek flew past my ears like an enraged hornet or a ricochet from a .45 caliber slug. Feely herself followed, knocking me out of the way with a wicked forearm.

In a lightning flash, she was in his arms and he in hers.

All, apparently, was forgiven.

Much as I wanted to gab with Dieter, I decided to leave the lovebirds alone. As far as I knew, they hadn't seen each other for a while, which meant that they would want to be alone to swap spit until they were caught up, or until they died of saturation.

In chemistry, the term "saturation" refers to the state of a compound at which all the units of affinity of the contained elements become engaged, and it is dependent upon both heat and pressure.

In this case, I could not have come up with a better definition if I tried. It was downright disgusting. I didn't want to watch.

I strolled casually out the door, whistling Thomas Morley's musical setting of Shakespeare's song "It Was a Lover and His Lass" from *As You Like It*, but I don't think either of them heard me.

Outside, the world seemed suddenly quiet in the warmth of a perfect English day. There was no one in the street, nor did there seem to be any further activity across the road in the churchyard.

I made my way round, under the quaint hanging signboard—THE OAK & PHEASANT, ARVEN PALMER PROPRIETOR—to the sunken garden at the back of the inn, to the enclosed area I had seen from my bedroom window.

"Go away!" said a voice.

I turned to find Daffy curled up with a notebook and a pencil, in a small bower behind the garden gate. I had walked straight past without seeing her.

"Go away," she repeated.

"Go away yourself," I said. "I am not your slave or your bondmaid, you know."

I stuck out my tongue at her to prove my point.

"Idiot," she retorted, and returned to her reading.

"Dieter's back," I said.

"*I* know that," she said. "He came round here to see me first. I told him where Feely was."

"I'm glad," I said. "I've missed him."

Daffy said nothing: a perfect indication that she had missed him, too.

"What are you writing?" I asked.

"None of your beeswax," Daffy said.

She had picked up some rather colorful American expressions from Carl Pendracka, one of Feely's—now supposedly unsuccessful—suitors.

"Oh, *here* you are, luv!" exclaimed Mrs. Palmer as she came bustling through the gate with a tray, upon which was a tall glass of milk and an artfully arranged stack of cucumber sandwiches.

I had already begun a grin, and had raised my hands to receive this most welcome feast, when the landlord's wife walked straight past me and put the tray down on Daffy's bower bench.

"I thought you were still in your room, and took it up there by mistake," she said, shaking her head in baffled amusement.

"Thank you, Mrs. Palmer. This is most kind of you," Daffy said in her smarmiest, stickiest voice.

I could have whacked her on the head with a warming pan.

"Would you like one, too, dearie?" Mrs. P asked, turning to me with dramatically raised eyebrows.

The lesson had not been learned.

"No, thank you," I managed to mumble, shaking my head.

"Headache warning still in effect, then?" she asked. Whatever she meant by that.

I nodded.

"I'll leave you to it, then," she said, and she was gone.

"You oughtn't to do that, you know," Daffy grumbled.

"Do what?" I replied, out of habit.

"Whenever anyone calls you 'dearie' you change instantly into a monster. It's like *Hocus Pocus!* or *Alakazam!* And—*poof!* You become *The Ineffable Flavia*."

"I don't know what 'ineffable' means," I said, although I had my suspicions.

"It means you're a beast. A chump; a bufflehead; a clam; a foozle; a proper dickey-dido."

I knew that, with Daffy, it was best to let her exhaust her storehouse of exotic insults. She would eventually, like an overwound alarm clock, run down and stop her clatter.

While I waited, I examined my fingernails—which I was now rather proud of. I had finally been able to break my habit of gnawing the old keratin to the gristle, and had grown, quite to my surprise and admiration, as slick a set of claws as had ever graced a maiden's hand.

"You've made a friend," I said when Daffy's jaw had tired.

"Huh?" she said, taken by surprise.

"Mrs. Palmer. She's your lapdog. Unlike me."

Daffy scoffed: a prolonged and horrible damp process involving her sinuses.

"She's a *published poet*," she threw at me. "Her work has appeared in the *New Statesman* and in *Blackwood's*. She's spent weekends with the Sitwells, for heaven's sake! What do you say to that?"

"I hope she enjoyed the blue cows," I said.

Sir George Sitwell had caused his cows to be painted in the blue and white willow pattern so as to look better in the green landscape. Or so the vicar's wife had once told me.

"A grand triumph of aesthetics over brains," Cynthia had remarked. "So remarkably rare nowadays."

"Besides," Daffy said, lowering her voice to an excited

whisper and scanning the horizon for eavesdroppers, "she's the author of *The Mussel Bed*."

"Zip-a-dee-doo-dah," I said.

"You're so ignorant!" Daffy spat. "*The Mussel Bed* was a literary sensation. It was short-listed for every book prize going but they could never discover who the author was."

She closed her eyes and recited:

"*On Monday morn*
The maid came up
And found him there in bed,
His jaw ajar,
His face affright,
All pale,
All cold,
All dead."

Daffy shivered.

"'Brilliant but chilling,' *The Times* called it. 'Folk *naïf*, but all the more effective because of it.' James Agate wrote: 'Raw, bleeding, essential,' and George Bernard Shaw suggested, mischievously, that he had taken upon himself the skin of a country barmaid and written the thing."

"And Mrs. Palmer wrote it?" I asked.

"She confided in me," Daffy said. "She made me swear never to tell, and I won't."

"You've just told me," I pointed out.

"Pfaugh!" Daffy said. "You're nobody. And if you ever tell, I shall pour poison in your ear while you're asleep."

I knew that Daffy was desperate. She was cribbing from Shakespeare: the scene in which Hamlet's wicked uncle, Claudius, pours hebenon into the ear of the sleeping king.

Hebenon, in my opinion, was simply a mangled form of henbane, misremembered by one of Shakespeare's acting pals when it came time to write down the plays. Either that, or the error was caused by a daydreaming typesetter.

My point being that the old poison-in-the-ear-of-a-sleeper was nothing new to me.

Daffy's threat was as empty as her hope chest.

"Ho-hum," I said.

But it was at that very moment that I realized something: Two pairs of ears were better than one and twice as likely to gather useful gossip.

Did that mean using my sister as a listening device?

Well, yes, frankly, it did.

We were in a strange place where we knew almost nobody. We would not likely be staying here any longer than required by the law. Time, therefore, was of the essence. I needed to collect as many ears as I could—as American soldiers were said to have done from the British during the American War of Independence.

I drew my forefinger across my mouth in the signal of the zipped lip, crossing my heart and holding my fingers up in the Girl Guide sign of honor (*Ha-ha!*), and said:

"I, Flavia Sabina de Luce, do most solemnly swear that I shall never reveal, upon pain of poison in the ear, those secrets which my dearly beloved sister Daphne de Luce is about to impart unto me."

I realized, even as I said it, that the "unto" was a bit rich, but I wanted Daffy to take me seriously.

"But why would she entrust her secret to you?" I asked. I needed to keep a bit of skepticism in the conversation, otherwise Daffy would suspect I was acting—which I was, but not in the way she thought.

"Because there are times," Daffy answered, choosing her words carefully, "when a woman needs to confide in another woman—and *only* in another woman. Doctors won't do, nor will an entire army of Freud's followers."

"True," I agreed, hoping to sound wise beyond my years.

"What would you know about it?" Daffy scoffed.

I shrugged, which was as good an answer as any. It got Daffy off my back and gave her a perfect opening to go on spilling her guts.

And it worked.

"The poor woman is petrified," Daffy told me. "It seems that her book cut a little too close to the bone. Some of the poems were far too close for comfort."

"To real life?" I asked. This could prove interesting. Especially in a town whose vicar had gone to the scaffold for vile crimes against women!

"Of course to real life!" Daffy said.

"Which poems were they—in particular?" I asked.

"She didn't tell me. I'll look them up when we get home to Buckshaw."

"You have a copy of *The Mussel Bed*?" I asked. Sometimes my sister amazed me.

"Of course," she said, "as does every discriminating woman in England. *The Times Literary Supplement* called it 'indispensable' and they weren't far off the mark."

It was at that moment that I vowed to get my hands as quickly as possible on this literary gem. Daffy's copy might be back at Buckshaw, but surely there was one within earshot of where we were sitting. In its author's bedroom, for instance.

She wouldn't have left a copy in the little library of the saloon bar of the Oak and Pheasant. No, that would have been too risky. But it was reasonable to assume that it wasn't far away.

"So no one knows that she wrote this book?" I asked. "Not even her husband?"

"No," Daffy said, glancing over her shoulder. "*Especially* not her husband."

"Then what's she got to worry about?" I asked.

Daffy bit her bottom lip as if she were making a critical decision, then beckoned me with a crooked finger.

I went to her side and put my ear close to her mouth.

"She's begun to receive blackmailing letters," she said.

"Somebody *knows*?"

I couldn't help myself.

"Shhh!" Daffy whispered. "Apparently so. Now promise you won't breathe a word."

I pantomimed the old sewing-the-lips-shut-with-an-invisible-needle-and-very-long-thread routine, which seemed to satisfy her.

"Now run along," she said, opening her notebook.

"What are you writing?" I asked. "Notes on the case?"

"No. It's a sonnet. You wouldn't be interested."

"Of course I'd be interested, Daff," I said. "I'm your sister, aren't I?"

She gave me a speculative look.

"Some say you are, yes."

"Come on, Daff. Let's hear it. I'll bet it's a killer. A masterpiece, I mean."

Vanity overcame her. She turned to a middle page.

I might not have thought of looking there.

"Well," she said, clearing her throat, "it might not be very good, but here it is—"

Why do so many poets apologize before reading their work aloud? I wondered. How many readings had we attended at St. Tancred's parish hall where the poet felt obliged to kill his own young before they ever drew breath?

"Get on with it!" you always wanted to shout—but you never did. Poets—other than the dreaded Millbank Morrison, of course, who had a hide as thick as a rhinoceros's in chain mail—were notoriously sensitive about their creations, whereas scientists never were.

Did Joseph Priestley apologize for discovering oxygen? Or Henry Cavendish for hydrogen?

Of course not! They fairly crowed about it.

"Pray go on," I said. "I'm listening."

Daffy cleared her throat again and began to read:

*"What pale-flesh'd slugs or graveyard grubs do mar
Thy fair and once beguiling former face?"*

"Stop!" I said, holding up a hand.

How *dare* she? How *dare* she trespass upon my personal territory? *I* was the expert on the business of the dead. *I* was the Doctor of Decay. How *dare* she?

"I'm sorry, Daff," I said. "You'll have to stop there. It's too real. You've made me queasy."

Daffy looked up, flushed with pride, then closed her book.

"Actually, that's all there is so far. I've only just begun, but I shall read you the rest of it when I'm finished."

"Don't wear out your pencil," I said as I walked out through the garden gate.

·TEN·

"Ah, Miss de Luce," said a voice before I'd taken half a dozen paces. "A word with you, if you don't mind."

It was Constable Otter, notebook and indelible pencil poised at the ready.

How long had he been lurking outside the garden gate? How much had he overheard?

I tried to sneak a look at the page to see if it was blank, but as I stepped forward, he stepped automatically back. What a canny customer he was!

"Yes, Constable?" I said. "How may I help you?"

"By not meddling," he replied, "in things you know nothing about."

Was this a threat? Was I being warned off by a village bobby?

"I beg your pardon," I said. "I don't know what you're talking about."

"I believe you do," Constable Otter said, shutting his notebook with an elaborate single-handed flourish and, with all the art of a well-drilled sailor loading a cannon, tamping it down into his jacket pocket.

"Yes, I believe you do," he went on.

I put on Innocent Face Number 5: the full-on expression that combines injured innocence with just the slightest hint of aggression, conveyed by the rolling-out of precisely four millimeters of lower lip. I had practiced it many times in a mirror.

The next move was his—and he took it.

"I've rung up Inspector Hewitt at Hinley," he said. "I am led to believe you're rather notorious in that neck of the woods."

In that neck of the woods? Was this country bumpkin suggesting that my small successes in the solving of crimes were limited to Hinley and environs? Had Inspector Hewitt neglected to tell him that I had been thanked—in person!—by our own dear (and now, alas, late) King George VI?

What was the inspector thinking of? Had he forgotten already that I had sent him—and his wife, Antigone, whom I adored—a wicker hamper of apples and oranges upon the birth of their daughter, and first child, in January?

Antigone, of course, had sent back a card thanking me for my thoughtfulness, but since then, I had heard nothing.

It was, I must admit, quite soon after Father's death, and the Hewitts, perhaps, had wanted to respect my family's privacy.

There had been a discreet card of sympathy, edged in

black, but that was all, which came as a keen disappointment when I had been expecting to be asked to stand as the baby's godmother: to stand with the child at the font as she was christened Flavia Antigone Hewitt.

And now this!

"*Notorious in that neck of the woods,*" the constable had said.

"Yes, Constable Otter," I replied. "I have been known to solve a crime or two."

The hairs on the back of my neck were fairly bristling.

"Perhaps you have, miss, but what makes you think that a crime has been committed here? What makes you think that the young man's death was anything more than misadventure?"

Sharp as a tinker's tack, this constable! He was giving nothing away.

Since I already knew that Orlando Whitbread was a young man, Otter wasn't being indiscreet. But, obviously, he wasn't yet aware I knew the dead man's name.

"I didn't *say* it was a crime," I shot back.

Two can play at this game, you saucy Peeler! I thought. Didn't he realize he was taking on a master?

"I merely observed that I have been known to solve a crime or two. Elsewhere. In the past."

That ought to put him in his place. I had given away nothing.

"Perhaps you have, miss," he said. "But in any event, it won't be called for in this case, will it?

"Besides," he added, almost as an afterthought, "the

Chief Constable doesn't fancy interference on his own turf. No, that he doesn't. Not by a long chalk."

There was no doubt about it. I *was* being warned.

Constable Otter knew a great deal more than he was telling, which was proper, I suppose, for a policeman, but still, if no crime had been committed, why had he gone to the trouble and expense of ringing up Inspector Hewitt to check on my background?

Something here was fishy, and it wasn't just Orlando Whitbread.

Or perhaps it was.

I needed to get to the bottom of this business about Blue Boy and his scarlet dancing slippers, but how was I to do so?

The answer seemed obvious.

The low-beamed kitchen of the Oak and Pheasant was hot and hellish, like some turkey-tainted inferno. Pots bubbled busily on the cooker, giving off odors of gravy, potatoes, and mushy peas.

In spite of it being midsummer, the pub seemed to be doing a roaring business in hearty meals. Who ate them? I wondered.

Could it be the local farmers, who came in starving from the fields? If so, I hadn't seen any tractors parked outside. Or the droves of tourists who, with petrol ration-ing ended, were everywhere in England, driving cars with names like Hawk or Snipe, suggesting that their tin wings could whisk you through the air over vast distances to anywhere your heart desired.

Perhaps the resting turkey on the sideboard was destined for the tummies of the roustabouts from Shadrach's Circus & Menagerie. Other than my brief encounter with Polka-Dot Kerchief at the fair, I hadn't had a chance to look into their presence.

I needed to ask some questions.

Brushing wet strands of hair out of her face, Mrs. Palmer looked up from stirring something that looked like a glue pot. She was not exactly delighted to find me in her kitchen.

I made an after-the-fact knock at the doorframe.

"Sorry to bother you, Mrs. Palmer," I began, letting the words gush out like water from a hose, "but I want to apologize for the way I spoke to you. It wasn't right. I don't know what got into me. It may have been the shock of finding the body of that poor drowned man on the riverbank, I don't know, but even that is no excuse. I beg your pardon and I promise it will never happen again."

I moved my hand closer to my heart to emphasize the point.

I was proud of myself! I had groveled, made good, and brought the subject round to the corpse all in one breath.

I lowered my head and stood there looking abject.

Who could resist?

Not Mrs. Palmer, at any rate.

Slowly, as if to savor the moment, she removed her oven gloves and, with an audible sigh, placed them tenderly on the table.

"Who told you to come in here?" she asked. "Your sister Daphne?"

Darling Daphne obviously had Mrs. Palmer eating out of her hand.

"No," I said. "I came of my own volition."

I don't know where the word came from. It popped out of me like the filling from a squeezed pimple.

"I don't believe you," Mrs. Palmer said, taking up her gloves again.

"You don't have to," I returned, taking the plunge. "But it's true."

It was masks off. Very seldom did I ever show the real Flavia de Luce to anyone, especially to strangers. But now? Well, she had asked for it.

"As Professor Cooke pointed out more than sixty years ago," I said, taking a deep breath, "you cannot unite the chemical elements in any proportion you please. Twenty-three ounces of sodium will unite precisely with thirty-five and a half ounces of chlorine to produce table salt. But if you have carelessly added an extra half ounce of either substance, Nature will set aside the surplus. All the wishing in the world cannot force the extra to mix."

Mrs. Palmer looked rather stunned. I think it was my use of table salt as an example that got through to her. She understood table salt.

"And your point is?" she demanded.

"I am here because I will myself to be here," I told her. "And all the king's horses and all the king's men couldn't keep me here if I didn't want to be," I said, waving my hands in the air to add a bit of drama.

"Well," Mrs. Palmer said, "if even half of what you tell me is true, I can only say that you're a Force to Be Reckoned With."

She spoke the last few words in capital letters. You could actually *hear* them!

I dropped my eyes modestly.

Spot-on! I thought. Her assessment was spot-on.

"Your sister told me you had dynamite for brains, but I had no idea—"

Dynamite for brains? Daffy told her that?

I might have to rethink my sister.

Mrs. Palmer seemed to have come to a sudden decision.

"Help yourself to the Mercy Seat," she said, pointing to the kitchen's only chair, an ancient wingback in the corner.

She saw my puzzled look.

"That's what Arven calls it—the Mercy Seat. He lugged it down from the attics. In case I ever took a break, he said. Not that I ever have, mind. Belonged to his father, the Old Gaffer. Go on, sit yourself."

I lowered my carcass reluctantly into the ancient upholstery, which reeked of departed dogs and so forth. I was expecting the chair to be uncomfortable and oppressive, but I was pleasantly surprised to find that it fit me like a glove. The Old Gaffer must have been quite slight of frame.

"I'll make you a nice cup of tea," Mrs. Palmer said, and I did not object. "Don't mind me if I keep working. To a cook, the world consists of open mouths.

"Not that I'm complaining," she went on. "Those lads from Shadrach's Circus shoveling in their pies and pints in the summer is what keeps us in coal in the winter."

Although Mrs. Palmer had not said so directly, it was obvious she had accepted my apology.

As she worked, she talked to me over her shoulder, clattering away like some wonderful automaton, bustling about the kitchen, lifting lids, sniffing sauces, pulling pies from the pantry, and dismembering the turkey. In an earlier century she might have been called *The Marvelous Mechanical Maid. Wind her up—see her sweep!*

People would have paid to see her, but now I had her all to myself.

I was trying to think of the best way to make my questions seem casual when she said suddenly, "You poor child!"

It took me a moment to realize she was referring to me.

"What a shock it must have been, finding Orlando's body like that, without any warning. Your fingers in his mouth, so to speak. Just the thought of it gives me the heebie-jeebies."

I nodded and widened my eyes a bit.

"Did you know him?" I asked.

"Orlando? Everybody knew Orlando. He was what you might call a local character."

"In what way?" I said.

"Oh, in every way: the way he behaved, the way he talked, the way he dressed. Orlando was an original—one of a kind."

"Wasn't he the son of a former vicar?"

"Dear old Canon Whitbread, poor lamb . . . dear old soul. God rest him."

Poor lamb? Dear old soul?

What kind of description was that? The man had gone to the scaffold for sending a clutch of communicants to an early grave by means of a poisoned chalice.

Poor lamb? Dear old soul? My great-aunt Fanny!

"God rest him," I repeated, making the sign of the cross on my breast. "A good man, was he?"

Mrs. Palmer put down a pot roast and dabbed at her eyes with the corner of her apron.

"He was a martyr," she said. "Put to death by the Powers of Darkness."

"The powers of darkness?" I asked.

"Clement Atlee," she said, "and the Labor Party. Curse them all!"

Mr. Atlee, the former prime minister, had, by only a slender margin, been defeated last autumn by Winston Churchill, who had returned for his second term.

Because I had been incarcerated in Canada at Miss Bodycote's Female Academy, I had heard little about Churchill's victory, although I was quite fond of the man himself, who had taken the trouble to attend my mother's funeral.

"Amen," I said, and Mrs. Palmer beamed upon me.

"Hanged by the neck until he was dead. An innocent old man led to the slaughter," she said, pulling open the oven to baste a large pan of roasting potatoes. "That's what some say—including me."

"But how is that possible? Surely someone—"

"Listen, sweetie," Mrs. Palmer interrupted. "When good old Gabriel blows his horn, 'Surely someone' will be the last words ever to be spoken on this earth. When nothing's left of the world but ashes and a smoking jawbone, that ruined mouth will still be croaking 'Surely someone . . .' You can count on it."

I had begun to like this Mrs. Palmer. Immensely.

It was as if, somewhere in our vast universe, a giant planet had rolled over in its sleep—some great force had shifted, quaked, and then subsided once more into silence.

It left me numb for a moment—but only for a moment. Until I realized that this innkeeper's wife, in her low, hot, greasy kitchen, had been the first person in my entire life to explain why there was a Flavia de Luce.

I was necessary. *I* was *Someone*.

I felt as if I had shed an invisible skin. A fresh layer of the onion had been exposed.

Had Mrs. Palmer noticed as the change came over me? Probably not. But if she did she gave no sign of it.

"Orlando had to live with that," she continued. "And so did all the rest of us. We knew we had to get on with our lives. That's why, when Orlando turned up to audition for the Puddle Lane Little Theatre just days after his father's funeral, he was welcomed with open arms."

"By everyone?" I asked.

"Well, almost everyone," she replied. "Poppy Mandrill grumbled a bit. But then she always does. Poppy has a remarkable theatrical career behind her, with emphasis on *behind*. She just doesn't realize it yet, as most faded actors don't. But I think she realized from the start that this rather unusual young man had what it took to be a star."

"And what about Canon Whitbread? Did he? Realize it, I mean?"

Mrs. Palmer shot me a penetrating look.

"About Orlando?"

I nodded.

"Canon Whitbread was under no illusions about anything or *anyone*. Including himself—or his son. Every canon, you must remember, has a cathedral somewhere in his past. The country canons are mostly lovely old gentlemen who have been given the title as a garment to keep them warm on their way to the grave, and no one was more aware of that than Canon Whitbread."

"And Poppy Mandrill?"

"Well . . ." Mrs. P said, letting the word out in a long breath, "our dear canon was under no illusions about her, either. *Particularly* about her. St. Mildred's is not exactly known for its High Church practices—not by a long chalk—and yet she insisted on his hearing her confessions every Saturday afternoon. 'The Saturday Afternoon Matinées,' he always called them."

"He told you that?" I gasped.

As the child of a devout Catholic family, I could hardly believe that a churchman would break his vows of silence. The sanctity of the confessional was sacred no matter what the circumstances.

"He was joking, of course. Poppy wasn't the only one of his flock who wanted to whisper in the vestry. We were very close, the canon and I," she announced, brushing up her hair with the back of a damp hand. "I served as vicar's warden when all but I had fled."

"The boy stood on the burning deck," I said.

Daffy had recited that horrific old potboiler to me when I was still in my pram, waving in great, swashbuckling circles around her head a smoking string mop whose strands she had set alight to simulate the breech-loading of Nelson's cannon at the Battle of the Nile.

I knew what Mrs. P meant, though. Suspected of murder, old Canon Whitbread must have often found himself alone in his protested innocence. Nobody wants to be on cozy terms with a killer.

"It must have been difficult," I remarked.

"Difficult is an understatement," Mrs. Palmer said. "At times, toward the end, it seemed as if it were the two of us against the world."

"What about Orlando?" I asked. "Surely he—"

"Orlando was estranged from his father, and had been for some time. Poor soul. He had a devil of a time trying to make both ends meet. He worked for a time delivering ale casks, but it got the better of him, if you know what I mean. And he filled in from time to time at the chemist's, but that—well, let's just say that didn't work out, either. I even gave him whatever work I could find for him washing dishes, but Arven didn't like having him underfoot, or so he claimed."

She sighed.

"Orlando lived in a boathouse down by the river—

Scull Cottage, they call it, although it's not quite so grand as it sounds. A leaky boathouse with a bed and paraffin camp stove is more like it."

She saw me looking at her.

"I only went down there once or twice," she told me. "Toward the end. To try to talk some sense into him."

"And did you?" I asked.

It was quite a long time before she answered. I could see her going over that visit, minute by minute in her mind.

"No," she said at last. "I didn't."

"You didn't?" the landlord said, appearing suddenly in the kitchen as if from a magic lamp. "You didn't what?"

"Oh, nothing, Arven," Mrs. Palmer said. "Dearie here was just asking me if I'd made her cucumber sandwich. It clear slipped my mind. Too many cooks."

How fascinating, I thought, *that she should both lie to her husband and, in the same breath, scold him for being in the kitchen.*

Or was she scolding *me*?

Whatever the case, I noted that she was a lightning liar. As a connoisseur of the untruth myself, I was quick to recognize the gift in others.

"Well, I'd better be going," I said, leaping up out of the Mercy Seat as if scalded (for the landlord's sake). "Thank you, anyway, Mrs. Palmer. I'll eat later. After I've picked up my snapshots."

It was far too early for Hob's photographs to have been processed: They would not be ready until tomorrow at the earliest. But it was a good excuse and I escaped with an—almost—clear conscience.

·ELEVEN·

WHEN YOU'RE PLANNING MISCHIEF, it's always a good idea to throw up a smokescreen in advance. Excuses made *after* the fact are seldom successful.

Which is why I made a point of mentioning to the Palmers that I was departing the Oak and Pheasant to pick up photographs. One would not ordinarily bother, or feel it necessary, to explain to a landlord where you were going or why. My real intent was to draw attention to the fact that I was taking myself elsewhere: which ought always to be your first concern when you plan to burgle someone's bedroom.

The second step is timing. It is only logical to plan your attack while the burglee is away from the intended target.

Say, for instance, that you were planning to rifle the bedroom of a country publican's wife in search of a certain book of poems. Logic would dictate that the best time to do so would be when the said publican's wife, being up to her ears in sauces in the kitchen, would be least likely to return to her sleeping chambers.

Which was now.

There wasn't a moment to lose.

Up the stairs I went, as if returning to my bedroom. At the first landing, I stopped to examine the shelf of books which Daffy had scoffed at.

Under Two Flags . . . *The Sea Hawk* . . . *Piracy* . . . *Eric Brighteyes* . . .

The titles alone made me seasick except the last one, which made me gag.

How could people waste their lives writing—or reading— such utter bilge?

There was no sign of anything slender enough to be poetry. Mrs. Palmer was not foolhardy enough to leave her explosive little book in plain sight where any commercial traveler might pick it up for a bit of bedtime reading. *Hide in plain sight* was a well-worn plot device used by legions of detective novelists, but not in this case.

Resuming my upward climb, I peered up through the old oak banisters and newel posts, but the landing above looked deserted. On tiptoe, I crept slowly up the last five steps.

The coast was clear.

The bedrooms rented out were at the front of the inn, facing the church, except mine and Dogger's, which both overlooked the sunken garden at the rear. This left only one room unaccounted for: the one I had decided belonged to the Palmers.

The door of this room was painted with buttermilk emulsion in a peculiar shade of blue, a color which reminded me not of buttermilk, but watery milk of the thin, skimmed variety: the skin of a decrepit duchess.

I pressed my ear tightly against one of the door panels. The only sound to be heard was that of my own heart.

I seized the knob and twisted. The door opened and I stepped inside.

How often fortune favors the brave!

In spite of its tall four-poster bed—which surely must be the very one that Good Queen Bess had slept in—the room was surprisingly small and crowded: clothespress, dresser, chair, table with alarm clock, faded red Turkey carpet on the floor, washstand, sink, shaving gear, skin cream. Aside from those few personal belongings, it was as spare as if the landlord and his wife were transients themselves, stopping overnight at the inn on their way to visit an expiring aunt in Exeter: hardly the room of a longtime landlord and his churchwarden wife who had lived here since the year dot.

The ancient wallpaper—surely no newer than the eighteenth century—portrayed a smoke-darkened Chinese landscape with repetitive fishing boats, mountains, cranes, bamboo, and pagodas.

I began my search for *The Mussel Bed* in the most obvious place: under the mattress. The high bedstead itself was shaky and precarious. Its elderly bed slats clattered horribly, like old bones raining down on a slate roof, and I eased the bedding back into its original position, hoping the noise would not be heard in the kitchen directly below.

I rifled the drawers of the dresser, fingering each item of clothing, and peered into the depths of the clothespress, plunging my hand into the deep pockets of the hanging bathrobes.

All to no avail.

I looked behind the curtains and under the carpet, behind framed pictures, and (against my will) into the flowered chamber pots.

I was about to turn my attention to the contents of the washstand when there was the creak of a floorboard: the sound of a footstep in the hall.

I froze.

Someone had paused at the top of the stairs. Another guest, perhaps, stopping to get their bearings in the dim, mazelike, up-again-down-again passageways of the old inn.

But then as I watched, the doorknob began—slowly—to turn.

I stepped back into the corner at the head of the bed. There wasn't quite enough material in the drapes of the canopy with which to wind myself a shroud.

I pressed myself against the wallpaper, hoping, somehow, miraculously to blend into those dreadful water-stained pagodas.

The door opened. A shoe appeared . . . a leg . . .

"What the devil are you doing in here?"

Needless to say, it was Daffy.

"I might ask you the same question," I told her, with a flick of my head so that my flying braids would give her a symbolic whip-lashing.

For a long moment, we stood there glaring at each other, both of us unwilling to give an inch.

De Luce v. de Luce, as the law liked to put it.

And not for the first time. Far from it!

There is an old scientific paradox: What happens when an irresistible object meets an immovable object? One solution to this stumper was proposed in a tale from Greek mythology in which an irresistible fox encounters an immovable hound—or vice versa. In that particular case, the great god Zeus turned both of them to stone, thus cleverly solving the problem.

And that was precisely what was happening here. My sister and I stood glowering at each other like a couple of calcified garden ornaments, a situation which persisted until I decided to give in. Otherwise, we would have still been standing there when we were gray-haired old ladies with hearing trumpets and china choppers.

"Looking for *The Mussel Bed*," I said, catching Daffy by surprise.

"So am I," she replied. "Let's search together."

I had begun listing all the places I had already looked when Daffy strode confidently across the room, climbed up onto the high mattress, and, standing fully upright, stretched her arm and felt along the top of the canopy.

"The spell for finding books," she whispered, closing her eyes before pronouncing the incantation: "*Abraca-dabra, Alakazam, Angela Thirkell, and Omar Khayyam.*"

I had never seen my sister so excited.

Slowly Daffy retracted her extended arm, and—to my

amazement—clutched in her hand was a slender book with yellow marbled covers.

"Eureka!" she said, for once not following the word with the usual offensive pun.

"How did you know it was up there?" I asked, not believing what I had just seen.

"When you have eliminated the impossible, whatever remains, however improbable, must indicate the four-poster."

"Huh?" I said, perhaps for the first time in my entire life.

"Elementary," Daffy said. "The Mussel Bed."

Only slowly did her words seep into the thinking part of my brain.

"Oh! I see," I said. "The Mussel *Bed*."

"Wonderful," Daffy echoed dryly, rolling her eyes up beseechingly to Heaven. "Now let's amscray."

Daffy had learned Pig Latin from Carl Pendracka and was inordinately proud of her ability to baffle Mrs. Mullet by lapsing into that tongue—or whatever you wish to call it—when she wished to convey a confidence, or deliver an insult.

"The eans-bay are urned-bay," she would say. "My ummy-tay is urning-tay to ar-tay."

Mrs. Mullet would beam upon her as if the king himself had complimented her on the glories of her cooking.

"Amscray," of course, meant "Scram."

"Ighty-ho-ray!" I said, and again Heaven was harrowed by my sister's scorching gaze.

Daffy held the slender volume up to her lips and blew. A small atomic dust cloud appeared and dissipated.

Then she tucked the book into the folds of her woolen cardigan. She had for the past six months or so begun complaining of the cold, even when the summer temperatures were tending toward the tropical, and never went anywhere without an old brown baggy knitted jumper which I realized only now, with a sudden shock, had belonged to Father.

I wanted to hug her but I didn't.

Hopping down from the bed, she gestured with her head and eyes that I was to follow.

Back in Daffy's room, we huddled over the book.

"The dust dictates that it has lain undisturbed. No fingerprints other than mine," she said.

"Which means that whoever is blackmailing her has their own copy," I suggested.

"Unless, of course, they borrowed it from a friend or from a library—or read it in a bookshop. The latter seems unlikely, though. A blackmailing letter is no casual thing. Like tough beef, it requires a certain amount of stewing on the part of the writer."

"Or cold-blooded calculating on the spur of the moment," I added.

This was a situation of which I had considerable first-hand experience.

"Precisely," Daffy said.

Precisely? Could this actually be Daphne speaking? To me?

To *me?*

Where were the razor words?—the acid accusations?

Had it come to pass that the fullness of time and a drowned dandy had finally brought my sister and me together? Was I witnessing a miracle?

And if that were true, was the miracle mine? Or was I merely caught in the crosswinds of someone else's heavenly intervention?

There was no time now to worry about such things. I would sort it out later.

But miracles, I knew, above all, required acknowledgment. Some sign must be given before the bestowing angel took it into his or her head to throw in the towel; to wander off in a sulk and give the gift to someone else instead, out of sheer spite, such as the ruddy traveling wine salesman in the room across the hall.

Accordingly, I crossed my eyes at Daffy.

If we were to be colleagues in crime—even just this once—then priorities needed to be established at the outset.

"Open the book," I commanded, perhaps a little too forcefully. "Let's get on with it."

She looked at me. I looked at her.

"I can't wait to hear your professional opinion, Daff," I improvised. "I'm a complete duffer when it comes to literary excellence."

With all the cool confidence of a Mona Lisa with all

the aces, she cradled the book in her left palm and opened it to the first page. She let out a whistle.

"Crikey!" she said. "Listen to this. It's the dedication. There's also a dedicatory poem:

> "*To Mine Own Leander.*
> *The copper mare and*
> *The brass stallion graze*
> *In Flecker's Field.*
> *He paws the turf,*
> *While she the wind tastes.*
> *And when he trots to her*
> *She turns tail.*"

"I don't understand it," I said. "Does it mean anything?"

"Only to the discerning eye," Daffy said.

"Then you'd better explain," I told her. "I have no time to piddle about with poetry."

"Pity," Daffy said. "You might learn something."

"Such as?"

I was already becoming impatient.

"To begin with, Leander was a character in Greek mythology. He fell in love with a nun named Hero."

"Hold on," I said. "Hero is a man's name."

"It is now, yes. But in those days, it was a woman's. Before men reduced real history to rubble, then raked over the ruins, like a dog burying and digging up its . . . well, you know."

"Bone," I said, but Daffy ignored me.

"This Leander tried to swim the Hellespont at night, but a storm blew up and drowned him."

Drowned? At night?

This was becoming intriguing.

"What about Flecker's Field?" I asked. "I've never heard of the place. Is it around here somewhere?"

"Possibly," Daffy said, "but James Elroy Flecker was the name of a poet who died during the Great War."

"In battle?" I asked.

"In bed," Daffy said. "Not in the field, but in bed. Of tuberculosis. In Switzerland."

"I don't see the point," I said. I was glad I had taken up poisons, rather than poetry, which seems to me more baffling than belladonna.

"The point is," Daffy said, "that Flecker's Field—in one of its senses—was poetry. You know:

". . . *Have you heard*
That silence where the birds are dead yet something pipeth
like a bird?"

Invisible feathers tickled my spine. I was going to have to look into this Flecker chap. Perhaps I was even going to have to rethink poetry.

"Aha!" I said. "I understand!" Although actually, I didn't.

"So obviously," she went on, "the reference could be to some poet other than herself."

"But wait!" I said. "If Flecker's Field refers to poetry,

then it might just as well be Mrs. Palmer's *own* field, since she's a poet herself."

Daffy gave me a skeptical look.

"Or," I said, holding up a forefinger to emphasize a brilliant idea, "it might be an *actual* field. Is there a field belonging to the Oak and Pheasant?"

"Hmmm, I doubt it." Daffy frowned. "Modern poets are seldom literal—unless they live abroad in the colonies, of course. Still, I expect your idea might be worth looking into."

"Do you think we might find a *real* copper mare and a *real* brass stallion? Maybe it's a horse breeder we're looking for—or a racetrack."

"Or a railway," Daffy added, clapping me on the shoulders. "The Iron Horse, and all that."

Although I nearly fainted with surprise, I bore up remarkably well.

"And what about the rest of it?" I asked. "All that pawing of the turf and the tasting of the wind, and so forth?"

Daffy got up from the bed and went to the window, peering down into the sunken garden where Feely and Dieter were strolling round and round in circles, arm in arm.

She turned and gave me a long, cold, calculated look as if she were weighing whether to entrust me with some deep, dark secret. After what seemed to me like hours, but couldn't have been more than a quarter of a minute, she said:

"Leave that to me."

"Righty-ho," I said.

We had agreed, Daffy and I, that each of us would follow her own lines of investigation.

Not that I intended to, of course. Not for a mayfly's
minute.

What Daffy didn't realize was that we were aiming at
two different targets. While her intent was to unravel the
mysteries of a book of poetry, mine was to catch a killer.

I had no idea what she knew about Orlando Whitbread, and I didn't want to ask her. With her nose forever
in a book, Daffy was no great authority on today's front
page—or yesterday's, for that matter.

In her estimation, the world had come to an end in
1870. Nothing worthwhile had been written or published
since the death of Charles Dickens on the ninth of June
in that year.

Although she read more modern works, it was simply
to exercise her eyes—or so she claimed.

And so it was I who scanned the morning papers for
the lurid crimes. I had begun, of course, with the ava-
lanches of ancient newspapers that tumbled out of every
cupboard at Buckshaw, many of which dated back a century or more. From their brittle yellowing pages I had read
with fascination about the cream of the criminal element:
Haigh, Armstrong, Crippen; the list went on and on.

Once begun, it was hard to break the habit, and I was
already hungering for much more current news. Mrs.
Mullet was only too happy to bring me the latest papers
every day, after her husband had finished with them.

"Alf gets up with the sparrows every morning," she
told me, "so as to be at the newsagent's when they rolls up

the blinds. Alf says 'e can't 'elp it. 'As to find out what they're up to at Westminster. That lot needs keepin' an eye on. Our Agnes says 'e's what's called an invertebrate reader."

Agnes Mullet had left home some years ago to study Pitman Shorthand, and had since come to be considered—at least by Alf and Mrs. M—the world's greatest authority on anything which involved printed matter.

Unlike the great Sherlock Holmes, I did not keep a commonplace book other than the one that was in my head. Who could ever forget, for instance, even the tiniest detail of the Acid Bath murders, in which John George Haigh dissolved as few as six and as many as a dozen bodies in vats of concentrated sulfuric acid?

At the risk of sounding ghoulish, I swear that these titbits were etched permanently into my brain.

To put it bluntly, I was more accustomed than Daffy to dealing with death, while she was more accustomed to dealing with Dickens—which is all right, I suppose, if you feel you might be seized suddenly by little red men from Mars in their flying saucers and transported back to Victorian times.

Which is why I decided to keep my intentions to myself.

By now, it was getting late in the day. If I got a move on, I might even be back at the Oak and Pheasant in time for tea.

·TWELVE·

SHADRACH'S CIRCUS & MENAGERIE, all in all, was rather a shabby affair. A half dozen ancient pantechnicons were drawn up in a rough circle round the market square, like a wagon train under attack. Although they had the appearance of military vehicles which had barely survived the First World War, these sagging vehicles were painted in gaudy colors with the name of the circus, as well as garish images and slogans: MAN-EATING TIGERS! LIONS! ELEPHANTS! SEE THE SAVAGE BEASTS!

All of these, and more, were portrayed on the panels with oversized heads, snarling mouths, and teeth the size of icicles. A crouching cheetah was preparing to bring down a white Arabian stallion, which was rearing up, red nostrils flaring and eyes rolling in terror.

What would Hob think of such a dramatic scene? I wondered. Or was it too unreal?

Nearby, in a wheeled cage, a rather moth-eaten lion was sleeping on its back with feet in the air. To one side of the cage, the lone elephant, still chained by its leg to a post in the ground, munched thoughtfully on a stray newspaper. There were no tigers in sight.

A steam organ, sadly out of tune and sounding like defective plumbing, was playing the opening theme song for the wireless program *The Archers*, which seemed especially pathetic: *DUM-dee-DUMP-ity-DUM-dee-DUM, DUM-dee-DUM-dee-DUM-dee* . . . and so on, almost to distraction. Every one of the piercing notes was a new assault upon my ears. It was like being under attack by a swarm of those wasps that drill through the skin of baby figs to lay their eggs.

On a raised platform, a tall, thin man with a bare chest, but wearing suspenders, was swallowing a sword for an audience of two small boys who were fighting over a bag of apples. The sword-swallower put down his blade and began juggling five metal rings, but it made no difference: The apple war raged on.

I was wondering where to begin my investigations when a voice behind me said, "Look who's here again. Missed us, did you?"

I spun round to find myself face-to-face with the man in the polka-dot kerchief. This time, he was with his two friends. I stepped back instinctively.

All three of them had their hands in their pockets and all three had something in their mouths: one a toothpick, one a wooden matchstick, and Polka-Dot a cigarette.

"Come to see the menagerie, 'ave yer?" Matchstick asked. "Come to see the man-eating tigers?"

Polka-Dot snickered and blew a showy smoke ring.

That did it.

"Actually," I said, "I'm looking into the death of Orlando Whitbread—the man who was fished out of the river this morning."

I realized as soon as I said it that this was a hugely risky business. I was not only tossing away my anonymity but also, possibly, putting my life in jeopardy.

What if one of these bruisers was the killer? What if one—or two—or perhaps even all three of them had dumped Orlando into the water? Any one of these muscle-bound hulks could have overpowered his thin body with ease.

I watched their eyes carefully for the slightest sign of alarm, but there seemed to be no reaction other than amusement.

"Friend of yours, was he?" Polka-Dot asked, looking from one to the other of his pals as if he had made a capital joke.

"A relative, actually," I lied. "A cousin. A distant cousin, to be sure, but a cousin nonetheless."

"Nonetheless!" Polka-Dot coughed out the word in a cloud of smoke. "Hark her, Nigel! Nonetheless! *Nonetheless*, she says."

"Nonetheless," Matchstick replied with a grin, and I deduced that he must be Nigel.

"One of the Torquay Whitbreads," I went on, ignoring their stupid banter. "On my grandmother's side, obviously. My aunt Gregoria always predicted that Orlando would meet a watery death. 'You can count on it,' she used to say. And she was right. Of course, Aunt Gregoria had more than a little of the psychic about her, which might have given her a bit of an unfair advantage, don't you think, Mister . . . ?"

"Terence," Polka-Dot said.

"How do you do?" I asked, sticking out my hand and trying not to gag.

Terence's paw was black with circus grease and grime and knobbly with hardened calluses. To the touch it was like hand-wrestling with an engine-room oiler.

I would need to concoct a disinfectant as soon as I got back to the Oak and Pheasant.

"And you are?" I asked, offering my tainted hand to Matchstick.

"Nigel," he said, taking my fingers in his fist, and I almost laughed. "You don't look like a Nigel," I said gaily. "More like a Pierre, or a Jean Baptiste. But perhaps it's your neckerchief."

His neckerchief was gaily striped with blue, white, and red, like the French tricolor flag. I suppose it could equally have been red, white, and blue, like the British, but I wanted to flatter him.

I held out my hand to the third ruffian—Toothpick— and raised my eyebrows. His light blue neckerchief matched his eyes.

"Cornell," he said quietly. "Pleased to meet you, Miss—"

"Dorchester," I said. "Arabella Dorchester. But you can call me Arab. Everybody else does."

"Hold on," Terence protested. "That's not the name your sister gave us."

I arranged my features into a look of surprise.

"Betty?" I asked, letting my mouth fall open in disbelief. "Oh, she's such an awful liar! She's always telling people she's Lady Lancaster, or Dame Agatha Dimbleby. Who did she tell you she was?"

"Ophelia de Luce," said Nigel, looking like a man bamboozled.

"That scallywag," I said, shaking my head. "I'm so ashamed of her. I really must apologize on Betty's behalf."

The three roustabouts were looking distinctly uneasy. I had deftly turned the tables on them and got the upper hand. There was no time to lose.

"Now then," I asked, taking command as if it were I who had arranged our meeting, "how long have you gentlemen been in town?"

"Three days," Cornell answered obediently. "Counting today, that is."

I shot him a beaming smile as a reward, and from that moment on the poor lad was eating out of my hand.

"And you," I said, turning to Terence. I had already sized him up as the ringleader. "Are you in charge of these great beastly machines?" I asked, waving a hand toward the parked pantechnicons. "Gosh, they must be jolly difficult to drive."

I almost reached out to feel one of his bulging biceps, but I restrained myself.

Terence drew in a deep breath.

I had him.

"Well, then," I said, rubbing my hands together. "About Cousin Orlando. I'm sure Aunt Gregoria would be willing to offer a generous reward for information. Just to put her mind to rest, you understand. Orlando was more or less her pet, you know. Actually, she spoiled him outrageously."

"We seen 'im round about—'ere and there," Terence said, shifting his shoulders and looking away, trying to disguise the telltale glitter in his eyes.

"I'm surprised to hear that," I said. "I should have thought you'd have seen a great deal more of him. Cousin Orlando was simply mad about circuses. More than mad: He had a bee in his bonnet about them. He didn't beg to run away with you, did he? To be trained as a clown? Offered to work for nothing?"

"'E never said anything like that to us," Nigel volunteered.

Which told me what I wanted to know: They *had* talked to Orlando. He had still been alive when they arrived in town the day before yesterday. More to the point, they had been here when he died.

"What did he say, then?" I asked, turning to Cornell.

"We had a few drinks with him is all," Cornell said, "at the Wooden Bird."

"The Wooden Bird?" I asked.

"The Oak and Pheasant. It's a kind of joke. We've always called it that."

"Why?" I asked.

Cornell shrugged.

"Who knows? Same reason the landlord is always

called Gov', no matter his real name. It's a tradition. You might as well ask why they always drop bread in the churchyard, or dance round the Maypole with wooden hobbyhorses!"

"Always?" I asked. "You've been here before?"

"Shadrach's has been stopping here since Napoleon was in nappies," Terence said.

"And which of you is Mr. Shadrach?" I said.

All three of them laughed at once, as if their mouths were tied together with a string.

"Mr. Shadrach went to his reward when Queen Victoria was on the throne, if you'll pardon the expression," Terence said.

Again came the clockwork laughs—but only two, this time.

"Then who's the proprietor nowadays?" I asked. "Cousin Orlando may have approached him."

"Approached *her*, you mean," Terence told me. "Mrs. Dandyman. 'Dreadnought Dandyman,' we call her."

The three of them broke into sniggers, and I noticed that Cornell looked cautiously over his shoulder.

"Because she's an old battleship," he explained. "A dreadnought is a battle cruiser from the time of World War One."

"HMS *Colossus* and HMS *Collingwood*, for instance," I said.

I'd show them I knew my peas from my pickles. I had often enough pored over the ancient picture magazines which simply bulged to bursting with photographs of British Naval Power.

Not one of the three seemed to be able to come up with a reply.

"And where might I find Mrs. Dandyman?" I asked, following the line of Cornell's glance, which was toward the largest of the pantechnicons—the one with the stallion and the cheetah.

"Over there—in Bucking Horse Palace," Nigel said. "Just don't tell her we told you."

"Bit of a tartar, is she?" I asked.

Terence gave off a noise that sounded as if his sinuses had collapsed.

"Judge for yourself," he said as he turned and walked away with Nigel and Cornell hard on his heels. Behind the backs of his two pals, Cornell twiddled his fingers goodbye.

A slight chill touched my bare arms as I stepped into the shadow of the pantechnicon. The sheer tonnage of the thing loomed over me like a vast red whale.

My first task was to find the entrance, which was not easy. The metal skin of the thing appeared to be seamless, and the enormous murals of the beasts made it even more difficult to find a door. After a complete walk-around without success, I finally spotted a small set of folding stairs, cunningly concealed among the roots of a painted jungle tree. Only then did I spot the door, its hinges hidden by the artist's idea of bark.

Someone, I thought, *is particular about her privacy.* And I couldn't help but wonder *why?*

I gave the steps a gentle pull—more as a test than anything—and was astonished when they folded out and down without a sound.

"Hello?" I called. "Mrs. Dandyman, are you there?"

Again in silence, the steps folded themselves up as they retracted and locked into place with a metallic *click*. It was as if they had never existed.

Hydraulic, I thought. *How clever*. They could be opened and closed from the inside as well as from the outside, which made sense.

All I needed to do was find the push button.

Which wasn't all that difficult once you knew what you were looking for.

And yes! Here it was: not a button, but a switch, cunningly disguised as one of the tiger's claws.

I looked round to see if anyone was watching me, but Terence and his chums had wandered away from the pantechnicon, leaving me alone in the shadow of the thing.

No one would see me climb aboard (if I was able to). If I vanished from the face of the earth, no one would ever know where I had gone. Orlando's fish-nibbled features sprang suddenly into my mind.

"Mrs. Dandyman?" I called again. "I'd like to speak with you."

When there was no answer, I reached out and flipped the switch.

The silent steps came down and, with the slightest hiss of air such as you might expect from an alien spaceship, like the one Michael Rennie stepped out of in *The Day the Earth Stood Still*, the metal door slowly began to open.

"Hello?" I called out into the darkness, placing a foot on the lowest tread.

When no one told me to keep out, or to go away, I took it as an invitation and climbed aboard.

To my right was a heavy hanging curtain. I pulled it aside—foolhardy, perhaps, but I did it anyway—and walked through.

I couldn't suppress a gasp.

The cavernous space—I hesitate to call it a room—was filled with paintings: a dozen or so, each on its own altar and each illuminated by a row of flickering candles.

A private chapel, I thought.

In one of the paintings, a man flayed to his bare muscles stood holding his own skin draped over his arm like a toga. In another, a nearly naked man was being grilled over a makeshift stove by men with lances. And in yet another, a woman armed only with a crucifix was using it as a blade to cut her way out of a dragon's belly.

"Chamber of horrors, isn't it?" said a voice. "Better run away before something nasty happens to you."

I hadn't seen her there, half hidden, as she was, by a hanging curtain.

She took a step toward me, a pointed object in her hand.

I was already preparing to take to my heels when I realized that her weapon was an artist's paintbrush.

As she stepped out of the shadows, I could see that the woman had been working on a canvas of a group of men, bound together by weighted chains, being tossed over the side of a ship and into the sea while, nearby on the shore,

another man hung from a cross surrounded by a swarm of
bees.

"They're beautiful!" I exclaimed. "Every one of them.
That's Saint Astius on the cross, isn't it? He was covered in
honey and left in the hot sun to be stung to death by bees."

The woman took another step toward me, her can-
dlelit face blazing like a comet in the half-darkness, her
gray hair streaming out behind her like the comet's tail.

Closer and closer she came until her nose was nearly
touching mine. The odor of garlic on her breath was so
overwhelming that when she spoke, I could smell every
word.

"Blimey!" she said. "You do know your saints, don't
you?"

I was afraid that her next question would be to ask my
name, but I needn't have worried.

"Who's this, then?" she asked, pointing to the group of
men who were being forced to walk the plank.

Was it my imagination, or did one of them look uncannily like Orlando Whitbread? I had only seen him dead,
of course, so it was difficult to tell.

"The seven martyrs of Dyrrachium," I said, ticking them
off on my fingers. "Germanus, Hesychius, Lucian, Papius,
Peregrinus, Pompeius, and Saturninus—alphabetically,
that is."

I did not tell her that I had once won a prize by being
able to regurgitate those names on demand. Poor Father
Duffy, back in Hinley, was probably still shaking his head
at the defeat of his house Goliath, Mary Rose Trethewey,

who had a photographic memory but whom Fate had dealt a losing hand when I was given her question by mistake.

Feely (who knew him from one of the music festivals) had tipped me off that Father Duffy was obsessed with the Albanian Martyrs, and that they were more likely than not to be hauled out of the hat like white rabbits, in order to defeat the Bishop's Lacey home team.

I had got their names off by heart by making a mnemonic of the first letters of the martyrs' names: **Give Him Large Portions of Potted Plums and Strychnine.**

G, H, L, P, P, P, S.

Germanus, Hesychius, Lucian, Papius, Peregrinus, Pompeius, and Saturninus.

Just like that, and I had come away with the trophy: a rather cheesy china teacup with my name (misspelled) painted on the back by Mary Margaret Tackaberry, the captain of the Crafts League.

I didn't notice until I got home that the Virgin Mary on the front of the cup was sticking out her tongue.

"Very impressive," Mrs. Dandyman said, turning to the skinned man.

"Saint Bartholomew," I said. "The patron saint of tanners."

"And this?"

"The bloke on the barbecue?" I asked, becoming more sure of myself by the minute. "That's easy: Saint Lawrence. I believe they still have the grill on display in a church in Rome."

166 · ALAN BRADLEY

Before she could question me further, it was time to gain the upper hand. I pointed to the woman escaping from the dragon's gut.

"Margaret of Antioch. The dragon is the devil in disguise. Serves him right. You'd think that he, of all people, would know that crucifixes are not just used against vampires."

Mrs. Dandyman lifted one of Saint Bartholomew's candles out of its socket and held it up in front of my face. For a long time she examined my features, moving her light from right to left.

"I've seen you before, somewhere," she said. "But I can't for the life of me remember where."

I shrugged.

"I'm just a girl," I said, hating myself even as I said it. "Ever so many girls have mousy hair. I'm just one of the mice."

Sometimes, you must manufacture camouflage with whatever is within easy reach, which, in this case, was my mouth. And my brain, of course.

I needed to divert her attempt to put a name to my face. She might have seen my photograph in the newspaper not long ago.

"I feel that I can trust you, Mrs. Dandyman, but you must give me your word that you won't share with a soul what I'm about to confide in you."

Who, in the entire history of the world since Adam and Eve, has ever been able to resist so downright juicy an offer?

"I give you my word," she said, already licking her lips in anticipation.

I touched the back of her hand with my fingers to change her promise into an unbreakable bond.

"I'm the one who found Orlando Whitbread's body," I said, and I watched her eyes. "I need to talk to you."

·THIRTEEN·

"ORLANDO?" SHE GASPED. "HE's dead?"

Even by the warm light of the flickering flames I could see the color draining from her face, an effect which is virtually impossible to fake—and goodness knows, I've tried.

If this woman wasn't honestly shocked, she was the greatest actress I had ever seen.

"When?" she asked. "Where? What happened?"

"This morning," I told her. "In the river."

"Was it suicide?"

I said nothing, a trick I had learned from Inspector Hewitt, which had proved to be one of the most useful weapons in my arsenal.

"But no, that's not possible," she said, answering her own question. "That's simply not possible."

"Perhaps it was an accident," I suggested, sparing her

what I believed to be the truth—at least for the time being.

"Not likely," she insisted. "Orlando grew up on the riverbank."

I continued my silence.

"He was always as much at home in the water as Mole and Ratty. Boats, swimming, fishing. I'm surprised he hadn't grown gills."

I recognized at once that she was referring to the animal characters from *The Wind in the Willows*.

"Always?" I asked, choosing my question with care.

"It seems like always. Shadrach's Circus has been coming here year in and year out since the old man himself—blast him—was alive."

"Your father?" I asked, meaning Shadrach, whomever he might be.

This produced an ironic and tight little laugh.

"My great step-uncle," she said. "He was a monster. Even the tigers lived in fear of him. In the days when we *had* tigers, I mean. Nowadays, we have only one: Saladin. Near-blind and toothless. He only growls because his bones ache."

"So you've known Orlando for a long time," I said helpfully.

"Since he was a boy, poor lad. He used to beg us to take him away with us. Not that he had any illusions of becoming a showman, but simply to escape from his father."

"Canon Whitbread," I said, matter-of-factly. "The one who—"

Mrs. Dandyman held up a restraining hand.

"Yes, *that* one. Say no more about it. I find it distressing."

"But I thought everyone loved Canon Whitbread."

"And so they did—until he did away with three harmless old ladies who dared disagree with him. Love can forgive only so many murders."

She was being ironic, I was quite sure of it.

Daffy had once explained to me that irony consisted of words from another world: that they did not seem to mean what you thought they meant, which was a contradiction in itself.

"They're words from the other side of the looking-glass," Daffy told me, "and ought always to be answered as such."

Could I trust Daffy? In cases like this, I had no other choice.

I took a deep breath, counted to three, looked Mrs. Dandyman in the eye, and asked: "How many murders have *you* forgiven?"

"None," she answered. "Nor will I—ever."

I was flabbergasted by her words. Here was a woman after my own heart! How I rejoiced in meeting her!

And yet I mustn't let her know.

In my own short life I had come to believe that murder is unforgiveable. Perhaps, in time, when I was older, I would come to see things differently, though for now, I was happy enough to be lumped with Saint Augustine, who prayed for purity—but, as he said, not yet.

"Who were they?" I asked. "The women he did away with, I mean."

"The Three Graces, we used to call them, if somewhat

inaccurately. Two Graces and an Annie, in fact, but there's no sense in nicknames, is there? Grace Willoughby, Grace Harcourt, and Annie Cray. Faith, Hope, and Treachery. The Weird Sisters, others called them."

"Were they actually sisters?"

"Good lord, no! It was just that they all stirred the cauldron of gossip more than was good for them—or for anyone else. There's nothing so deadly as an acid tongue driven by a pious mind. That's what Canon Whitbread said in one of his last sermons."

"Just before he poisoned them?" I asked.

"Some say that, yes."

"And you?"

"I keep to myself," Mrs. Dandyman replied.

She turned back to her easel and I suspected I was being dismissed.

I was, after all, trespassing.

"Why martyrs?" I blurted. "Why do you paint only martyrs?"

"This world we live in," she said, keeping her back to me, "is made up of saints and sinners. And of the two, there's a shortage of saints. It's as simple as that."

But was it? Did her words—which seemed to me to come too easily, as if she'd been asked this question before—mean that she saw it as her duty to supply the world with saints, even painted ones?

Or to rid the world of sinners?

Flavia, I thought, *you are developing a suspicious mind.*

"One more question, if I may," I persisted. "And then I'll leave you to your work."

She didn't answer, so I asked it anyway.

"Who hated Orlando enough to kill him?"

Mrs. Dandyman spun round and dropped her brush, splattering the hem of her dress and the legs of the easel with an ax-murderer scarlet.

"Nobody!" she exclaimed. "And don't you dare suggest otherwise. Don't you dare even think about it."

"What about Poppy Mandrill?" I asked brazenly. If I were to be tossed out on my ear I desperately needed one last morsel of information.

"Out!" Mrs. Dandyman shouted. "Out with you before I call the police."

I wondered idly how she could carry out this threat with no telephone in the pantechnicon, but it was no time to anger the woman further.

"I'm sorry," I said, and walked out the door, down the folding steps, and into the sunshine, my head in the air, not sorry in the least.

On the far side of the market square, Constable Otter was engaged in conversation with the three roustabouts, Terence, Nigel, and Cornell.

I put on a carefree expression and, with a careless whistle, became absorbed in kicking an empty ginger-beer bottle ahead of me as I walked. The greatest thing about being twelve is that you can turn it on and off as the situation requires.

The instant Constable Otter spotted me, he touched the front of his helmet with a long forefinger and made a beeline toward me. I angled away slightly—not too obviously, I hoped—and began to tack back toward the Oak and Pheasant.

It was no use. The blasted man had me on his radar and changed course even as I did. He reminded me of Inspector Bucket in *Bleak House,* that relentless hound who seemed to be everywhere at the same time.

"Miss de Luce," he called out.

Picking up speed slightly and changing direction again, I pretended I hadn't heard him.

"Miss de Luce!" he called again, more persistent this time.

I couldn't possibly evade him without breaking into a full gallop.

By now he was at my heels, and with my peripheral vision, I could see that he was reaching for my arm. I did the only thing I could think of: I stopped dead in my tracks.

Constable Otter crashed into me at speed, and down I went, ark over teakettle into the dust.

Intentionally, of course.

I lay there looking dazed—allowing the man to scramble to his feet, pick up his helmet, dust himself off, and regain his dignity. Meanwhile, I began, slowly and painfully, contorting my limbs into the most bizarre angles I could conjure up on a moment's notice from my monkey ancestors.

Laboriously, I hauled myself to my knees.

I set my drooping head to vibrating at high speed, like the clanger on an alarm clock, as if I were on the verge of a seizure, all the while groping for my elbows, knees, shoulders, and giving off a few pitiful moans.

"Are you all right?" he asked. "I'm sorry, but—"

"Shappened?" I said, slurring the word and letting my tongue thicken and loll out the corner of my mouth. "Hoss hit me?"

It wasn't a bad plan to raise the specter of concussion right at the outset.

"I'm sorry," the constable said again, reaching for my elbow to help me up, but I shook him off.

A small crowd had begun to gather. I gaped at them blearily, letting my eyes roll a little, as if I had never seen human beings before.

I grasped Otter's hand and hauled myself agonizingly to my feet.

"What's she done, then, Constable?" a man in rubber boots called out. "Broke into the Bank of England?"

In spite of my grave injuries, most of the onlookers laughed at this sudden flash of wit.

"He attacked her!" called out a small birdlike woman with white hair and spectacles the thickness of railway signal lamps. "I saw it with my own two eyes!"

Another laugh went up.

"Pick on someone your own size, Jimmy!" the rubber-booted man called out.

I could see that, round his official police collar, Constable Otter was turning red as rubies. I decided that he had had enough.

"Sorright," I said. "My fault. I tripped. I shurrna stopped so . . . so . . ."

I rolled my eyes again, fishing for an elusive word.

"Fasht," I concluded triumphantly.

There! I had done it!

Constable Otter was suddenly beaming upon me like some pagan Sun God of beaten gold.

"Are you all right?" I asked, reaching out a solicitous (but trembling) hand toward him for extra points.

I shook my head to clear it and then I took his arm.

"I'm still a little shaky," I said. "Perhaps you could walk me back to the Oak and Pheasant, and you can question me over a nice cup of tea."

That's how it's done.

At least in *my* books.

And so it came to pass that PC Otter and I were alone at last in the saloon bar of the Oak and Pheasant, safely away from any danger of being overheard.

"Please have a seat, Constable," I said. The place was my residence, after all, even if only temporarily. Besides, it cost nothing to be polite.

"Thank you, miss," he said, pulling his inevitable notebook from his pocket. "But I'm on duty."

"I hope you won't mind if I sit," I said. "I'm sorry to be so much trouble. I expect your wife will be wondering what's become of you."

"No, she won't," he replied, "as I don't have a wife. Now then, about the . . . uh . . . deceased, which you discovered in the river this morning."

"Orlando Whitbread?" I asked, as if I had an endless

string of corpses up my sleeve, which I suppose in a way I did.

"How did you know his name?" he pounced, his pencil poised.

"Poppy Mandrill was screaming it. You could hear her a mile away. Besides, everyone in the county knows it by now."

Constable Otter made a brief scribble in his notebook as he arranged his features into a look of Official Gravity.

"You're not withholding anything from me, are you, miss?"

"Withholding?"

I wanted to add *"What could I possibly be withholding?"* but with the slip of paper from Orlando's trousers still soggy in my pocket, I didn't want to say too much.

I was beginning to learn that in criminal investigation, as in chair design and poetry, less is more.

At that moment, the landlord appeared with the tray of tea I had ordered on the way in.

"I've brought a few shortbread biscuits," Mr. Palmer said. "Some people like a few shortbread biscuits with their tea."

Since neither I nor the constable said anything, he gave the table a quick wipe and left us to our discussion.

I took a biscuit and dipped it into my tea. Etiquette be hanged.

"I expect Scotland Yard will be arriving at any moment," I remarked pleasantly. "And I shall be grilled again. It's such a bore, isn't it?"

"Scotland Yard?" Constable Otter said, not touching his tea. "Why would we bring in the Yard? They're not called out for every little accident, you know."

He shook his head and gave me a rueful smile.

"What would they think if we bothered them with every bruise—every skinned knee?" he said, glancing pointedly at my own knee which was scraped raw from my tumble. I hadn't even noticed.

So he still believed Orlando's death to be an accident, did he? Not worth reporting.

Investigation wrapped up in ribbons by the local constable. A discreet inquest which would find that the victim met his death through misadventure. A trip in the dark. Nobody's fault. Case closed.

Which left the field to me.

If I played my hand properly, I would get to the bottom of this affair, and present it myself—solved—to the appropriate inspector at the Yard. Providing I could discover who he was.

And perhaps—yes, perhaps—I could ring up Inspector Hewitt and lay the whole thing at his feet much as a dog brings a bone.

The important thing was to lie low; to say nothing to anyone.

From here on in, I would be as silent as the tomb.

I took a last sip from my teacup, and set it back on the saucer, taking great care to let my hand shake enough to produce a noticeable clatter of chinaware.

"I'm afraid I'm not as well as I thought I was," I said to

Constable Otter, summoning up a sickly, insipid smile. "I still feel quite shaken. If you'll excuse me, I think I'll go to my room and lie down."

I could see the relief on his face.

No more competition, he was thinking. *No more interference from that de Luce brat.*

In his eyes, I was already a dead duck.

Well, *"Quack! Quack! Quack!"*

I had just reached the top of the stairs when Mrs. Palmer came suddenly out of her room. She seemed surprised to see me.

"Oh, there you are," she said. "Did the undertaker find you?"

"Undertaker?" I asked, genuinely puzzled.

"Mr. Nightingale. He was looking for you. Arven told him you were in the saloon bar with Constable Otter. Didn't he look in?"

"No," I said. "Perhaps he didn't want to disturb us. Did he say what it was about?"

"He was looking for his son. Thought you might have been the last to see him."

My heart gave a leap.

"Is he missing?" I asked.

"Only in a general sort of way," Mrs. Palmer replied. "Hob is not your usual boy. Without a mother, and his father busy with the graves and so forth, he comes and goes when he pleases. He wouldn't if he were my son. I'd put a string on him."

I was reminded instantly of Hob and his kite. And his camera. Perhaps I could kill two birds with one stone by locating the little boy—probably gone back to Shadrach's Circus, I thought—and by retrieving his processed film from the chemist's shop.

But here was a pretty kettle of fish: Why would Mr. Nightingale keep clear of me when he knew I was with Constable Otter? Wasn't the constable, after all, the official eyes and ears of Volesthorpe, who probably knew to within a square yard the location of every single inhabitant at any given moment—as well as what they were up to?

It simply didn't make sense.

I vowed then and there to ask Mr. Nightingale that very question as soon as I was able to locate him. I was confident that he would give me a frank answer.

Undertakers were, I had discovered, decent men. Once you had got past the black crepe, the polished ebony, and the closely shaven chins, they were a tribe of hail-fellows-well-met, who enjoyed a joke as much as the next fellow, and sometimes more.

But aside from that, and perhaps more importantly, they knew—not to put too fine a point upon it—where all the bodies were buried.

I needed to buff up my acquaintanceship with Hob's Da, I realized, and I needed to do so immediately.

And this was the perfect opportunity.

"Thanks, Mrs. Palmer," I said. "Hob can't be far away. I saw him just a while ago. He's probably gone back for another squint at the elephant."

*

Outside, in the garden bower, Feely and Dieter were still clutching both of each other's hands, each gazing into the eyes of the other as if they were about to burst into song, like Jeanette MacDonald and Nelson Eddy in *Maytime* or one of those boring but unsettling films featuring advanced wrestling holds.

They didn't even see me.

Which was just as well, because I didn't wish to be seen.

An older sister in love is an unexploded bomb (UXB) at the best of times, but when she's just been reunited with her intended mate after a nerve-shredding separation of more than half a year, she's as touchy and unstable as a rusty bucket of old nitroglycerine ($C_3H_5O_9N_3$), and consequently best steered clear of.

I made my way back to the high street and to the premises of Wanless & Sons Dispensing Chemists, taking great care by stopping to gape like a tourist at the half-timbered shops and the tiny leaded windows of the adjoining houses.

I dawdled on the pavement for a couple of minutes, shaking my head at the quaintness of it all.

And then I stepped casually into the dimness of the shop.

"We're closed," said the man in white behind the counter. He looked as if he hadn't budged since I was here hours ago.

"I'm sorry," I replied. "But I wondered if there's the slightest chance my prints are ready? I don't mean to bother you, but there's been a family emergency and we've been summoned home immediately."

"Summoned" was a perfect choice of words, I thought. It added such great gravity to the situation.

He gave me that stare that chemists have.

"I don't know," he said, "but I doubt it. I had to step out for a while, you understand. We're very busy.

"Howland!" he bellowed, but this time there was no reply from the underworld.

He stamped on the floorboards. "Howland!"

"Would you mind checking?" I asked. "I'm afraid that it's . . . it's . . ."

I stifled a sob. Pressure works best when applied at precisely the right moment.

The chemist clicked his tongue with that sound which is usually written "Tch," and which suggests martyrdom: "Give me the strength to suffer this fool gladly."

Bending down, he pulled at an iron ring that was inset into the trapdoor and lifted it, revealing the top of a steep and narrow set of stairs—more of a ladder than anything.

I leaned round the wicket for a better view, but the chemist, with that crablike secrecy natural to his profession, scuttled down the hole, pulling the hatch closed behind him, and I, tiptoeing as silently as I could, stepped onto it.

I'd have to be quick.

A lightning scan of the counter did not reveal what I was hoping to find. An apothecary's pill roller of wood and marble and a brass balance were on one side and a paper-dispensing roll on the other.

No, it wasn't here. It would be put away somewhere out of sight, as official objects often are.

I pulled out one of the two deep drawers in which were a surprising number of loose coins, bills, and a few slips of scribbled paper which I guessed to be IOUs.

Don't touch, Flavia, I thought. *Fingerprints and so forth.*

I closed the first drawer and pulled out the second.

"Fortune favors girls with guts," some ancient Roman had once written, or ought to have written, because it was true.

I was instantly rewarded: There before my very eyes was a tall, black slender volume. *Sale of Poisons Register Book* was stamped on the cover in gold letters.

I hauled it out and opened it, fingerprints be hanged. It couldn't possibly be a crime to examine an official document. Could it?

I turned the pages with trembling fingers, beginning at the back, where the latest entries were written in a black and official-looking ink.

Each page had space for four entries, each detailing the date, the name and address of the purchaser, the name and quantity of the poison sold to them, the purpose for which it was required, and their signature, along with the name of the person who had introduced the purchaser to the chemist, which, in most cases, had been signed or initialed by the chemist himself: E. B. Wanless, presumably the name of that white-jacketed gentleman who was presently rummaging around somewhere in the depths beneath my feet.

My eyes widened as the secrets of Volesthorpe were laid bare. Here, in page after page, among the purchases of lead and opium to treat spasms, were the names and addresses of everyone who had bought sixpennyworth of rat poison and mouse poison; arsenic for psoriasis, or—four pounds of it at a time!—to tan or cure skins; potassium cyanide to destroy wasp's nests, or for photographic purposes.

As I leafed back toward the entries of two years ago, a notation fairly leapt at me off the page: HCN.

Prussic acid!

An ounce of the stuff had been sold to the Volesthorpe Constabulary. My pulse leapt as I read the reason given for the purchase: "Poison injured dog," it said.

And it had been signed for by J. R. Otter, Constable 997.

A wooden clatter beneath my feet indicated that the chemist was coming back up the ladder.

There was no time to waste: I shifted my brain into its speed-reading setting, tuning my eye for any occurrence of HCN, prussic acid, or cyanide.

And there were, I'm sorry to say, many—most requiring an ounce to poison a dog or a cat. And Hob's photographer brother, Pippin Nightingale, had, in an entry dated 1st November, 1949, signed for two ounces of "Cyanide of Potash," his given reason being "Silver Bath."

And in August of the same year, Canon Whitbread, of

"The Vicarage, St. Mildred's" had bought two ounces of potassium cyanide for the purpose of "destroying wasps' nests."

I touched the dead man's signature with my forefinger. I pictured him standing here at this very wicket as the cyanide was handed over. What was in his mind? What was in his heart?

I remembered, too, that according to Mrs. Palmer, Orlando had worked part-time at the chemist's shop, but as far as I could see, he had never signed this register, either as a buyer or a dispenser of poison. Which made sense, I suppose, since he was not licensed as a pharmaceutical dispenser.

The floor was now beginning to quake beneath my feet as the chemist applied his shoulder to the trapdoor. A string of muffled, but still clearly naughty, curses filtered up through the heavy floorboards.

"Hello?" I called out, injecting a note of surprise into my voice as I slipped the poison register back into the drawer and shoved it shut with my hip. "Is something wrong?"

At the same moment, with both feet still firmly on the trap, I bent down, seized the iron ring, and gave it a jolly good rattling.

"Blast!" I said in a frustrated voice, kicking at the ring. "I think it's stuck."

More chemical profanity floated up from under the floorboards.

"Hold on," I shouted. "I need to get something to lift it."

A few more heavy but useless heaves from below convinced my captive that I was telling him the truth.

I smeared a bit of dust from the floor onto my cheekbones, tousled my hair, then bent and threaded one of my pigtails through the ring. Then, in one single and continuous motion, in a fluid movement that would have delighted both Sexton Blake and Philip Odell, the BBC wireless detective, I stepped off the trap and pulled open the hatch, using my hair as a rope.

I stared down for a moment into the lobster-red face of the chemist.

I held the pose just long enough that the astonished Wanless could see what I had done. Then, freeing my hair from the ring with a flick of my head, I stuck out a helping hand and began to haul him up out of the hole.

"Oh, you poor soul," I cooed, hoping it would sound genuine. "The beastly ring was jammed. I had a very dickens of a time getting it open. How brave of you not to have panicked! If it were me"—I shuddered—"I should have shed a kidney."

I know . . . I know. But sometimes it's necessary.

I steadied his shaking arm as he came scrambling up out of the open hatch like a sailor escaping a sinking submarine.

It was easy enough to see that the man had worked himself up into a tizzy. *Claustrophobia,* I thought. *No point in staring and embarrassing him.*

"I'll just take my prints, then, and be on my way," I said, in that cheery voice that makes people want to strangle you.

I was simply dying to whistle "Someday My Prints Will Come," but I thought better of it.

"There are no prints," Wanless muttered, running his finger round the inside of his collar.

"They didn't turn out?" I asked. My heart began to sink.

"I expect they did," he said. "Howland had to charge extra for the expedited service."

"That's all right," I said blithely. "I don't mind paying. How much will it be?"

"You don't understand," the chemist said. "Howland must have dealt with it while I was out. They've already been picked up. Picked up and paid for. Less than an hour ago. It's marked in his receipt book."

He pointed toward the cellar.

My jaw fell open.

"Picked up by whom, may I ask?" I demanded, stiffening my spine like Aunt Felicity. I'd show this impertinent tradesman a thing or two! "They were *my* photographs."

But wait—best not to get too shirty. Perhaps Hob had picked up the snapshots and was lurking somewhere, chortling at the thought of surprising me with the finished prints.

"Ah," I said, relieved at the idea. "My friend—the little lad . . ."

Wanless gave me a quizzical look.

"They were signed for by Constable Otter," he said.

How did Otter know about the prints? I thought. *Had Hob told him? Or had he spotted the camera at the riverbank after all and decided to let it lead where it may—as I should have done, in his boots.*

I tried not to gulp. I mustn't panic. If Hob's aerial photographs showed anything at all—which I wasn't sure of—I didn't want them falling into the hands of Constable Otter.

I'll admit my reasons were selfish ones, but Otter had the full force of the law at his command, while I had only my wits. Would he have been so bold as to open the envelope and have a peep at someone's private prints? If he was any kind of investigator, he almost certainly would. I had already noted his keenness.

One thing was certain: I needed to find Constable Otter immediately, and to recover the photographs without arousing suspicion.

I have always believed that it's better to seize the bull by the horns than to be bitten in the backside. At the risk of dragging in too many animals, I would beard the lion in his den.

And, like Daniel in the book of the same name, I would trust in the Almighty to zip the lion's lips.

·FOURTEEN·

THE VOLESTHORPE CONSTABULARY—A DANK and moss-covered stone guardhouse—was located in the market square. It must once have been used as the village lockup.

One could easily imagine a set of wooden stocks at the door, facing the village green, where the village rowdies and hotheads were left to cool their heels—and their heads—until the alcohol wore off.

Attached to the rear, as an afterthought, were what I took to be the bachelor living quarters of Constable Otter: a wooden lean-to built along the lines of a Quonset hut cut in half and rammed up against the original medieval jail.

The constable's bicycle, with his rainproof cape lashed to the carrier, was parked out in front under the blue lamp.

The lion was at home.

I threw back my shoulders and straightened my back. "Don't slouch," Daffy was always telling me, "otherwise you'll look like me."

My sister affected a scholarly slouch of which she was particularly proud. "Bent under the burden of knowledge," she was fond of saying. "A cripple for culture."

I took a deep breath, stuck out my chin, stuffed make-believe shoulder pads into my blouse, arranged my features into what I thought Joan Crawford might look like in such a situation, and marched in the door.

Constable Otter looked up from the battered-looking counter at which he was writing.

"Well?" he asked.

"I believe you have my photographs," I said coldly, holding out my hand, palm up, to receive them.

"Have I, now?" he asked in a teasing tone.

So! It was going to be one of *those* conversations. A catalog of condescension.

Well, two could play at that game. I was glad I had been alerted so early on.

"Yes," I said. "You have. The chemist gave them to you—to give to me."

I moved closer and stuck out my hand again—too close to his face to be ignored.

"Is that what he said?"

Actually, he hadn't. I was bluffing and he knew it.

We were eye to eye. Which of us would blink first?

"Well?" he asked again.

Maddening.

He pulled them from under the counter, running a finger teasingly along the flap of the envelope, as if he was about to open it and remove the prints. The man was toying with me. I had to do something—and quickly.

"Constable," I said, "I wish to remind you that those photographs are my personal property. As such, they are protected by several Acts of Parliament. Unless you are seizing them in evidence, you have no right of possession. You are breaching my privacy."

Otter ought to have known better. I saw a slight haziness come into his eyes, like a scattering of cloud beginning to cross the moon.

I had made him think.

I was still bluffing, of course, but that's just part of the game and, in my opinion, one of the most enjoyable. She who bluffs last bluffs best.

Taking care not to lay it on too thick, I moved my hand even closer, making it easier for him to give up the envelope.

He began to gnaw, almost invisibly, at his lower lip.

"And did you take these pictures yourself, miss?" he asked, thrusting his face forward in a determined manner.

Of course I had taken them. Hadn't I removed the film cartridge from Hob's camera with my own hands?

Does God forgive you when you intentionally pretend to misunderstand? This was probably one of those questions that tormented the ancient saints in their lonely cells in the tiny hours of the night.

Would the Creator actually cast you, forever, into Hell's deepest coal cellars, merely for using the wits that He gave you?

It seemed most unlikely.

And yet, I didn't want to perjure myself—at least not officially—by lying aloud.

I would compromise.

"Surely, in your profession, Constable," I said, "you will recall the case of *Nottage v. Jackson* (1883), in which Justice Bowen ruled that the prints taken from a negative are to be appropriated to the use of the customer only."

It wasn't for nothing that I kept a complete set of the *Encyclopaedia Britannica*, Eleventh Edition, in the eastern upstairs loo at Buckshaw.

Were the constable's eyes clotting, or was it just my imagination?

"You're a regular clever clogs, aren't you?" he said at last.

"No, Constable Otter, I am not," I replied, holding out my hand again. "But I *am* a girl who knows her rights. My pictures, if you please."

And by the jingling Jeremiah, he handed them over, holding the packet between his thumb and middle finger as if it had suddenly begun to reek.

I offered up a rapid prayer of thanks to Bernardine of Siena, the patron saint of bluffers and gamblers.

"Thank you," I said, removing the envelope slowly from his hand, and trying to keep my voice from sounding too shirty.

No need to rush. Keep a cool head, Flavia.

Taking my time, I looked slowly round the barren room, then back to the glaring policeman.

"Quite a nice place you have here, Constable Otter. But I think a few flowers would vastly improve it."

I left him to work out what I meant.

And then, shooting him a horrible smile that was a half inch short of a grimace, I sailed out the door of the constabulary as grandly as if I were the *Queen Elizabeth*.

I had made an enemy. I just knew it.

I was strolling up the high street, looking for a place to study the snapshots undisturbed. Because of the circus, I supposed, there were little knots of people everywhere, with privacy nowhere in sight.

I was walking past a shop whose window was full of yarn: skeins and balls of yarn of every color imaginable—and a few shades that weren't. I had just paused for a closer look at an antique colander full of wicked-looking knitting needles, when a voice said:

"Pssst! Flavia."

I spun round. There was no one there. No one within fifteen or twenty feet of me.

"Pssst! Flavia!"

More urgent this time.

Failing any other choice, I looked up: up into the branches of a plane tree that overhung the pavement. And there, perched like a cocky sparrow, grinning down at me, legs dangling from a limb, was Hob.

"Come on up!" he hissed, making the universal beckoning signs with his hands and fingers.

I made a hasty reconnaissance of the street to make sure no one was watching, then, with a sudden leap, hauled myself up amongst the branches and settled on the limb beside him.

It was like a cool, green cathedral here in the tree. A slight breeze stirred the leaves, providing a welcome refreshment from the hot, tired air of a summer afternoon.

"Oh, good! You got the snapshots," Hob said, reaching for the envelope. "Let's have a look and see how they turned out."

Something in me resisted handing them over, but I realized at once that in spite of Constable Otter, in spite of *Nottage v. Jackson,* and in spite of Justice Bowen, when it came to Hob's ownership of these snaps, I hadn't a chance.

My inner dog-in-the-manger crawled back into its bed of straw.

"Of course!" I said, overcompensating with cheerfulness. "You go first."

I passed him the envelope and watched impatiently as he slowly lifted the flap, peered into the envelope as if he were applying his eye to a telescope, looked up to grin at me, stuck two fingers into the packet, and pulled the photos halfway out.

I could have strangled him.

And yet, in my heart, I remembered having done things every bit as maddening myself on many occasions. Manufactured mysticism was such a wonderful way of stretching a happy instant to the breaking point; a way of

194 · ALAN BRADLEY

causing a brief moment of sharing to form even a fraction of some new infinity. And I realized now, for the first time, that these brief and fleeting joys were little more than sadness with a mask on.

"Let's have a dekko," I said, pretending to grab for the photos, but Hob jerked them away, giggling.

"Bags it me," he said, settling the matter beyond dispute. It is a fact of life that, among civilized people anywhere in the world, a basic "bags it" trumps everything, including, I suspect, even Judgment Day.

Pretending to be bored, I gazed off into the distance, waiting impatiently for Hob to thumb his way through the prints.

He made a rude noise with his mouth.

"Spoiled," he said. "All of them."

"Oh?" I said airily. "Why?"

"The camera moved. They're blurry."

"What do you expect when the camera's bobbing around on the end of a kite? Let's have a look."

Hob handed over the photos with no further interest.

"You have to wait until the string tied to the shutter is already tight. You mustn't jerk it too hard. I tried to wait until the wind was pulling steadily."

"Well, there wasn't much of a wind, as I recall," I said, thumbing through the photos.

Hob was right. Most of them were no more than hopeless smudges of light and shadow.

All except one.

"Hold on," I said. "This one's almost perfect."

Hob leaned over for a second look.

"It's looking in the wrong direction," he said. "I was trying to take a view of the river and the circus."

"And so you did," I said, pointing to the foreground. "Look: Here's our punt on the river. That's me dabbling my hand over the side."

I did not draw attention to the dark submerged mass in whose dead mouth my fingers were firmly hooked.

"Pfah!" Hob said. "You can have it. That's not what I wanted."

How well I knew the feeling! As a scientist, I'd learned to incorporate unexpected results into my data. There was, for instance, the time I had charged Feely's hot water bottle with a mixture of naphtha and turpentine, both of which are capable, after a certain delay, of dissolving India rubber. Although Feely had been too embarrassed to report the outcome, I knew by her looks next morning at the breakfast table that I was the prime suspect.

When I retrieved the wreckage later that day from the refuse bin, I found that I had accidentally discovered what I believed to be a previously unknown solvent, a single whiff of which was powerful enough to strip paint from battleships at a distance of six miles.

Spirit of Flavia, I intended to call the stuff, but not until I had got around to writing it up for the chemical journals. So far, I simply hadn't had the time.

I slipped Hob's print into my pocket. I would study it later at my leisure under a magnifying glass.

"Did your father find you?" I asked, trying to change

196 · ALAN BRADLEY

196 · ALAN BRADLEY

196 · ALAN BRADLEY

196 · ALAN BRADLEY

the subject and—yes, I admit it—draw attention away from the photographs.

I had almost forgotten that I'd been looking for Hob when I happened upon him.

"No," Hob said.

"Then you'd better run home," I told him. "He was asking for you at the Oak and Pheasant."

Hob sniffed.

"I'm not a boozer, you know."

"Perhaps he'd looked everywhere else," I suggested. "Perhaps he thought someone had seen you."

"He's checking up on me," Hob said, examining his fingernails. "He's afraid I'm hanging round the circus."

"Like Orlando Whitbread?" I asked. The words slipped out before I could stop them.

Hob's mouth fell open.

"How could you know that?" he asked. "Are you a witch?"

"Yes, I am," I told him, enjoying the moment. "I practice a specialized kind of witchcraft called thinking. It's a very mysterious power. Quite unknown to the average person."

I wiggled my fingers at him like a nest of little worms, as if casting a spell. "Now then, tell me about Orlando Whitbread before I turn you into a turnip."

Hob shrugged, unimpressed.

"Orlando played the Widow Twankey in the panto. He pulled a string of sausages out of the horse's—well, you know. I'm not allowed to say the word."

"Bottom?" I suggested.

He nodded furiously.

"He made me laugh until I sicked," he said. "Da had to take me home. I ruined the new jumper I got for Christmas."

I wrinkled my face in appreciation.

"'Cause we had spaghetti for dinner," he added, trying to outdo himself.

Although, like Mr. Gradgrind in Dickens, I have always had a fondness for facts, this was a little too much sauce even for my liking.

"What a good memory you have," I said, trying to be encouraging, but not *too* encouraging.

It was odd. Although I had never experienced such a thing before, I was suddenly feeling the need to display a certain maturity. I must tread carefully.

"What did Orlando do when he wasn't pulling sausages out of horses?" I asked. "Did he have a job?"

"He walked by the river," Hob said. "Talking to himself—or someone invisible. Waving his arms around."

"Is that all?"

"I guess so."

It seemed obvious that Orlando must have been either a madman or an actor rehearsing his lines.

"Well, I'd better be on my way, then," I said.

The day was getting on, and the heat was having its effect. I suddenly wanted nothing more than to put my head on a cool pillow and allow my thoughts to collect themselves.

What a disaster it would be—and how embarrassing—to fall out of a tree from fatigue.

I needed to eat and I needed to sleep.

Murder would simply have to wait.

"Wait," Hob said, as I began to pick my way down the tree.

"What?" I asked snappishly.

"Nothing," he said, seemingly hurt. "I just didn't want you to go."

I felt like a heel.

I was beginning to feel a headache coming on, and this time it was genuine. I could already feel the invisible octopus wrapping its tentacles round my temples.

I'd barely eaten for hours, I realized. Even in a young person such as myself, the finely tuned chemical factory that is the human body cannot run forever on cheese and pickled onions.

Little has been written about the exhausting effects of a late summer afternoon's heat, but I intend to do so. Like the weather, everyone knows about it, but no one does anything about it.

I would use myself as a guinea pig. Yes, that was it! With proper microscopic examination of blood samples taken at regular intervals and chemically analyzed at every step, I would show that lack of food in a hot environment and in the presence of mental stress could result in a kind of blood poisoning.

It was a brilliant insight and I couldn't wait to get back to Buckshaw.

"Hold on," I said, brightening suddenly. The word "poisoning" had triggered something in my mind. "You said Orlando walked by the river. *Where* by the river, in particular?"

Hob shrugged.

"In the churchyard. By the dock."

"Waving his arms and talking to himself."

"Mostly," Hob said.

"What do you mean, *mostly?*"

"Just hanging around. Like he lost something. Staring at the water."

Cold fingers caressed the back of my neck. There is an old saying or belief that a criminal always returns to the scene of his crime. Whether this is true or not I have no way of knowing, but the tired old idea was suddenly speaking to my blood. Could it be that Orlando was drawn back to the spot where his father was supposed to have ditched the silver chalice? The same spot where Fate would later, eerily, arrange for me to find his corpse? Had Orlando's death been staged to make it seem like suicide?

I nearly lost my grip on the branch.

"Hob," I wanted to say, *"you are a treasure. A bucketful of gems. Your price is far above rubies."*

I also wanted to hug him.

But I didn't, of course.

"Hmm," I said in what I hoped was a disinterested voice. "Anything else?"

Hob shrugged.

"Sometimes he helps Da in the shop. He used to, I mean. Da said it didn't work out."

·FIFTEEN·

THERE WENT ANY IDEA I'd had of sleep. Farewell food, and farewell cool pillow, also. There wasn't a minute to be wasted.

The way ahead was marked in my mind as clearly as a map drawn in flame.

Having thanked Hob, I made my not-so-graceful exit by parachuting down out of the tree and into the street. Thankfully, there was no one about to witness this display.

I would return at once to the Oak and Pheasant. I would quiz Dogger about his day's investigations, then turn my attention, full force, to the late Orlando.

But back at the inn, disappointment awaited me. Dogger was nowhere in sight. And the Rolls was gone, which meant, I hoped, that he had uncovered something interesting.

I went to my room to wait for him.

I sat for a time on the edge of my bed, drumming impatiently on my knees. My stomach was giving off noises like a jungle at sunset and could no longer be ignored. There was nothing in the room to eat but fingernails.

Had Dogger been there, I'd have asked him to fetch me up a whole hog on a plate, which I'd tuck into with fangs and flying fat, like Henry VIII. I would let out a belch of gratitude, and then we'd be off, renewed: a pair of old hounds hot on the trail of a cold-blooded murderer.

When I opened my eyes, I was lying on my back and the room was suffused with a gray and watery light.

I thought at first that I had been deprived of color vision as punishment for some forgotten sin.

I struggled into a sitting position.

Beside me on the table was a packet wrapped in wax paper which, when I opened it, turned out to be a cold ham sandwich, with salt, pepper, and mustard, just the way I preferred it.

"Bless you, Dogger," I said aloud, and fell upon the food.

Henry VIII, by the Grace of God King of England, France, and Ireland, Defender of the Faith, and of the Church of England and also of Ireland on Earth Supreme Head, would have been proud of me.

I washed down the feast with the cup of cocoa—still slightly warm—which Dogger had left. He had been here not so long ago.

I gave my arms and legs a good waggle to shake off sleep.

202 · ALAN BRADLEY

In spite of the weather, it would be chilly outside in the early morning. I dug a wool jumper out of my suitcase, a garment insisted upon by Aunt Felicity:

"Only a fool would go without wool," she had said.

It was almost a poem, and having once remembered it, I could not get the blasted thing out of my head.

"Only a fool would go without wool," I said to myself as I shrugged into the jumper.

"Only a fool would go without wool."

I wondered idly if Mrs. Palmer had ever written so instructive a poem, or whether she confined herself to obscure musings about wild animals, such as copper mares and brass stallions.

Hold on, I thought. Hadn't there been a rearing Arab stallion painted on the side of Mrs. Dandyman's pantechnicon?

My heart accelerated at the thought—although it might have been the sudden influx of ham.

I switched off the bedside lamp. No need to signal to anyone outside that I was up and about. One of the prime rules of sneakiness is to attract no undue attention.

I opened and closed my door soundlessly. The stairs were in darkness so that I had to make my way down, step by step, holding on tightly to the banister.

Clinking noises from the direction of the kitchen told me that Mrs. Palmer was already up and preparing for another busy day.

I slunk with ferret footsteps across the entranceway and eased myself out the door.

Well done, Flavia, I thought. Even a ghost could not have made a more soundless exit.

It was only when I was outside, breathing the chill morning air, that I came to my senses and realized I didn't know where I was going.

Scull Cottage, I knew, was somewhere on the river-bank, but on which side and in which direction?

Mrs. Palmer had said that it was little more than a boathouse, and that it was leaky. How many structures of that description could there be? I could hardly barge into the kitchen now and ask for directions.

No one must know what I was up to.

I would simply have to flip a mental coin and proceed by elimination.

I glanced up quickly at the casement windows, hoping my face wouldn't show up white in the half-light of the early morning. Feely would not be awake yet anyway, I decided. Courting is strenuous work, and if I knew my sister, she would now be snoring away like half a hundred pigs, her mouth gaping open and her hair a buzzard's nest.

Having decided I would begin in the churchyard and work my way downstream, I was partway across the gravel sweep when I heard the sudden and unmistakable sound of car tires.

Someone was coming and there was nowhere to hide. In the open road I would be a sitting duck.

I did the only thing that I could think of: I froze.

It is a well-known law of nature that a moving object attracts more attention than one which is motionless.

Every rabbit and every squirrel—in fact, every living creature subject to being eaten by predators—is born with the ability to freeze instantly when danger is detected.

I was standing there awkwardly in mid-stride, trying not to blink—not even to breathe. If my strategy worked, whoever it was would drive by without noticing me.

The crunching sound came closer and closer. It was eerie. Even in the silence of the morning I could hear no motor.

Crrrunch!

And then it stopped.

There was a soft thump, as of a sturdy door coming open, followed by the sound of boots on gravel.

I turned my head slowly, like an owl, hoping the whites of my eyes would not give me away.

Dogger was standing beside the Rolls, holding the door open for me. The car's sidelights glowed with a soft, warm welcome.

"Good morning, Miss Flavia," he said. "I trust you slept well?"

"Very well, thank you, Dogger," I answered. "I knew you'd be waiting for me."

It was a bluff. Dogger knew it and I knew it, but in spite of that, it somehow served as a bond between us.

To those of us who truly love one another, the occasional flaming fib serves only to strengthen the ties.

"Scull Cottage, please," I said, climbing into the front seat of the car's deliciously toasty interior.

"Indeed," Dogger said as he let in the clutch and we floated away in near-silence from the inn.

"You will have already had a good look round," I remarked, as we drove along the deserted high street—in the opposite direction, actually, of the way I had intended to go.

"I'm afraid not," Dogger said. "I did make something of a reconnaissance, but I'm afraid I was spotted by a neighbor."

"Spotted?" I asked. That could mean anything from a quick glance to the ringing up of Constable Otter.

"Recognized," Dogger elaborated, looking straight ahead. "A person from the past."

Aha! I thought. Dogger had already admitted to having been here before. "In another life," as he had put it.

"A woman?" I asked, staking everything on a wild surmise.

"I'm sorry, Dogger," I threw in at once. "I have no right to ask that. It just slipped out. Forget I said it."

Dogger turned and smiled.

"As it happens, you're right. A dear friend, merely, but one, I'm afraid, I have—"

"Never mind," I interrupted, still embarrassed for my breach of manners. "Let's talk about something else. Orlando Whitbread, for instance. Shall I tell you what I've found out about him?"

Dogger shook his head.

"Not until later, Miss Flavia, if you don't mind. After we've had a look round. I've found it useful to come at things with an untainted mind."

Even though I agreed with his principle—indeed, Inspector Hewitt had once told me much the same thing—it did not occur to me until later that Dogger had already visited Scull Cottage. This would be his second look.

Dogger turned off the road and onto a narrow track—no more than a cow path, really, that ran along the edge of a field, at the far side of which it began to slope downward toward the river.

Ahead was a grove of willows, which, in the first light of day, clustered together in the slight fog with a vaguely literary look. Beyond these, a hawthorn hedge blocked the view of the water.

Dogger brought the Rolls to a stop and engaged the parking brake.

"This is as far as we can drive," he said.

As we climbed out of the car, I had a good look at our surroundings: at the bottom of the sloping field, glimpses of the river through the trees and bushes; above us, the greater expanse of the field. No houses were visible. In fact, no structures of any kind. In the pale light of the early morning, the entire landscape seemed composed of water, earth, and sky.

What a remote place, I thought, *for skulduggery.*

How odd it seemed to find such a wilderness on the very doorstep of a busy market town.

"This way," Dogger said, leading me along a barely visible path which appeared to lead directly into the heart of the hawthorns.

What seemed at first to be an impenetrable tangle opened quickly up into a pleasant track among the trees that ran down to the water's edge, and to a quaint but sadly neglected structure.

"Scull Cottage," Dogger said, almost to himself.

The place had the look of an abandoned pagoda. Its sagging roof, curving down in a swayback shape, was decorated, at the end of each joist, with a carved dragon's head. Once painted Chinese red, these formerly fearsome creatures were now sadly weathered and peeling, their wooden faces looking half hopeful, as if they were awaiting rescue.

We walked slowly round the structure, taking it all in: the mossy shingles, the drooping window frames, and the general air of brackishness.

The cottage itself might have been some relic of a drained Atlantis: a greenish, almost shapeless mound, a loaf of forgotten bread caught in the act of moldering back into the earth.

As in the presence of all fungi, there was a feeling of slight but detectable uneasiness about the place.

At the water's edge, beneath the trees, a dock of decomposing planks was crumbling quietly into the river. Beyond it, a stile marked the end of an overgrown lane: a former towpath, I guessed.

Old boards groaned as I stepped onto the porch.

"Careful," Dogger warned.

I nodded to indicate that I was heeding his words. The hush of the place was uncanny.

It was like that weird poem of the German hero-adventurers so admired by Daffy in which "all seemed quiet in the iland"; in which "no bird sang in the bushes"; in which "no tree rustled in the breeze"; and in which "no beast brushed athwart the thicket."

Even the thought of the words made me shiver.

I cupped my hands against one of the grimy windows.

It was useless. With the dishwater light of the early morning behind me and darkness within the cottage, I could see nothing of its interior.

"Were you here yesterday, Dogger?" I asked. It was just a sudden feeling I had, and I wondered why I was whispering.

Dogger nodded his head. He did not elaborate and I did not ask. It seemed somehow wrong, in this strange place, to make a sound.

I pressed my nose to the glass again, hoping for miraculous vision to be suddenly bestowed upon me.

Something touched my elbow and I nearly leapt—like Saint Bartholomew—out of my skin.

I whipped round, wide-eyed, to find Dogger offering the torch. I had not noticed him bringing it from the Rolls.

With a curt, professional nod, as if leaping out of my skin were part of my plan and no more than an everyday occurrence, I took it from his hand, switched it on, and held the light against the windowpane.

A woman's face was staring back at me from the darkness.

"Bugger!" I said—regretting it at once.

Get a grip, Flavia, I thought. Dogger was here. What possible harm could come from a moldering old house on the riverbank?

The house of a dead man, some part of my mind insisted. *The house of a murdered man.*

"Look here, Dogger," I said, pretending to sound no more than mildly interested, even though it took every ounce of my willpower to keep from taking to my heels.

Dogger stepped carefully up beside me on the porch and applied his eye to the window.

"Interesting," he said. "I should imagine 1910, or thereabouts."

I placed my eye next to his, our faces next to one another against the glass.

In the yellow light of the torch, I could see that we were looking at a large theatrical poster pasted to a wall. On it, in garish colors, a woman in a Victorian girdle, and not much else except for a few ostrich feathers, swung upon a trapeze, her painted lips open in simpering laughter.

"A bird in a gilded cage," Dogger said softly at my ear. "Back then, women were often portrayed as captives, their cages being life upon the stage."

"Did they ever escape?" I asked, instantly aware that we had slipped into a topic in which I was out of my depth.

But I would persist. Perhaps I would learn something.

"Some did," Dogger said. "This one—if I'm not mistaken—"

He took the torch from my hand and directed its beam to the bottom of the poster.

Lady Babylon, it said, in garish yellow lettering of a theatrical nature, *A Musical Play Written and Composed by Leonard Bostwich. Sung and Performed by Miss Poppy Mandrill.*

"Gosh!" I said.

"Quite," Dogger agreed.

"Is that actually her?" I asked. "She was a stunner when she was young."

Dogger did not reply.

I could now see in the gloom of the interior that there were many more posters and photographs of a similar nature covering the walls. In fact, the place looked more like a picture gallery than a home.

Had Orlando actually collected these relics himself and constructed a shrine of sorts to his mentor?

I was pressing my face flat against the window to permit a better view of the far corners when a voice said:

"Arthur?"

I spun round, startled by the sound.

In the dawn, a woman was standing at the stile, a hoe in her hand.

I'll admit I must have gaped.

She was dressed in rubber boots and a pair of muddy trousers tied at the waist with binder twine. A khaki shirt, open at the neck, was obviously a military castoff, as was the broad-brimmed, sweat-stained hat, which would have been more appropriate in the jungles of the Far East than in this remote British backwater.

"Arthur?" she said again, and it was only then I realized she was talking to Dogger.

Dogger lowered the torch and began to turn round, but I noted the slight hesitation, as if he needed to gather his wits before answering to his Christian name. His jaw muscles were ever so slightly tightening.

"Claire?" he asked, turning fully to meet her gaze at last.

Dogger was always a man of few words, and never more than now.

The woman had put down her hoe and was climbing over the stile. A moment later she stood facing us, a definite blush creeping up her tanned neck from the depths of the khaki shirt toward her glorious red hair.

"I thought it was you," she said, gulping to keep her voice calm.

As a female myself, I knew instinctively that she was fighting back an almost irresistible urge to hug him. The joy in her eyes stood out like diamonds.

"I saw you here yesterday," she said. "I couldn't believe my eyes. I thought I must have been mistaken. I called out to you from my garden, but you mustn't have heard me."

She spoke with an accent which I couldn't immediately identify: the vowels tightly wound, like Cockney, but even more so.

"No, I heard you, Claire," Dogger said. "You must forgive me. I was unprepared—"

"Nonsense!" Claire exclaimed. "You mustn't explain. I understand perfectly."

And I could tell from the calmness creeping back into Dogger's face that he believed her.

"It has been a long time," he said. "A very long time, indeed. How have you been?"

I couldn't help noticing his deliberate choice of words: "How have you *been*," rather than "How *are* you?"

How she was *now* was evident to everyone for a quarter of a mile: Even in the early light, her smile was a hundred suns.

"Getting by," she said. "Same as always. And you?"

"I manage," Dogger said, and I knew in my heart that he was telling this woman the brutal truth.

I couldn't help myself. I slipped my arm in his.

Could it be jealousy, this creeping in my throat? This almost imperceptible swelling of my brain?

Is this what the green-eyed monster looked like from the inside?

"Dogger has been of very great service to my family," I heard myself saying. "He has been a rock."

I wanted to say more but I didn't. I wanted to quote one of Daffy's favorite lines from *Cyrano de Bergerac*: "... A rock, a crag, a cape! ... Say rather ... a *peninsula*!"

But Dogger would have been embarrassed and so would I.

I was learning to keep my mouth shut.

"Miss Tetlock," Dogger said, "may I introduce you to Miss de Luce."

"Flavia," I said, sticking out my hand and seizing hers, not caring about the agricultural debris with which it was covered. How very different, I thought, from the black and unpleasant handshake Terence had given me at Shadrach's Circus.

This handshake was, by comparison, wholesome, and I beamed my approval toothily at this woman, in spite of the fact that we had only just been introduced.

"Claire," Miss Tetlock said, tightening her grip to show she meant it. "Call me Claire."

For a moment, we all of us stood there, as if in a tableau or a trance, waiting for the next word to come, and yet each of us reluctant to be the one to speak it.

"Well, then," Claire said at last, "I expect you'll be wanting to have a look through Orlando's belongings. Such a tragedy."

She saw my jaw drop open in disbelief.

"It's all right," she continued. "Orlando entrusted me with a key. I kept an eye on the place when he was away and he, in return, drove off invaders, human or otherwise, from my allotment garden."

She waved in the direction of the stile.

"Constable Otter may not approve," Dogger said. "But if you insist—"

"Hang Constable Otter," Claire cut in, to my surprise. "I don't mean that literally, of course, but there are times when, in order to be maintained, the law must be broken.

"Or at least *bent*," she added.

I beamed upon her as she stepped up onto the creaking porch and pulled a key from her shirt pocket. This was a woman from the same mold as myself.

"All I expect is justice," she said, as she turned it in the lock. "Orlando is going to need all the help he can get."

What a curious thing to say about a dead man, I thought.

A moment later we were inside.

·SIXTEEN·

HANGING ALMOST OVER THE water as it did, Scull Cottage had a brackish smell, like an aquarium that belonged to an absentminded fish enthusiast.

I shivered as I recalled my fingers caught in the dead Orlando's mouth: good experience, to be sure, but not one that I would care to have often repeated.

"I'm sorry there's no electricity laid on," Claire told us. "The place is really little more than a converted boathouse. If the truth be told, no one is supposed to be living in it. Orlando had his ups and downs with the authorities, but Orlando being Orlando . . ."

She let her voice trail off to end in a wry smile.

"What was he like?" I asked suddenly, taking advantage of the opportunity.

"He was a clergyman's son, the son of a canon," Claire replied, "which ought to explain everything, but doesn't.

That he enjoyed telling people he was a son of a gun is perhaps more revealing."

I grinned because I knew she wanted me to.

"A joker," I said.

"Not entirely. An attention seeker, perhaps, which is often the force driving those who seek the stage. His mother died when Orlando was a baby."

"A very good actor, I understand."

I did not bother mentioning where I had heard this, but Daffy had once told me that all actors and all murderers are attention seekers.

"The only difference," she had said, "is that the one fulfills his fantasies in a darkened alley or a shabby room, while the other does it on a raised platform in full public view."

"Astonishing," Claire said, interrupting my thoughts. "Anyone who saw him as Eliza Doolittle in *Pygmalion*, or as Hamlet, realized that Orlando was larger than the stage itself. He was not just *touched* with genius, but totally saturated with it."

"Eliza Doolittle?" I asked. "He played the role of Eliza Doolittle?"

"And on less than an hour's notice," Claire told me. "Millie Plumb, who works part-time at the chemist's, fell suddenly ill after rehearsing the part for months. Orlando stepped in and . . . well, the rest is—or ought to be—theatrical history. Those of us who saw the performance knew that something far more than greatness had been revealed to us. I still have to pinch myself to realize I didn't dream the whole thing."

"Genius is often accompanied by an inexplicable chill," Dogger observed. "Professor Merlino of Mantua published some most suggestive notes upon the topic, but they have gained little attention outside of Italy."

"Didn't Orlando also help out occasionally at the chemist's?" I asked. I didn't want to interrupt Claire's story, but the coincidence popped into my mind.

"Did he poison Millie to get the part, you mean?" Claire smiled. "Because Orlando's name was involved in both cases, that very point was raised at the inquest into the deaths of three old ladies who died quite soon after his singular performance. The coroner, quite rightly, refused to hear it."

"Canon Whitbread," I said, wanting to let her know I hadn't just fallen off a lettuce lorry.

"Canon Whitbread, indeed," she said.

Dogger had all the while been standing quietly by, listening with great interest but saying little.

"As a trial run," he said. "Both to secure the role for himself and to practice up his poisons."

"Something of the sort," Claire said. "It was later proven—by a chemical analyst employed by Scotland Yard—that Millie's gastric catastrophe had been caused by a surfeit of green apples: the result of courting in an orchard with the wrong sort of person and the wrong sort of fruit."

"The old, old story," Dogger said.

"Yes, the old, old story," Claire echoed, and for a moment there was silence.

"Listen," she said abruptly, fidgeting with her collar.

"How would you like to come over to my cottage for a cup of tea? Quite frankly, this place gives me the jim-jams."

She jabbed a thumb in the direction of Poppy Man-drill, who from her painted poster was grinning horribly over Claire's shoulder.

"Very kind of you," Dogger said. "But since we're here, we'd like to have a look around, don't you think, Miss Flavia?"

I nodded agreement, torn between the two of them, but drawn most powerfully to the prospect of having a good old rummage through Orlando's goods.

"I'm sorry," Claire said. "I was being selfish."

"Not at all," Dogger said. "It gives me the jimjams, as you say, also. But your assistance would be of immense help. Perhaps with the three of us, things will proceed more quickly."

"What are we looking for?" Claire asked. "Is it something I may already know about?"

"Letters," Dogger answered. "Address books, tele-phone numbers, bottles, books, and refuse. Anything that will give us insight into the life—if I may say so—of the deceased."

Could this be yet another of what I took to be Dogger's jokes?

He's enjoying himself! I realized. In spite of the gravity of the situation, and of our many troubles, dear old Dogger was having the time of his life.

It did my heart good.

But at the same time it made me break out into a cold

sweat, since in my pocket was the slip of paper I had removed from Orlando's corpse.

Should I confess to withholding evidence and hand it over?

It was no wonder that so many of the ancient philosophers had spent so much time and ink chewing over—digesting and redigesting—moral issues.

Philosophy had always seemed to me like the four stomachs of a cow, but now I might have to rethink my position.

Was I guilty or was I not? And if so, of what?

I suddenly knew how poor old Plato must have felt, and in that moment, I made my decision.

"Look at this," I said, pointing to a black-and-white photograph of the young Poppy Mandrill on a bicycle, her skirts raised to show a risky bit of ankle.

"It's signed: 'To my Pegasus, from Poppy.' Inscribed with a Biro. Much more modern than the photo."

"Good lord," Claire breathed, shooting a look at Dogger.

Pegasus, I recalled from hearing Daffy read aloud some of the steamier passages from *Bulfinch's Mythology*, was the winged horse in Greek mythology who sprang from the soil stained by the blood of the decapitated Medusa.

We British are far behind other countries when it comes to inventing stories.

Still, was it any accident that Poppy Mandrill handed out autographs to a horse, while Mrs. Palmer wrote poems to one?

Well, stranger things have happened. You never knew

what you were going to run into in the English country-side.

As Dogger shone the light from wall to wall, the shadows dissolved, revealing poster after ancient poster, photo after curling photo, all of them of Poppy Mandrill.

"She must have been very famous," I remarked.

"Incredibly famous," Claire said. "She was the toast of the London stage. It was said that gentlemen drank champagne from her silk slippers and snippets of her hair were auctioned off to millionaires."

"But what happened to her?" I asked, thinking of the old woman hunched in her bath chair, directing amateur plays in a backwater town.

"Poppy committed the deadly sin of growing old," Claire said. "The gentlemen slunk away to sip from other slippers. Millionaires have no interest in gray hair."

"Rather like Medusa," I said. "Orlando was to be her winged horse, wasn't he? The one who flew to new heights from her wreckage?"

"Flavia," Claire said, "you fascinate me. You really do. You also frighten me."

I tried not to look too smug.

"I have very clever sisters," I said modestly, including both of them at the last minute for good measure. A handful of flattery, spread like seed, costs nothing.

As no one said anything, I continued snooping round the little cottage. Aside from a cubicle containing a WC, it was all one room, with a bed and books in one corner, and a small kitchen area with a primitive paraffin cooker, kettle, cup, and saucer.

The little larder, housed in a tin tea chest, consisted of bread, milk, cheese, and half an apple.

Had Orlando gone to his death hungry? I wondered.

This riverside shanty must have been a comedown from living in the vicarage.

"How did he get on with his father?" I asked. "Orlando, I mean."

"Remarkably well," Claire replied. "Canon Whitbread had sufficient knowledge of human nature to leave well enough alone. He knew that genius cannot be put in a box."

"But sometimes in a bottle," Dogger said, holding up a bottle with a glass stopper. He held it out toward my nose.

"Paraldehyde," I said. I would recognize the sharp unpleasant smell of acetic or ethanoic acid from across a cricket pitch. It was vinegar with a chip on its shoulder.

"Where did you find it?" I asked Dogger.

"Behind the Bible on the bookshelf," he said. "The hiding place most often chosen as the spot least likely to be searched."

I rewarded him with one of Winston Churchill's famous two-fingered "V for Victory" signs.

Now that the stuff had come to light, there was no further point in trying to hide my light under a bushel.

"I smelled it on the body," I explained to Claire. "At the riverbank."

"As did I," Dogger said.

You could have knocked me over with a shadow! Whatever detailed observations Dogger had made as we were fishing Orlando out of the river, he had kept the specific details to himself.

But hadn't we agreed to do so?

Although I was agog at his powers of observation, I decided not to draw attention to them.

"And what did you conclude?" I asked.

"That the poor young man had most probably been treated clinically for alcoholism, most likely in a private hospital. That a course of paraldehyde injections had been prescribed—perhaps something on the order of five to ten cc's—but that, as is often the case, he had become addicted to the very stuff that was meant to cure him."

"You deduced that based simply on the smell?"

"It is another old, but sad, story," Dogger said. "One hypothesizes certain fixed outcomes.

"As if that weren't enough," he added, "there was also the evidence of the skin: the allergic rash and the yellowish discoloration, the latter appearing also, although to a lesser degree, in the eyes."

"Drat!" I said. "I missed that entirely. I knew that certain people became addicted to it, but I didn't know why."

"It is much like a drawing room puzzle," Dogger said. "The more pieces you put into position, the larger the picture becomes."

"I think I can add a piece, too," Claire said. "Now that Orlando's dead—and because Arthur and I are old friends—I suppose there's no harm in telling you . . . as long as you keep it confidential."

She said this looking at me.

I crossed my heart and gave the Girl Guide sign of honor. Not that it counted: I was an outcast.

"Orlando did receive treatment at Dollylands for his drinking . . . difficulties. It's a very discreet private hospital in Highgate, founded by Sir Ernest Dolly to treat wealthy Victorian . . ."

She paused.

"Unfortunates," Dogger supplied.

"Thank you, Arthur." Claire nodded. "Yes, unfortunates. A precise description of Orlando."

"They'll have wanted to keep that quiet," I remarked, "what with his father being a canon, and so forth.

"But," I added, my curiosity suddenly tickled, "how did *you* find out about it, then?"

"Because my profession required it," Claire answered. "I was formerly a nurse."

Eureka! I thought. As Dogger had said, the more pieces that fall into place, the bigger—and clearer—the picture becomes.

I slapped my stupid brow. How could I not have realized?

"Of course," I said. "You're Australian! You were in the Australian Army Nursing prisoner-of-war camp!"

Daffy had once scared me silly—beneath the blankets and well after lights-out—by telling me how Japanese soldiers had machine-gunned the brave Australian nurses at Bangka Island, off the coast of Sumatra.

It was a topic never again to be spoken of aloud: not then, not ever.

I glanced at Dogger to see how he was taking it.

I shrank inside.

Dogger's eyes were in the past. They had taken flight at my words, and gone to another place.

Please, God, I prayed. *Don't let him have another of his episodes.*

I reached out and took his hand—squeezed his fingers fiercely.

"Dogger," I said, "I'm sorry. I didn't mean to—I didn't mean to—"

"Sit down, Arthur," Claire said, pulling out a chair from under the rickety table. She took Dogger's elbow and guided him into the seat.

She did not look at me.

Slowly, and with great gentleness, she began stroking the back of his hand.

"The trees are lovely this time of year," she said, "don't you think?"

Dogger looked up at her, seemingly dazed.

He opened his mouth and then, after what seemed like simply ice ages, said: "Yes . . . yes . . . So they are."

"I'm sorry," I said, forming the words silently.

It had all happened so quickly. One moment we had been efficiently searching Scull Cottage and the next my impulsive mouth had flung Dogger into some deep hell of the past.

For someone like myself who is used to having her own way, there is nothing worse than the feeling of helplessness, of not knowing what to do.

All I could think of was to touch the back of Dogger's neck. Perhaps the warmth of my fingers would calm his brain.

I noticed, as I made contact, how neatly barbered he was. When had he got a haircut, and where, I wondered? I supposed he had been clean-shaven back and front for as long as I could remember, and yet I couldn't recall his ever visiting a barber.

There was so much I didn't know about the man!

At the touch of my hand, Dogger turned his head slowly round, looked up at me, and smiled. Well, perhaps it wasn't quite a smile, but the corners of his eyes wrinkled slightly.

"Thank you," he said. "I shall be all right in a few moments."

"Shall we take a little stroll?" Claire suggested. "Over to my place? It's not far—just beyond the stile. I'll make a nice cup of tea.

"This place is not conducive," she added with a shiver.

Even though I didn't know the meaning of the word, I knew what she meant.

"Besides," she continued, "we don't want to be caught tampering with the evidence, do we?"

I questioned the wisdom of having to move Dogger so soon after his "turn," but wasn't Claire, after all, a nurse? Mustn't she have been accustomed to Dogger's episodes, and how best to deal with them?

She was already helping Dogger out of the chair.

"A stroll in the fresh air will do us all some good," Claire said, with a glance at me, and I felt a flush of shame arising.

"It's such a lovely day," she added, opening the door.

Outside, the sun had suddenly sprung up as it does in midsummer, as if night had never existed.

We stepped out onto the porch and she turned the key in the lock. "What is it Housman said about such beautiful summer weather?

"'June suns, you cannot store them / To warm the winter's cold . . . ' I forget the rest."

"'The lad that hopes for heaven,'" Dogger said, "'Shall fill his mouth with mould.'"

"Of course!" Claire said. "Your memory always amazes me, Arthur."

By now we were approaching the stile. I lifted down one of the crosspieces and we stepped over easily without having to scramble across like a herd of schoolboys.

We stopped for a few moments under the willows to admire a mute swan with its two cygnets, both of which were dabbling about in circles.

"The mute swans belong to the king," Claire told us. "They're his personal property. At least, they did. Now they shall belong to the queen. How very odd it will seem to have a Queen Elizabeth on the throne again after three hundred and fifty years! It's going to take some getting used to, I expect."

A metallic clatter behind us made me turn round. Through the hanging branches I could see Scull Cottage, and someone dismounting from a bicycle.

"Shhh!" I said. "It's Constable Otter."

"Just in the nick of time," said Claire.

·SEVENTEEN·

CLAIRE'S COTTAGE WAS EVERYTHING Orlando's wasn't: neat, compact, and filled with the morning light. A pair of wingback chairs, upholstered in cheery chintz, faced the fireplace. Dogger, with deliberate movements, lowered himself into one of them and I took the other.

Claire made herself busy with the teapot and the kettle, setting out three cups and saucers on the blue-painted kitchen table.

"Pleasant," Dogger remarked.

I was happy to see that he seemed to be recovering himself. Having been exposed to his terrors in the past, I knew that they might be mild or severe, and of either short or horrifically long duration.

At least this time he hadn't been haunted by visions.

As Claire was pouring the tea, I had a sudden vision of

my own: of the Rolls sitting parked in the field beyond Orlando's cottage.

Before I could say anything there came the clatter of boots on the porch and an abrupt, official-sounding knock on the door.

Claire seemed in no hurry to answer it.

"Yes, Constable?" she asked. "Is there a problem?"

Constable Otter made no secret that he was craning his neck to look past Claire to Dogger and me, who were still seated at the fireplace.

"I wondered, miss," he said, "if you had noticed anyone about in the past twenty minutes or so?"

I knew perfectly well that he had spotted the Rolls in the field, and had done as any good policeman would do: checked the temperature of the radiator. He had estimated the time based upon the cooling rate and the time of day, taking into consideration the outside temperature.

Not bad, I thought. As I had noted before, young Otter was going places.

"No one other than my two guests, Constable. We're just sitting down to a cup of tea. Would you care to join us?"

"Not while I'm on duty, thank you, Miss Tetlock," he said.

Constable Otter was *definitely* going places.

"Anyone at Scull Cottage, I mean."

"We walked through the property," I volunteered, "on the way here."

Careful, Flavia! I thought. *Don't slice it too fine.*

"We parked in the field beyond," I explained, hoping to shift attention from the cottage.

With great ceremony and a few fancy flourishes, Constable Otter produced his little black book and made a note.

"Miss de Luce and Mr. Dogger," he said, pronouncing our names as he wrote them down.

Which seemed to satisfy him.

He closed his notebook and looked narrowly from one of us to the other. I recognized the technique.

Was the constable trying to intimidate us—or simply to assert his authority?

He turned as if to go, then paused and looked me in the eye.

"You seem to get about a good deal, Miss de Luce."

"We're on holiday," I replied. "Trying to see as many of the sights as we can, yet remaining ready to hand, should you require us."

That "ready to hand" and "require us" were both masterstrokes. They suggested availability and a willingness to please without actually fawning.

Still, I mustn't risk being too clever with this man.

But then he turned and was gone.

Dogger, I realized, had said nothing during the constable's visit.

I stared at him, wondering how he was feeling.

"Better, thank you," he said.

It was remarkable! Dogger and I were as attuned to each other as two wireless sets operating on a private frequency.

At the same time, I could tell that he needed time to recuperate. It would be up to me to make good use of the meantime.

"I must admit I'm curious," I said to Claire, who had come to stand behind Dogger. Although she appeared not to be, she, too, was keeping a close eye on him.

"About the Three Graces, I mean."

"Ah, the Three Graces," she said. "Miss Willoughby, Miss Harcourt, and Miss Cray. Where did you hear about *them?*"

"Mrs. Dandyman at the circus told me about them. I didn't want to pry too much."

"Probably a wise choice," Claire remarked, and left it at that.

"We should be happy to hear their story," Dogger said, settling back into his chair.

This was an excellent sign, and I could see that Claire thought so, too.

"Well," she began, "it all had to do with the church. St. Mildred's had just begun to drag itself out of the Middle Ages. For the first time since the Creation, women were beginning to take on certain roles—not ordination, to be sure, but important roles nevertheless."

"Such as vicar's warden," I said.

"Precisely. And as you can well imagine, because of the very novelty of these appointments, the competition to fill them was fierce. Until this time, Miss Willoughby, Miss Harcourt, and Miss Cray had been the greatest of friends—cronies, you might have called them. They played bridge and euchre together, they took holidays together, they made up half of the Volesthorpe 'Bitter Knitters,' as they called their little circle—jokingly, of course, but as you know, a joke, in order to be effective, must be at least half true.

"And then there was the gossip. It was said that those three had refined rumors into razor blades. There was nothing they didn't know and weren't willing to talk about: from the color of Annie Trout's knickers, which were said to be Venetian red, to the precise amount to the penny in little Albert Morrow's piggy bank . . . two shillings, fourpence, ha'penny.

"But when the vicar's warden, dear old Dr. Glandley, died suddenly after catching a chill during a midnight house call, everything changed.

"It wasn't exactly open warfare, but it wasn't far from it. Oh, they were still polite enough to one another when they met, but it was as if each of them had mysteriously grown bristles. There were odd visits in odd hours to the vicarage: forgotten gloves, borrowed books, promised recipes . . . any pretext to get Canon Whitbread alone and press their case."

"Who was it that called them the Three Graces?" I asked.

"Funnily enough, it was Canon Whitbread himself. Initially, I think, he tried to make light of the situation, but he finally realized that it was no joking matter. In the end, he said, he had to fall back on the wisdom of Solomon and let them take turns: a year for each, in strict rotation."

"And what about Mrs. Palmer?" I pressed. "She told me she was vicar's warden, too."

"And so she was," Claire said. "Although that happened a bit later—after Miss Cray came down with a severe colic."

"Colic?" I asked. "I thought that was something babies got."

"In adults," Dogger said, "it may, among other things, be caused by kidney stones or gallstones."

I couldn't help shooting him a beaming smile.

"At any rate," Claire went on, "Canon Whitbread ruled that, rather than disrupt the business of the parish with 'temps,' as they call them nowadays, a fourth volunteer be appointed to step in when any of the 'Three Graces,' as he called them, was indisposed."

"That doesn't make sense," I objected. "A fourth person serving part-time would be no less disruptive than one of the other three filling in."

"That very point was raised at a meeting," Claire said, "but the canon pointed out that a temporary substitution, based upon the random bouts of illness in another, might result in an unjust division of duties. Or so he claimed. Frankly, I think he was not above inventing convenient excuses.

"The Three Graces had to pretend to be satisfied with that solution, and so Greta was allowed to join their company."

"Greta?" I asked.

"Greta Palmer. Your present landlady."

"Did anyone object to that?" I couldn't resist the question.

"Oh, there was some grumbling, mostly among the Graces. There was the usual chin-wagging that Greta wasn't as good as she ought to be—that there was some past scandal that hadn't been properly aired—"

"And was there?" I interrupted.

Claire paused and looked up toward the ceiling as if to find an answer.

"And of which of us is there not?" she asked, finally.

I had to admit she had a point. Even *I*, Flavia de Luce, have done certain things in the past of which I am not particularly proud, although I don't need to bother listing them here.

"I suppose," I agreed, a little too weakly for my own liking.

"Now then," Claire said, "I expect you're wanting me to get on with it—to get to the poisonings."

This woman knew me like the inside of her eyelids.

I shrugged.

"If you wish," I said, the best I could do on the spur of the moment.

She laughed: not a laugh as of silvery bells, as you might expect, but a wholehearted guffaw that grew from the gut and exploded into the room.

Dogger smiled.

Life had never been sweeter.

"The poisonings," Claire said, as if she were reading aloud the title of a scientific paper at the beginning of a speech. "It was given in evidence at the trial of Canon

Whitbread that on the morning of the murders, he got out of bed and, having overslept, put on his vestments at the vicarage, rather than in the vestry of the church, as he usually did."

"Was it a Sunday?" I asked.

"Yes, it must have been. St. Mildred's has not conducted early Communion services on a weekday for as long as I can remember—except on certain occasions."

"Such as when Christmas falls on a weekday or a Saturday," I said.

Claire nodded and went on.

"He left the vicarage directly—without breakfast, as is usual for one about to partake in Holy Communion—and hurried across to the church. He was several minutes late, a fact which was later confirmed by members of the congregation."

"Was Orlando living with his father at the time?" I asked.

"As a matter of fact, he was," Claire said. "Although it was claimed by the Crown Prosecutor at Canon Whitbread's trial that he had taken the 7:02 up to London the previous evening."

"Hmmm," I said. I would need to look into this later, I thought. Alibis involving railway timetables do not happen nearly as often in real life as they do in detective novels. Not that it much mattered now anyway, since Orlando was dead.

Or did it?

"Sorry," I said to Claire. "I was woolgathering. Go ahead."

234 · ALAN BRADLEY

"Well, Canon Whitbread began the service. The congregation was sparse, as it so often is on early summer
mornings. No more than a handful of people."

"Including the Three Graces, obviously," I said.

"Obviously. None of them would ever dream of missing a service. Couldn't allow the other two to get one up
on them. It might have been funny if it weren't so pitiful.

"Everything was quite normal right up to Communion.
Miss Willoughby, Miss Harcourt, and Miss Cray came up
to the rail together, Canon Whitbread administered the
Sacraments, and they returned to their pew."

"The same pew?" I asked.

"Oh yes—they always sat together."

"Who else?" I asked. "In the other pews, I mean."

"Only three others. Lettice Farnsworth and her husband, Hugo, and . . . oh yes, the undertaker's lad."

"Hob Nightingale?"

"Yes, that's right. The little lad. Sat in the front row
out of habit. Anyway, it wasn't long—no more than a
couple of minutes—before the Three Graces began dropping like flies. I'm sorry to put it so crudely, but that's how
Lettice described it at the inquest."

Lettice Farnsworth was to be congratulated. She had
given a remarkably vivid—and accurate—description of
cyanide poisoning.

In its most lethal form, hydrocyanic acid (HCN), in
sufficient dosage, can kill within a minute. It does so by
paralyzing the central nervous system and, perhaps more
important, by paralyzing the heart directly.

It is always pleasant to reflect, also, that the same cyanogen is found in the kernels of peaches and cherries, and that the glucoside amygdalin, which is contained in the essential oil of bitter almonds, as well as in the kernels of plums and apricots, is converted into hydrogen cyanide in the presence of certain enzymes and a bit of moisture, and is often used to provide the characteristic taste and odor in the manufacture of certain sweets.

Do I enthuse too much? Very well, then, I enthuse too much.

The point is that, by dropping like flies, the Three Graces reacted exactly as I should have expected.

"Mrs. Farnsworth didn't go up for Communion herself?" I asked Claire.

"No," Claire said. "She was made to sign the pledge with the Band of Hope when she was a child that liquor would never pass her lips."

"Not even when it's the blood of our Lord Jesus Christ?" I asked.

"Not even," Claire said, shaking her head.

"What about her husband? What was his name . . . Hugo?"

"Poor Hugo has had his struggles with alcohol, but he's been abstinent for years. He and Lettice go to church for reasons of their own, but when it comes to Holy Communion, they both sit on their hands."

"It seems un-Anglican," I said.

Claire laughed that laugh again.

"Someone once said that all Roman Catholics are Roman Catholics for the same reason, but every Anglican is Anglican for reasons of their own."

Dogger smiled. In spite of his silence, he was following our conversation intently.

"Now then," Claire said. "Let me get on with my story, and you can save your questions for later."

Had I just been put in my place?

If so, she had done it so gently that I could hardly take offense.

I gave her a grin, to show that there were no hard feelings.

"Dropping like flies," I prompted.

"Oh, yes—dropping like flies. Well . . . Canon Whitbread had returned what remained of the consecrated elements to the altar. Before they could finish the recital of the Lord's Prayer, the Three Graces were dead."

How fascinating, I thought, *that "Feed on him in thy heart" and "preserve thy body and soul unto everlasting life" would be the last words that the Three Graces would ever hear in this life before the cyanide froze their hearts, and they were plummeted into Eternity.*

But what could they have done to deserve so dire a death?

"Hold on," I said. "One more question: Why would Canon Whitbread poison three harmless old ladies? What was his motive?"

"Well," Claire said, "it came out at his trial that there had been some jiggering of the church funds. Not a great deal, mind, but enough that the various vicar's wardens could no longer ignore it. They had decided to join together as a body"—*how apt,* I thought—"in order to confront him."

"Was Mrs. Palmer one of those?" Dogger had been sitting so quietly I'd almost forgotten he was in the room.

"Yes," Claire answered. "They arranged to meet in the vestry. Canon Whitbread reportedly didn't take it very well."

"All of this came out at the trial, I presume?" Dogger asked.

"Yes, and most—but not all—of it was reported in the newspapers. The Church still has long arms where certain interests are involved."

Dogger nodded, satisfied, and subsided into his thoughts.

"Now comes the interesting part," Claire went on, resuming her story. "After the Three Graces had collapsed into their pew—like circus contortionists, Lettice told me later—Canon Whitbread went on to the Gloria and the Blessing. He didn't come down from the altar until he had completed the service."

"To give the cyanide time to work!" I exclaimed. "He wanted to be certain they were dead."

"So the Crown Prosecutor suggested at his trial. But the defense suggested—quite brilliantly, at least in this instance—that the older clergy had been taught to carry on 'come hell or high water,' as he put it (begging M'lud's pardon) and citing the instance of the Vicar of Chittleford who, despite a direct hit on the nave of his church during the Blitz, had gone on to the completion of Holy Communion though not a single member of the congregation remained alive. The defense then, changing course slightly, began to put forward an argument for shock, but the judge was having none of it. In the case of the Three Graces, no one from the congregation had come to their assistance until it was too late."

"The Farnsworths and Hob Nightingale, you mean," I said. "It wouldn't have mattered much if they had— unless they'd just happened to have three doses of the antidote to cyanide up their sleeves, and got to the victims within seconds."

"I suppose," Claire said. "But Lettice claimed that they hadn't really noticed anything untoward until Hope Harcourt slipped out of her pew and crumpled to the floor. It is not uncommon for elderly ladies to doze off at early morning services on warm summer mornings—not uncommon at all.

"Although they don't anymore," she added. "Since the Three Graces died, it's believed bad luck to sit in that pew. Some say it's haunted, some say you can still smell the poison."

"Hold on," I said. "What about Hob—did he see them fall?"

"Hob didn't give direct evidence. He's underage. But he gave a statement to the police saying that, since he was seated in front of the three victims, he would hardly have noticed anyway. Smart as a whip. A very clever thinker, our Hob is, for so young a lad."

I realized that no matter how fascinating Claire's story might be, there were several things I needed to do at once. I could always catch up on the details later.

"I'm sorry," I said, glancing at Dogger, "but I think it would be best if we got back to the Oak and Pheasant."

Dogger, bless his finely tuned soul forever, nodded assent and began to get up out of his chair.

"I wonder if I might trouble you to drive?" I asked Claire.

She scrambled to her feet and took Dogger's elbow, as if in friendship.

"Of course," she said.

And a few minutes later we were riding in comfort back toward the inn, with Claire at the wheel and Dogger beside her.

"I shouldn't feel right riding in the passenger compartment," Dogger had insisted.

"First time I've ever driven a Rolls-Royce," Claire told us. "Actually, it's the first time I've ever *ridden* in one. I shall be spoiled forever."

I glanced over at Dogger, who was gazing out with seeming disinterest at the passing riverbank.

"I shall see you in, then take the shortcut home."

"No need," Dogger said. "I am quite all right. It was pleasant seeing you again, Claire."

He offered his hand and she took it.

I'd swear that a look passed between them, but I couldn't be sure. My heart gave a little lollop.

Had I been witness, this morning, to a carefully produced drama? Had Dogger staged an episode in order to be in the company of Claire Tetlock? Would Dogger even be capable of such a thing?

There are times when eyes and ears are not enough, times when you need to go inside yourself, to listen to the Whisperers in the Pit who, although they may sometimes shock you, are very seldom wrong.

After seeing Dogger to the door and waving goodbye to Claire, I made a beeline across the road to St. Mildred's.

I needed to be alone.

·EIGHTEEN·

THE CHURCH, AS I had hoped it would be, was empty.

Inside, I made a slow circuit of the nave and the chancel, reading the ancient memorial marble tablets that seemed to cover every inch of the walls, and a grim old lot they were, most of them recalling in stifling detail the lives of military men back to the time of "William Conker," as Mrs. Mullet referred to the tour operator who had brought the de Luces to England in 1066.

Everything was coated heavily with dust, some of it, I knew, the remains of those happy warriors and their loved ones, who must be jammed, judging by the number of plaques, heel-to-jowl inside the walls and underneath the floor's stone slabs. You couldn't walk down the aisle without having Sir Morton Stackpole and "Maud his dearly biluved wife" rise up in a cloud to greet you, as if they had been too long without company, and settle in a chummy way on your hands, your face, your neck, and in your hair.

On the Epistle side of the church, just outside the chancel, let into the floor at the foot of the lectern, was a bit of stone: a gray-flecked square of marble, no more than three and a half or four inches on each side. In the crumbling antiquity of the church, its relative lack of age had caught my eye. In short, to someone with my powers of observation, the marble stuck out like a sore thumb: too new, too polished, too freshly chiseled.

I got down on my hands and knees to examine the surface, On it, carved in half-inch letters, was the word G.L.O.W.

Glow?

What on earth could that mean? Could it possibly be a family name? I had never met or heard of anyone with the surname Glow, but in England such a thing is not beyond belief. Or was it, perhaps, a discreet marker placed by some organization, such as the General Laborers and Office Workers, to commemorate a certain occasion, or a gift of money to one of the church funds?

There was no point wasting time in speculation. I would simply ask the present vicar for an explanation: Clemm, I believe Mr. Palmer had said his name was—the plump gentleman who had come to the riverbank with Constable Otter.

I made a second circuit, pausing this time to run my fingers along the back of the pew—the second row from the front—where I deduced from all accounts that the Three Graces must have met their end, or ends. There wasn't a trace left of their passing—which in a few cases can be remarkably messy, cyanide working as it occasionally does. If such was the case, someone had done a wizard job of mopping up.

I slid gently sideways into the pew, closed my eyes, clasped my hands, and tried to project myself into the past: into the minds of those three old ladies at the very moment the poison had taken hold.

There would have been, at first, the realization that the sacramental wine was stronger than usual. Perhaps a cracked or otherwise defective cork, overlooked by Canon Whitbread, had allowed it to go sour—although I recalled from my chemical readings that, in 1922, the Holy Office had given permission to the Archbishop of Tarragona, in Spain, for the sacramental wine to be treated with either sulfurous anhydride or potassium bisulfite to keep it from going off.

That, of course, was the Roman Catholic Church, which is far more advanced in such matters than the Church of England.

After that first taste, there would have been a couple of blissful moments which would, alas, be their last; and then the sudden onrush of sensations: the taste of bitterness, the burning in the throat and bowels, the tightening of the jaw, the foaming at the lips, the perspiration, the inability to move any of the muscles—not even time, probably, for a final "Uh-oh."

How pleasant it is, as you sit in an ancient church, to ponder poisons, surrounded as you are by the towering toxicity of the stained-glass windows. The yellow cloak of that staring saint, for instance, was most likely achieved by adding cadmium, which, with its several compounds, is quite poisonous; whereas the startling emerald green of all that glassy grass at Galilee is most likely due to arsenic.

To say nothing of the lead.

Such happy thoughts are proof that I have become an adult. I am now ruled by not only what I see, what I hear, what I taste, and what I smell, but also, and perhaps most important, by what I think.

That very thought in itself ought to be certain proof that my brain has developed satisfactorily.

Pleased with myself, I turned the attention of my expanding brain to my surroundings.

Old churches, like old humans, give off occasional creaks and groans as bits of dried wood and old stones shift in their sockets. Also like old humans, they tend to hum a bit, although it's nothing to be alarmed about.

The slightly sickening smell of long-departed lilies and longer-departed perspiration hangs like an invisible mist in the air. There is an almost imperceptible whiff of roast beef, as if the ghosts of John Bull and his fellow squires were banqueting in the crypt. Added to this, almost as an afterthought, is the dry, pious odor of Bibles and hymnals.

Why do the printers of these books use so sober-smelling an ink? Why don't they stir your nostrils and your imagination with the sharp, tantalizing stink of, say, the *News of the World,* or the *Daily Mirror?*

To verify this observation, I reached out and lifted a Bible from the book rack of the pew in front of me, and gave it a sniff. Slightly moldy, but still recognizable as a

Bible. I'd put money on being able to identify one in the dark.

As is almost always the case, the book was bound in black, the title stamped in gold on the cover and spine. This particular edition contained not only the Bible, but also the complete *Book of Common Prayer*, along with maps of the Holy Land, charts of weights and coins of Scripture, and botany of the Bible (from which I was delighted to learn that the Vine of Sodom in Deuteronomy is in fact a kind of giant milkweed with poisonous juice which, in spite of its tasty appearance, dissolves, upon being bitten, into smoke and ashes): all of this in one handy—although slightly bulky—volume. It was a churchgoer's dream, a Boy Scout knife for Bible class.

But something had caught my eye. The word "poison" had leapt at me off the page.

Yes, here it was: Deuteronomy 32, verses 32 and 33:

For their vine is of the vine of Sodom, and of the fields of
   Gomorrah: Their grapes are grapes of gall, their
   clusters are bitter:
Their wine is the poison of dragons, and the cruel venom
   of asps.

If I had stuck my finger at random into the Bible as fortune-tellers do, I couldn't have hit upon a more apt entry. Wasn't this a direct warning against poisoned wine?

Could "the poison of dragons" and "the cruel venom of asps" refer to gossip?

Both passages were underlined in pencil.

Scarcely daring to breathe, I turned slowly back to the flyleaf, almost afraid of what I might find.

Written in black gall ink, the words made my eyes swim:

Anne Elizabeth Cray,
Hassock Cottage, Volesthorpe

Annie Cray! Of the Three Graces: "Faith, Hope, and Treachery," Mrs. Dandyman had called them.

And of the three, Annie Cray was Treachery.

Was it possible that she had brought this Bible to church the day of her murder, and that it had lain here unnoticed ever since? Two years had passed since Annie and her fellow gossips had been trundled off to meet their Maker. Could it be that the police—the whip-smart Constable Otter included—had overlooked the harmless Bible nestled in its book rack, not two feet from where the dead women would have lain?

Obviously, it was. Hadn't Claire Tetlock told me that the pew was believed to be haunted? That no one would sit in the spot where I was sitting now?

Besides, a Bible or a hymnbook is as invisible in a church as the walls and windows. No one would think to take a second look at the contents of the book rack.

It had lain there all this time, untouched, waiting for someone with the eyes to see.

Waiting for me. Flavia de Luce.

As I flipped the pages idly, the names of the books in the Old and New Testaments, the page numbers, as well as the numbers of the chapters and verses, fluttered by

like those animated cartoons which you make by drawing, in the corner of each page with a pencil, a slightly
different sketch of a galloping horse or a stick man having
his hat blown off by the wind.

I was riffling through Revelation when I had one.

A revelation, I mean.

It must have been the flying numbers, racing by before
my eyes at dizzying speed: Perhaps not, but something
in my freshly attentive brain went *Click!* as clearly
audible—inside my head, at least—as the slow breathing
of the ancient oaken beams above my head.

For an instant, I felt as if I myself had swallowed cyanide:
My mouth went dry and my breath snagged in my throat.

Slowly, so as not to break the spell, I reached into my
pocket and pulled out the crumpled bit of paper I had
found in Orlando's pocket.

The numbers danced before my eyes: 54, 6, 7, 8, 9.

I had supposed them at first to be the numbers of
hymns, but I was wrong.

What if they were books, chapters, and verses?

With trembling hands I turned to the general index.
Beginning with Genesis, I counted off the entries. The
fifty-fourth book of the Bible was the First Epistle of Paul
the Apostle to Timothy.

I followed my finger to chapter 6, and then to verses 7,
8, and 9:

For we brought nothing into this world, and it is certain
we can carry nothing out.
And having food and raiment let us be therefore content.

248 · ALAN BRADLEY

*But they that will be rich, fall into temptation, and a
snare, and into many foolish and hurtful lusts, which
drown men in destruction and perdition.*

A passage about drowning found in the pocket of a
drowned man?

It was beyond coincidence.

But what did it mean? Could it have been a warning?
A threat? And if it was, who gave it or sent it to Orlando,
and how did it come to be in his pocket?

I read the remaining lines of Timothy, which, although
they were few, contained the famous saying that the love
of money is the root of all evil, and that those who covet
it have pierced themselves through with arrows.

Poor Orlando was fortunate, in a way, that whoever
had it in for him hadn't used a crossbow.

But what had it all to do with money? As far as I knew,
Orlando had been as poor as a church mouse, brought up
by a rural clergyman who had to embezzle funds from the
collection plate in order to heat the vicarage.

There were so many unanswered questions. Why, for
instance, had someone chosen Saint Paul's First Epistle to
Timothy as a warning? Surely, there were many much more
threatening passages in the Old Testament, such as those
in which God is shaking His fist at Moses and his tribes.

Could it be that the Timothy letter was the only reference in the entire Bible to drowning? If that was the case, it
would prove beyond a doubt that Orlando's killing was med-
itated. It takes a certain amount of calculation to select a
biblical text and then plan and execute a murder to match.

It would have been too much to ask—too much of a coincidence—for the fat black volume in my hands to contain a Bible Concordance and, of course, it did not. I would need to get my hands on one of these at the earliest possible moment to check out the drowning angle.

Again I opened the pages of Annie Cray's Bible in search of inspiration. Anything would do: I needed help.

Like the attached Bible, *The Book of Common Prayer* contained a great deal of reference material: a calendar of the church year, including the various saints' days; a table of the Moveable Feasts according to the several days that Easter can possibly fall upon; a complicated set of tables of rules for finding the Golden Number and, once having found it, determining the date of Easter in any given year.

It was like a holy treasure hunt.

Fortunately, I had learned something about the topic from our own vicar, Denwyn Richardson, in Bishop's Lacey, who, having caught me fishing—illegally—in the river behind St. Tancred's, had sat down beside me in the warm summer grass and begun rattling on about one of his greatest enthusiasms: *The Book of Common Prayer* and How to Use It.

He had delivered several sermons upon the topic, not only from the pulpit, but also at various meetings and functions in the parish hall. If there was a single topic which the Anglican parishioners of Bishop's Lacey were prepared to be quizzed upon at the Golden Gate, it was *The Book of Common Prayer*.

Not only were there charts and tables of the saints' days and holy days, but also complex decrees about which chapters and verses of the Old and New Testaments were to be read aloud as lessons, depending upon the calendar and the time of day.

"It may seem rather left-handed," Denwyn had said, "but it's all perfectly logical. It all comes down to the moon, Flavia, when you stop to think about it."

Which, I suppose, is as good a thing to base a religion upon as any.

But just when I thought I had wrapped my mind around the codes and calendars of Christian prayer, Denwyn had mentioned, almost apologetically, that there was also an alternative table of lessons, and it was this which we used at St. Tancred's, rather than the original.

"But why?" I asked.

"Because the bishop wishes it," he had said, slipping me a furtive wink after a hasty glance round to make sure that no one was watching.

So there it is, then, I remember thinking. *Down here on earth, a bishop is mightier than the moon.*

Although this was an obvious case of misguided thinking, I did not say so to Denwyn. The poor man had a living to earn.

I dragged my mind back to the present—to the Alternative Tables.

If St.-Mildred's-in-the-Marsh used the same timetables we used in Bishop's Lacey, I ought to have an answer in two flicks of a dead lamb's tail.

Timothy 1 ought to be easy enough to spot.

I let my eyes float slowly down the long columns, like a deflating balloon, beginning with the first Sunday in

Advent, which, of course, would be in December—then onward through Christmas, Epiphany, Lent, and Easter.

Surprisingly, Timothy did not make his appearance until several Sundays after Trinity, at which time he was taken out for a rather good trot.

Ah! Here he was: First Timothy, chapter 6, verses 7 to 9—the very verses I had found listed in the dead Orlando's pocket!

My blood was already beginning to jingle.

With the knowledge absorbed during Denwyn's riverside lecture, as well as various exposures at Girl Guide meetings, I was able to work out—with remarkable speed and efficiency—the precise date of that reading in the present Year of Our Lord, One Thousand Nine Hundred and Fifty-Two.

But they that will be rich, fall into temptation, and a snare, and into many foolish and hurtful lusts, which drown men in destruction and perdition.

Those now-chilling words would be read aloud from the lectern as the Second Lesson of Evensong on the third Sunday after Trinity. Here, at this very spot, they would echo among these very stones and hammer beams.

June the twenty-ninth. Tomorrow evening!

The first Sunday—and just two days—after I fished Orlando Whitbread's drowned body out of the river.

Had it been planned?

Was this a message—or a warning to others—from Orlando's killer?

·NINETEEN·

THE TIME HAD COME to "shrug off the mantle of the present," as Daffy puts it when she's reading her beloved Dickens, and project myself two years into the past to the morning of the three earlier murders.

The successful solving of any crime depends, more than anything, upon accurate reconstruction, which is the closest thing we have in the modern world to time travel. Most detectives wouldn't admit that it's a form of self-hypnosis, but they have their reputations to think of.

Think how the court would laugh—even the magistrate on the bench in his wig and robes—if the detective, asked how he came to a certain conclusion, replied: "I put myself in a trance, M'lud."

There wouldn't be a dry eye in the house!

I squirmed and settled myself into the pew, closed my

eyes, and folded my hands daintily in my lap. In my mind, I let the pages of the calendar tear loose and fly away, one by one, month by month. June of 1952 became May, then April, and so forth.

Christmas flew by and I was back in 1951: November, October, September, the months of summer, spring, then Christmas again.

It was 1950. I allowed the pages to slow a little: I didn't want to overshoot.

August . . . July . . . June . . . and here we were.

I took a deep breath and slowly opened my eyes.

The church was the same as it always had been, but then it would be, wouldn't it?

There was a stir of air behind me as the door opened and the Three Graces entered: Grace Willoughby, Grace Harcourt, and Annie Cray, looking much as I remembered them from the grainy photographs on the front pages of the tabloid newspapers, except that now their faces were in color.

Grace Willoughby, as tall and slender as her name, was wearing a smart black tailored suit with a cameo brooch at her throat, and had perched on her head a curved winglike thing which looked as if it had been forcibly detached from a duck. Grace Harcourt, somewhat shorter and broad-shouldered, with grayish-blond hair, wore a summer dress of dusky rose and a smart straw hat, while Annie Cray, dark, short, and squat, and rather toadlike, I thought (uncharitably, seeing as she was dead), had draped herself in a kind of loose rug or blanket in which holes had been cut out for her head and arms. A floppy-brimmed black hat gave her the appearance of a villain in a cowboy film.

I slid over to make room for them as they entered the pew. Even though the poor creatures couldn't see me, I didn't want to be caught staring.

More footsteps at the rear and the clatter of kneeling benches announced the arrival of Mr. and Mrs. Farnsworth—Lettice and Hugo—and moments later, the much lighter footfall of Hob Nightingale.

Because of the summer season, and the sparseness of the congregation, there would be no processional this morning: no choir, no organ—just the bare bones, so to speak.

As far as I knew, the entire cast of characters—with the exception of Canon Whitbread—had now taken up their positions to act out the tragedy.

And now—yes!—here comes Canon Whitbread, hurrying in from the vestry: late for the service, just as Claire had told me he had been, and empty-handed.

Which meant that the wine and wafers were already in the tabernacle on the altar.

In my mind, I lit a flame in the altar lamp to indicate that fact.

I would need to check these details later with the witnesses, of course, but lighting a flame with the mind is a powerful aid to understanding.

The canon genuflected before the altar, and without further ado, launched into the Holy Communion service.

With my acute hearing, I could actually hear his dusty words.

After the Lord's Prayer, he began the Collect:

"Almighty God, unto whom all hearts be open, all desires known, and from whom no secrets are hid . . ."

What had Almighty God seen that morning, I wondered, as He looked into the secret hearts and desires of those three women who were about to die, and into the heart of the clergyman who was about to murder them?

Now Canon Whitbread had begun the recital of the Ten Commandments.

Well, there was no need to re-create the entire service. The part I was most interested in wouldn't come until near the end.

In my mind, I sped up the action, so that Canon Whitbread was racing through the order of service like the Keystone Kops.

It might have been funny if it hadn't been murder.

I waited until he and the little congregation dropped to their knees for the general Confession, then reduced the speed to normal.

Turning to face the people, Canon Whitbread now begged God to pardon and deliver them from all their sins, confirm and strengthen them in all goodness, and bring them to everlasting life.

As he did so, I was able for the first time to study his face.

My immediate impression was that the man was *tired*; that he had been awake for much of the night. One of his eyelids twitched incessantly; the other seemed to droop a little. The hollows of his rather gaunt face showed up as shadows, his chin and cheeks darkened with new whiskers. There had been an unsuccessful attempt to hide the morning's bristles with a rose-tinted talcum powder. He had not taken the time to shave.

My second impression was that this was not the countenance of a killer. I had several times come face-to-face with killers. Not one of them had had the gentle features of this rather worried-looking man.

I was recalling his face, of course, from the dozens of black-and-white photographs I had seen in the newspapers, but never until now did it ever occur to me that an innocent man might have been sent to the gallows.

The very thought of it caused my blood to bubble.

I focused my attention on the hands of the man at the altar.

Having transformed the host and the wine into the body and blood of Christ, Canon Whitbread genuflected deeply and administered Communion to himself, consuming the broken host and draining the chalice. I knew already that there was no danger of his poisoning himself—that he would go on living until the day he died at the hands of the hangman.

But now he was turning again to the altar—turning his back upon those of us seated in the pews. I watched, transfixed, as he brought reverently out from the tabernacle the silver vessel—the ciborium—which contained the wafers.

I could hardly believe it! They had been there all night!

I froze the action to let my mind catch up.

Normally, with a decent attendance, Canon Whitbread would have consecrated only as many of the hosts as were needed. Any remaining would be kept in the tabernacle for use during the week, including visitation of the sick and so forth.

But this morning, with only a handful in attendance, he would make use of the hosts that were already consecrated. Of course, he had newly consecrated one of the larger wafers for his own consumption, but the rest of the congregation would be given the leftovers, so to speak.

The point was this: The hosts and the wine which were about to be administered to the unsuspecting congregation had been left in an unlocked church overnight—and perhaps even longer.

Anyone in England—and perhaps even beyond—could have sneaked in the old cyanide.

This case was becoming far more difficult than I could ever have imagined.

I needed to find out—and as quickly as possible—whether the poison had been contained in the wine or the wafers—or both.

With mounting horror—and, I must admit, with mounting excitement—I watched as he turned to face us. Annie, who had been last into the pew, was already hoisting herself to her feet and shuffling sideways into the aisle.

In her mind, there was probably some imagined heavenly prize for being first at the rail.

Well, she'd soon find out, I thought.

The two remaining Graces, Harcourt and Willoughby, were breathing down her neck.

I slowed the image down a little. I didn't want to miss a single detail.

It flashed briefly into my mind that I could stop their motion and reverse it like a comic film, but I quickly dismissed the idea. I could only make them walk backward out of the church and home again, bottoms first. I could not really change what had already happened. I was unable to save these three women from a certain death.

"These are but shadows of the things that have been," as the Ghost of Christmas Past told Ebenezer Scrooge.

I could not change their destiny. I might as well sit back and learn from it.

Now they had reached the rail and were kneeling. Grace Willoughby, in spite of being the last at the Communion rail, was the first to receive the host from the hands of Canon Whitbread. She crossed herself rather showily. Now it was the turn of Grace Harcourt, and finally Annie Cray.

Even though Annie's back was still toward me, I could tell by the sudden slump of her shoulders that she was miffed, as First Place in Heaven was snatched unfairly out of her grasp.

And now for the wine. Or should I say, the Blood of Christ?

It all depended whether you accepted the hotly disputed doctrine of transubstantiation: the actual transformation of fermented grape juice into the Holy Blood of the Son of God.

It was a subject upon which I had already come to my own conclusions.

Six months ago, at a greatly trying time in my life and racked by loss of faith, I had whisked away—by a method which I'm still ashamed to reveal—a sample of the consecrated wine from Holy Communion at St. Tancred's, and taken it home to my laboratory, where I had subjected the supposedly holy liquid to the most rigorous analysis known to organic chemistry. I had compared the fluid and its constituents at various stages of my experiment with control samples of the ordinary, or unconsecrated, wine, nicked from the same church, I must confess, at a somewhat earlier date.

I had recorded the results—which were indisputable—in the back pages of one of Uncle Tarquin's bulging notebooks, to be discovered at some future date when the world is better prepared to receive my earth-shattering findings.

I forced my mind back from these researches to St. Mildred's, and the imminent demise of the Three Graces.

Because there were no deacons in attendance to assist with the Holy Communion on this sunny summer morning, it was left to Canon Whitbread himself to deliver both bread and wine, and I had to admire the quiet efficiency with which he administered the hosts to each of the three communicants before returning briefly to the altar to replace the ciborium in the tabernacle and to take up the chalice.

And now here it was: the moment I'd been waiting for. I took a mental snapshot of the scene.

Canon Whitbread stood poised, chalice in hand, facing the three communicants, whose heads were bowed in preparation.

I felt a shiver run down the back of my neck, down my arms, and into my elbows.

I was about to witness murder.

But whether Canon Whitbread was the killer or not, I could not yet tell. And yet he was certainly the instrument by which cruel Fate had chosen to deliver their deaths to these three unsuspecting chatterboxes.

Reluctantly, wanting to treasure the moment, and yet impatient to see the results, I allowed the action to resume.

Again, Grace Willoughby was first. She tilted her head back slightly. I could not see her mouth but I knew by the angle of her jaw that it had opened. She lengthened her life by a fraction of a second by crossing herself again. But Canon Whitbread's hand moved swiftly, and the deed was done.

He was already moving sideways to confront Grace Harcourt.

Grace, too, went like a lamb to the slaughter.

Kaboola!

Just like that. With death in her mouth, she was already halfway to her feet.

Now it was the turn of Annie Cray.

Why did I feel so suddenly sorry for this pathetic little figure in her Mexican donkey blanket and silly hat? Why did I want to rush up to the rail shouting "No! Stop!

Don't swallow that! *Spit it out!*" Why did I want to grab her by the arm and haul her out of the church to safety?

These, I would realize later, were probably the kinds of afterthoughts that came to old misers as they lay dying alone in the night, clutching at straws of salvation.

If only I had thought to . . . if only I had . . . if only . . .

But I was neither old nor a miser—nor was I dying.

Fate undoubtedly has her reasons, and I was merely a girl who had been sent by her to solve a mystery.

And, by Saint George and his dragon, and his white horse, Uffington, that's exactly what I intended to do!

I studied their faces carefully as the Three Graces arose from the Communion rail and turned toward me. Was there anything in their expressions to indicate that they smelled a rat, so to speak? That they had detected even the slightest taste of bitterness?

It was difficult to tell. There is something about receiving Holy Communion which causes even the most jolly person to look as if their face has just been suddenly and unexpectedly starched and hung out on the line to dry. The face of the average communicant is not a happy one, and the faces of the Three Graces were no exception. Pious, is the word I'm looking for.

Although it may be blasphemy to say so, the features of these three women as they made their seemingly sightless way back to their seats reminded me of nothing so much as that famous painting *The Blind Leading the Blind* by Pieter Bruegel.

I watched intently as they shimmied hip to hip into

262 · ALAN BRADLEY

the pew. With a muffled *thump* the kneeling bench went down and they were on their knees.

Less than a minute to zero hour, I remember thinking, as I began counting.

The first sign came precisely thirty-three seconds later as Grace Harcourt let out a slight hiccup. She covered her mouth quickly with a white-gloved hand and kept it there. Her other hand was at her heart.

Potassium cyanide—when changed to hydrogen cyanide by the body's stomach acids—is one of the swiftest of the deadly poisons. Only carbon monoxide and some of the other gases kill so quickly. Unconsciousness can occur within seconds. Even so, I was surprised at the speed with which it took her.

Grace slumped farther forward, her right shoulder coming to rest against the back of the front pew. I watched as she drew a couple of noisy breaths and collapsed slowly sideways, her summer hat falling to the floor, her chin coming to rest grotesquely against the polished oak seat of the pew, her eyes staring blindly up at the hammer beams above.

While I was still marveling at the sight—and still fighting the instinct to leap to her assistance, as I had done once before with a victim of cyanide—Grace Willoughby jerked suddenly halfway to her feet, looked round in wild-eyed panic, and flopped, backward at first, and then sideways, into the pew.

She seemed unaware of her already dead friend beside her.

One of her legs twitched, then kicked convulsively—and was still.

It was not a graceful death.

Now only Annie Cray remained, still on her knees, her eyes fixed fiercely on the altar, upon which Canon Whitbread was replacing what remained of the consecrated Elements.

Then Annie, too, crumpled: slowly, beautifully, lightly, like a falling leaf that has detached itself from the parent bough and launched itself upon the air, rocking slightly from side to side, lower and ever lower, until settling on the welcoming earth.

It was just that easy.

I was happy that none of them had died that ghastly, frothing, foaming death that sometimes signals cyanide.

And now, Canon Whitbread turned toward us and began to pray:

"Our Father which art in Heaven . . ."

If there was, actually, such as place as Heaven, the Three Graces were already safely in it. I couldn't help smiling at the thought as the canon went on:

"Hallowed be Thy name. Thy kingdom come, Thy will be done in earth, as it is in Heaven. Give us this day our daily bread. And forgive us our trespasses, as we forgive them that trespass against us."

Had God already forgiven the trespasses of these three gossips, even as they lay entangled among the furniture of a country church? Was forgiveness as fast as cyanide?

For their sakes, I hoped so.

264 · ALAN BRADLEY

*"And lead us not into temptation, but deliver us from
evil . . ."*

Yes, that was the thing, wasn't it? To deliver us from
evil, which was surely still among us. Somewhere, not far
from this very spot, was the person—or persons—who
had callously murdered Grace Willoughby, Grace Harcourt, Annie Cray, and—yes, I was now quite sure of it—
Canon Whitbread himself, albeit in a very complicated
way.

To say nothing of his son, Orlando.

Father, Son . . . and Holy Ghosts.

In a weird way, it had all begun to make sense.

Not seeming to have seen what had happened before
his very eyes, Canon Whitbread recited quickly, and
quite quietly, the prayer of thanksgiving. He then began
the closing prayer:

"Almighty and everliving God, we most heartily thank
Thee, for that Thou dost vouchsafe to feed us," and so
forth.

As he spoke, I turned to glance at Lettice and Hugo
Farnsworth, who were clutching one another, wide-eyed,
like a pair of frightened monkeys in a tree. In front of me,
Hob Nightingale was fiddling idly with the buttons of his
jacket, apparently lost in some kind of boyhood daydream.

I turned my attention again to Canon Whitbread as he
gave us the final Blessing:

"The peace of God, which passeth all understanding,
keep your hearts and minds in the knowledge and love of
God, and of His son Jesus Christ, our Lord: and the bless-

ing . . ." (here, he made the sign of the cross) ". . . of the Almighty, the Father, the Son, and the Holy Ghost, be amongst you and remain with you always. Amen."

Only then did he let out a howl of such unearthly agony that surely it must have been heard in the farthest reaches of Hell.

When I summoned up the courage and turned to look at the Three Graces, I saw to my amazement that they had begun to become transparent; to shimmer and to dim. I could clearly see the floorboards and part of the kneeling bench through Annie Cray's feet and legs.

Loss of opacity, I remember thinking. *A slight change in the index of refraction. A trick of the light.*

But in spite of my clutching at scientific straws, the Three Graces were becoming ever less and less substantial, fading away before my very eyes.

Even as I watched, they had become vague and indistinct, like receding nebulae in the haze of the starry heavens, until at last they gave a faint and final shiver . . . and were gone without a trace.

And to tell you the truth, I was devastated by their loss.

On the verge of tears, I sat there motionless for many long minutes in a perfect vacuum which, although previously unknown to science, is now known to me.

It was as if the world around me had darkened. My vision narrowed until only the altar remained visible at its center, lighted now by the low rays of the suddenly cold, weak sun lancing in through the stained-glass windows.

Somebody seized my shoulder.

·TWENTY·

WITH A DEAFENING WOODEN-SOUNDING *Bang!* I shot
up out of the pew like an overcharged skyrocket, my feet
tangling with the kneeling bench.

"Are you all right?" inquired an unfamiliar voice.

"What the blue blazes do you think you're doing?" I
shouted, church or no church. "You might have given me
a heart attack!"

I added a couple of other choice words which I will not
quote here, as I am not proud of them.

I spun round to face the intruder, who withdrew his
hand from my shoulder instantly. His pale face stared
back at me, mouth hanging open in disbelief. Except for
the white dog collar which completely encircled his neck,
he was the spitting image of Humpty Dumpty.

It was the vicar: the same roly-poly gentleman I had
seen talking to Constable Otter as I waited with Orlan-

do's body on the riverbank. A Mr. Clemm, if I remembered rightly.

He had cut himself shaving, I noticed. A small scrap of bloodied tissue peeped out distastefully from his wilted white clerical collar. What could it mean?

Was he careless? Distracted? Shortsighted? Lazy? Forgetful?

These and other possibilities flashed through my mind. It's amazing what even the slightest glimpse of animal blood can do to the human brain.

On the one hand, I felt sorry for the vicar in a complicated way. I wished I hadn't seen his careless toilet habits. At the same time, I wished he hadn't let me see them.

Which of us was guilty of this small— but important— breach of good manners?

I couldn't possibly know. I wasn't old enough and hadn't enough experience.

So the fault must be his.

We stood there, the two of us, staring at each other with bug eyes, like rival dogs, each of us unwilling to be the first to speak. I could feel my hackles rising at the back of my neck, feel my nostrils flaring.

I wanted to bite him.

Mr. Clemm was as astonished by my ferocity as I was.

"I . . . I'm sorry, young lady," he began. "I thought you might have been in some distress."

You clever old hound, I thought. *Some distress* indeed!

This was a game, and both of us knew it. The next move was mine.

Hadn't Mr. Clemm been the assistant to Canon Whitbread at the time of the murders? Where had he been that fateful morning? Surely he must have been among the suspects. Until this very moment, that thought had never crossed my mind.

I pressed my wrist—first the back of it, then the front of it—to my forehead, then lowered myself gingerly into the pew.

Mr. Clemm sank slowly down beside me. He placed his hand on my shoulder.

"Here," he said, offering me a white linen handkerchief. "Wipe your nose and tell me all about it."

I was about to give him a piece of my mind when I realized my nose was running.

"Thank you," I whispered, and put the cloth to work with a surprisingly loud *honk*. When I was finished, I handed it back to him with a weak but appreciative smile.

"You may keep it," he said, with a glance at the thing. "You might need it later."

Was this a threat? Was I sitting here cheek to cheek in a pew with a mass murderer?

A mass murderer? *That's a good one, Flavia.* Even in the heat of the moment I made a mental note of my little joke. I would tell it to Dogger, and he would smile— perhaps even give a little whistle—at my brave wit even in the face of peril.

"It's just, you see," I whispered confidentially, "that I need to be able to lay the ghost of my great-auntie to rest. I thought that if I could see the spot where she . . ."

"I understand," Mr. Clemm murmured, patting my hand. I resisted the urge to pull away.

He had probably been made to take classes at divinity school in the art of Sucking Up to Survivors.

I gave a frail smile and went on, just to encourage him a little.

"I couldn't believe it when I found that we had landed our punt almost at the very spot where . . . where—I thought it wouldn't hurt to come inside and say a little prayer for Great-Aunt Grace."

I raised my eyes to the stained-glass windows, as if to Heaven.

Don't whimper, *Flavia,* I thought. *She was supposed to be, after all, only a great-aunt, a distant twig on the family tree . . .*

I did what any intelligent girl would do: I batted my eyelashes becomingly and lowered my gaze modestly toward the floor.

When God has given you a great brain and long lashes, they may sometimes be the only weapons you have at your disposal, and it is best to know how to use them effectively.

"God hears all prayers," Mr. Clemm said. "Prayers both great *and* small."

"Thank you," I whispered, dabbing furtively at my eyes with his handkerchief, which was still clutched in my hand.

"You must have been shaken by your discovery," Mr. Clemm said, referring, I assumed, to Orlando's corpse laid out like a salmon in the grass.

"You can't imagine," I said, nodding frantically with rolling eyes, covering my mouth with the handkerchief and stifling what I hoped he would mistake for a sob.

Like most men of the cloth, Mr. Clemm had no idea how to deal with a damp and distressed female.

Round one to Flavia.

"Actually—" I said.

All great lies begin with the word "*actually*," and this one was no exception.

"Actually," I said, "one of the three ladies who died so dreadfully here was a relative of mine: my great-aunt Grace."

"Grace Willoughby?" he asked.

I shook my head. "Grace Harcourt," I told him.

I'd better tread carefully, I thought. I must remember that this man, after all, had known each of the deceased personally. The fact that he had mentioned Grace Willoughby's name first probably meant that he had known her better than Grace Harcourt.

Which is why I plumped for Grace Harcourt.

Rather than volunteering any information, as I hoped he would, Mr. Clemm gave up only a sad, knowing nod.

I needed to prime the pump.

"Anything you can tell me about her last moments will help ease the pain," I said, touching his sleeve to reinforce my pleading eyes.

"I'm afraid I can't be of much help. You see, I was rather . . . ah . . . indisposed myself that morning."

Indisposed? What did he mean by that? Had he been tippling the sacramental wine the night before? Not very likely, I thought, otherwise he'd be out in the churchyard pushing up petunias rather than sitting here evading my questions.

Unless, of course, the cyanide had been introduced

just minutes before the Communion, which would have pointed to Canon Whitbread as the killer—or to one of the Three Graces, all of whom might have assisted in the vestry before the service.

Hard to believe, though, that any one of them would have poisoned herself. Unless, of course, it was murder/suicide.

My head was spinning.

"Indisposed?" I echoed solicitously, letting the word hang in the air.

One has to be careful about inquiring too closely into another's indisposition. You never know what torrents of ucky and disturbing detail might be spilled.

Mr. Clemm looked away—looked back—then looked away again.

"Loss of faith," he admitted, biting his lip. "I had been at that time suffering a very great loss of faith, you see. It wasn't right that I should administer Holy Communion in such a state. George was very good about it. Canon Whitbread, I mean. He told me I must confront it head-on: chin up, stiff upper lip, talk to God, 'man to Man to Man to Man,' as he put it."

"Oh?" I asked with raised eyebrows, a response which is nearly impossible to ignore.

"Yes . . . well, you see . . ."

His words trailed off in a mumble as he looked away.

"Love, was it?" I blurted, taking a shot in the dark. Still, I reckoned I had a less than fifty-percent chance of being wrong. Clergymen do not come undone over football, for instance, or even money. Jealousy, greed, revenge, and love were the usual motives, judging by the newspapers, but the greatest of these is love, as Saint Paul so wisely foresaw.

And when you boiled them down, jealousy, greed, and revenge went usually hand in hand with love.

Quod erat demonstrandum, as Archimedes said, except that he said it in Greek.

Mr. Clemm gasped.

"How could you possibly know that?"

"Feminine intuition," I replied. Which was an outright lie. Feminine intuition is no more than an acceptable excuse for female brains.

I turned the famous de Luce blue eyes upon him with full force.

Suddenly he laughed.

"All right, it *was* love. You have a very persuasive way about you, Miss . . . ?"

"De Luce," I said. "Flavia."

He had thrown in the towel with surprisingly little effort on my part. I needed to be wary. I continued my stare.

"George was an understanding man. He told me I needed not to condemn myself, but only to amend my ways."

"Surely this must have come out at his trial?" I blurted. I couldn't help myself.

"It did—in a way," Mr. Clemm answered. "However, the coroner was one of our sidesmen here at St. Mildred's. And so, of course, he didn't want to add unnecessarily to the scandal."

"But why are you telling me this?" I asked, suddenly suspicious.

"Ah," Mr. Clemm breathed. "We are taught to confess, to bewail our manifold sins and wickedness, and what better way than to confess them to an innocent child such as yourself?"

I restrained a snort and favored him instead with a smile.

"Go on," I encouraged.

"Sorry," he said. "No names, no pack drill. Forgiveness," he said with a little wink, "does not demand the dirty details."

I was shocked. How could he possibly keep back the interesting bits? It wasn't fair!

"I understand," I lied, returning to the game.

All in due time, I thought.

"Come," he said. "Allow me to show you round the church. We can talk as we walk. Quite frankly, I find the atmosphere of this particular pew oppressive."

I was actually relieved to have him move. I hadn't realized how uncomfortable it had become having my escape route to the aisle blocked by a rather large clergyman.

And yet, if I wanted information, I was going to have to talk to him. Time was running out, and I was still baffled about so many points.

"This stone," I said, pointing. "It seems rather new. Stands out in such an old church. I wondered who it was?"

"A former rector," Mr. Clemm said, and began to move away.

"G.L.O.W.," I read aloud from the stone. "George L. O. Whitbread."

There was a silence of several centuries before Mr. Clemm said, "George Lancelot Orlando Whitbread. I am being very honest with you, Miss de Luce. I hope you'll not let me down."

Was he still holding me under the Seal of Confession?

"*Wark! Wark!*" I remembered Daffy barking, as she flapped her flippers together.

"But he was hanged!" I said. "How can he possibly be buried here?"

Mr. Clemm gave me such a long, sorrowful look that I almost forgave him his razor cuts and his shabby collar.

"Vanity," he said. "Mistakes are made. But as Jeremiah the prophet tells us, 'They are vanity, and the work of errors: in the time of their visitation they shall perish.'"

As if that explained everything.

Whom was he referring to? Who would perish? Those who made the mistakes? Or those who were their victims?

"Then it *wasn't* Canon Whitbread who killed the Three Graces?"

It was as blunt a question as I'd ever dared ask in my life.

Mr. Clemm stared at me as if he was torn between two answers. And then:

"Come," he said. "There's something I want you to see."

And without another word, he turned and walked

briskly away from me down the aisle. And I, without giving it another thought, followed him.

At the front of the church he turned sharply to the right and vanished up a steep stone staircase.

"Mind your head," his voice came echoing back between the walls of the narrow passage.

In spite of the summer heat outdoors, the staircase had a dank, musty, tonsil-clogging smell, as if it were a chimney for the churchyard.

I set my foot on the bottom step and began to climb: up and up and round and round. Because these early churches had also served as fortresses, the towers were designed to be defended. The circular staircase, with its tall risers, made fighting far more difficult for an attacker coming up the stairs, and easier for the defender fighting downward and backward, since it gave him the advantage of height and a free sword hand.

It reminded me of the mistaken belief that water went down the drain counterclockwise in the northern hemisphere and clockwise in the southern, as well as the doctor's symbol of a serpent twisting round a pole: the Staff of Asclepius, Dogger had told me it was called, and I wondered idly, as I climbed, if snakes slithered up trees counterclockwise in the northern hemisphere and clockwise in the southern.

"Are you coming?" Mr. Clemm's voice echoed from somewhere far above. He sounded impatient.

"Yes," I called up to him, wondering what he wanted to show me.

When I reached the top of the staircase and stepped out onto the flat roof, Mr. Clemm was nowhere in sight.

A dilapidated wooden structure, rather like a misplaced garden shed, stood in the very center of the roof, blocking my view of half the horizon.

I peered over the crumbling parapet at the scene below.

To my right, the river, slow and silent, glided like a lazy brown snake through the landscape, its lush willow-lined banks giving it the appearance of wearing an exotic green feather boa which had been flung aside perhaps, by some aging music hall star.

Poppy Mandrill came to mind.

From this altitude, the view was similar to the one taken by Hob Nightingale with his homemade kite camera.

A shock of remembrance rushed through my brain: *the photograph!*

I had shoved the snapshot into my pocket when Hob handed it to me in the tree, and with all the excitement, I had, quite frankly, forgotten about it.

Was it still there?

I shoved my hand carefully into my pocket and felt with my fingers.

Yes! I could feel the crisp edges and shiny surface of the photographic paper, still safely nestled where I had placed it.

Careful, Flavia, I thought. *You don't want to drop it over the edge and into the churchyard.*

Not that it would harm the photo, but I wanted to keep its existence to myself.

"Are you coming?" Mr. Clemm called again. "I'm round the other side. Round the back."

The back of the tower, I remembered, faced another stretch of the river with a view of the fields and a distant wood. More immediately, although I could not at the moment see them, it loomed directly over the lead roofing slates of the body of the church: the nave, the transept, and the chancel.

"As soon as . . . I catch . . . my breath," I called out, panting for effect like a dog in the desert.

What I needed to do needed to be done now, and I had to be quick about it. With Mr. Clemm breathing down my neck, I couldn't possibly compare Hob's snapshot with the view from the tower.

As I put my elbows on the parapet, a bit of Norman brick sheared off and went plummeting end over end into space.

"Watch out below!" I wanted to shout, but I didn't. If Fate had decided to clobber some deserving character in the churchyard below, who was I to interfere?

Besides, until I had examined the photograph, I needed to maintain silence.

As we had been taught to do in map-reading in Girl Guides, I rotated the photograph until it aligned with the landscape below.

Yes—here it was: Beyond was the dock where we had landed, and the grassy edge of the graveyard where Orlando's body had lain. The path along which Constable Otter and Mr. Clemm had come was clearly visible, a gash of gravel in the grass.

And here it was in Hob's photo. And here was our punt. Feely's sun hat was clearly visible in the bow. The pages of Daffy's open book caught the light amidships, and there was Dogger, poling us toward the riverbank.

The huddled lump in the stern was me, one arm outstretched. The ripples which trailed from my hands were due to the corpse of Orlando Whitbread. If I squinted, I could just make out his dark outline beneath the surface of the water.

I glanced rapidly back and forth from landscape to photograph. To my left—but hidden by one of the transept walls—would be the market square and Shadrach's Circus and, further along, Scull Cottage.

If I leaned over and out a bit, I could see—another stone dislodged and fell.

No time to look.

In my mind, there had been something else—

Aha! Just out of sight from where I now stood, hidden by one of the stone walls of the transept, the path began a long and gentle curve, through the churchyard, among the tombstones, toward the door.

In the photograph, a dark shape showed clearly against the light gray of the gravel.

A wicker bath chair!

And not just a bath chair, but an *empty* bath chair!

And just there, in the snapshot, look: lurking among the tombstones, the unmistakable form of the crouching Poppy Mandrill. Even from the kite's altitude, her Norfolk jacket was easy enough to see, and the bun of her white hair might as well have been a signal flag.

From behind a tall tombstone, she was watching us land the body of Orlando Whitbread.

Was her presence a coincidence, or had she herself been searching for Orlando?

On the path beside the church stood Hob, looking expectantly upward, the string of the kite and its release cord clutched tightly in his hand.

"What have you got there?" demanded a voice at my ear, and I spun round to find Mr. Clemm sticking his neck over my shoulder, trying to get a gander at Hob's photograph.

"It's just a snapshot," I said, shoving the thing quickly back into my pocket. "What did you wish to show me?" I asked, taking the offensive.

"You'll have to come round the other side of the tower," he said. "You can't see it from here."

"You go first," I said as I picked an excuse out of the air. "I'm terrified of heights."

My real reason was that I didn't want anyone between me and the top of the staircase.

"Always guard your exits," Daffy had once told me during one of our frank talks. She had been reading an English translation of an ancient Chinese text on military strategy, and was adapting its teachings to everyday life. "You never know," she warned, "what each new wind will bring."

And she was right. A light breeze had now begun to stir the flag above our heads, bringing with it the sound of faint music from Shadrach's Circus and, if I was not mistaken, the sharp odor of wild animals.

"Come," said Mr. Clemm, beckoning with a forefinger.

I followed him cautiously round the shedlike structure. The view, I must admit, was spectacular.

Far, far below us, at the bottom of a dizzying drop, were the lead roofs of the church, jutting every which way at sharklike Gothic angles.

"Behold," Mr. Clemm said, pointing, as he swept his arm round half the horizon. "All the wicked world."

Was he being facetious? Perhaps not. The man was, after all, an ordained minister of the Church of England and, as such, licensed to hear confessions. If anyone in Volesthorpe had the worldly goods on everyone, it was probably Mr. Clemm.

Perhaps even more so than Constable Otter.

"Over there," he said, pointing to the dock at the edge of the churchyard, "was where the poisoned chalice was found."

I nodded knowingly. I'd almost forgotten the poisoned chalice. Who had put it there, I wondered, after the tragedy of the Three Graces?

"*And also,*" he drew the words out with great emphasis, "the spot where you recovered the body of Orlando Whitbread."

He leered at me.

"Could it be, do you think, a coincidence?"

Was the man trying to tell me something? Was he trying to tip me off about something he had been told in confidence, without actually betraying the Seal of the Confessional, which, Daffy had told me, although it was a popular plot device and dear to the hearts of grubbing novelists and foreign film directors who were completely devoid of imagination, did not actually exist in law—not, at least, in England?

"Huh?" I said.

Mr. Clemm had on his face a look which I took to be exasperation.

"Is it not odd," he asked, moving a little closer, "that Orlando Whitbread should be found dead at precisely the same spot at which the murder weapon, so to speak, used by his own father was found?"

"Now that you mention it," I said, "I suppose it is."

"Look—Miss de Luce—" the vicar said. "I know who you are. There's no point in pretending with me. Your reputation has preceded you. I know where you've been and what you've done."

He was referring, I supposed, to my successfully solving a number of crimes which had perplexed the police. I couldn't help preening a little.

"Constable Otter has enlightened me—" he went on.

I held up a modest hand to stop him.

"What is it you wished to show me, Mr. Clemm?" I asked.

One of the greatest accomplishments of the detective's art is in learning to seem obtuse.

Another is in learning to provoke at precisely the right moment.

"Or did you simply want to get me up here alone?"

It was a bold move and, as I suspected it would, it took him by surprise.

He took another step toward me.

I stepped backward and away from him—toward the parapet.

"Hello the tower!" called a voice from somewhere below. "Miss Flavia!"

I risked a rapid glance over the edge.

Harriet's Rolls-Royce was parked on the gravel path, and beside its open door stood Dogger, calling up to me through the megaphone of his cupped hands.

·TWENTY-ONE·

IT IS UTTERLY IMPOSSIBLE for anyone ever to know what Dogger is actually thinking.

Except for me, of course.

Because of the great hardships to which he was subjected during the war, Dogger wears nothing on his sleeve but cloth. He can seem as blank as a newly whited wall, and yet—

I have learned to observe, by the minute movements of his eyelashes, the degree to which he parts his lips when he speaks, the caliber of his nostrils, and the tension of the skin at his temples (a sure indicator, which cannot be suppressed or modified by even the greatest actors of stage and cinema), his innermost thoughts.

In spite of that, the two of us always observe the ritual courtesies with each other.

"I hope you'll forgive my raising my voice, Miss Flavia," he said, as he met me at the door. "St. Mildred's has an uncommonly high tower for a fourteenth-century church. A hundred and thirty-five feet, I should say."

"A hundred and thirty-six," I told him. I had seen this fact inscribed on the tablet in the porch. "But perhaps, over the years, it has sunk a foot into the churchyard."

"Perhaps," Dogger said.

I had left Mr. Clemm on the roof to his own devices. I paused for a moment to listen for his footsteps on the winding stone staircase, but the old church was in silence.

"Dogger," I asked as we walked slowly to where the Rolls was parked, "has it ever occurred to you that Canon Whitbread may have been innocent?"

"It has indeed, Miss Flavia," he said. "It was, in fact, one of the reasons I suggested visiting Volesthorpe on our little holiday."

"You didn't!" I said, knowing perfectly well that he had. Dogger had put forward several excellent-seeming reasons for selecting this part of the river rather than Oxford or Cambridge, and in the end, even Aunt Felicity had been swayed.

"You astonish me!" I said.

"Yes." Dogger smiled.

"But," I said, remembering my visualization of the crimes from the pews of St. Mildred's, "if Canon Whitbread didn't kill those three old ladies, then who on earth did?"

"Someone," Dogger said, "who had something to hide. Someone who feared being found out."

"The poor man!" I said, thinking of Canon Whitbread.

"If that should be the case," Dogger went on, "then a very grave miscarriage of justice has occurred. Very grave indeed. Judicial murder."

"But whatever made you think so?" I asked.

"It was perhaps the speed with which he was arrested, tried, and executed," Dogger answered, holding open the front door of the car for me. "There is, of course, the so-called three Sundays rule which suggests—although not officially, of course—that three Sabbaths must be allowed to pass between the putting on of the judge's black cap and the drop from the scaffold, but still . . ."

"So much death," I said.

"Yes," Dogger agreed. "Too much death."

Without another word, he eased into first gear, and we rolled silently out of the churchyard.

"Have you had an interesting day?" I inquired.

"Most interesting," Dogger replied. "A day at the circus can be remarkably instructive."

"And not because of the elephant," I said, teasing a little.

"Not *because* of the elephant." Dogger smiled. "But perhaps in spite of it."

"Meaning?" I asked.

Before answering, Dogger turned the Rolls around and pointed its bonnet to the narrow dirt road that led along the riverbank. I knew enough to keep silent.

"In all walks of life and in all professions," he said at last, "there are those whom we might call the Invisible

Ones. No one remarks upon the presence of a clergyman at a funeral, or a policeman at the scene of a crime. No one thinks it strange to find a surgeon in the operating theater."

Although I could quite agree with him, I didn't see exactly what—or who—Dogger was driving at in this particular case.

"I suppose we usually look for the person who is out of place. *'Cherchez le stranger,'* Daffy would probably say."

"Precisely." Dogger nodded. "And often quite wrongly. Although we have no way of knowing who might or might not have been present at the death of a man in blue silk and red ballet slippers, we may be permitted to make certain deductions."

I loved it when Dogger talked like this. It made me feel that we were partners.

That we were equals.

It made me feel grown up and appreciated. It made me feel wanted.

A momentary pang struck at my heart. How could I possibly withhold from this kind and generous man the fact that I had picked the corpse's pocket as I waited on the riverbank?

Should I own up to Dogger and be done with it?

How could I admit that there was part of me that— quite desperately!—needed to have the upper hand, to intentionally withhold information: information which would all but guarantee that I should be the one to solve the murder of Orlando Whitbread?

In the Roman Catholic Church, I remembered, a sin is

covered by the grace of sacrament until you get around to confessing it, but in criminal investigation, it's an entirely different matter.

The answer was clear: I would confess later.

"Do you suppose there's any connection between Orlando's death and the deaths of the Three Graces?" I asked Dogger.

"I could hardly be persuaded otherwise," he said. "Multiple deaths in a tight-knit community prove often to be links in a single chain, however obscure that chain may seem to be. Miss A, for instance, might stab Miss B in the heart with an ice pick for love of Mr. C, while Miss D or Mrs. E might pine away in silence for the same unwitting gentleman."

"Mr. C would have a great deal to answer for," I said, "even if he was unaware of the facts."

"In a chemical reaction, I believe, the catalyst need not be aware of the reactants. It is little consumed itself, and often only a minute quantity is required to cause an infinitely larger effect. Of course, you'd know much more about this than I would, Miss Flavia, but you take my point."

Of course I did! Dogger was brilliant!

What smoldering embers had lain beneath the surface of this sleepy town, waiting only for the tiniest flash of flame to ignite the tinder?

I thought at once of Mrs. Palmer and the brass stallion in her poem. Who had he been, and who had resented him?

And the Three Graces: What tales had their tongues tattled to result in their triple murder?

288 · ALAN BRADLEY

"Why isn't Constable Otter investigating Orlando's death as suspicious?" I asked. "Why is he so anxious to treat it as a simple drowning?"

"The police move in mysterious ways," Dogger said. "Their wonders to perform."

Which opened whole realms of possibilities. Was Dogger hinting that Constable Otter himself might be involved? Could the constable be the brass stallion of the poem?

Or could it have been Orlando?

This was the most complicated case I had ever come across. Four people dead—five if you counted Canon Whitbread, who may have been wrongfully executed— and hardly a sensible clue to be had.

Everyone in town, it seemed, within the past two years, had bought cyanide for one reason or another: none attracting the slightest bit of attention, apparently, except for the good Canon Whitbread, whose campaigns against the humble wasp had resulted in a noose around his neck.

Even Mrs. Dandyman, of Shadrach's Circus, who came to Volesthorpe only once a year, seemed obsessed with ridding the world of sinners and replacing them with painted saints.

Perhaps it was too much for me, I thought. Perhaps I ought to ring up Inspector Hewitt, dump my basket of undigested trifle at his feet, and let him apply his superior brain to the evidence.

Should I? In a pig's parlor!

I would never live it down.

Flavia de Luce Fails! the headlines would scream. *Copper Solves Shocking Case Single-Handed.*

"I shouldn't worry about it," Dogger said, breaking into my thoughts. "Inspector Hewitt would be as baffled as we are."

"How did you know I was thinking of Inspector Hewitt?" I asked, taken aback.

"You straightened your hair and then you bit your thumbnail."

"Marvelous, Holmes!" I said, even though I felt like an idiot for being so transparent.

"No more so than your working out the state of my . . . health," Dogger said, with a sideways smile.

I had to laugh.

"You're observing me observing you observing me. Is that the way the world works?"

"Largely," Dogger said. "Yes."

We fell into one of those warm silences that I live for, and I stared out at the passing willows as the road narrowed to little more than a footpath.

"Where are we going?" I asked. "Back to Scull Cottage?"

"No," Dogger said. "Miss Tetlock has kindly arranged for us to visit the formidable Poppy Mandrill. We're to pick her up. They are, apparently, old friends."

I gasped.

"I told her I was keen on the history of the London stage. I'm sorry for speaking such an untruth, but I couldn't see any other way around it."

"But *are* you?" I asked. "Keen, I mean?"

"I have seen a few shows in my day. I shall manage."

"But," I said, my mind reeling, "Poppy Mandrill might well be our prime suspect."

And although I had vowed to keep back my confession until later, the whole sad story of how I had deceived him came suddenly pouring out: not just my rifling of the corpse's pockets and my finding of the crumpled paper, but also Hob Nightingale and his camera, the chemist, the aerial photos, the empty wheelchair—all of it in one breathless blurt.

I was ashamed of myself.

"Well done!" Dogger said, shaking his head.

Claire Tetlock was waiting for us at the edge of the field. Dogger got out of the Rolls and opened the back door for her.

"I feel like visiting royalty," she said, settling back into the soft leather upholstery. "Hello, Flavia."

I twisted round from my usual seat beside Dogger and gave her my warmest smile.

"Hello, Claire," I said, remembering she had given me permission to use her Christian name.

The first time I had seen her, Claire had been hot from hoeing, damp under a tropical hat. But now—dressed to kill, I thought—in a bluish-green belted summer frock with a bit of lace at the throat, she looked like nothing so much as a visiting duchess. Maureen O'Hara astray in the English countryside.

I couldn't take my eyes off her.

"I'm quite looking forward to this," she said. "I haven't

visited with Poppy for ages. She's quite a character, you know."

"I hadn't realized you were such good friends," I said, recalling how uneasy Claire had seemed at Scull Cottage in the presence of Poppy's ancient theatrical posters.

"Not quite friends," Claire corrected. "I had occasion to call upon her as a nurse. It was more of a professional association."

My ears perked up. Was Claire aware that Poppy Mandrill was able to get out of her wheelchair when the occasion demanded?

"Poor soul," I said. "She's not quite well, is she?"

Which Claire could take in any way she wanted.

She laughed.

"Poppy is an actress," she said. "And a very great one, at that. The London stage did not misjudge her. In her day she was a Titan . . . a Titaness. Or a Poppaea. That's her name, you know. Poppy. Poppaea."

Poppaea Sabina, I recalled, from Daffy's sometimes daring chatter at the breakfast table, was the woman who schemed her way into a marriage with the Roman emperor Nero, who later (Daffy had whispered over the kippers) kicked both her and her unborn child to death.

Perhaps in part because we shared the middle name Sabina, I had always felt an invisible kinship with this determined and yet somehow tragic woman. Being married to Nero must not exactly have been a piece of cake.

After turning it round, Dogger negotiated the Rolls along a narrow lane that rose, gradually, away from the river, ending in a shady grove where the yaffling call of a green woodpecker rang out among the trees like a series of rapid ricochets in an elderly Western film. Only the puffs of smoke were missing.

"Alhambra House," Claire told us. "Named after the theater."

There was nothing quite so grand about this place. A dank-looking pile whose weathered white plaster front was so cracked with an overgrowth of ivy that one longed to slash at it with a sword-stick, as Queen Mary, the Queen Mother, was said to be so fond of doing.

A couple of once-impressive pillars marked the entrance, their peeling paint betraying that they were composed of no more than worm-eaten wood, from which ants came and went in busy funeral processions.

"Poppy has fallen upon hard times," Claire said. "This place was once the Mecca of the theatrical world. Noel and Larry simply begged to be allowed to sit at the feet of the *grande dame*."

Which reminded me of something.

"What happened to her leg?" I asked.

"It was a national calamity," Claire replied. "An accident with a piece of stage machinery. Poppy's greatest, most famous scene at the end of the play. She was swinging high above the stage on an iron crescent moon when the rigging somehow failed. Although it was later determined to have been an accident, some said that the gear had been tampered with. At any rate, the heavy contraption, in falling, acted like the blade of a scimitar and . . . well . . ."

I didn't need Claire to describe the scene. I could picture it all too well: the crashing down of the mechanical moon; the single horrible, bloodcurdling scream; the audience, electrified, leaping to their feet; the hundred gasps; the hands raised to cover mouths; the sudden dimming of the stage lights; the curtain gliding slowly down to hide the blood.

"How ghastly!" I gasped.

"Quite," Claire said. "And yet in spite of it, just six weeks after the amputation, Poppy returned to the stage as Long John Silver, the one-legged pirate in *Treasure Island.*"

"Good lord!" I said, and I meant it.

"It was one of the greatest moments in theatrical history. She still sometimes makes use of the battered wooden crutch she used so effectively in that role. She keeps it hidden in the depths of that ridiculous old bath chair, but pulls it out at dramatic moments. As I say, Poppy's a very great actress. But don't let her fool you. You'd be surprised what she's capable of."

No, I wouldn't, I thought, but I didn't say so.

I was thinking of the bruise on the back of Orlando's neck.

·TWENTY-TWO·

OUR RING AT THE rusting bellpull was answered by a surprisingly crisp young man in a blue cardigan and a yellow tie.

"Miss Mandrill is expecting you," he said, stepping aside to let us in.

"Thank you, Coatesworth," Claire replied, with a barely perceptible wink. "I hope we're not too early."

"Not at all, Miss Tetlock," he answered. "Miss Mandrill has made her preparations."

Preparations? What did he mean by that? *Was the woman compounding poisons in her kitchen?*

We'd better keep a sharp eye on the tea and biscuits.

Although her name had not appeared in Mr. Wanless's poison register, Poppy Mandrill did, after all, have indirect access to cyanide through Orlando, who worked occasionally at the chemist's shop. And Canon Whitbread's wasp killer would have been kept somewhere in the vicarage—probably the greenhouse—and any of the vicar's wardens, including Mrs. Palmer, would have had no trouble pinching enough of the stuff to do whatever nefarious deeds they had in mind.

"She'll see you in the second parlor," Coatesworth said as he led us past an open double door, through which I had a glimpse of a dusty parquet floor, high moldings, and a number of grim green hangings.

"Just in here," he said, showing us into an altogether smaller room.

I could see at a glance that sunlight was not welcome here. The windows were covered with blackout paper, sections of which were visible behind a set of heavy, dark curtains.

Three chairs had been arranged in a dead straight line at the edge of a threadbare Turkey carpet, upon which had been centered a small table, set with a vase of old-fashioned pinks and a large brass carriage clock. In the silence, I could hear its self-important ticking.

The spicy clove scent of the flowers overpowered even the moldy atmosphere of the parlor. I was reminded of a sickroom—or perhaps an undertaker's shop.

"Please be seated," Coatesworth said, fussing with a fully set tea trolley which stood parked on one corner of the carpet, as if on a stage set. "Miss Mandrill will be with you momentarily."

I raised an eyebrow at Dogger, who had once told me that the word meant "briefly," rather than "soon," and was best avoided if one didn't want to be mistaken for an

American. But Dogger was wearing his unreadable poker face, and I was left to feel superior all by myself.

"Thank you, Coatesworth," Claire said as we took our seats.

There was a feeling of expectancy in the room, as if even the wallpaper were listening to our every word. We sat in silence, hands folded, and we waited.

And waited.

Claire shot me a half smile before she returned to contemplating the carpet.

It seemed as if the lighting in the room was changing. Surely the shadows of the vase and clock were shifting slightly across the silk tablecloth?

How many shoe soles had that shabby old carpet seen in its day? I wondered. What famous feet had worn away its pile? Had murderers stood chatting upon its once-red nap?

There was a slight scurrying sound in the corner: the sound that a couple of mice might make when caught with the cheese, followed by a hollow groaning.

Poppy Mandrill's ornate wicker bath chair came sailing smoothly into the room like some ancient wooden ship under full sail, coming to anchor on the Turkey carpet between the table and the tea trolley.

Surely the lights were brighter at that spot than they had been when we came into the room; surely we were now sitting in a slightly greater darkness.

But it was the woman herself who commanded attention. I wouldn't have believed it if I hadn't seen it with my own eyes.

This was not the elderly invalid who had accosted me in the churchyard! Nor the same harpy who had hissed into my ear in the pews of St. Mildred's.

This was an Edwardian beauty in the full flush of high-colored womanhood. Her skin was like peaches and her eyes sparkled like happy diamonds.

Belladonna, I thought, but I pushed it out of my mind at once. It would be a sin to penetrate such artistry: an affront to decency. We were entranced, and I knew it.

Poppy Mandrill looked slowly and deliberately at each of us in turn: from Claire to Dogger, and then to me, her piercing eye relishing—no, not relishing, but positively *feasting upon*—our reactions.

She was coolly judging her effect upon our widening eyes, making us her mirror.

Her transformation was remarkable. From a frail and elderly invalid, this woman had summoned up a goddess.

I'm afraid I gasped.

"Welcome," Poppy Mandrill said in a voice like ancient honey, extending her arms, her palms upturned in a gesture of hospitality. "I bid you welcome to Alhambra House."

Now I wanted to applaud. I was in her grip already and I knew it; under her spell.

But I didn't care. It was as if the very nature of time itself had shifted and taken us with it: a slice of time in which we sat frozen in a pretty little tableau; living insects in amber.

Poppy was dressed in a classic white drapery, which I guessed was modeled on the Greek, overlaid with a large, dangling Art Deco necklace of shiny Bakelite lozenges, each of a different vivid color: a necklace for which the Duchess of Windsor would happily have sold herself— several times over—into slavery.

We sat suspended for several very long moments in this charmed state until Dogger broke the spell.

"Thank you for inviting us to visit, Miss Mandrill," he said. "It is most gracious of you to share your memories."

Already her eyes were glittering like a snake's. This woman's metabolism burned recognition in the same way that an automobile burns petrol.

She tittered slightly.

"You mustn't press me too much, Mr. Dogger, for I am of frail and tender years."

It was a joke, I suppose, and Dogger smiled dutifully.

"*Hypatia of Alexandria*," he said. "Act One, Scene One."

"You surprise me, Mr. Dogger," Poppy said.

I turned to stare at him but caught myself just in time. Dogger had surprised me, too. Just when I thought that I had got the measure of the man, he would reveal an entirely new and unsuspected side.

"As a student, I was fortunate enough to take up residence in a theatrical boardinghouse," Dogger said. "Complimentary tickets often served as the common currency."

Poppy Mandrill laughed a throaty laugh.

"In exchange for what, Mr. Dogger?"

"Favors," Dogger answered. "Friendship. Do you remember Frederick Linden-Smith?"

Poppy's face became a sunbeam. "Of course! He was Adagio in *Return of the Homing Angel*. Wonderful reviews. Wonderful. And Carlyle Quinn in *When the Sleeper Awakes*. Were you acquainted with him, Mr. Dogger?"

"I was," Dogger said quietly. "He died a prisoner of war in Burma."

Dogger did not mention his own captivity.

He was risking a great deal by opening this line of conversation, I realized, when even the slightest trigger—the most casual reference—could set him off on a nightmare journey of flashbacks to his own torture.

"Yes, I believe I heard something to that effect," Poppy remarked. "Poor chap, Freddie. He had a great future."

I bit my tongue, and from where I sat, it looked to me as if Dogger was doing the same.

"I believe he was once your protégé," Dogger said. "As was Orlando Whitbread."

Something glistened at the corner of one of Poppy Mandrill's eyes.

"You mustn't be too hard on me, Mr. Dogger," she said. "The flame must never be blamed for the death of the moth.

"Help yourselves to tea," she added, covering her own cup with an open hand when Claire offered to pour.

Dogger inclined his head, accepting the rebuke graciously. Was he trying to encourage her to talk?

"All the world envies a woman like me," she said, when we were settled. "They think it heaven to have been the quarry of every male, young or old, who ever laid eyes upon her. Let me tell you it is not. The bull's-eye on a target range has fewer holes than the heart of a woman on the stage. 'Oh!' you will say, 'but what about

the gifts: the flowers, the food, the jewels . . . the attention . . . the applause?' Well enough when you are young,
I suppose, and still blinded by your own beauty. But to
someone of my present age, it is quite frankly sickening.
One comes to fear the corpulent clergyman as the apple
fears the worm."

Aha! I thought. *The present vicar, Mr. Clemm, and his
loss of faith.*

How my heart was suddenly breaking for him—and for
her!

Claire, who had not spoken to this point, got up from
her chair and moved toward the woman in the wheelchair.

"No!" Poppy said, holding up a forbidding hand. "Sit
down. The priestess must never be approached upon the
altar.

"We must honor our traditions," she added.

Although she said this in rather a wry tone, almost half
joking, her meaning was unmistakable.

Claire returned to her seat. "Tell me about Orlando,"
she said softly. "I haven't yet been able to grasp—'

And in that instant I suddenly saw through her. She
and Dogger had planned this interview as precisely as a
pair of generals craft a battle plan. They had rehearsed
this conversation even before we set out for Alhambra
House! They had rehearsed this little scene as carefully as
any opening night in the West End.

I kept my mouth shut in admiration.

"Ah, Orlando." Poppy shook her head. "Dear Orlando.
He was too good to live. The world did not deserve him."

What was this? Was the woman confessing to murder?

"He was paying you a tribute, was he not?" Dogger asked. "I recognized the red ballet slippers and the blue silk costume at once as one of yours. *Pierrot in the Underworld.* One of your greatest roles. A record run at the Aldwych. I remember it with great pleasure."

Poppy's only response was to touch her upper lip with a startlingly long forefinger, and for a fleeting moment, her face was that of Pierrot—as if the character had been flashed upon her face by some cleverly concealed magic lantern.

"He was going to re-create my role . . . *we* were going to re-create my role. To astonish the world. There would be no denying his talent."

"You understood him," Dogger said. "Where others failed him."

Poppy nodded. It was easy to see how touched she was at even the mention of Orlando's name.

Which didn't mean that she hadn't killed him.

"Orlando's life was not an easy one," she said quietly. "His mother died before she could begin to love him. His father resented him in the beginning—hated him in the end."

"But why?" I couldn't resist.

"There are children," Poppy said, "whose lives are shaped by the minds of their elders. It matters not a jot what they are in actuality, but what they are *thought* to be. Orlando was such a child—and such a man."

"Sad," I said, because I knew exactly what she meant.

"Infinitely sad," Poppy said, "because Orlando had in

him, as I have said, the power to be the greatest actor of his generation. A gift from the gods."

"He must have been the envy of Volesthorpe," I said, putting it as gently as I knew how.

"Haw! Haw!" Poppy cried, her voice like that of an enraged hawk. "There were those who resented—"

"The Three Graces!" I blurted, as if I had just thought of it. I needed to flush this conversation out into the open to keep it from creeping back into the bushes.

In spite of that, I did not say what was actually on my mind.

"—his ease with women," Poppy went on.

Meaning what? I wondered. Was it possible for one woman to hate a man because of his ease with another? This was a question that was far beyond me. I tried to think of an equivalent problem in the world of organic chemistry, but I could not.

I would ask Daffy, who had read *Lady Chatterley's Lover* and accordingly knew everything there was to know about such things.

I turned my mind back to the Three Graces and their swift departure from the earth.

If not Canon Whitbread, who then had poisoned the chalice? Who, indeed, had dumped it in the river after the killings of the Three Graces?

"Look for the Invisible Ones," Dogger had told me.

And who could be more invisible in a parish than the minister's son? My heart fluttered at the thought. Was it possible that Orlando had poisoned the cup of the village gossips? He may well have had good reason to.

"Where was Orlando on the Sunday morning—the day of the three murders?" I asked.

Poppy was suddenly a hawk again, her wild eyes staring directly—perhaps too directly—into my mind.

"He was with me," she said.

I shot a glance at Claire. Hadn't she told me Orlando claimed to have taken the 7:02 up to London the previous evening? She gave me an eye shrug.

"Rehearsing," Poppy added unnecessarily. "And I testified to that fact at the time."

"What actually happened that morning, Miss Mandrill?" Dogger asked, with a little shake of his head. "One reads the papers, of course, but I have never quite been able to get it straight in my mind."

"You are a clever man, Mr. Dogger. And a very pretty trap you have laid. But obviously, since I was with Orlando, I could not possibly know what took place in the church."

"Quite right," Dogger agreed, not fazed in the least. "I thought it might have been spoken about in Volesthorpe."

"And so it was," Poppy answered. "It was also widely reported in all the newspapers, which you admit to having read—as did I—as did we all."

"May I help myself to more tea?" Claire asked brightly, getting to her feet and reaching for the silver pot.

How much of this conversation had she and Dogger anticipated? I wondered. How much of it was spontaneous?

"You've come to me under false pretenses, Mr. Dogger," Poppy said in a scolding tone, as if he were a naughty boy. I saw that the spark had returned to her eye. "I fear your interest in my theatrical experiences was merely a ruse. Your motives are not those of the theatrical historian, nor are they of the merely curious."

Dogger did not protest, as I might have done if I were him.

"I offer my apologies if I haven't made myself clear," he said. "But as a once-avid student of the stage, I couldn't help being struck by the remarkable similarities of the murders to your role in *Mildritha Kinbote*. The three poisonings from the common cup were particularly suggestive. There is also the coincidence of the name: St. Mildred's."

The silence that fell clotted the air of the drawing room. I hardly dared breathe.

And then there came an insistent "SSS-SSS-SSS." Poppy Mandrill was hissing like a kettle through her teeth.

"You must forgive me, Mr. Dogger," she rasped, pulling a handkerchief from her sleeve and wiping at her mouth. "Perhaps you won't believe me, but that similarity had never occurred to me. Not until this very moment. You are quite right, of course. Do you suspect some connection?"

"No," Dogger said. "I was merely pointing out the remarkable coincidence. In my experience, murderers in real life have neither the wit nor the ingenuity to plot and plan such literary crimes, let alone carry them out. Killers do not read books, nor do they frequent the theater. They are more often to be found in cinemas, or wrapped in the *Daily Mail*."

Poppy Mandrill let out a dry chuckle.

"Touché, Mr. Dogger," she said. "I am properly chastised. I should have known better than to bait you. Your point, of course, being that such fiendish killings occur only in the books of Mrs. Christie and her ilk?"

Dogger gave her a slowly beatific look. His face was suddenly that of a weary but understanding archangel.

"And, of course, in Volesthorpe," he said.

Although I could see that they were both taking a certain pleasure in the duel, it was time to remove Dogger from the line of fire. I knew the signs all too well.

I reached for my teacup and as I raised it to my lips, I let out the most appalling, gut-grinding belch.

It was an art that Daffy had taught me as a child, and one which I had perfected over the years in the privacy of my bedroom and my laboratory. My belches were not for the faint of heart.

"I'm sorry," I gasped, covering my mouth and holding my breath just enough to make my face go a convincing shade of red. "I suddenly don't feel well. The piggies-in-a-blanket at breakfast, perhaps."

I let out another train of injured air.

Dogger and Claire were on their feet at once, bustling me toward the door and making their apologies.

It was a performance worthy of Poppy Mandrill herself. *Had she spotted it as such?* I wondered.

I kept my shoulders hunched like a vulture and my hands over my mouth until we were in the Rolls and safely away from Alhambra House.

Only then did Claire and I burst into hysterical laughter.

Dogger smiled a tired smile and I realized that it really was time to get him home.

After dropping Claire off at Scull House ("Just leave me at the edge of the field," she had insisted), we drove back to the Oak and Pheasant in near-silence.

"Phew!" I said as we got out of the car. "It's been a long day already. I think I need a rest. You might as well have one, too, Dogger."

"Thank you, Miss Flavia," he said. "I believe I shall."

In my room, I stood on my head on the bed as I sometimes do when I need to concentrate my thoughts.

Why hadn't I asked Poppy Mandrill about Orlando's paraldehyde habit? I'd certainly had the opportunity. It was almost as if some powerful hand had held back my questioning—and perhaps for good reason.

"All's well that ends well," Shakespeare had said and, as usual, the wily old bard was right. It might not have done at all to let Poppy know how much I already knew about the characters in the case.

When I woke up, the shadows of late afternoon had subtly rearranged my room.

I got up, washed my face, and brushed my teeth. Daffy had become remarkably fussy about personal hygiene in the past several months, and I didn't want to give her an excuse to carp.

·TWENTY-THREE·

I TAPPED LIGHTLY AT Daffy's bedroom door with my fingernails. One long followed by two short: a Morse code letter *D* for Dickens, the password we had agreed upon during one of our rare truces.

After a moment, I heard the key turn in the lock.

"Well?" she demanded, peering out at me with one eye through the crack of the opening door.

"How are you getting on with the poems?" I whispered, keeping my voice down in case Mrs. Palmer was within earshot.

Daffy eased the door open wider—just enough to let me squeeze in—then closed it behind me.

"Listen, Nugs," she said, putting her hand on my shoulder, and my heart leapt up. She had not called me Nugs for years—not since we were children.

308 · ALAN BRADLEY

"Listen, Nugs, these are deep waters and dangerous. You'd be a fool to become involved."

I was too stupefied to speak. Daffy led me over to her bed, patting the quilt to indicate that I should sit.

Mrs. Palmer's book, *The Mussel Bed,* lay open face-down on the counterpane—which ought to have told me something in itself, since Daffy had raged more than once that anyone who left a book in that position ought to be flayed, hanged, drawn and quartered, and dragged by four black horses to the four corners of the globe, their tattered remains roasted and the ashes cursed and scattered to the winds.

Daffy snatched up the book and read.

"This one, for instance, about the copper mare and the brass stallion. Remember?

"The copper mare and
The brass stallion graze
In Flecker's Field.
He paws the turf,
While she the wind tastes.
And when he trots to her
She turns tail."

"Of course I do," I said. "It's about Leander, the ancient Greek chap who drowned trying to reach his lover, Hero, who was a nun."

"It's about horseplay," Daffy said. "And not the kind you're thinking. James Elroy Flecker died in bed, remember?"

"I don't know what you're talking about," I said, and I didn't. Daffy's mind and mine do not function in the same way.

"Do you remember *Madame Bovary?*" she asked. "Remember Rodolphe? The gentleman in the yellow gloves and the green velvet coat?"

"Holy moly!" I said. "You don't mean—?"

"Indeed I do!" Daffy said with a leer.

"Mrs. Palmer?" I asked. "I don't believe it!"

I still wasn't exactly sure what Daffy was referring to, but I didn't need the details.

"With whom?" I asked, managing to keep my head grammatically.

"With her Leander. The one who drowned."

"Hold on!" I protested. "She wrote this poem and published it ages before Orlando died."

"Which can mean only," Daffy said, "that she either foresaw his death or was herself the instrument of his demise.

"Ah!" she said. "Is there true love beyond the grave? Does the drowned hero await in some violet-scented afterlife? 'Fraid not, Flavia. Marvell said it best:

"The grave's a fine and private place,
But none, I think, do there embrace.

"Nope, you can count on it, little sister. The woman's either a psychic or a killer."

"Top drawer, Daff!" I shouted. "You ought to be in the detecting business yourself!"

I was amazed to recognize that there was no resent-
ment whatsoever attached to my words. My sister deserved all the praise and encouragement I could give her.

"Go on," I urged. "Is there more?"

"Tons more. Steaming cartloads of it."

That did it. I vowed there and then to take up the
study of poetry at the earliest possible convenience.

"I'm all ears," I said, putting my forefingers behind my
ears and pushing them forward until I looked like Dumbo.

"Well, this, for instance," Daffy said, turning to a new
page and striking a dramatic stance.

Her voice was different, I noticed, when she read poetry.

> "'Tis not the hawk that frightens but the shadow of the
> lark—"

"She is more afraid of the songbird than the raptor," I
interrupted. "I wonder why?"

"The Linnaean classification of the skylark is *Alauda
arvensis,* meaning 'field lark.' *Arvensa* is the Latin word
for 'field,' recalling both Flecker and the field in which
the copper mare and the brass stallion graze. And our
trusty landlord Palmer's Christian name is Arven. It's on
the hanging signboard out front."

Of course it was! Hadn't I seen it with my own two
eyes?

That did it. I resolved to take up the study of Latin as
soon as we were back home. I was already drooling at the
thought of those mountain torrents of leather-bound

texts in Buckshaw's overflowing library. What juicy secrets lay hidden in forgotten names!

"Sorry," I said. "Go on."

Daffy gave me an amused raised eyebrow and began the poem again:

*"'Tis not the hawk that frightens but the shadow of the lark.
Most melancholy bird of all espies us in the dark."*

"An owl!" I said. "Owls can see in the dark! Someone has spied on them in Flecker's Field!"

"Partially correct," Daffy said. "Someone *has* spotted them. But it's not an owl."

She closed the book, sniffing at its sandwiched pages as if gratefully savoring the knowledge they had given up.

"'Most melancholy bird,'" she said, "is an allusion to a poem by John Milton. Surely you've heard of *Paradise Lost?*"

Heard of it? I had *lived* it! *Paradise Lost* was the story of my life!

"Vaguely," I said.

"Excellent," Daffy said. "The reference to a melancholy bird, however, as every schoolboy knows, is from one of his earlier poems, 'Il Penseroso,' which, roughly translated, means 'The Thinking Man.'"

"And what is the thinking man thinking about if he's not referring to an owl?" I asked.

"It's a poem about his muse, and how she meets her lover."

Daffy fell into her rich, dark reading voice:

"Oft in glimmering bow'rs and glades
He met her, and in secret shades
Of woody Ida's inmost grove . . .

"Quite frankly, Flavia, it's about an assignation."

Well! That put a whole new light on things. Had Mrs. Palmer's husband realized what was going on and killed the man who was meeting his wife "in secret shades," whatever that meant?

"And the bird?" I asked. I was not about to be thrown off the track by a lot of nauseous lovemaking.

"A nightingale," Daffy said. "The melancholy bird of which the poet speaks was a nightingale."

There are times when the breath is sucked out of your lungs as, in an instant, a forest fire consumes the living air.

Giddy and light-headed, I made my excuses (sudden fatigue) and fled the room.

"Wait!" she called after me. "There's more!"

But my head was spinning. I needed to be alone. Now.

When all else fails, there remains a single spot on earth where one can be alone: a place where teeming thoughts can be rounded up and organized; a place where one will never be imposed upon by the inhabitants.

And, as if of their own accord, my shoes were already making their way across the road to the graveyard. All I needed to do was to keep my feet in them.

Here I could collect my thoughts among the ancient stones.

Would I sit here with Fanny Greatorex, spinster of this parish, who departed this life on the third day of April, in the Year of Our Lord Nineteen Hundred and Six, or over there on that mossy bank with Thomas Button, Gent, whom "life abandoned" on November thirty-first (that's what it said) in the fifty-ninth year of the reign of our Sovereign King George III?

Since Fanny looked a little more welcoming, and somewhat less damp, I chose her. I settled myself among the lichens on her slab.

There is something mystical about sitting on a stone. It not only provides firm support for one's bottom, but also seems almost miraculously to stimulate the brain.

It was obvious that Orlando Whitbread was central to what I had already begun to think of as the Volesthorpe Mysteries: as tangled a knot of death as I had ever seen. The man himself was dead, as was his father, as well as the three village women who had perhaps gossiped too much about him for their own good.

The good canon had gone to the gallows for the deaths of the latter three ladies and now his son would be joining him—more or less—in the grave.

There was so little left to go on. Perhaps it was too late, anyway. Perhaps we should simply pack our picnic baskets in the Rolls, drive off into the sunset, and leave these dead to their own devices. Given enough time, it wouldn't matter anyway.

Or would it?

Would Flavia de Luce blot her heavenly copybook by overlooking a crime?

"*Four crimes!*" a little voice cried within me.

Would all the saints, when I arrived in Paradise, rub forefingers together at me as if starting a fire with sticks, and cry out to me "Tish! Tish! Tish!"? Would a choir of angels chant, to the tune of some grand and previously unknown melody by Bach or Handel, "Shame! Shame! Shame! Shame! Flavia's going down the drain!"?

With Heaven, you never knew. It was better not to take any chances.

A twig cracked and before I could even think someone seized me from behind and covered my mouth. I had only a flashing impression of rough red hands and a hot rasping breath at my ear.

"Keep quiet," hissed a voice.

My eyes must have been bugging out above the restraining fingers. I did the only thing I could think of. I bit them.

"Oww!" shrieked the voice as I was abruptly released. "You filthy little minx. You've bitten me! I'm going to lose a finger!"

I spun round to see Mrs. Palmer. She was staring at her bleeding hand, which had distinct teeth marks on the web between her thumb and forefinger.

My instinct was to make a break for it and run for my life, but her next words stopped me.

"Wait. I probably deserved it. I was simply trying to keep you from crying out and attracting attention. It's my fault entirely. I should never have followed you in the first place. I thought we could have a quiet talk."

She looked at her injured hand in a way which I believe is called rueful.

"Why didn't you simply walk up to me?" I asked, handing her the handkerchief Mr. Clemm had thrust upon me. "Why didn't you just hail me from a distance?"

"I thought you'd run away," she replied. "I thought you'd think I was going to kill you—just as I killed Orlando."

"*Did* you?" I asked. "Kill Orlando, I mean?"

"No," she said, wrapping her damaged hand in my now-ruined handkerchief. "I most certainly did not. But you *believe* I did."

"Do I?" I challenged.

The conversation was becoming like one of those absurd French dramas in which the characters stand about swapping nonsense dialogue while the audience pretend they know what's going on.

She did not reply to my question but dug deep into the pocket of her apron with her undamaged hand and pulled out a roll of banknotes.

"Here," she said, holding it out. "Take it. It's all I have. I can get more later if you insist."

I looked at her blankly.

"Just leave. Go away. Ask no more questions. Leave us in peace."

It took me several moments to see what she was getting at.

"Are you offering me a bribe?" I asked.

She shook the money in my face, then tried to press it

into my hands in what, because of her injured hand, was rather a gruesome gesture: all blood and banknotes.

I did not take them from her, but neither did I refuse. I needed to keep this conversation alive until I had what I needed.

"Who else is blackmailing you?" I asked. Because I had broken into her bedroom, it was probably not a good idea to bring up the brass stallion and the copper mare. I didn't want her to think me a snoop.

"Ah!" she said with a wry grin. "I see you've been talking to your sister Daphne. Serves me right. I ought to have known better than to trust anyone who reads Trollope."

There was a long, uneasy pause and then she reached with her good hand into her apron pocket and pulled out a packet of cigarettes and a book of matches. She made a clumsy effort to get one alight, but her fingers were shaking badly. I lit a match and held it for her in spite of my aversion to the habit.

There we were, inches apart, staring into each other's eyes.

"Orlando," I said, and I watched as her tears welled up instantly at the sound of his name. Surely this woman could not have—

"Orlando was a very special soul," Mrs. Palmer said. "He did not belong upon this earth."

"Who killed him?" I persisted, thinking of her husband.

She took a deep drag on her cigarette, sizing me up with tired eyes.

"You shouldn't listen to gossip," she said, exhaling a trumpet of smoke brutally. "Gossip kills."

"Sometimes there is no other choice," I insisted, "when you can't get at the facts."

I was quite pleased with myself for having thought of this.

She was already halfway through her cigarette, staring now at the horizon.

"Orlando, like many artists, was not strong-willed. He suffered from an abundance of addictions."

Which was rather a neat way of putting it, I thought: wine, women, and song, and paraldehyde—all without actually mentioning any of them: all swept under the carpet with all the efficiency of Mrs. Mullet on a Saturday morning and Aunt Felicity arriving unexpectedly from London.

"Talent is a terrible taskmistress," I remarked, picking this shockingly trite bit of rot out of thin air. I was ashamed of myself, but still rather proud.

"It is, indeed," Mrs. P said, dabbing at her eyes with her bandaged hand. "His father was so very, very proud of him, and yet—"

"It must have been very difficult for Canon Whitbread," I said. It is often best to lead with a general remark and leave the other person to release a flood of details. But in this instance, it didn't work.

"Yes, it was," she said, and left it at that.

I detected some awkwardness developing. I needed to be more personal.

"Mrs. Palmer—" I said.

"Greta," she blurted. "Please call me Greta."

She was as anxious to be chummy as I was. Chummi-ness invariably leads to confidences being exchanged, which, when you get right down to it, is what the art of detection is all about. Sleuths learn nothing by being aloof. It was the one thing that the great Holmes got wrong.

"Greta," I said. "I'm curious about just one point. Per-haps you can set my mind at ease."

Brilliant, Flavia. Make it sound as if I'm the one who is discommoded (which doesn't mean what you probably think it does).

Before she could even think about it, I fired away.

"Where was Orlando on the morning the Three Graces died?"

I already had two answers to this question. Poppy Mandrill claimed he had been with her. Canon Whit-bread's prosecutor insisted he had gone up to London.

"Presumably at home at Scull Cottage," Greta said. "He had just come down from London the day before."

"Hold on," I said. "Gone *up* to London, you mean. Sat-urday. The night before the murders."

That's what Claire had told me.

Greta laughed.

"You see how stories get muddled in a time of murder? He had, as I say, come *down*. I know because I picked him up at the station."

"From Dollylands," I said. "He had just been released from the private clinic."

"Yes," she agreed.

"Then this is my question," I persisted. "Was his treatment successful? Or was he still under the influence of paraldehyde?"

"What would you know about that?" she demanded. If she'd had feathers, they'd have been ruffling.

I shrugged. I needed to find out if Orlando, at the time of the poisonings, was shot full of paraldehyde, and in the grip of the delusions and hallucinations that sometimes accompany its use.

I could feel the resistance. She did not want to reply.

"It all came out at the time of his father's conviction," she said bitterly. "You can read about it in *Great Trials*."

"I don't have a copy of *Great Trials*," I said gently. "And besides, I'd rather hear it from you."

"Why are you doing this, Flavia?" she asked, fumbling for another cigarette.

"Because I trust you," I rejoined, suddenly inspired.

That did it. Greta began to talk.

"Orlando had been in and out of several institutions and private hospitals, all of them promising, but none, in the end, providing a cure. Dollylands was the end of the line. They admitted only the most badly addicted patients. He came down on the Saturday evening train, went straight home to Scull Cottage, and, as far as I know, injected himself with the stuff immediately. He came into the Oak and Pheasant an hour later and I bustled him out the back door into the garden. You could smell him from across the room. He was extremely agitated. Went on and on about his reputation ruined, his good name grabbed from him by gossips. He was receiving vile letters. Said he had no choice but to involve the police. I told him to go home and sleep it off. It was dreadful. He cried. And so did I, but not until later."

"And did you see him on Sunday?"

"No. Apparently no one did. He claimed to have been lying in Scull Cottage in a stupor until the Monday morning after the murders."

"Thank you, Greta," I said. "You've been a great help." And I meant it.

"I'm glad of that," she said. "And now I want you to drop the whole thing. Orlando is dead but there are still many secrets in Volesthorpe. Some of them will come out and some will not. None of us need the trouble. Take this, go home, and forget about us."

Again she held out the roll of banknotes.

"Keep the money," I said. "I don't take bribes. I'm not that kind of person."

"What kind of person are you?" she asked, and I could see that she was offended.

"I'm the kind of person who is going to make a difference in the world," I told her. "As soon as I get rid of my braces."

Greta began to laugh a low, slithery laugh, like a snake in the grass. But the laugh died in her throat like a shot pheasant.

A man's voice, nearby, was calling out "Greta?"

She seized me by the arm and pulled me roughly down behind a weathered tombstone.

"It's Arven!" she hissed. "My husband. He's come after me. He's going to kill me!"

"Why would he want to kill you?" I whispered.

"You don't want to know," she whispered back, clutching my elbow to her chest as if it were a life jacket.

I did not bother telling her that I already did.

I peered round the edge of the tombstone. Arven Palmer was standing about thirty yards away, looking round, scratching his head.

"Can you see him?" she whispered.

I nodded yes.

"Just keep still," she pleaded. "Arven has no patience. He'll give up and go away before he'll search the churchyard."

"You know him very well," I said.

She shot me a grim grin.

"Too well," she said. "He may have no patience but he never forgets a wrong . . .

"*Ever!*" she added.

We sat for perhaps ten minutes in silence, our backs against the tombstone, before Mrs. P scrambled to her feet.

"I'm leaving now," she said, brushing off her skirt. "I'll go the long way round. But promise me this, Flavia . . ."

She waited until I met her eye.

"When Constable Otter gets round to questioning you, don't mention my name. Please. I beg you. I thank you. Goodbye."

She touched my hand and then she was gone. I lost sight of her before she reached the river.

·TWENTY-FOUR·

I HAD HOPED THAT Hob would be at his father's shop. It would have made things so much easier.

As things turned out, it was probably as well he wasn't.

I stood in the street gawking for a few minutes, as I always do when I want to be taken for a tourist. There were no funeral notices in the window of the Nightingale shop, which came as no surprise; a set of faded and threadbare purple curtains hid whatever lay behind the plate glass. I cupped my hands against the window and peered through them, hoping to somehow see what lay inside.

Nothing but a brace of dead flies.

I tried the door, but it was locked. No point in going round the back, then. I didn't want to be seen trespassing upon private premises.

What was I to do?

As so often happens when you are a girl of intelligence, the answer was already right there in my head, ready for immediate use, like a celestial screwdriver.

I remembered sitting once, only half attentive, through one of Denwyn Richardson's lazy summer sermons on the Book of Matthew. Perhaps it was because Denwyn often recirculated his winter preachings that they were sometimes so memorable. In any case, it was a message I had heard more than once:

Ask, and it shall be given you; seek, and ye shall find; knock, and it shall be opened unto you: For every one that asketh receiveth; and he that seeketh findeth; and to him that knocketh it shall be opened.

What a wonderful text it was—and how appropriate. I closed my eyes, folded my hands, and asked.

It was in that instant that I remembered the wool shop just down the street. I turned away and strolled casually toward it.

The bell over the door rang, and I stepped into the shop.

"Good day to you," said the woman behind the counter. She was sitting in a chair, knitting. I couldn't help thinking that she was vaguely familiar until I realized that she looked uncannily like a sheep herself.

I pretended to interest myself in her balls of wool.

"Do you knit?" she asked.

"Not myself, no," I said. "But my aunt Felicity does. She's a wizard knitter. She's promised to knit me a Fair Isle pullover if I can find some wool of my favorite color."

"Which is?" the woman asked.

"Peacock," I said.

The woman put down her knitting and began to haul herself out of her chair.

"Peacock?" she asked.

"Yes," I said enthusiastically, "it's one of my school colors."

"And your school is?" she asked skeptically.

"Miss Bodycote's," I said.

"It's Canadian," I added, as if that explained everything.

Without another word, she shuffled off toward a little back room, as I had desperately hoped she would.

In a flash, I had seized a couple of crochet hooks from a display on the counter and rammed them into my pocket.

I could have paid for them, of course, but I didn't want to leave such an easy trail of evidence, should I happen to be caught. I would balance the books later.

The woman—blast her—was back in a jiff. She dumped half a dozen balls of wool on the counter.

"Peacock," she said proudly. "It's on sale. I can let you have the lot for six shillings."

I picked up a ball and fingered the wool.

"Oh, dear," I said. "I'm afraid this is Indian peacock. Miss Bodycote's is Javanese peacock. Miss Bodycote herself, you see, was brought up in Batavia. The Javanese peacock is said to have derived its unique green color from the volcanic nature of the soil there."

I gave her my most horrid, know-it-all leer, as if to confirm this mixture of fact and fiction. At the same time— although I could hardly believe I was doing so—I offered up silent thanks to my obnoxious cousin, Undine, for her endless prattling about wildlife in Singapore and the former Malaya.

"That's fine, then," the sheep-woman said in that voice which means that it isn't, really. She stuffed the wool under the counter and resumed her knitting.

"Thank you," I called loudly and cheerily as I walked out the door. "Lovely shop."

I took my time walking back along the street to the Nightingale establishment.

Pausing again to look at nothing in the window, I stood with one hand idly in my pocket, bending one of the crochet hooks into a letter *L*.

When it seemed about right, I took it out and applied it to the lock, using the other hook as if the two of them formed the jaws of a pair of pliers.

Dogger had given me extensive training in the art of picking locks. This was just one of the many accomplishments he had picked up in his earlier life. I would have loved to ask where, and how, and why, but of course one doesn't do that sort of thing. One merely listens and observes.

As if by magic, there was a deeply satisfying *click* and the knob turned easily. After a quick glance up the street and down, I stepped inside the shop.

This was not the first time in my life I had reconnoitered an undertaker's shop. The trick of it was, of course, to find out what I needed to know without being caught. Although it might seem like a good idea at the time, meddling with corpses is difficult to explain in the cold light of day.

First thing, then, was to determine if Orlando's body was actually here.

An arched doorway to the right led to a small chapel in which several rows of straight-backed chairs faced an empty wall.

Nothing here. To the left were a pair of double doors which caused my heart to beat a little faster: double doors are made for the wheeling in and out of things that cannot walk themselves.

I tapped lightly on the paneling just in case someone was inside. I could still explain my way out of this. I was looking for Hob. I had found the front door ajar, and so forth . . .

I pushed the door open and peered inside. This was more like it! The inner sanctum: the control room for the Empire of Death.

Two tilted slabs of porcelain with drains stood side by side, both of them, unfortunately, empty. Glass reservoirs of what I knew to be embalming fluid were close at hand, their contents tinted the shade of candy floss to restore in the subject what was believed to be a healthy complexion.

On a wall, stainless steel surgical instruments—one of them a colossal syringe with a snout like some prehistoric mosquito—stood ready to extract stomach contents, and so forth.

I gave a thought to the dead Orlando, and to the contents Dogger and I had analyzed from his stomach. What were they called? Diatoms! Yes, that was it, diatoms: those microscopic creatures whose sandy skeletons had told us whether Orlando had been dumped dead or alive into the river.

In any case, he wasn't here, as I had half expected he wouldn't be. I was beginning to get that familiar feeling at the back of my neck: not out of fear, but out of a sense that your hunches are more than hunches.

I backed out of the room and turned to face the remaining door which must lead, I knew, to the workshop, which I had already seen on my previous visit.

Again I knocked out of courtesy, as I make it a point never to startle a man with a hammer in his hand.

The same dark and beautifully polished coffin stood as it had before, on trestles in the middle of the workshop. I flicked the finish with my fingernail. Mr. Nightingale had certainly put a lot of work into this masterpiece of the carpenter's art. Again, I wondered who it had been made for.

In a far corner of the room was a desk, bulging with papers and letters, which spilled out of its many pigeon-holes in a most haphazard manner.

As I took a step toward it, I brushed against a chisel which had been left lying atop a wooden trestle. It went clattering to the floor—and I froze.

The Nightingales' living quarters were probably upstairs over the shop.

Had I been heard?

I stood listening for several endless moments, but all I could hear was the pounding of my heart.

I tiptoed my way to the desk.

By their dry, faded paper, I could see that these documents stretched back over many years. It appeared as if Mr. Nightingale had begun filling the top left pigeon-holes in the early days of his business and moved on from side to side, over the years, and down.

The freshest-seeming envelopes were in the bottom right compartment, spilling over onto the desktop. I pulled the drawers out, one by one. These, too, were jammed with bills and invoices.

I pulled one out at random. It was three years old.

The next drawer down was a complete surprise. It was filled—almost to overflowing—with loose race cards: cheaply printed greyhound racing programs from Wimbledon, Harringay Arena, Southend Stadium, and the White City—certain dogs in each race checked off in pencil, presumably to win, and every one of these, I realized, purchased with the wages of death.

With races on weekdays and at weekends, afternoons and evenings, and the sheer amount of travel involved, his commitment in time must have been colossal, to say nothing of the money wagered.

And suddenly I knew. Mr. Nightingale was no angel. He was also in deep trouble.

It was just then that something caught my eye: a fat, solemn-looking ledger that lay flat on the top shelf.

I reached for it and took it down, my hands trembling.

Inside the front cover, on the flyleaf, in a remarkably ornate hand, was written in businesslike black ink (oak gall, I thought) *F. T. Nightingale.*

The first entry in the book was dated thirteenth September, 1922, and had to do with the funeral of an infant named Margaret Rose Cawfee.

In meticulous copperplate script were written the details of the transaction:

Attendance at The Laurels, 10/, pine coffin, £8, shroud 7/, ribbon, 2/, motor hearse and driver, £2, opening grave, bearers & sexton, £2, undertaking, £1.

All of it coming to about £14.

Poor little Margaret Rose Cawfee. Had anybody loved her? They surely must have: The ribbon told the tale.

I turned toward the back of the ledger which was not quite filled. There were only a few blank pages left.

The last entry had been made two years ago.

I whistled.

Canon G. L. O. Whitbread!

The bill had been paid in full by H. M. Prisons. The cost had been five hundred and sixty pounds.

There were no details.

And there hadn't been a single entry since.

With fingers flying, I leafed back to the previous page, and there they were—the Three Graces: Miss Willoughby, Miss Harcourt, and Miss Cray.

All on the same day.

It must have been a bumper season for Mr. Nightingale. But why, then, had his business so suddenly failed? Why had he only carried out four funerals in the past two years?

I needed to dig deeper into his personal papers. If only I could find his checkbook, or perhaps his diary. Even the mail that he had received might well shed some light on his most peculiar business.

I was trying to decide where to begin on this mountain of papers when I spotted something on the floor: something which had been flung carelessly toward the wastebasket but had fallen short, almost hidden behind the leg of the desk.

I picked it up with my fingernails.

Unfortunately, it was blank. Just a piece of blue-lined paper from which a portion had been torn.

Sometimes, out of the heavens, the Great Gods will drop something unexpectedly into our laps. It's their way, I suppose, of saying "Thank you for your custom. Thank you for believing in us." It is their way of throwing us a bone.

The only word that can adequately describe our feelings when this happens is "thrill," which ought to be spelled with a couple of Z's instead of L's, since it has the same effect as sticking your finger into an electrical receptacle.

I put the scrap on the desk and reached into my pocket, smoothing as I pulled out the piece of paper I had found in Orlando's pocket.

54 6 7 8 9, I read.

Same ink, same written numerals as those in Mr. Nightingale's ledger.

I pushed the two torn edges of the papers together. It was a perfect fit. I pocketed both pieces.

Well done, Flavia! I thought.

There was a step and a stir behind me, and as I whirled, something rough was clapped over my face, covering my nose, my mouth, my nostrils. I was filled instantly with a sickeningly sweet, stinging, and pervasive odor which I recognized at once as diethyl ether. Oddly enough, I even managed to remember the chemical formula of the stuff—$(C_2H_5)_2O$—and the fact that it could be obtained by distilling a mixture of ethanol—common drinking alcohol—and sulfuric acid.

I struggled to break free, but it was no use. Whoever had seized me was stronger than I was.

I clawed at the wrists that were pressing against both sides of my neck, realizing even as I did so that it was a lost cause. Carried by the breath, diethyl ether, like those poisonous clouds in a cheap thriller film, swirls up the nose and goes directly for the brain. There is nothing subtle about the stuff. Its smell is so powerful that the odor of a single drop can fill a room, and I remembered reading somewhere that a cat would refuse to eat the flesh of an etherized rabbit, even after it had been boiled.

I knew that there were just a few seconds left before I lost consciousness. The telltale buzzing in my ears—like a swarm of invisible insects—had already begun.

Half in a haze, I felt myself being lifted bodily in someone's arms, lugged across a crazily spinning room, and dumped heavily like a bag of bones into what looked, to my burning bulging eyes, like a large wooden box.

That—and then something that seemed to sound like coffin screws biting into wood.

On the one hand, it was the most terrifying thing that had ever happened to me in my entire life and yet, on the other, the most strangely satisfying.

Here I am at last, I thought. *Now I know what it is actually like.*

It was, in one sense, as if I had crossed some mystic finish line and had come home at last in a blaze of great glory, but yet in another, as if I were back at the beginning, tensed, waiting for the starter's pistol: about to die, yet about to be born again.

What would I be, I wondered, *if it turned out there really was such a thing as incarnation: a dweller in a grass hut, perhaps, like one of those carefree tribal beauties I had seen in the cinema travel films, whose only desire in life was to pull the most frightening faces for the white man's camera?*

Or a slave, perhaps, in ancient Egypt, milling corn on a slab for the flatbread which would feed the hordes of sweating slaves who were hauling stones to build the pyramids?

But perhaps not. The world was changing and I, whatever I was, was changing with it. By the time I came around again I might well be a famous scientist—a chemist, of course—calibrating the controls of some new and, as yet, undreamt-of device, which would permit me to peer into the most secret heart of the universe.

But first I had to suppress the feeling of panic that was rising in my chest. I fought frantically to swim to the surface of my senses. The first of these to return was memory.

It is a fact that oxygen deprivation begins damaging the brain after less than five minutes. I had learned this by studying the notebooks of my late uncle Tarquin, who had participated in several experiments with John Scott Haldane, the renowned Scottish physiologist. Haldane had famously sealed himself inside specially constructed glass chambers in order to observe, firsthand, the effects of certain gases—including ether—upon his own brain.

Haldane had come to the conclusion that lack of oxygen does not stop the machinery—meaning the brain—but destroys the whole apparatus.

I also remembered, although rather vaguely, that Haldane had analyzed the air in the sewers beneath the House of Commons.

It was not easy, though, to think. The ether was making it difficult to distinguish between thought and reality. Was Haldane a thought, or was he one of the faces that was now rushing toward me through a swirling tunnel at the speed of the Flying Scotsman?

Because my body failed to respond, I couldn't leap out of the way. Was I moving sideways or merely thinking about moving sideways? There was no way of knowing.

I felt oddly like Alice, falling endlessly . . . endlessly falling, floating, rocking from side to side like an autumn leaf, down the rabbit hole, but with nothing to grab: no cupboards or bookshelves, no jars of marmalade to seize.

Now I was becoming aware of a stinging tingle around my mouth and nose, as if the middle of my face had been held too close to a campfire.

Diethyl ether does that, I found myself thinking idly, as if someone else were thinking my thoughts. *It irritates the skin.*

I forced open my burning eyes, but could see nothing. Nothing but total darkness.

Have I been struck blind? I remember wondering idly, as if it didn't matter.

Consciousness must have been returning by then, although I didn't think that at the time.

I am in a box, is what I thought in actuality. *A coffin.*

For an instant, the odor of pine overwhelmed the chemical smell of ether.

But what are its dimensions? How much air is available—and how long will it last?

The standard coffin, I remembered, measured about five and a half feet by two by one and a half, which made a little over sixteen cubic feet, if my woozy mind was any judge.

Minus, of course, the volume of my own body, which was roughly half that of the coffin. I didn't actually work this out in my misfiring brain, but it made sense that the size of any container is proportional in some way to its intended contents, except in the case of breakfast cereal, of course.

If the average person breathes, say, seven liters of air per minute, that would work out to about half an hour's oxygen remaining.

I must not panic.

I must breathe slowly . . . shallowly . . . evenly . . . regularly. I must feed my brain without wasting oxygen on useless muscle movement.

This is easier said than done when the mind is already flying ahead to vivid images of a black and desiccated corpse being dug up in some remote forest, its features frozen in horror, its fingers worn to stubs by frantic, fruitless clawing at the lid.

No point in pounding at the wood, or screaming out my burning lungs. My attacker, whoever he or she might be, was still in the room, and would be the only person on earth who could possibly hear my cries for help.

Besides, I thought, if I made too much noise, they might well decide to take certain other steps to speed my death. Although I didn't want to dwell on this idea, I have to admit that fire—or water—crossed my mind.

A person locked in a wooden box is a sitting duck, so to speak, to flame and flood.

Better to keep quiet. Better to play dead.

I winced as the inevitable ether headache wrapped a rope around my temples. I had read about this effect, of course, but this was the first time I had ever experienced it.

How fortunate I was not to be suffering that other complaint which ether often causes: gut-wrenching vomiting. At the moment, in spite of the danger of the situation, I could think of nothing worse than to be locked in an airless box filled with my own stomach contents.

I reached up slowly, tentatively, with my fingertips. As

I had known it would be—feared it would be—the lid was right there, inches above my face.

"Don't dwell on claustrophobia," a voice said quite clearly from somewhere close by—or was it in my head?

My wits were beginning to return. Although there was still the stink of ether inside the coffin, it was not nearly so noticeable—or so I thought—as it had been.

As a scientist, I knew that things must be dealt with in logical order: A helter-skelter chain of thoughts would result in my death. It was as simple as that.

The first requirement was oxygen. Without it, there would be no second requirement. I focused upon oxygen and how to get it.

A breathing hole would solve the problem: Even a tiny one could be breathed through in a pinch. All that was needed was some small metallic tool to work through the wood.

Unfortunately, I had refused to wear my braces on this summer holiday.

"Put them in your pocket, dear," Mrs. Mullet had insisted. "You can wear 'em at night in bed when no one's lookin'."

But I had sauced her dreadfully, and how I regretted it now!

I wiped away a tear which, I realized, hadn't been caused by the ether.

I took silent inventory: no braces, no hairpins, no pens. Even my little silver crucifix with its concealed magnifying glass and switchblade knife had been left at home through my own stupid fault.

If ever I escaped this predicament, I decided, I was going to acquire a ladies handbag with a tool kit that would cause any burglar to drool with envy. I would never, in future, go anywhere without it. Not even to the WC.

No wonder women lugged all that stuff around on their shoulders! It was necessity—not vanity—that determined what you carried in your kit.

But wait!

What about the crochet hooks in my pocket? I had almost forgotten them.

Taking care not to exert myself—*keep calm, Flavia!*—I worked one hand slowly into my pocket. My fingers touched the L-shaped hook.

Slowly . . . gingerly . . . I extracted it and, anchoring its business end against the side of the coffin, began a twisting motion.

After only a few minutes my fingertips were throbbing. The awkwardly shaped hook was going nowhere. The varnish was too hard, the coffin wood too thick.

As I had noticed earlier, this was a well-made coffin. Too well made for my liking.

I mentally cursed Mr. Nightingale for various reasons, and as I did so, the crochet hook snapped in half.

Son of a sea-cook!

Although each half now had a sharper end than before, they were both too short to get a decent grip on.

I reached for the second hook. Perhaps the sides of the coffin were thinner. Lids and bottoms would be the thickest because, well, we wouldn't want any unpleasant accidents during funerals, would we?

I shifted myself to one side and resumed my drilling motion, but I soon realized it was in vain. The hook was slipping in my sweating hands.

I was breathing too rapidly.

How stifling it was in the coffin, and how heavy my lungs had suddenly become.

No point in using up whatever remained of the oxygen. How much time remained?

Twenty minutes? Less, perhaps, because of my exertions.

Time to face reality. It was now quite clear that if rescue were to come, it would come from the outside. I had exhausted my resources.

I shifted my head slightly, first to the right and then to the left, pressing my ear softly against one side of the coffin, and then the other.

As I knew from years of listening at doors, an ear to a wooden panel amplifies the slightest sound remarkably. If anyone else was in the room, I would certainly hear them.

Thank heavens, I thought, that my attacker had chosen a coffin which had not yet been lined with decorative padding of muffling silk or satin. Even a single layer of fabric, such as curtains, for example, can be frustrating to an eavesdropper.

But outside the coffin, the room sounded as silent as the tomb.

A breath caught in my throat as I tried to ration the air.

All right, I admit it: I wanted to weep for myself. I wanted to explode with fury.

Surely, I was entitled to that? A little display of fire-works to celebrate my entry into the afterlife?

Even a condemned killer was entitled to a last supper, as pointless as it may seem. To the best of my knowledge, no one had ever died from going hungry to the gallows.

Which turned my mind back to Canon Whitbread. What had *his* last meal consisted of?

Had he ordered up a banquet of roast beef with all the trimmings or had he humbly settled for Holy Communion, and gone to the grave with the taste of sacramental wine on his lips, as had his victims, the Three Graces?

Suddenly, everything began to fall into place. I remembered Daffy once reading aloud from Boswell's life of Dr. Samuel Johnson, in which that ancient bore had said, *"Depend upon it, Sir, when a man knows he is to be hanged in a fortnight, it concentrates his mind wonderfully."*

Although I had at the time thought this the most awful load of rubbish, it turned out to be true after all. The prospect of my own immediate death washed windows in my mind which must have become clouded over with the scum of my own accumulated pigheadedness. At that very instant, I made a solemn vow. Should I survive this day, I would never, ever scoff at anything or anyone again.

And—by all that's holy—it worked!

Suddenly—just as the good Dr. Johnson had said it would—the darkness had lifted and my mind was sparkling with remarkable clarity. It could not possibly be due to the ether, which is known, in fact, to have quite the opposite effect.

My spirits rose. I would go out in a blaze of glory.

Hang the exhausted air in the coffin. I might be dying, but I would die a de Luce. I would die defiant!

How proud of me my mother, Harriet, would have been. How proud my father, also.

In a very few moments now I would be rejoining them.

Farewell chemistry, I thought. Besides my parents, I would also be greeted by some of the greatest chemical minds of all time: Humphry Davy, Henry Cavendish, Edward Frankland, Ernest Rutherford. How proud I was of my country.

Die I might—but I would die British.

How exhilarating that decision was! I lay rigidly at attention, my arms straight down at my sides, and began to sing:

"God save our gracious King!
Long live our noble King!
God save the King!"

Although King George VI, my dear and beloved old friend, had died four months ago, his daughter, Princess Elizabeth, had not yet been crowned queen.

But she would be. Oh, yes, she would be! Before my bleached bones had settled into the English soil, Queen Elizabeth II would be seated on the throne and the world would be fresh again.

And now I was bellowing the words, the tears springing hot to my eyes:

"Send her victorious,
Happy and glorious,
Long to reign over us,
God save the Queen."

Now only darkness and death remained.

I awaited them, my head held as high as I could manage.

Someone was hammering . . . hammering . . . hammering. I wished they would put an end to it and leave me in peace.

"Go away!" I wanted to shout, but my tongue was dry and swollen in my mouth.

Then came the nauseating grinding sound of protesting wood. I tried to wet my lips but there was no moisture left.

In the darkness, I was being jerked and jolted, like shot game in a hunter's bag.

Stop it! I thought, since I couldn't form the words.

A sudden blaze of light caused me, in spite of my weakness, to throw up my boneless hands defensively in front of my face.

Someone was wrapping their arms around me. I struggled to fight them off, but it was no use. My entire body was an unpleasant, reeking jelly.

"Flavia?" said a voice, and I tried with all my strength to force one eye open against the stabbing pain of the light.

Again: "Flavia!"—more insistent this time.

As things swam into focus, I saw a face looming above me: a huge, round face, its features grossly distorted as if viewed through a fishbowl.

It couldn't be! It was impossible!

"Flavia," Dieter said as I threw up on his cashmere jumper. *Pity*, was my only thought. *It was such a beautiful robin's-egg blue.*

"Sorry," I mumbled, as he lowered me gently to the floor and propped me against the wall. I looked wobbly-eyed round the room in amazement.

Feely was bending over the prostrate Mr. Nightingale with a rubber mallet clutched like a cricket bat in her hands and, from the rising red welt on the back of the undertaker's neck, I knew that she had recently used it.

The poor man wouldn't have stood a chance against Feely's anger.

"How dare you manhandle my sister?" she shouted, seizing the man by the collar and giving him a shake that would have loosened a monkey in a tree. "How dare you attack my fiancé?"

Nightingale seemed not to be hearing her.

"How . . . ?" I asked weakly, waving one of my flippers at the open coffin. "Did Dogger send you?"

"We were outside in the courtyard," Dieter said, coloring slightly, highlighting the fresh abrasion on his chin. "Feely and I. Behind the coffin cases. We wished to—you know—to be alone. We thought no one would ever—"

"Dieter!" Feely snapped, her cheeks like Mary Poppins's. "That's enough!"

In spite of the risk to his life, Dieter shot me a secret wink. I wiped off my mouth and did my best to grin.

"Ring up Dogger and have him bring the Rolls around," Feely said, pointing to the telephone on the desk. "Then call the police. They'll know what to do with him."

"Don't count on it," I managed to say.

The rest of that evening is best left to the imagination, except to say that mops and buckets played a prominent part. Who would have believed that a girl could sleep so much in June?

·TWENTY-FIVE·

I HAD BEEN UP since long before the sun. The sickly
sweet effects of the ether had still not worn off completely
and my stomach felt like a seagoing barge.

We were going home today, but before we left, I had
several things to do, one of which was to telephone Inspector Hewitt. I agonized about how best to manage this.

I had covered a sheet of paper with scrawled notes,
with headings such as "Opening Pleasantries," through
"Topics for Discussion," all the way down to "Thanks and
Closing Remarks."

But what if the inspector didn't want to talk to me?
What if he decided that unsolved murders were not a per-
missible topic for discussion with a member of the public?

I would simply have to take my chances. The worst the
inspector could do, I suppose, would be to tear a strip off me
and hang up in my ear. I'd have to prepare myself for that.

The hours seemed to drag by, as if they, too, had been soaked with ether. Dawn took forever.

When I told her I needed to make a personal call, Greta Palmer had kindly offered the use of the telephone in the private cubicle tucked away beneath the stairs, where I would be free from prying ears.

"It's on the house," she had said. "After all, we're sisters under the skin."

She must have seen my puzzled look.

"'The Colonel's Lady an' Judy O'Grady are sisters under their skins,'" she said. "Rudyard Kipling. The sly old bird knew more about women than he's been given credit for.

"I'll leave you to it," she said as she closed the door. "I don't fancy a lot of embarrassing gush so early in the morning."

I grinned, even though she was already gone.

Just after sunrise, I put through a call to Bishop's Lacey.

"Hello? Mrs. Mullet? It's Flavia. I hope I didn't get you out of bed."

"Lord, no, ducks! I was peelin' parsnips for Alf's soup before I go out. Where are you? Is everything all right?"

Poor Alf! I thought. His life was measured in parsnips.

"Yes, thank you, Mrs. M. We're still at Volesthorpe, but we're coming home today. I thought we'd better let you know."

I didn't tell her that I desperately needed to hear her voice.

"It's good of you to think of me, dear. I shall peel some extra parsnips. Did you 'ave a nice holiday?"

346 · ALAN BRADLEY

"Quite pleasant," I said. "We viewed the church, and so forth."

"I missed you," she said suddenly, almost reluctantly. "Missed 'avin you underfoot and stickin' your fingers in my custard mix. I shall be glad when you're home."

"Thank you, Mrs. Mullet," I managed. "So shall I. I trust you're keeping well?"

"Same as always. But I have to go now, dear. My friend Mrs. Waller 'as a prolapsed eucharist and I promised I'd bring 'er round some water biscuits for breakfast. 'Er doctor says she needs to stay off 'er feet."

I expressed my sympathies, we said our goodbyes, and I rang off.

I waited until I could no longer stand the tension. Was there the slightest chance that Inspector Hewitt had come in early to work? There was only one way to find out.

I wiped my sweating hands on my jumper and reached for the phone.

"I'd like to speak with the Hinley Constabulary," I said. "Inspector Hewitt."

There were various electrical clicks, hums, buzzes, and disconnects before a powerful, weary voice which could only belong to a police sergeant answered.

"Who shall I say is calling?" he asked.

"Flavia de Luce," I told him, and there was—at least I *think* there was—a fleeting silence.

After what seemed like an eternity but which must have been, in reality, no more than twenty seconds, the phone was picked up.

"Hewitt," said that familiar voice: that voice of which I realized I had been far too long deprived.

"Inspector Hewitt," I said, "this is Flavia de Luce speaking."

"Oh, yes, Flavia. How are you?"

At least he hadn't forgotten me!

"Quite well, thank you," I replied. "I should like to report a murder. No—four murders."

Curses! I'd forgotten to ask about his wife, Antigone, and their baby.

"Where are you?" he asked.

"Volesthorpe," I told him. "At the Oak and Pheasant."

"I'm afraid that's rather off my turf, Flavia," he said. "Perhaps you should get in touch with the station there?"

"I'm afraid I can't do that." I lowered my voice. "You see, I have reason to believe that the police themselves may be involved."

Did I actually think that? Or was my mind doing acrobatics?

"I see," the inspector said. "Tell me a bit more."

"Do you remember the Canon Whitbread affair several years ago?"

"Yes."

He was being noncommittal.

"He was hanged for the murder of three of his parishioners. Cyanide," I said.

"Yes?" he asked.

"He was innocent," I said. "He didn't do it."

"He confessed, as I recall," Inspector Hewitt pointed out. "They had no choice but to hang him, did they?"

I laughed, perhaps a little too loudly. The inspector was pulling my leg—making a joke—and I wanted to show him it hadn't gone over my head.

This little witticism was a remarkably good sign. Police inspectors do not make jokes with those they do not view as equals. At least, I hope they don't.

"Begin at the beginning and go on until you come to the end, Flavia. Then stop."

And so I did. I told the inspector how I had entangled my hand with Orlando's dead body in the river; of how Dogger and I had fished him out and laid him on the bank.

I even confessed to finding the rumpled piece of paper in the dead man's pocket.

"Interfering with a dead body at the scene of a crime can be a criminal offense, Flavia," he said, not in an accusing way, but matter-of-factly, as if he were examining his fingernails.

"I thought he might still be alive," I protested, rather lamely.

"And you'd bring him back to life by rifling his pockets?" Inspector Hewitt asked. "A most novel method of artificial respiration, and one I've not heard mentioned before."

I did not tell him about my interviews with Claire Tetlock and Greta Palmer. It was not necessary. They had told me things in confidence, and I mustn't violate their trust. He would find out all he needed to know about Orlando during his own investigation.

"The point is," I continued, "Canon Whitbread didn't

poison those three old ladies. His son, Orlando, did. They had been gossiping about him. He was a paraldehyde addict. I could still smell it on his body."

"I see," Inspector Hewitt said. I pictured him making notes.

"And who killed Orlando?" he asked, as I had hoped and prayed he would.

"Nightingale, the undertaker. He tried to kill me, too. He overcame me with ether and sealed me in a coffin to die."

"Good lord," Inspector Hewitt said, and my heart soared. "Are you all right now?"

I realized, even as I spoke, that the tears were welling up. I hadn't realized until now how close I'd come. I began to shake like a December leaf.

I could hear the legs of the inspector's chair grating on his office floor.

"Stay where you are," he said. "Don't talk to anyone. Don't go outside. I shall be there as soon as I can manage."

"Thank you," I whispered.

"Oh, and Flavia . . ."

"Yes?" I barely managed to whisper.

"Well done," he said.

Precisely eighty-nine minutes later—I had Dogger time it with his watch—Inspector Hewitt's blue Vauxhall pulled up and parked beside the Rolls in the forecourt of the Oak and Pheasant. Two minutes later, the three of us, with me wrapped in a blanket and sipping a cup of hot Oxo, faced one another across a table in the privacy of the saloon bar.

"You must tell me everything," the inspector said. "Even those things you might not wish to."

I looked at Dogger. Dogger nodded solemnly, and I began to speak.

It all came pouring out. Our chemical experiment with the diatoms, our visit to Scull Cottage, Poppy Mandrill, all of it. Even Constable Otter.

"Constable Otter is very ambitious," I said. "He keeps insisting Orlando's death was a drowning accident. I think he's covering up: protecting someone—or himself.

"The constable was involved in the arrest and trial of Canon Whitbread, who's buried under the altar, by the way, in spite of being a convicted murderer. I don't have the means of finding out why, which is partly why I rang you up, Inspector."

"I see," he said. "But, if such *should* prove to be the case, I must place both of you under a pledge of secrecy. This could have grave implications at the highest levels. *Very* grave implications."

"I promise," I said, and Dogger nodded assent.

"You see, Inspector, Canon Whitbread was . . . *framed*, I believe, is the word you use. A number of people knowingly gave false evidence against him. One of these was Constable Otter. A great many falsehoods were put about and allowed to spread. Orlando's train trip to London, for instance. Why? I can't begin to understand it all, but I have good reason to believe that blackmail was involved—as well as a certain amount of hanky-panky. Orlando had threatened to involve the police in certain letters he had received—which can be interpreted in more ways than one. But I must leave such delicate matters to you, Inspector."

Greta chose that moment to come bustling into the room and my heart almost stopped. I simply didn't have it in me to tell the inspector that she herself had met Orlando's train. She would need to make that—and other equine matters—part of her own confession.

"Would anyone like a bite to eat?" she asked, putting her hand on my shoulder. "This little girl's looking peaky."

I could have killed her!

"No, thank you, Mrs. Palmer," Dogger replied. "A quiet place to talk is all we require."

Good old Dogger.

"Very well, then," she said, seemingly reluctant to let go of me. She drew in a great deep breath as if coming to some decision, then said: "But when you're finished here, Inspector, I should like to have a word with you myself. In private."

I gave her an encouraging smile, in spite of her recent remark. I was grateful that it would be she who would explain to him that business of the brass stallion and the copper mare. When it comes to poetry, I'm way out of my depth.

The inspector watched her leave, and then said, "Tell me more about Orlando Whitbread. I assume you've compiled quite an impressive dossier on him."

Now here was a man who knew how to give credit

where credit's due. I tried, by lowering my eyes, to look properly humble.

I took the crumpled bit of paper and its matching mate from my jumper and placed them on the table.

"This was in Orlando's pocket," I said. "The numbers refer to the book of Timothy: 'But they that will be rich, fall into temptation, and a snare—' "

" '—and into many foolish and hurtful lusts which drown men in destruction and perdition,' " Inspector Hewitt finished for me.

With no more than a quick inspection of the paper scraps themselves, he extracted a glassine envelope from an inner pocket and slid them neatly into it.

"As you have suggested," the inspector said, "he was being blackmailed."

"Yes," I replied. "I believe he murdered the Three Graces in revenge and to silence their gossip, although I suspect his fears were greatly magnified by his use of paraldehyde."

"What makes you think that?" the inspector asked.

"Hob Nightingale saw him talking to himself on the riverbank. People assumed he was rehearsing some theatrical role, but to my mind, Inspector, he was having hallucinations. Paraldehyde, especially in large quantities, has strange effects upon the human brain, of which religious visions and hallucinations are an excellent example. He might even have fancied himself to be some heavenly avenger."

The inspector looked me in the eye and hauled out his Biro.

"Go on," he said.

"Paraldehyde addiction may result in delirium tremens and delusions. In severe cases, it may result in complete moral deterioration."

I let my words hang in the air.

"I see," Inspector Hewitt said.

"It's in *Medical Jurisprudence*. I can show it to you, if you wish."

"Thank you, Flavia," he said. "I take your point.

"Back to your dossier," he added, almost absentmindedly.

"Well, Orlando was an extraordinarily gifted actor," I said. "He was planning to re-create one of Poppy Mandrill's greatest stage successes, with himself in the starring role."

One of Inspector Hewitt's eyebrows went slowly up, like a hawk rising on the wind.

"I see," he said.

"In some ways," I went on, "he was like a child. Wanted to run away with the circus. Which is why his father was so protective of him."

"To the extent of going to the gallows in his place?"

"The canon was a martyr," I said. "Someone will have to make amends."

As the inspector made another note, I glanced over at Dogger. If eyes alone could signal approval, that was the message he was sending.

"In spite of his addiction, Orlando had many friends. Everybody loved Orlando."

Inspector Hewitt made a note. "Just so," he said. "But he obviously also had several enemies."

354 · ALAN BRADLEY

"The Three Graces?" I asked. "Well, yes."

"I recall the case," he said. "Something of a landmark. So you believe it was Orlando who poisoned the Communion wine?"

"Yes. Dogger told me that we must keep an eye out for the Invisible Ones. And who is more invisible than the rector's son at a vicarage? Especially one who lives scarcely a mile away in a tumbledown boathouse."

Dogger was sitting with his hands folded, listening. He was leaving things to me.

"Orlando allowed his own father to be hanged for the crime. It was all too fatally easy. He was supposed to have been in London at the time."

"Hmmm," Inspector Hewitt said.

"Since then he'd been enormously wracked by guilt. So much so recently that, several nights ago, he returned to the very spot where he had ditched the poisoned chalice, and swallowed cyanide. It was to be an act of repentance. Very dramatic. In keeping with his talents."

I saw a certain light come into the inspector's eyes.

"Unfortunately, he was spotted," I went on. "Someone saw him and clubbed him, not realizing the poor creature had already poisoned himself."

"And so," Inspector Hewitt said, "we come to Mr. Nightingale."

This was the moment I had been waiting for, and I meant to relish it.

"Well, you see, Inspector," I said, "when I saw that highly polished coffin in his workshop, I knew that he was in trouble. The finish was too hard. He had not conducted a funeral for a very long time—two years, in fact.

"As you know, the French polished finishes involving shellac and methylated spirits take a remarkably long time to dry, which is why they are so seldom used. Coffins tend to be required on short notice, and there's no time for fine finishes. That coffin, Inspector, had been in his workshop for simply ages. I wondered why."

"Whoa! Let's back up a little," Inspector Hewitt said. "But I see what you're getting at. You believe that it was Nightingale who killed Orlando Whitbread."

"Yes," I said.

"And his motive?"

"Money. Undertakers are the only ones who profit from every death. Mr. Nightingale has had no income since the deaths of the Three Graces two years ago. Except, of course, for Canon Whitbread's burial, which was paid for by His Majesty's Prisons—which seems suggestive in itself, don't you think?"

"That's quite a leap, Flavia," he pointed out.

"Yes," I agreed, "—but I'm quite a leaper."

"I can vouch for that, Inspector." Dogger's face gave away nothing.

"Of course, the undertaker is another of the Invisible Ones," I said. "No one thinks anything of it to find them in the church or the churchyard. Oh, dear, what's going to become of poor little Hob?"

"We shall cross that bridge when we come to it," Inspector Hewitt said. "But tell me this: Did Nightingale say anything to you before his attack? Before he overcame you and put you in the coffin?"

"Nothing," I told him. "I didn't even see him. He came at me out of nowhere."

"For no particular reason?" the inspector pressed. "Entirely unprovoked?"

"Except that he must have known I was on to him."

"Yes, there might be something in that," Inspector Hewitt said, closing his notebook.

How maddening this man could be!

"Well, then," he said, getting to his feet. "I shall have to leave you now. I have certain—ah—inquiries to make."

Which meant arranging with the local authorities to have Nightingale—and possibly Constable Otter—clapped in irons.

"Crikey!" I exclaimed, clapping my hand to my head. "Where *is* Mr. Nightingale?"

"I should be surprised if he's not having a nice cup of tea with Mr. Dieter and Miss Ophelia," Dogger answered. "They offered to keep an eye on him until Inspector Hewitt arrived. I don't expect he'll give them any trouble."

When the inspector had gone, Dogger and I sat for a time in silence at the table. As an old clock ticked slowly and companionably on the mantel, I suddenly understood—*really* understood—the meaning of time.

"Dogger," I said, "I want to go home."

"As you wish, Miss Flavia," he said. "Buckshaw is at its most convivial in the summer months."

I nodded in agreement as I allowed the dear old place to come flooding back into my consciousness for the first time in ages. The estate was now entirely mine to do with as I pleased: I could keep it, or sell it, or give it away. Aunt Felicity be blowed!

There had been recent indications that all the long years of legal wrangling would soon be coming to an end. The fortunes of Buckshaw would be entering into a new age.

The last pieces of the puzzle had suddenly fallen into place while I was lying only partly conscious in Nightingale's abominable coffin. Were they the remnants of a dream? A fantasy? A vision of the future?

I would probably never know how inspiration came to me, but it was no less real for all that.

"Dogger," I said. "We're going to have a brass plate made and mounted on the gates. Very discreet, of course. Very tasteful."

With Feely soon to be married, it made perfect sense. Of course it did! And hadn't Daffy just demonstrated her unsuspected genius at solving difficult puzzles?

My heart began to hum like a spinning top as I added names to the register: Aunt Felicity, of course; Mildred Bannerman, the once-convicted murderess and former teacher at Miss Bodycote's Female Academy; my old friend and would-be associate Adam Tradescant Sowerby, the florarchaeologist; and, yes, even my obnoxious little cousin Undine, whose weird enthusiasms and uncanny persistence could, in time and in the right hands, be put to good use.

358 · ALAN BRADLEY

"A brass plate, Miss Flavia?" Dogger asked.

"Yes," I said, drawing a rainbow in the air with my spread fingers. "And on it we shall have these words: *Arthur W. Dogger & Associates—Discreet Investigations.*"

"Hmmm," Dogger said. "It does roll off the tongue, doesn't it, Miss Flavia? *Discreet* is such an elegant touch."

ACKNOWLEDGMENTS

At the end of any long journey, the traveler cannot help but look back and remember with great affection all those who, somewhere along the way, have helped to lighten the load. Quite often—and quite surprisingly—these kindred souls do not realize either the timeliness or the importance of their assistance. Although they have sometimes even forgotten their contributions, the grateful author has not: They have become as much a part of the finished book as its pages and binding.

All thanks, then, to Eileen Roberts, of St. Hilda's College, Oxford, for her friendship, and for the many stimulating conversations about the rivers in our midst, and the role they play in detective fiction. Eileen's delight about everything from residential trapezes to toxicity has so often been the necessary tinder to my flame.

And to Doug Bell, whose generosity and patient companionship is embedded invisibly throughout this book.

To friends Doreen and Geoff Dixon, for putting into my hands so many rare and fascinating books—and always at precisely the moment when they were most needed. It's beyond synchronicity: It's downright spooky! Doreen and Geoff have also very kindly, and so frequently, taken me places I needed to go. Driving with them in the rain to discover junk shops and overgrown churchyards is simply delicious: like wine to the wicked.

Special thanks to Marie-Andrée Lamontagne of the Montréal International Blue Metropolis Festival, and grateful acknowledgments to the Canada Council for the Arts, the Embassy of Canada in Rome, and the Délégation du Québec à Rome for making it possible for me to meet so many Flavia fans in Italy.

To Beatrice Orlandini for being herself: a beautiful and most charming shepherd.

And to Marella Paramatti, of the Festivaletteratura di Mantova, and interviewer Chiara Codecà; and to Laura Grandi and Luisa Rovetti, of Grandi & Associati, in Milan: a thousand thank-yous would never be enough.

To the memory of my cousin, the late Bill Bryson, and his wife, Barb, for providing important photographs and documents, and for bringing me home again through time to my childhood.

To Denise Bukowski and Stacy Small, of the Bukowski Agency, Toronto, for handling all the really important matters with such efficient grace and good humor.

Once again, to Roger K. Bunting, Professor Emeritus,

Department of Chemistry, Illinois State University, whose wise counsel has saved me from excessive chemical mischief.

My chemically inclined readers will have spotted at once that I have taken certain liberties with the Levine-Bodansky method, by which the presence of paraldehyde is detected in biological fluids. I can plead only that great simplification is sometimes necessary, even with the most fascinating procedures.

And finally, as always, to my wife, Shirley, who has allowed Flavia to occupy our days, our nights, and our home for nearly ten years. If anyone deserves a medal, it is Shirley, and so I hereby award her the first and only Companion of Valor, First Class, for love and patience and tolerance far, far beyond the vows of marriage.

Isle of Man

Maundy Thursday, 2017

If you enjoyed

The **Grave's** *a* **Fine** *and* **Private Place,**

read on for an excerpt from

The **Golden Tresses** *of the* **Dead**

by Alan Bradley

the beguiling next installment in the award-winning,
New York Times bestselling Flavia de Luce series.

·ONE·

I'D LIKE TO REMARK at the outset that I'm a girl with better than an average brain. Just as some people are given the gift of a singular and often quite remarkable talent—such as Violet Cornish's uncanny ability to break wind to the tune of "Joy to the World"—I myself, in much the same way, have been blessed with the power of logical thinking. As Violet could easily confirm, it's something you're born with, and then improve upon by much practice.

The many occasions upon which I had been consulted by the constabulary had sharpened my already considerable detection skills to the point where I had little choice but to turn professional. And so, I had set up with Dogger, my late father's valet, gardener, and all-round sounding-board, a small agency to which we gave the name—to signal respectability—Arthur Dogger & Associates.

Little did we know that our very first case would be so close to home.

But I'm getting ahead of myself. Let me begin at the beginning.

My sister Ophelia's wedding was spoiled only slightly by someone calling out coarsely, as the bride floated in modest beauty up the aisle of the ancient church, "Hubba, Hubba, ding-ding, twenty years in Sing Sing!" The culprit was Carl Pendracka, one of Feely's former suitors. It was his Cincinnati accent that gave him away.

We all of us pretended we hadn't heard, except my odious, moon-faced cousin, Undine, who let out one of her long, wet, horrible, slobbering snickers, such as might have been made by a herd of cannibal cows.

More troubling, though, was when, just a few moments later—at the precise moment the vicar addressed the congregation: "If any man can shew any just cause, why they may not lawfully be joined together, let him now speak, or else hereafter forever hold his peace"—one of the carved and painted angels, from its place high among the roof-beams, cried out suddenly, in the voice of a certain cinema cartoon character, "*I* do! *I* do! Call the police!"

It was Undine, of course, who, bored by lack of attention, decided to practice her ventriloquism—which she had been studying for some time from a sixpenny book.

Aside from that—except for the human remains—it was a beautiful ceremony.

Preparations had been begun far in advance. First there had been the cake.

"The weddin' cake must be laid down 'least six months before the nup-chools," Mrs. Mullet had said, waving a batter-coated wooden spoon at me in the kitchen. "Else the marriage'll be poisoned."

The mention of poison captured my undivided attention.

"What kind of poison?" I asked.

"The worst kind. The poison of leavin' things to be done on the spurt of the moment. Just look at that Lucy Havers, as was, and then talk to me about darin' the devil. Left it till the day before 'er weddin' to 'ave 'er cake baked at that Bunne Shoppe in 'Inley, if you can credit it, an' look what happened to 'er!"

I raised my eyebrows in a "What happened to her?" signal.

"'Er 'usband—one o' them Simmonses, 'e was—run off with a tart from the Bunne Shoppe the day after they got 'ome from their 'oneymoon in 'Astings."

"If it were me, I'd have run off with an apple pie," I said, pretending I didn't understand her meaning, a tactic I am increasingly forced to employ in order to protect my alleged innocence.

Mrs. Mullet smiled at my modesty.

"Like I said, a weddin' cake must be laid down six months ahead o' time and left to sleep in the larder till required," she said, returning to her theme. Mrs. Mullet could be uncommonly informative when allowed to lecture uninterrupted, and I pulled up a chair to listen.

"Like layin' the keel of a battleship," she went on. "You mustn't leave it till the enemy's in sight."

"Who's the enemy?" I asked. "The groom?"

Mrs. Mullet laid a forefinger alongside her nose in the ancient sign of secrecy. "That's for every woman to find out for 'erself," she said, tapping the finger and causing her nose to give off an alarming hollow knocking sound. She lowered her voice. "And till she does, she needs all the spells she can get to keep away the Old Ones."

The Old Ones? This was becoming truly interesting. First poisons, and now malevolent supernatural spirits. And it wasn't yet ten o'clock in the morning!

Mrs. Mullet was now scraping the batter out of the bowl and into a large cake pan.

"Here, let me help you," I said, reaching for the oven door.

"Not yet," Mrs. Mullet said, surprisingly short tempered. "First things first: Grab an 'andful o' them sticks and toss 'em on top of the fire."

"In the basket there," she added, pointing with the spoon, as if I hadn't seen them.

A wicker basket beside the cooker was half-filled with a tangle of twigs and branches. "Run a bit of water in the sink," she said. "We wants 'em good an' damp."

I did as I was told.

"To make steam?" I asked, wondering how the steam was going to make its way from the firebox to the oven chamber.

"Somethin' like that," Mrs. Mullet said, as I opened

the firebox and threw the wet wood on top of the fire. "An' somethin' else besides."

Again, the finger beside the nose.

"Protection," I guessed. "Against the enemy?"

"That's right, dear," Mrs. Mullet said. "'Azel and 'aw-thorn. I gathered 'em with my own 'ands in Gibbet Wood. Now, one more thing an' we're ready to pop in the cake."

She pulled a sprig of needled leaves from the pocket of her apron. "Rosemary," I said. I recognized it from the kitchen garden.

"That's right, dear," Mrs. Mullet said again, as the warm spicy odor of the herb filled the kitchen. "To re-mind Miss Ophelia of 'er 'ome, and all them as 'ave ever loved 'er. Rosemary in the oven for the cake and rosemary in 'er bouquet. It also 'elps keep off the 'obgob-lins."

"I thought rosemary was for funerals," I said.

I remembered that because Daffy was always quoting Shakespeare.

"An' so it is, dear. Funerals and weddin's both. That's why it's such an 'andy 'erb to 'ave around the 'ouse. Which is why we grows it in the kitchen garden. If we wants it for weddin's we soaks it in scented water and braids it into the bride's veil and bouquet. For funerals, we wets it with rainwater an' tosses it into the open grave on top of the coffin."

"We also tucks a bit of it into the shroud," she added. "If we 'ave one, of course, which most of us doesn't nowa-days, what with it bein' charged as an extra expense by the undertakers."

"And the hazel sticks?" I asked.

"Guarantees descendants," she said, her face suddenly serious.

Poor Feely I thought. Alone upstairs at this very moment, innocently picking her pimples in a sterling silver hand-mirror without the faintest idea that the cook was in the kitchen, already fiddling with her future. It almost made me feel sorry for my sister.

"Now don't ask me no more pesky questions," Mrs. Mullet said. "I've got four more layers to bake an' dinner to get started for you lot."

"What about the hawthorn?" I asked, even though I already knew the answer. It is believed by some—but not by me—that the haws, or berries and the flowers of the hawthorn, preserve in their smell the stench of the Great Plague of London, whereas I, with my scientific mind, know perfectly well that both haws and flowers of the tree contain a substantial quantity of trimethylamine, which is the chemical compound responsible for the smell of putrefaction.

"Never you mind," Mrs. Mullet said. "Ask me no questions and I shall tell you no lies."

It was her standard response to any question whose expected answer had to do with the birds and the bees.

"Thanks, Mrs. M," I said cheerfully. "It's just as I suspected."

And I skipped out of the kitchen before she could fling a piece of pastry at me.

Anyway, as I was saying, the wedding was . . . well . . . interesting.

Although it was autumn, St. Tancred's was decked with exotic flowers: early narcissi, show pinks, and snapdragons, all flown in for the occasion from the Isles of Scilly by Feely's godfather, Bunny Spirling, a dear old friend of our late father. Feely had asked Bunny to give her away.

"If only it were for keeps," I had remarked when she told me the news.

"Silence, you suppurating cyst!" Feely had shot back. "What makes you think it won't be? You may never ever see me again."

"Oh, you'll be back," I told her. "There are two things in life that can be counted upon to return: a married sister and the smell of drains. Quite frankly, I'd prefer the drains."

I shot Dieter a sidelong wink to let him know I bore him no hard feelings. You can't punish a basically decent chap simply for marrying the resident witch.

But to get back to the wedding . . .

There had been a last-minute panic when it was discovered, ten minutes before the scheduled time, Dieter's best man had still not arrived.

"He'll turn up," Dieter said. "Reggie is an honorable man."

"Like Brutus?" Daffy had blurted. Daffy sometimes has the habit of putting her mouth in gear before engaging her brain.

Reggie Mold was the British pilot who had shot Dieter down and was, therefore, the cause of Dieter's remaining in England after the war. They had since become fast

friends and shared, like all pilots, that mystic brother-
hood of the air.

Dieter took the two of us aside.

"You mustn't be surprised when you meet Reggie. He's
a member of the Guinea Pig Club."

We both of us looked at Dieter blankly.

"After he bagged me, Reggie himself went down into
the Channel in flames. He was very badly burned. He
spent ages in Queen Victoria Hospital. You have probably read about it."

We shook our heads.

"Dr. McIndoe worked miracles with skin grafts . . ."

A shadow crossed his face.

"But still . . ." he added, trailing off into some silent
memory of his own.

"Don't stare," I said, grasping his meaning immediately.

Dieter's face lit up in a glorious grin.

"Exactly," he said. "Look. Here he comes now."

An ancient green MG with a blatting exhaust was
looming at the lych-gate, and a young man extracted
himself gingerly from the low-slung cockpit.

He came slowly toward us through the churchyard.

"Tally-ho!" he shouted as soon as he spotted Dieter.

"Horrido!" Dieter replied.

St. Horrido, I recalled Dieter telling me, was the patron saint of hunters and fighter pilots.

The two men hugged and slapped one another on the
back—carefully, I noticed, in Dieter's case.

"I thought I'd put paid to you the first time I had you in

my sights," Reggie laughed. "Now I'm back to jolly well finish off the job properly."

Dieter laughed graciously, as he had learned to do since meeting my sister. "I'd like to introduce to you my sisters-in-law," he said.

I was grateful that he hadn't said "future."

Even though I had been forewarned, as Reggie turned, the air went out of me.

His face was a ghastly blank: a grotesque mask of dry and fragile sheeting, as if someone had coated his skin with papier-mâché and painted it white, and then red. His mouth was a round black hole.

Only the eyes were alive, sparkling mischievous fire at me from their raggedly deep dark sockets.

"Charmed," Reggie croaked. His voice was that of a man who had breathed flames. "You're the Shakespeare authority," he said, offering Daffy a handshake.

"Well, not actually," she began as Reggie turned to me.

"And you're the poisonous one. We must have a chat before I leave."

Then, assuming a hissing, bloodcurdling, snakelike voice, he added: "I have dark designs on several of my lesser enemies."

He needed to say no more. He had won my heart.

"Wizard!" I said, with a grin like the blazing sun, and trotting out the only bit of RAF slang I could remember at the moment.

Dieter then introduced Reggie to Aunt Felicity, who, offering him a cigarette, launched into a questionable RAF joke, which rather shocked me, but which I realized was meant to set Reggie instantly at ease, and to make the two of them forever comrades-in-arms.

Dieter's parents had flown over from Germany to attend the wedding. Although his father was a publisher and his mother an archeologist, they stood off to one side at the church door, not forgotten, but too exotic, perhaps, to be casually chatted up by the villagers.

I wandered over for a few words, having learned earlier that both spoke excellent English.

"Dieter must have learned to sing at twenty-thousand feet," I said.

They looked at me blankly.

"From the angels," I explained, and they both laughed heartily.

"We thought we had lost him to England," Dieter's mother said, "but it is comforting to know that someone has already found him."

I wasn't quite sure that I understood completely, but we all beamed at one another like fellow magistrates.

"Your English weather is quite like our own in autumn," Dieter's father observed, gesturing to the beautiful day around him.

"Yes," I said, not having enough international experience to form an opinion. "Have you been here before?"

"Yes," Dieter's father replied. "My wife and I both read Greats up at Oxford."

Which shut my mouth.

Dieter, meanwhile, was engrossed in animated conversation with Reggie Mold, their hands tracing out zooming, swooping angles in the air.

"We'd better go inside," I said. "Feely will be thinking we've abandoned her."

And so it all began.

A church is a wonderful place for a wedding, surrounded as it is, by the legions of the dead, whose listening bones bear silent witness to every promise made—and broken—at the altar.

Dead now, every single one of them, including the man who invented the rule about not putting your elbows on the dinner table. Most of these had taken their vows at this very altar and each in his turn, reduced by life and time at first to juice . . . and then to dust.

As Daffy once pointed out to me, the Latin word *carnarium* can mean both "cemetery" and "larder," which shows that the Romans knew what they were talking about. The function of a churchyard—and the church itself, to some extent—is to digest the dead: there's no point in pretending otherwise.

After Undine's shocking outburst of ventriloquism, the ceremony itself went relatively well. Feely, although it pains me to say so, was radiant in a wedding dress that had belonged to our mother, Harriet. Radiant or not, it gave me the shivers.

When all of the proper words had been spoken, rings and vows exchanged, and the register duly signed, the vicar, Denwyn Richardson, held up a hand signaling us to remain in our seats.

"Before walking down the aisle and departing upon

their newly married life, Mr. and Mrs. Schrantz," he said, "have prepared a personal thanks—a little gift—to each and every one of you, who have come from near and far to share their happy day."

It took a moment for me to realize that "Mr. and Mrs. Schrantz" meant Feely and Dieter, who were already moving towards the grand piano which had been carted from Buckshaw to the church in the early hours of the morning.

Feely, flushing furiously in her billowing white wedding dress and veil, fiddled annoyingly, as she usually does, with the height of the piano stool, twisting it this way and that in a series of ever-diminishing adjustments until it met the stringent requirements of her fastidious backside. Then she sat down and opened the lid.

There was a long, expectant silence and then, at last, her hands fell upon the keys and she began to play.

A series of descending chords, following one upon another, joined in a melody of childlike simplicity.

Dieter stood stiffly at the foot of the piano which, to my way of thinking, looked in the shafts of light from the stained-glass windows uncommonly like a polished black coffin. He shoved a hand in the front of his morning coat, and began to sing—in German:

"Fremd bin ich eingezogen . . ."

It was "Gute Nacht," from the song cycle *Winterreise*. I recognized the song at once as one of Franz Schubert's lieder, those songs of love and longing so popular in the

last century, yet still so beloved by *The Third Program*, on the BBC wireless Home Service.

"I came among you as a stranger," the song began, and went on to tell the sad tale of a love-struck young man, standing in the snowy darkness at his lover's gate. He dares not disturb her dreams, but instead, writes on her gate the words "Good night," so that when she awakes, she will know he was thinking of her.

Even though Daffy had explained the whole thing to me in great detail, I didn't then—and still don't—understand how it is that love feeds so voraciously on sadness.

Come to think of it, Dieter *had* come among us as a stranger—a prisoner of war, in fact—but had long since been welcomed with open arms. He was now as much a part of Bishop's Lacey as the tower of St. Tancred's. Had he chosen to sing this particular song at his wedding as a way of expressing the fate he had so narrowly escaped?

The sound of Dieter's voice made my hair stand on end. His rich baritone filled the church with a warmth that made you turn and smile at your closest fellow man: in my case, Cynthia Davidson, the vicar's wife, who wiped away wet tears from each eye. Cynthia, too, and her husband, in the tragic loss of their first child, had known grief of that same intensity of which Dieter was singing.

I caught Cynthia's eye and gave her a wink. She returned a sad, wry, silly smile.

Schubert's melody line was rising like a stairway to heaven. In spite of its melancholy words, the music was

that of hope, ever and ever higher, ever and ever more haunting.

It was, I realized with a gasp, the story of my life to date, and I was suddenly finding it difficult to breathe.

Great music has much the same effect upon humans as cyanide, I managed to think: it paralyzes the respiratory system.

Get a grip on yourself, Flavia, I thought.

I had heard stories of people flying to pieces at weddings but had never imagined it could happen to me.

Was it the sudden realization that after today Feely would be gone forever from Buckshaw? It seemed unthinkable.

The two of us had waged war upon one another since the day she had first overturned my pram. What would I do without her?

I twisted round in the pew and glanced back at Dogger, who had chosen to sit with Mrs. Mullet and her husband, Alf, (he in a new suit with a chest full of medals) at the back of the church.

We had tried to insist upon them sitting with the family—which consisted today of just Daffy, myself, and, unfortunately, Undine.

But Dogger had demurred.

"I shouldn't feel comfortable, Miss Flavia," he said. When he saw my disappointment, he had added, "One must be free to be oneself at weddings, despite the fal-lal and flap-doodle."

I knew that he was right.

All too soon Dieter's song came to its inevitable end.

It was greeted with an explosion of applause from nearly everybody, an ear-splitting two-fingered whistle from Carl Pendracka, and an inexplicable wail—that of a wolf-howling-at-the-moon—from Undine.

I was about to pinch her when she bared her little fangs at me in a werewolf grin, and I let my hand fall to my side.

"*Gute nacht,*" she whispered in a rasping, guttural voice that could be heard as far away as the font.

Someone giggled, but it wasn't me.

Feely closed the piano lid, screwed down the seat of the stool, strode back to the top of the aisle and reassumed the role of a blushing bride.

Transformations, I thought, *are everywhere. We are all of us in the process of becoming someone—or something—else. If only we knew it, there are probably people all around us who are in the process of becoming dead.*

Later, I wished I hadn't thought that.

Well, almost.

After Feely finished fussing with her dress almost as much as if it were a piano stool, she was ready to begin her walk down the aisle.

As the organ struck up—something from Wagner, I think—she seized Dieter's arm and began her stroll to the door, taking her own good time about it. I could see that she was having her day and was going to make the most of it.

Feely had originally asked Daffy and me to be her bridesmaids, but we had both declined: Daffy because she believed bridesmaids at a wedding to be superstitious hokum ("Originally meant to scare away spooks," she said) and me because I wasn't going to climb into ballet garb just to pander to a sister's whim.

"What a relief!" Feely had told us. "I didn't want either of you anyway. I asked only out of courtesy. Actually, I've promised Sheila and Flossie Foster since we were toddlers, and I couldn't possibly back out now—not that I'd want to, anyway."

And that was that. I have to admit that the Foster sisters lent glamour to the occasion. Having put away their chewing gum and tennis rackets for a few hours, they were radiant in autumn-colored faille frocks with Elizabethan collars, sweetheart necklines and full skirts.

And, I might as well mention that, in order not be outdone, they both also wore tiaras, with Juliet caps embroidered with pearls and silver beads.

Not that I care a rat's whiskers what they draped themselves with, but I'm always trying to sharpen my already powerful powers of observation.

I, having fallen in behind, was able to follow the procession closely down the aisle to the porch, where the Misses Puddock, Lavinia and Aurelia, perched on matching shooting-sticks, had already staked out their vantage point.

Cameras large and small flashed and clicked as the happy couple paused in the porch and smiled out upon the assembled villagers, some of whom, although not present in the church for the ceremony, had gathered in the churchyard to cheer and tug their forelocks in respect, and as a way of getting an hour or so off work with hopes of a free drink or two.

When the wedding was being planned, the Misses Puddock had tried to horn in, as they always did, by offering to perform one of their dreary musical offerings free of charge.

"Oh, no," Feely had told them. "You must be at the door to catch my bouquet."

Now, with a modest, maidenly backhand Feely tossed her bouquet into the air. For a girl who could bowl a cricket ball with the best of them when she felt like it, it seemed a frail and puny effort.

Although Miss Lavinia and Miss Aurelia were both in their seventies, and well past the age when most females traipse to the altar, hope still burned eternal, apparently, in their respective withered breasts, these two ancient sisters shot off their respective shooting-sticks as if they were ancient skyrockets, and fell upon the flowers like hounds upon the fox, clawing and hissing at one another as if it were a catfight rather than a celebration of Holy Matrimony. Blows and several shocking words were exchanged. It was not a pleasant spectacle.

The real horror, however, was not to come until the reception.

ALAN BRADLEY is the internationally best-selling author of many short stories, children's stories, newspaper columns, and the memoir *The Shoebox Bible*. His first Flavia de Luce novel, *The Sweetness at the Bottom of the Pie*, received the Crime Writers' Association Debut Dagger Award, the Dilys Award, the Arthur Ellis Award, the Agatha Award, the Macavity Award, and the Barry Award, and was nominated for the Anthony Award.

alanbradleyauthor.com
Facebook.com/alanbradleyauthor